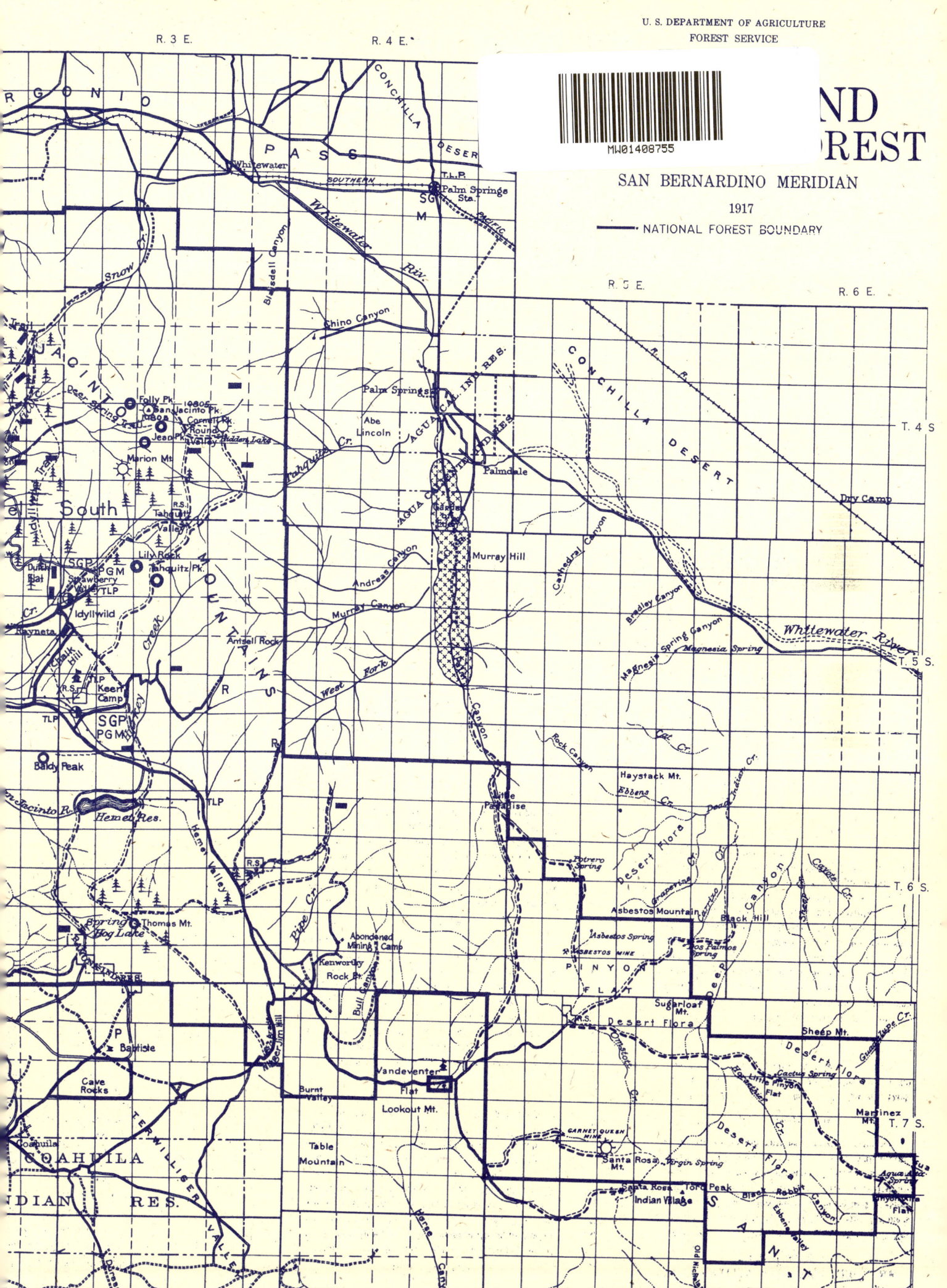

THE
SAN JACINTOS

The Mountain Country from Banning to Borrego Valley

John W. Robinson

and

Bruce D. Risher

Natural History by Elna Bakker

1993

Big Santa Anita  Historical Society

All photographs not credited are from authors' collection.

Frontispiece: **After the storm, Lily Rock.** – ROY MURPHY

Published by the Big Santa Anita Historical Society
7 North Fifth Avenue   Arcadia, California

Copyright © 1993 by John W. Robinson and Bruce D. Risher
All rights reserved.

1st Printing – August 1993

ISBN No. 0-9615421-6-0

Pacific Typesetting, Monrovia, California

ACKNOWLEDGMENTS

Uncovering the rich heritage of the San Jacinto and Santa Rosa mountains has been a rewarding experience, thanks largely to the generous help we have received from so many people. A mountain history such as this would be far from complete without the support of those who have lived part of the mountain saga, those who have previously done some of the historical spadework, and those who have so willingly shared photographs or provided access to newspaper files, personal papers, documents, and other materials that shed light on what has occurred in years past.

We owe most to Glen Owens of the Big Santa Anita Historical Society, who has long given unwavering support for our efforts to tell the story of the Southern California mountains – first with the San Gabriels, then the San Bernardinos, and now the San Jacintos. Without Glen and the Society, none of these books would be available.

David Scherman of Yucaipa, great-grandson of lumberman Anton Scherman and keeper of the Scherman family records, gave us invaluable help. David, who knows the San Jacintos as few others do, accompanied us on numerous trips into the range, pointing out sawmill sites, introducing us to Indian friends on the Santa Rosa Reservation, and helping us trace the old Anza trail.

We are indebted to Richard C. Davis, whose doctoral dissertation provided our most important source for our "Game Refuge, State Park, and Primitive Area" and "Tramway and Wilderness" chapters.

Jack Garner and his daughter Meg showed us the Garner Ranch and related much of the mountain cattle story.

Fanny Contreras and her niece Dolores Arnaiz told us much about the Arnaiz, Contreras, Hamilton, and Wellman families, early ranching pioneers in the San Jacintos.

Bud Clark revealed to us the stories of his father Frank Clark, and uncle Fred Clark, and their cattle drives down Coyote Canyon.

Ernie Maxwell, "Mr. Idyllwild," founder and long-time editor of the *Town Crier*, provided valuable information on the saga of Idyllwild, particularly the years since World War II. Other long-time Idyllwilders who gave generously of their time and knowledge were Bob and Virginia Gray, Nell Emerson Ziegler, Margaret Humber, Mary Sigworth, Inez Wilson, and our good friends Charles and Mary Ann Miller.

We appreciate the help so willingly given by Bill Jennings, Hemet historian and newspaper columnist. Bill read over many of the chapters and offered constructive suggestions.

Phil Brigandi, curator of the Ramona Bowl Museum and an outstanding historian by his own right, shared his knowledge of the Juan Diego killing, Helen Hunt Jackson and the *Ramona* story, and various other happenings. Phil saved us from the pitfalls of error that have so long plagued the "real" *Ramona* saga.

We owe heartfelt thanks to Sally West, assistant archivist of the San Diego Historical Society, who painstakingly searched for and made available many documents and other items in the Society's splendid collection.

Our understanding of the mountain heritage was broadened by several people interviewed in the 1970s who have since passed on: Charles Van Fleet, Louis Ziegler, and Lela Lockwood Noble of San Jacinto; Clarence Swift of Hemet; Jim Wellman of the 101 Ranch; and Richard Elliott of Idyllwild. Particularly valuable were the long interviews with Harry C. James, sitting before his warm fireplace at his Lolomi Lodge above Lake Fulmor. James talked of his Cahuilla Indian friends, and detailed his efforts to preserve the San Jacinto high country and the struggle to prevent the building of the Palm Springs Aerial Tramway.

Dorothy "Peg" Cowper, archaeologist and historian, helped us identify aboriginal sites in the San Jacintos and Santa Rosas.

The personnel of the San Jacinto Ranger District, San Bernardino National Forest, have our gratitude for the many favors they granted us. We want to particularly thank Kathy Valenzuela of the Idyllwild Ranger Station and Bob Will, attached to Ryan Field in Hemet.

Mike Hamilton of the James Reserve and Duane Lawson of the Riverside County Visitor Center in Idyll-

The Angel of Mount San Jacinto. — DONALD DUKE

wild gave us important information.

Heartfelt thanks go to Larry Burgess and the patient staff of the A. K. Smiley Public Library in Redlands, Ronald Baker and the staff at the Riverside City and County Library, Jo Daugherty and the very helpful ladies of the Hemet Public Library, and the friendly staffs of the Idyllwild Public Library, the San Diego Public Library, the Banning Public Library, the San Jacinto Public Library, the Palm Springs Public Library, and the Henry E. Huntington Library in San Marino.

The hundreds of historical photographs used in the book were provided through the courtesy of numerous individuals and institutions. We wish to particularly thank William Dugan of the San Jacinto Museum, Phil Brigandi of the Ramona Bowl Museum, Richard Buchen and Ligia Perez of the Southwest Museum, Sally McManus of the Palm Springs Historical Society, the *Idyllwild Town Crier*, the Henry E. Huntington Library, the Idyllwild Public Library, the San Diego Historical Society, the United States Forest Service, David Scherman, Laura Swift, Bill Jennings, Bob and Virginia Gray, Charles Van Fleet, Nell Emerson Ziegler, Fanny Contreras, Bud Clark, Jack Garner, Peg Cowper, Duane Lawson, Sandra Smith, David Wendelken, Virginia Garner, and ISOMATA.

We are deeply indebted to Roy Murphy of Covina for his beautiful mountain pictures and his superb photocopy work.

Larry Jones of Costa Mesa earns our gratitude for his accurate maps, and Jill Cremer for her superb diagrams.

In the production of the book, we thank George Brown and Anne Penney of Pacific Typesetting and Clifford Lee, Robert Bos and Carl Bennitt of Pace Lithographers.

John W. Robinson
Bruce D. Risher
June 22, 1993

CONTENTS

ACKNOWLEDGMENTS iii
INTRODUCTION 1
CHAPTER
  1. NATURE'S HANDIWORK by Elna Bakker 5
  2. EARLY PEOPLES 23
  3. SPANISH EXPLORERS, MISSION RANCHOS AND MEXICAN LAND GRANTS 31
  4. GOVERNMENT EXPLORERS AND MAP MAKERS 41
  5. CHARLES THOMAS AND HIS RANCH 49
  6. CATTLE AND SHEEP 55
  7. KENWORTHY 77
  8. FELLING THE MOUNTAIN FOREST 87
  9. ORDEAL OF A PEOPLE 101
10. STRAWBERRY VALLEY, IDYLLWILD AND KEEN CAMP 123
11. MOUNTAIN ROADS 145
12. LAKE HEMET 155
13. THE SANTA ROSAS 163
14. GUARDIANS OF THE FOREST 177
15. SAN JACINTO PEAK 191
16. HIGH COUNTRY 197
17. GAME REFUGE, STATE PARK AND PRIMITIVE AREA 205
18. TRAMWAY AND WILDERNESS 215
19. MOUNTAIN COMMUNITIES 225
20. THE CHALLENGE OF TOMORROW 241

BIBLIOGRAPHY 243
INDEX 247

Garner Valley – ROY MURPHY

INTRODUCTION

Travelers heading east through San Gorgonio Pass are treated to an awesome panorama. To the left, dominating the northern skyline, is the abrupt south slope of the San Bernardinos, crowned by the long gray ridgeline of San Gorgonio Mountain. To the right, ahead, towers a stupendous rock escarpment, soaring almost 10,000 vertical feet in five horizontal miles. This mountain wall is the northeast face of 10,804-foot San Jacinto Peak, as rugged a precipice as exists anywhere in the United States outside of Alaska. Somber gray in summer and fall, gleaming white in winter, snow-streaked by late spring, San Jacinto's vaulting desert face has fired the imagination and artistry of many a painter and photographer, and awed countless desert visitors.

San Jacinto, as is true with most mountains, has its gentle as well as its rugged features. The southwest flank of the mountain mass is made up of rolling hills and ridges that rise from the San Jacinto Valley and become progressively higher and steeper until they culminate at the summit. Scenic highways traverse the west and south slopes, winding through verdant stands of pine, incense cedar and oak, crossing streams that sparkle with icy-cold water, and giving access to mountain communities. Idyllwild is the largest of these resort villages, nestled in beautiful Strawberry Valley. To the southwest is Garner Valley, sage covered and dotted with pines, wedged between the Desert Divide, San Jacinto's southern spine, and the long hogback of Thomas Mountain. And south of all this are the mysterious, desert influenced Santa Rosas.

This is inviting mountain country, and humans, for various reasons, has long been attracted to it. The Cahuilla were here first, a culturally-rich native people who found sustenance in the varied flora and fauna and looked upon the mountain with spiritual reverence. Spanish padres and Mexican Californios used mountain water to nourish their ranchos but apparently stayed clear of the high country. Anglo and Spanish speaking pioneers grazed cattle, cut timber, formed Lake Hemet to irrigate valley towns and farms, and vainly sought gold. To modern civilization, the San Jacintos provide mountain homes, recreation, and solitude. All of this human activity is worth recounting, for it tells something of ourselves: our hopes, our efforts, our successes and frustrations, our reasons for living.

It may be best to first define the San Jacintos. Geographers consider them a northern extension of the Peninsular Ranges, an 800-mile mountain backbone that extends the length of Baja California and into Southern California as far as the Santa Ana Mountains. But just what mountain lands are part of the San Jacintos have long been a subject of dispute among geographers and writers. All agree on the main mountain mass extending from San Gorgonio Pass southeastward to the head of Palm Canyon. Many include the Garner Valley and the long Rouse Hill-Thomas Mountain ridgeline, to the southwest. Some extend the range to include Anza Valley and Cahuilla Mountain. Until the turn of the century, many maps included the Santa Rosas as part of the San Jacintos.

We have included *all* of this vast mountain country, from Banning to Borrego Valley. We have done this because the history of the region is integrated and cannot be segregated by an arbitrary boundary line of any particular ridge or valley. How can you discuss the Mountain Cahuilla without including the Santa Rosas? How can you describe Anza's journey across the mountain without taking in Coyote Canyon and Anza Valley? The whole world learned of the San Jacintos through the *Ramona* story, whose tragic climax took place on Juan Diego Flat below Cahuilla Mountain. Cattlemen ranged their herds far and wide over the southern San Jacintos, through the Santa Rosas, and as far south as Borrego Valley. And the San Jacinto District of San Bernardino National Forest envelops not only the main mountain mass, but Rouse Hill, Thomas Mountain, Cahuilla Mountain, and the northern part of the Santa Rosas.

We have made a sincere effort to relate the mountain saga as accurately as possible, to separate myth from reality, to consult both the printed word and human memory. It has not been an easy task. Despite the vast amount of written material, there remain mysteries unsolved. What was the cause of the strange rumbles so often reported by early mountain visitors? How did Hemet Valley get its name? Who first suggested the name Idyllwild, or Idylwilde as it was once spelled? Just what is the "real" Ramona story and why do so many writers come up with so many different versions? Do the Pegleg Smith and Fig Tree John legends of lost mines hold any truth?

Parts of this saga have been told many times over – the culture and traditions of the Cahuilla people, the Anza journey, the Ramona story, for examples. Other parts have been all but ignored. Although Cahuilla culture and aboriginal background have been well covered in a number of books, Cahuilla history since the 1860s has, with a few notable exceptions, been neglected. The turmoil leading up to the killing of Will Stanley, agent for the Cahuilla Reservation in Anza Valley, and an Indian policeman is related here for the first time. The ordeal and eventual triumph of the Soboba is likewise told here.

We have not told everything. A complete history of these mountains would be a monumental work, involving many volumes this size, covering not only the documented activities but the rich folklore of the range.

To set the stage for the long human drama, Elna Bakker, renowned California naturalist and author of *An Island Called California,* gives us a fascinating view of the geology, flora and fauna of the San Jacintos and Santa Rosas.

We hope that we have, in these ensuing pages, given the reader a balanced view of human use – and sometimes overuse – of this magnificent mountain country that lies between Banning and Borrego Valley.

Crossing Hidden Lake Divide, Mt. San Jacinto State Park.

Suicide Rock from Devils Slide Trail. – ROY MURPHY

Desert calm, Alpine tempest. Looking up Snow Creek.

1

NATURE'S HANDIWORK
by Elna Bakker

From the jagged crest of the San Jacintos to the flat expanse of Coachella Valley, the awesome powers of nature have rent asunder the ancient landscape to form this spectacular partnership of mountain and desert. Nowhere else in the long backbone of the Peninsular Ranges, which stretch from the tip of Baja California into Southern California, is there a mountain so high nor such a precipitous drop from peak to desert floor.

It is indisputable that the geologic story of the San Jacinto and the neighboring Santa Rosa mountains cannot be told without discussing the mountain chain whose northern end they dominate. The core of the Peninsular Ranges is composed of a series of granite-type rocky bodies, or plutons, that form collectively what is termed a batholith. How these masses of once-molten rock came to be here is quite a story in itself. It requires knowing something about how our planet's surface was put together.

Plate Tectonics, the New Geological Science

We know very little about the first two billion years of the earth's geologic history, but we are quite certain that we are on the right track about what followed. The earth's crust is cracked like an eggshell in careless hands. The pieces, called plates, have come together and spread apart, sometimes joined in huge supercontinents, at other times, like now, spread apart by intervening oceans.

It wasn't until the 1950s that geologists realized that the ocean floor was not a litterbin of the remains of sea creatures and other debris collecting through the centuries. The floor of the Pacific Ocean is composed of a number of crustal plates, each traveling somewhere at the supersnail pace of 3 or 4 inches a year! New floor is added to the plates where molten basalt flows out of great mid-ocean rifts or cracks. It cools, solidifies, and becomes part of the plates, which, like giant conveyor belts, continue moving to their encounter with other crustal plates.

Here several things can happen: gigantic continental collisions like those which created the Himalayas, the world's tallest mountains, sideways or horizontal motion like that along the San Andreas fault where two plates are grinding past each other and subduction where heavier oceanic plates dive beneath the edge of lighter continental masses.

Subduction

Subduction zones have several interesting features. Some of the world's deepest ocean trenches are where subducting slabs of ocean crust bend under continental edges. All kinds of rocky debris pile up in this entry zone basin, stuff scraped off the top of the subducting slab as well as dibs and dabs of rock chiseled off the continental rim. California's coastal ranges are in part composed of just such rocky rubble compacted when subduction was in progress off the coast back in dinosaur times.

One of the most important results of subduction is the formation of volcanoes. When the upper side of the subducting slab heats up because of friction generated by scraping against the overriding continental plate, its rocks begin to melt. Buoyant with heat, masses of molten rock move up to the earth's surface where, escaping as lava, they build up volcanic cones. Retained as magma under the surface, they form plutons that cool very slowly into solid crystalline rocks. This awesome process is responsible for much of the geologic history of the Peninsular Ranges, as we shall see.

The steep eastern escarpment of the San Jacintos is very evident in the picture taken from Keys View in Joshua Tree National Monument. The San Andreas fault runs through the Coachella Valley in the middle distance. The Indio Hills are in the foreground. – ROY MURPHY

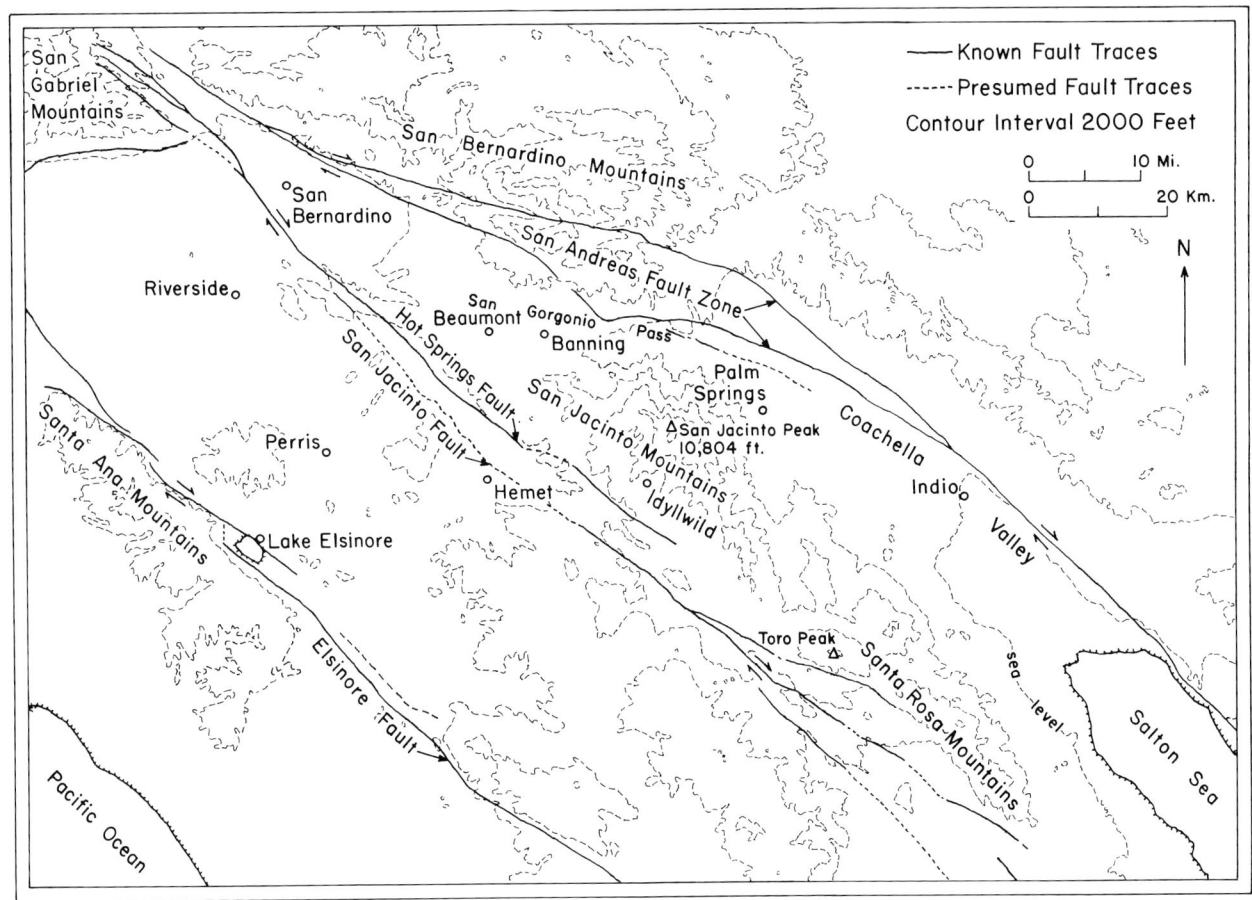

This map shows the major faults that have moved the northern Peninsular Ranges to their present location.
— LARRY JONES

Diagram showing a generalized subduction zone. A slab of ocean crust is diving under the edge of the continental plate. Erosion has removed the volcanoes, but the underlying magma, now crystalized, forms the core of the San Jacintos. — JILL CREMER

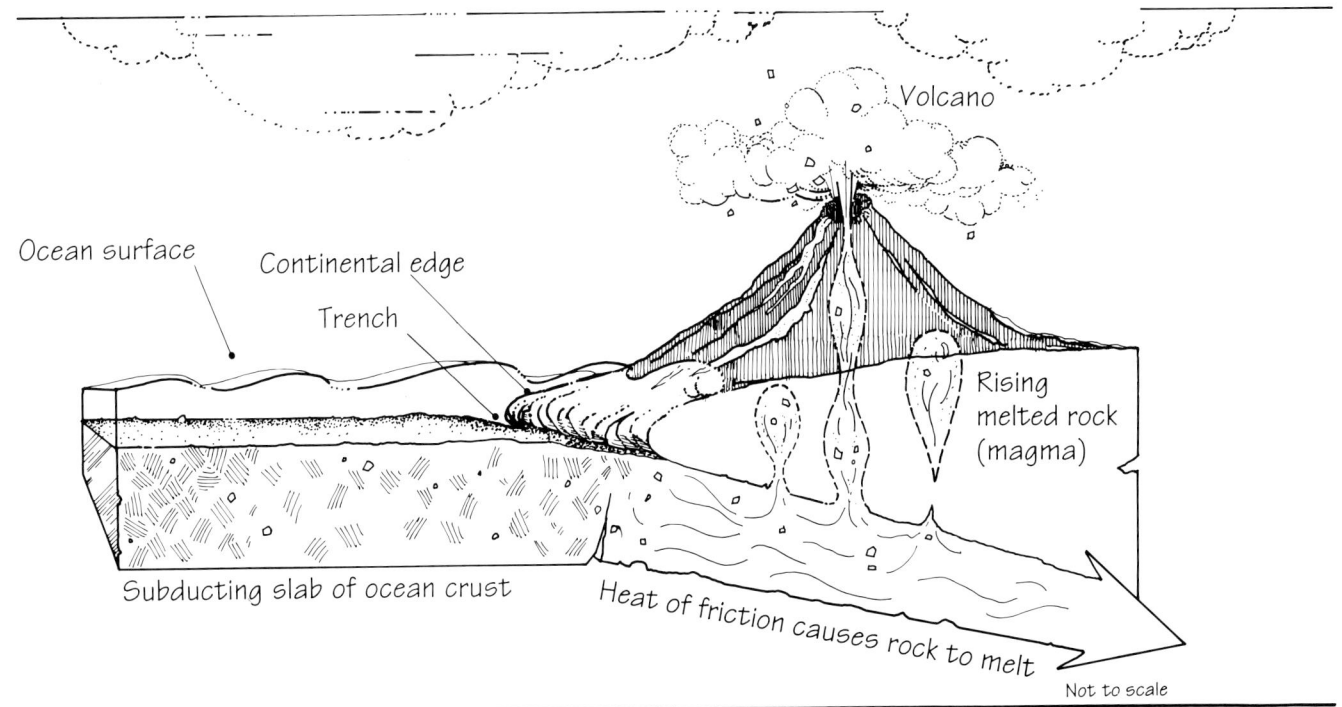

Metamorphosed rocks that were once deposits on an ancient sea floor are exposed in an outcrop along State Highway 243 above Banning. — ROY MURPHY

With this as background it is time to flip the mental switch to "rewind," back to 400 or 500 million years ago when life was just emerging from the sea but before the dinosaurs evolved to assume their masterful roles. The western edge of the ancient North American continent was far to the east. California as a piece of real estate did not exist. Some of its rocks were yet to be formed. Some had to come in like baggage carried along on those great conveyor belts, moving crustal plates. Other rocks began as sand, silt and other deposits on the floors of ancient seas.

Ancient Seas

And, indeed, this is where our story begins. Some 400 million years ago there was only a shallow sea where the San Jacinto and Santa Rosa mountains are now located. Its waves lapped up on a shoreline somewhere far to the east, perhaps not too distant from present-day Phoenix or Tucson. Under these quiet waters, beds of mud, sand and other sediments piled up on a continental shelf that deepened as it extended west from the coastline of the ancient North American continent. These shelf deposits were cooked in a process called metamorphism, which changes both the appearance and composition of the original rocks. Outcrops of these altered rocks are exposed in roadcuts along the Palms to Pines Highway where it switchbacks just before entering the straight stretch to Palm Desert.

Subduction Begins off California

Some 230 million years ago, around the beginning of the Dinosaur Age, huge alluvial deposits and other rocky debris began collecting in an ocean basin west of the shallow sea of the old pre-dinosaur times. This basin was probably part of a subduction zone, possibly a trench, the first indication that one of the great geological processes that rearrange our planet's surface was beginning. Sure enough, on the west side of the Santa Ana Mountains, little brother of the San Jacintos over in Orange County, are outcrops of these basin deposits – slate, limestone, quartzite and other weakly metamorphosed rocks. Just east of them are exposures of typical volcanic material, the next big clue that subduction was involved in building California as we know it today.

These early volcanoes were part of an island chain, much like the group of islands forming Japan. Along with their accompanying sediment-filled basin they were carried to the east "piggyback fashion" on a

Lily Rock, an imposing landmark above Idyllwild, looms in front of Tahquitz Peak, seen from the Wellman Cienega trail. Granitic outcrops in the San Jacintos remind the visitor of the Sierra Nevada.

subducting slab of ocean crust. Eventually this subduction zone collided with the edge of the North American continent and was welded to it. The Golden State was beginning to take shape!

Fast forward to about 140 million years ago. The dinosaurs were in full swing by then, but, unfortunately, very few bones have been recovered from Southern California, so we don't know much about their history here. From about 140 to 70 million years ago subduction continued to be king of west coast geology. It was responsible for building two new chains of volcanoes, one along what was to become California's eastern border and another south along the western edge of Mexico, reaching into tropical latitudes. Today those volcanoes have been almost entirely eroded away, but their plutons, or magma bodies once deep underground, are very much a part of our local landscapes. The domes, cliffs and peaks of the Sierra Nevada are carved from these batholithic rocks now shoved thousands of feet above sea level. Similar granitic-type rocks under the volcanoes of western Mexico formed the Peninsular Ranges batholith. In the San Jacinto-Santa Ana mountain complex the plutons punched their way through the host rocks described above, the buried beds of the ancient sea floor on the east side of the range and the older subduction zone basin deposits and volcanic rocks of the Santa Ana Mountains.

Uplifts and Faults

From now on the story is less about subduction, which quit anyway not long after the demise of the dinosaurs though it is still going on offshore parts of the North American continent, building the Pacific Northwest's Cascade Range and creating the volcanoes of Mexico and Central America. It is more about uplift and erosion, other great geologic processes that shape the land. The earth's surface is constantly vibrating in one place or other as seismic waves generated by fault motion pass through its crust. Some of this activity shifts crustal plates around in their endless slow dance; other motion is responsible for lifting mountain ranges. We would not have many clues about the geologic history of the rocks of the Peninsular Ranges if they had not been lifted and exposed to our view.

There are several kinds of faults important to the geologic story of the San Jacintos and Santa Rosas. The type of fault with which we are most familiar is the lateral or strike-slip fault whose prime example is the San Andreas and is the kind of fault that produced the great Landers earthquake of June 1992. Motion along the fault face is horizontal, one side moving past the other along the direction of the fault line.

Ramp-like thrust faults and other rifts along whose inclined traces upward motion takes place are also encountered throughout much of Southern California. Most of the uplift responsible for our local mountains occurred on faults of this nature. Rock above the fault line rides up much like a truck ascending a freeway onramp or a cable car climbing a steep slope.

The San Andreas Fault

By far the most prominent tectonic feature of the entire area is the San Andreas fault zone, which cuts California in two pieces from where it exits into the sea north of San Francsico to its termination near the Mexican border. It is a classic strike-slip fault with right-lateral motion, that is, a viewer facing the fault sees all the land across the fault as moving to the right. One major branch slices east-west just north of the northern face of the San Jacinto Mountains and then veers in a more southerly direction past the eastern edge of the Salton Sea. Another major strand, the historically active San Jacinto fault, extends from the San Gabriel Mountains and passes through the Peninsular Ranges to roughly define the western edge of the San Jacintos and Santa Rosas.

Strike-slip faults change the earth's surface in many ways. Not only is there horizontal crustal movement during earthquakes, but curves or bends in the fault trace create depression and uplift – basins where the land is stretched and highlands where it is compressed. Such tectonic processes have been important in the geologic history of the San Jacintos and Santa Rosas.

Looking north across San Gorgonio Pass to the San Bernardino Mountains. A branch of the San Andreas fault follows along the northern edge of the pass.
— ROY MURPHY

The Great Trek

About 30 million years ago subduction was no longer an important force in shaping Southern California. Tectonic activity changed to another system, that of right-lateral strike-slip motion. One plate, the Pacific, is edging to the northwest along the San Andreas fault past another plate, the North American. Geologists differ on how much motion has occurred, but there seems to be general agreement that the Pacific plate has moved to the northwest about two hundred miles. Evidently motion began in the southern part of its trace with the ripping open of the Gulf of California about 5 million years ago. Keep in mind that all of the land west of the fault has been on the move to the northwest, which means that everything on this sliver of the earth's surface was once south of its present position. The San Gabriel Mountains were part of a land mass situated near the Mexican border, and the San Jacintos and other ranges in the Peninsular system were originally located in western Mexico. How far south is under considerable debate.

Moving up in the World

Three important things took place during this northward journey:

• The ripping apart of western Mexico, creating the Gulf of California and the Baja California peninsula.

• The activation of the southern part of the San Andreas fault, which joined the northern part of the rift in shoving all of the land west of it to the northwest.

• The development of two large bends in the fault, forcing it to take a more east-west trend between the Tejon Pass in southern Kern County and Indio in northern Riverside County. As noted above, bends create compressional stress that is being relieved by upward motion on thrust and other types of faults – the foothill fault system. It includes the Cucamonga, Raymond Hill and other faults along the southern base of the San Gabriels. Similar faults have raised the San Bernardinos to their present elevation, and others are no doubt partly, if not wholly, responsible for the rise of Mount San Jacinto some 10,000 feet above the Coachella Valley. The main bulk of the San Bernardinos is *east* of the San Andreas fault. This range has been rising in place for a million or so years, standing guard, as it were, while the San Gabriels moved past it to their present position and the San Jacintos advanced as trailblazer of the Peninsular Ranges' great trek to the north.

Erosion, the Great Leveler

Movement along faults greatly weakens the rock bordering their traces, crushing and breaking it up. Erosion

Soboba Hot Springs resort, pictured here in 1924, lies along the Hot Springs fault, a major branch of the San Jacinto fault. Soboba and other nearby hot springs are caused by water seeping up along the fault line.

more easily attacks weakened rock, and slot-like valleys develop where faults break the earth's surface. Deep Canyon, south of the Palms to Pines Highway, is such a valley as is the canyon of the San Jacinto River which follows a strand of the Hot Springs fault. One of the traces of the San Jacinto fault system, it is named for a series of hot springs, some now resort locations, along the southwestern base of the San Jacinto Mountains. Springs and seeps are common features of earthquake faults. Ruptured bedrock provides channels through which ground water can reach the surface.

Erosion usually begins by weathering. Once bedrock is exposed it is attacked by the elements. Freezing water caught in rock cracks expands, forcing the fractures apart. Weakened by this breaking up, as well as chemical dissolution, the exposed rock is eroded into rounded contours. Many of the roadcuts along the highways traversing the San Jacintos have been sculpted in this way. Lily Rock, that prominent landmark above Idyllwild, was produced by the same type of erosion responsible for the domes of Yosemite, a sort of peeling off of overlying rock.

Basins also developed during the long geologic history of these mountains, trapping sediments eroding from canyons and slopes. The beds of the Mount Eden Formation on the northwest "corner" of the San Jacintos have retained some remarkable evidence of life as it was long before the first American Indians set foot on the continent. Fossil leaves of semi-desert plants indicate that the climate was becoming drier even as far back as 5 million years ago. (Tropical forests once grew near the location of San Diego some 40-50 million years ago.) San Jacinto Valley, location of the towns of Hemet and San Jacinto, is a pull-apart basin. Strain near bends in local faults created an elongated valley running parallel to the San Jacinto fault.

The Final Stage of the Journey

The San Jacinto fault had one other role. Since the land to the east of it is moving to the southeast – it, too, is a right-lateral fault – the San Jacintos and Santa Rosas were once farther to the northwest than they are today and were moved into their present position by motion on the San Jacinto fault. This settling into place created the deep embayment of the Borrego Valley. During this late period of geologic history, tectonic forces dropped the Salton Trough. The same type of rifting that formed the Gulf of California is taking place right now under the Salton Sea. Heat from molten rock in the rift is cooking overlying, brine-laden sedimentary deposits, hydrothermally altering, in other words, metamorphosing them less than a mile beneath the earth's surface.

Summing Up

• About 400 million years ago a wide shelf extending west from the ancient North American continent was covered by a shallow sea whose floor was littered with sedimentary debris. These beds hardened and then were changed by heat and pressure into metamorphic rocks now exposed in the northern and eastern flanks of the San Jacintos.

• Subduction began offshore what was to become California in early dinosaur times and welded a part of a

Exposures of granitic-type rocks that date from dinosaur times have been sculpted by erosion. These jagged rocks are above the Devils Slide Trail. — ROY MURPHY

volcanic chain and its attendant trench deposits to the growing continent. These rocks now appear in the Santa Ana Mountains.

• Subsequent subduction created new chains of volcanoes along the western edge of the continent whose plutonic foundations of cooling magma became the granitic-type rocks of the Sierra Nevada and Peninsular Ranges.

• Subduction ceased and right-lateral strike-slip faulting moved the rocks of the Peninsular Ranges north some 100 miles. Subsequent motion on the historically active San Jacinto fault moved the San Jacintos and Santa Rosas south to their present location. Basins and valleys developed in response to bends in local faults that were filled by sedimentary deposits eroding off the now-rising mountains.

• Compressional strain near bends in the San Andreas fault created ramp-like faults responsible for the uplift of many of Southern California's mountains, including the San Jacintos and Santa Rosas. Erosion has since carved out deep canyons and sculpted peaks, creating the rough terrain so characteristic of Southern California's mountain landscapes.

Post-script

Recent work by a group of geologists hints of a much longer journey for the rocks of the Peninsular Ranges. Though their research is still controversial, it should be mentioned. When rocks are formed any particles of iron in them are aligned relative to the magnetic North Pole. By using sophisticated methods to "read" this until now hidden history, some geologists believe they can determine the rock's original position. They think there is a growing body of evidence that many of the rocks of the Peninsular Ranges were at one time far to the south, the latitudes of present-day Central America according to one school of thought. If this is the case, then some of the geological episodes described above were not off-shore future California, but took place near the shoreline of a continental mass much farther away. The journey north covered a distance of a thousand miles or so, not mere hundreds. Presumably the transport was accomplished by strike-slip faulting or conveyance on plates of oceanic crust moving to their subducting destinations.

Mountain Life

Like other mountainous regions of Southern California, the San Jacintos and Santa Rosas are "highland islands" of predominantly cone-bearing trees that are surrounded by seas of scrub and other brushy vegetation. Yearly rainfall averages of 28 to 30 inches, twice as much, if not more, than the amounts received by neighboring lowlands, allow the growth of pines and firs, trees typical of 6,000 feet and above.

Most of Southern California's winter storms originate over the Pacific Ocean. They sweep in from the south or west, rising above the local ranges. As they ascend they meet the cooler temperatures of thinner air. Cold air cannot hold as much water vapor as warm air, and the storm clouds are wrung almost dry of moisture as they travel inland. This means very little rainfall remains for

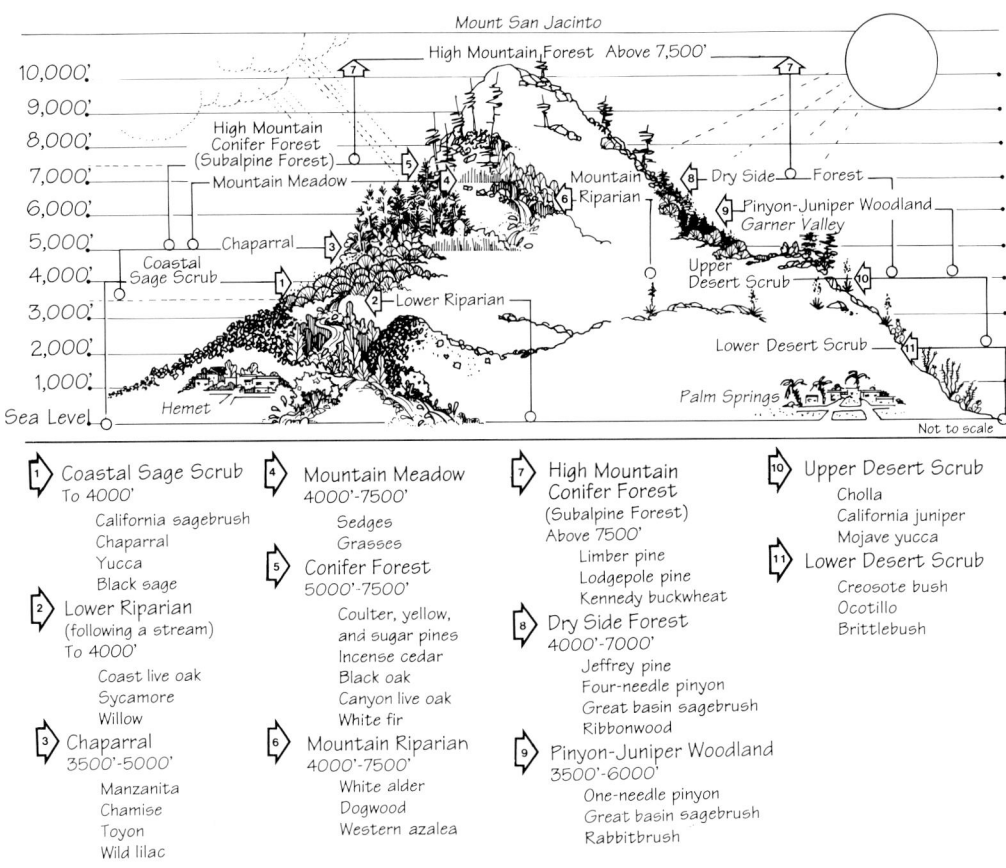

Diagram of vegetation zones characteristic of the San Jacinto-Santa Rosa mountain region. — JILL CREMER

the land to the lee of the San Jacintos and Santa Rosas, thus helping to create the desert east of these ranges.

California's Peculiar Climate

Unlike parts of the world where warm weather and rainfall are climatic partners, California's summers are dry. Most precipitation falls in winter when cool temperatures limit plant growth. Drought during the warm season is tough on plant life, forcing adjustments to the lack of moisture during the hottest part of the year. Indeed, it is amazing that California has developed such a rich flora (the sum total of species found in a particular area), but the state is home to one of the most varied groups of plants in the world. About half of California's plant species occur nowhere else, that is, they are native to what botanists call the California Floristic Province. The San Jacinto-Santa Rosa mountains are at the southern end of this province and share its fascinating diversity.

There are a number of reasons for this variety, most of them physical in nature. Though the overall climatic pattern is described as Mediterranean – dry summers and wet winters – environments vary locally because of differences in latitude, elevation, direction of slope face, terrain, exposure, availability of water and soil type. Specific plant associations, or communities, have developed in response to these differences. Desert scrubs and foothill grassland, for example, are adjusted to drier sites, whereas redwood groves and red fir forests require regions of higher rainfall. Some communities are comfortable in acid soils, others more tolerant of alkaline soils. Fire has been a partner of plant life for millions of years. A pattern of unique adaptations to and following its occurrence is a hallmark of California's flora.

In many respects the San Jacintos and Santa Rosas are microcosms of the state as a whole. Coast-facing foothill plant life is quite different from counterparts on the desert side; vegetation changes drastically as elevation increases; ponds and creeks encourage riparian (streamside) trees and shrubs; drier sites support only scrub and brush. Fire, as noted above, has played an important role in cyclical changes in vegetation and will continue to do so.

Local climatic variations, however, are important. Moist air masses often invade Southern California's Peninsular Ranges in summer, drifting in from Mexico or the Southwest and bringing measurable amounts of warm weather rainfall every year. It and fog, which moves in from the coast on most summer evenings, help plants survive the dry season, but the searing Santa Ana winds of autumn are particularly hard on the already summer-stressed vegetation. Years of prolonged drought and spells of severe cold weather bring additional hardship.

Fire on the chaparral-blanketed west slope of the San Jacintos endangers forest, life, and property. However it is a normal part of the mountain ecology.
— IDYLLWILD TOWN CRIER

The handsome, brilliantly red snowplant is a delightful surprise in shady groves of yellow pine and white fir.
— ROY MURPHY

As unique as the plant life are the animals of these "highland islands." Prey and predator weave their webs of food dependency through each living community, making homes, raising families, and finally relinquishing life, so that nature can recycle the resources essential to existence. Ranging from red-tailed hawks to western rattlesnakes, deer mice to Jerusalem crickets, the rich assortment of animal species is another wondrous facet of mountain life.

Diversity of Plant Life

To better appreciate the diversity of life in the San Jacintos and Santa Rosas, let's take a more or less imaginary trip, starting in the San Jacinto Valley and, crossing the crest, head down to Palm Springs. Part of it could be coincidental with existing highways such as the Palms-to-Pines or any of the roads leading up to Idyllwild on the west or north side of the range.

Before we begin, it might be well to review what plants must do to cope with drought. Most plants make food through the chemical magic of photosynthesis, using the energy of sunlight with the aid of the plant's chlorophyll to combine water and carbon dioxide for the production of simple sugar and oxygen. Water enters the plant through its roots, and the carbon dioxide enters through tiny pores in the leaves. It is unfortunate that water vapor escapes through these same pores, but drought-tolerant plants have developed ways to reduce the loss of water from their leaves.

On the left, a chaparral-covered slope quickly recovers from a recent fire. To the right, California lilac needs fire to either stimulate seed germination or promote new growth from the root top. — ROY MURPHY

Coastside Scrubs, Brush and Woodland

The first community zone we enter as we ascend the mountain slope is *Coastal Sage Scrub,* characterized by what are called subshrubs, plants with soft, thin leaves and flexible stems growing out of a woody base. Examples are California sagebrush, black and white sages and yerba santa. The sagebrush, in particular, makes a drastic adjustment to this hottest and driest of all coast-side environments. It is summer-deciduous. That is, its leaves dry out and drop off as the summer progresses, freeing the sagebrush from its water-spending foliage. These little shrubs remain dormant until the rains return. Then they grow new foliage and go about the business of food-making as if summer drought was of no concern.

At about 3,500-4,000 feet, higher in elevation than the scrub below and thus benefitting from slightly cooler temperatures and an increased rainfall, there is a subtle change to true *Chaparral,* the stiff-twigged, evergreen brush so typical of California hillsides. This vegetation has developed ways to cope with summer drought without resorting to leaf loss. It can be divided into two groups, the tiny leaved and the larger leaved. Those with very small leaves include California buckwheat, also common in the sage scrub, and chamise, both of which have bundles of tiny leaves that are only fractions of an inch in length. Small size means fewer leaf pores, those pesky water-losing features. The shrubs with larger leaves such as scrub oak, toyon (Christmasberry), sugar bush, manzanita, holly-leaved cherry, mountain mahogany and wild lilac have developed other adaptations to help them cope with summer drought:

• Thick and leathery leaves that are commonly waterproofed with a waxy substance.
• Sunlight-reflecting foliage.
• Hairs on the leaves that cast shade like tiny umbrellas.
• Small plant size, reducing the amount of water-wasting foliage.

The two brushy communities – coastal sage scrub and chaparral – share many of the same animals. Resident birds include California thrasher, brown towhee and wrentit, a little gray wisp of a bird whose cheerful trill accelerates as it works through the brush. California ground squirrels sun themselves by the roadside, whisking into burrows if red-tailed hawks, western rattlesnakes or other predators threaten. Nighttime will see California mice brave these brush slopes, alert to great horned owls and coyotes. Elegantly attired scrub jays, rufous-sided towhees and California quail are more typical of chaparral as are mule deer, gray foxes and California pocket mice. Gnatcatchers are more common in the sage scrub.

One lowland community makes no effort to emulate the Draconian drought-abating strategies of the communities described above. It doesn't need to, as its plants grow where water is available throughout the year either on the surface as stream flow or just beneath. This is *Riparian Woodland* whose thickets of large-leaved, water-wasting trees such as sycamore, Fremont cottonwood and willow provide welcome shade on hot days. Mid-elevations supply white alder, another characteristic riparian tree. Winter- rather than summer-deciduous, these species are among the few native trees in low-elevation Southern California that behave like the hardwoods of eastern states, turning bronze or richly gold in late fall before dropping off at the advent of winter.

Often found on shelving canyon slopes and as part of river bottom vegetation is coast live oak whose small, stiff, prickly leaves are well adapted to withstand drought. At mid-elevation they consort with bigberry manzanita and other shrubs in an *Oak Woodland* of their own. Acorn woodpeckers glide through these shady groves in black, white and red arcs, scolding as they go while titmice and bushtits work over the oak bark for tasty insects. Black-headed grosbeaks are summer nesters here as well as in the conifers above.

The attenuated stream floor oases also harbor rich bird life, particularly in spring. Here one can find Wilson, yellowthroat, yellow and other warblers as well as colorful orioles and western tanagers. Thirsty animals in the vicinity visit the stream during their active hours. Evening may see raccoons playing in the water with their hand-like paws and mule deer drinking on their way to browsing on the tender leaves of spring foliage. Salamanders and other amphibians are denizens of these moist places as are aquatic insects.

The Piney Woods

Approaching the *Conifer Forest* in the heart of the range, manzanitas and other shrubs of the upper edge of the chaparral zone gradually open their ranks to several kinds of oaks whose distribution often depends upon terrain type, soil depth and the direction of slope face. Black oaks, handsome winter-deciduous trees with large, thin leaves, tend to remain on gentle slopes with deep soils. Interior and canyon live oaks, whose small, leathery leaves are well adapted to drought, are capable of occupying steeper sites with shallower soils. All three seem to favor north-facing slopes, where sunlight is less intense and the soil retains moisture past the start of the dry season.

At about 5,000 feet the vegetation begins to have the character of a real forest – close-knit trees that, like the oaks, often fit neatly into a site-determined mosaic. The

Riparian growth along Fuller Mill Creek. Numerous streams encourage alder, willow, and other moisture-requiring trees along their banks. Western azalea is very much at home here. – ROY MURPHY

Pines and other conifers along with black oaks crowd the hillside above Lake Fulmor, a popular fishing spot on the Banning-Idyllwild Highway. — ROY MURPHY

trees are in fierce competition for water, a very limited resource, and they manage to divide up the landscape between them according to their individual moisture requirements. Coulter pine, famed for having the heaviest of all pine cones, is the first of the conifers to invade the manzanita-clad slopes of upland chaparral. It appears content with the "sunny side of the street," south-facing slopes and exposed ridgetops and knolls. The less drought-tolerant white fir and incense cedar are comfortable in canyon bottoms or on north exposures, while Jeffrey and yellow pines, like their Coulter cousin, make do on dry and rocky slopes. California bay has a scattered distribution on this edge of the coniferous zone. Big-leaf maple and big-cone Douglas-fir, though common throughout much of Southern California's mountainous country, have limited distributions in the San Jacintos and Santa Rosas. A stand of this type of Douglas-fir grows on a ridge south of the town of Mountain Center.

Bracken fern is understory in moister places of the conifer forest while mountain chaparral continues in drier sites such as steep slopes with south exposures. Spiny snowbush, snowberry and bush chinquapin enrich the shrub cover in many places. The rose sage excites the eye with spikes of purple bracts and the nose with a highly aromatic scent. Common wildflowers growing in the forest litter include the brilliantly red snowplant, a member of the heather family that is totally lacking in chlorophyll thus incapable of making food. It relies instead on decaying vegetation for sustenance. Lilac-tinted mariposa lilies and the vividly orange-red San Gabriel and Bridge's penstemons brighten the more open forest floor. The latter are sure to be visited by hummingbirds, including the striking rufous hummer whose male is as richly hued as the flowers he seeks for nectar. The pale pink Grinnell's penstemon and four wildflowers in the yellow part of spectrum – goldenbush, golden yarrow, bush monkey-flower and blazing star – bedeck the roadcuts at these elevations. If you are fortunate you may meet the aptly-named showy penstemon and guard lupine both resplendent with rose-and-purple hues. The true reds are provided by paintbrush and scarlet bugler, another penstemon.

Three other environments enrich the overall pattern of vegetation at these elevations – seep, riparian and meadow. Seeps are concentrated around springs and other wet places. This is a major habitat for lemon lilies, one of our most spectacular wildflowers. As cleanly yellow as their namesake fruit they gleam through the shadier nooks of the forest. Rein orchid and twayblade, diminutive orchids that often get lost in the herbaceous cover of these damp places, occur here as well.

Riparian vegetation follows stream courses such as Strawberry Creek. This is the place to look for western azalea whose gold-and-white, sweet-smelling flowers often grow under western dogwood, splendid in spring with flower-like clusters of white bracts and just as glorious in fall when its leaves turn burgundy-red. Scarlet monkeyflower and western columbine cheer these shady thickets with colorful bloom.

Meadows are rare in most of Southern California's mountains. A few, however, are located near Idyllwild. These open places support tangles of wild rose, sedges, rushes and the smiling faces of buttercups. Pale-pink wild hollyhocks called checkerbloom are often meadow dwellers. Several native grasses such as pine bluegrass and mountain brome are at home in the more open areas of the forest. They have persisted even though foreign grasses such as wild oats have long since pushed most of California's native species from their original habitats.

Common birds of the piney woods include the brilliantly attired western tanager, Steller's jay, whose rasping calls rival those of its chaparral-dwelling cousin, the scrub jay, western bluebird, mountain chickadee, pigmy nuthatch, olive-sided flycatcher – its "hick-three-beers" is unmistakable – and Oregon junco. The colorful mountain kingsnake used to quite plentiful, but over-zealous collectors have taken their toll. Gray squirrels and Merriam's chipmunks are locally abundant rodents. Coyotes, bobcats and gray foxes use these forests frequently as well as the brushy cover below.

Going Higher

The San Jacintos and Santa Rosas are not high enough in elevation for true timberline and alpine rock fields to have developed. Above 9,000 feet, however, cold temperatures, constant drying wind and fierce winter blizzards often impose severe climatic conditions. Here and there lodgepole and limber pines, conifers of higher altitudes throughout much of the mountainous West, exhibit some contorting, and Kennedy buckwheat and other low-growing shrubs are frequently cushion-shaped or mat-like, keeping a low profile in response to the harsh climate.

The Dry Side of the Mountain

Descending to the desert side of the range on the Pines to Palms Highway one soon encounters trees typical of the dry side of the range. Jeffrey pines gather around the edges of Garner Valley, towering over Great Basin sagebrush that intermingles with a ground cover of grasses and other low growth. Summer flaunts some showy wildflowers well worth a trip to see – richly pink mountain sand verbena, sapphire-hued wool star and the flamboyant apricot mallow.

Pinyon Woodland joins the Jeffrey pines at the south end of Garner Valley where it introduces a rare California native, the four-needled pinyon, a nut pine that is

Jeffrey pines tower over meadowlands in Garner Valley. — ROY MURPHY

Looking down over Fuller Ridge from the Deer Springs Trail, well up in Mt. San Jacinto State Park. Chinquapin, snowbush, and other high country shrubs form a ground cover beneath white firs.

Ribbonwood's feathery green leaves and peeling red bark are colorful roadside companions along parts of State Highway 74. It blankets the slopes around Santa Rosa Summit on the Palms to Pines Highway. — ROY MURPHY

native to the southern San Jacintos and the Santa Rosas. Pinyons are common through out much of the arid west. California has two species, the single-leafed pinyon, which reaches north from the Peninsular Ranges into the inner Coast Ranges as well as along the eastern side of the Sierra Nevada, and four-needled, or Parry, pinyon. This species poses a problem for botanists who find it difficult to tuck into a taxonomic niche. The latest thinking has it a type of three-needled Sierra Juarez pinyon, a newly designated species found in Baja California. Since researchers have found specimens of Parry pinyon with only three needles, perhaps this is the solution to the problem.

Within the pinyon woodland, Great Basin sagebrush, also common on less well-watered slopes in the conifer forest, associates with rabbitbrush whose crowns of yellow-gold flowers gleam through this grey-foliaged landscape in early fall. One of the most arresting plants of drier slopes is ribbonwood, unmistakable with its richly red shreds of thin bark and clumps of feathery, light green foliage. It is rare in Southern California, occurring only in this region, a few places in the Santa Monica Mountains and locally in interior Santa Barbara County. Palmer oak is a small tree occasionally encountered in pinyon woodlands and other desert margin communities.

A number of shrubs showing characteristic adaptations to aridity enter the woodland near Pinyon Flats. The tall stalks of nolina and desert agave mingle with goat nut, Mojave yucca, silver cholla, Mojave prickly pear, desert scrub oak, antelope brush, Mormon tea and California juniper. Many of these plants exhibit the same kind of drought-tolerant features as those of sage scrub and chaparral. The leaves of Great Basin sagebrush are small, very light in color and somewhat hairy. Even more drastic adaptation includes prickles and spines instead of leaves and succulent tissue that stores up needed moisture.

Several animals are typical of pinyon woodland: sage sparrow, pinyon mouse and pinyon jay, a gray-blue bird whose calls sound like those of an angry cat! Horned larks and western kingbirds are often seen on these dry, open slopes.

Cactus wrens and ladder-backed woodpeckers are typical species of the desert floor, but they are also regular visitors to its higher edges. Horned lizards are almost invisible when they retreat into sandy soils if disturbed. Woodrats seem to prefer building their huge nests, in reality collections of twiggy litter, at the base of California junipers. Desert cottontails and deer mice also utilize these brush thickets.

The Desert Base of the Mountains

On the semi-barren rocky slopes just above the desert floor ocotillo, creosote bush, and brittlebush, a wild bouquet of brilliant yellow in spring, join jumping cholla and cat claw in typical *Desert Scrub*. Some of

What appears to be one blunt pine needle separates into four needles, a characteristic leaf arrangement of the Parry piñon. A few of these four leaf piñons occur along the Palms to Pines Highway just east of Anza Valley Road junction. – ROY MURPHY

these plants are so inconspicuous they are barely noticeable against the brownish colors of the surrounding metasedimentary rock, the ancient sea beds that form their backdrop. Chuckawallas, large lizards that depend on a plant diet, have been seen sunning themselves on nearby rocky ledges, and zebra-tailed lizards and round-tailed ground squirrels should not be too far away.

Several native *Palm Oases* occur along the desert base of the mountains. Watered by streams flowing off the higher elevations or from fault-fed springs, these handsome trees as well as cottonwoods and other plants of the desert riparian environment sheltered the original palm springs, the inviting resting places that inspired the world-famed playground now spread over the desert to the east.

Desert-dwelling animals have made many adjustments to their stressful environment. Few expose themselves to the heat of a summer noon but prefer to spend the hotter part of the day in underground burrows or shady places. Water strategies differ. Kangaroo rats never seek water but produce it metabolically from the food they eat. Others rely on juicy vegetation.

A Meeting Ground

The San Jacinto and Santa Rosa mountains have the southernmost concentrations of Sierran-type coniferous

Palm Canyon, one of the many oases of *Washingtonia filifera*, native fan palms, along the eastern base of the San Jacinto and Santa Rosa mountains.

The rare lemon lily is found near seeps and springs in the San Jacintos. — ROY MURPHY

forest. They are not as rich in species because scantier rainfall precludes such luxuriance, but they are the end of the line for a number of species, including meadow rue, western dogwood, bitter cherry, bush chinquapin, lady fern, mock orange, western columbine, Sierra gooseberry and several willowherbs. On the other hand, some species more typical of Mexico have come this far north, Parry pinyon – probably related to the Sierra Juarez pinyon – and a type of Horkelia, for example. A number of plants are endemic to the San Jacinto-Santa Rosa mountain area. They include two subspecies of a type of monardella, an attractive member of the mint family.

Fire and the Mountains

All of the biotic communities of the San Jacintos and Santa Rosas have been affected by fire in one way or another. Sweeping through a brushy hillside, it destroys the greenery, turning it into a nightmare landscape. But regeneration soon follows, encouraged by ash-enriched soils. Concentrations of wildflowers, some of them capable of germinating only after a blaze, are as colorful as carefully tended gardens. The brush recovers eventually, either sprouting from fire-stimulated seed or still-living root crowns. Vegetation patterns often develop. Patches of wild lilac prevail on steep, dry, south-facing slopes that are frequently burned, while black oaks somehow manage to create conditions that deter fire. Their litter is relatively inflammable and their shade discourages easily burned undergrowth.

These, then, are the San Jacintos and Santa Rosas. Built and moved into position by tectonic forces, sculpted by rain and snow over eons of time and graced with a fascinating diversity of flora and fauna, these ranges are a unique yet integral part of Southern California's environment. To learn what humankind has wrought on this magnificent landscape of mountain and desert, turn the ensuing pages.

Bighorn sheep on a rocky hillside in the northern Santa Rosa Mountains. These statuesque animals favor arid, precipitous terrain over gentle forest. — BONNER BLONG

Nolina thrusts stalks of creamy white blossoms amid a stand of ribbonwood along the Palms to Pines Highway near Santa Rosa Summit. — ROY MURPHY

A Cahuilla woman grinding meal.
— SOUTHWEST MUSEUM

2
EARLY PEOPLES

Untold centuries before the first European explorers arrived, Southern California was the home of primitive peoples. Unfortunately, the archaeological evidence regarding these early humans is scanty, and the time of their arrival is subject to speculation.

Some archaeologists believe that "Calico Man" (referring to the location where ancient stone artifacts were found) dates back 48,000 years.[1] "Laguna Woman" and "Los Angeles Man" have been dated at 17,000 and 23,600 years respectively.[2] There is much disagreement among archaeologists regarding these "early man" date estimates.

The difficulty of precise dating of habitation sites is due primarily to the interpretation of the meager archaeological finds. Some proponents of ancient inhabitation in Southern California rely on the dating of stone artifacts which are interpreted by others as being naturally eroded rather than fashioned by human hands.

It is, however, widely accepted that aboriginal peoples have been here for at least 10,000 years. At that time, the environment was more moist and cool, and several ancient lakes were still to be found in the Mojave and Colorado deserts. The San Dieguito peoples, consisting largely of small, mobile bands of hunter-gatherers, were the earliest documented group known to have inhabited the area.[3] Archaeological interpretation of artifacts indicates that during the San Dieguito occupation of much of Southern California, their projectile points became quite refined and their stone tools quite varied in both style and function. Knives, scrapters, planes and choppers, all made from stone, have been found in several scattered locations.

About 6,000 years ago, the local environment began to fluctuate between cool and wet, and warm and dry. During this period, the native peoples began to occupy seasonal sites as climatic conditions dictated. Although animals remained the main source of food, plants were beginning to assume more importance. Food processing tools such as *manos* and *metates,* used to grind seeds and other vegetal materials, appeared.[4]

During the period from about 3,200 to 1,400 years ago, the environment became much the same as it is today. The Pleistocene lakes dried up and the climate, except along the coast, became generally warm and dry. The use of the bow and arrow seems to have begun during this period, a significant improvement over the thrown spear that had previously been used. This change in hunting weaponry was probably dictated by a growing scarcity of game animals as much of the land became arid.

The peoples occupying the San Jacinto Mountains and neighboring areas at the time of European contact were the Cahuilla, unrelated to the ancient San Dieguito culture. According to archaeologists, the Cahuilla arrived in this mountain and desert region some 2,500 to 3,000 years ago.[5] They may have migrated from the Great Basin area to the northeast, or possibly from the desert plateau region of what is now Arizona and southern Utah.

Linguistically, the Cahuilla language was one of six of the *Takic* family of the Uto-Aztecan stock. The Takic family of languages included those spoken by most of the Indian peoples of Southern California, including the Gabrielino and Fernandeño (Los Angeles County), the Juaneño (Orange County), the Serrano (San Bernardino County), and the Luiseño, Cahuilla, and Cupeño (Riverside-San Diego counties). This indicates that all these native peoples were closely related.

The Cahuilla were divided into approximately a dozen independent clans, politico-religious kin groups, each having its own name, territory, and common ancestry, and ruled over by a nominal leader known as a *net*. Each clan was further divided into a number of lineages, or family groups. Each lineage occupied a particular village site and claimed a specific tract of land for hunting and gathering purposes.[6]

Anthropologists, starting with William Duncan Strong in the 1920s, have somewhat arbitrarily divided all the Cahuilla into three territorial groupings: the Western or Pass Cahuilla, the Desert Cahuilla, and the

A Cahuilla seed gatherer beating bushes with a racquet-shaped beater. She is holding an open basket to catch seeds as they fall. When the basket is full, she places the seeds into the large basket on her back, slung in a carrying net suspended from her forehead. — SOUTHWEST MUSEUM

Mountain Cahuilla. The Western or Pass Cahuilla lived in San Gorgonio Pass, the upper Coachella Valley, and in the palm canyons on the desert slope of the San Jacintos. The high San Jacintos were apparently within their seasonal domain. The Desert Cahuilla were found primarily in the lower Coachella Valley and in the eastern canyons of the Santa Rosas. The mountain Cahuilla inhabited the Cahuilla (Anza) Valley, the Santa Rosas, and Coyote Canyon as far south as the edge of Borrego Valley.[7]

The Cahuilla were keenly aware of their environment. Permanent villages were located near sources of both food and water, usually near a spring or at the mouth of a watered canyon. Besides the dozens of permanent locations, there were seasonal sites higher in the mountains, used for hunting and gathering purposes during the warmer months. The Cahuilla territory varied greatly in topography, climate, and vegetation, perhaps more so than any other Southern California native people. Their lands ranged from 270 feet below sea level in the Salton Sink to 10,800 feet above sea level on San Jacinto Peak.

Important Mountain Cahuilla villages were located at *Paui* (Cahuilla) in the Anza Valley, *Pauki* in Terwilliger Valley, *Saupalpa* near Tripp Flats, *Kewel* and *Kolwoyakut*, both known as Old Santa Rosa, in upper Rockhouse Canyon, *Sewiu* (Old Santa Rosa #2) high on the western slope of Santa Rosa Mountain, *San we yet* or *Sowis is pakh* (New Santa Rosa) on Vandeventer Flat, *Natcuta* just above Horse Canyon, and at various sites in Coyote Canyon.

Along the desert base of the San Jacintos were Western Cahuilla villages at *Tetcanaakiktum* in Snow Creek, *Wakaxix* in Blaisdell Canyon, *Mala* in Chino Canyon, *Sec he* at Palm Springs, *Kakwawit* in Tahquitz Canyon, *Panyik* in Andreas Canyon, *Eit* in Murray Canyon, and at *Tatmilmi* in Palm Canyon.

Most of the Desert Cahuilla villages were in the Coachella Valley and Salton Sink areas; two of them were close to the northeastern base of the Santa Rosas: *Mauulmii* (Toro) and *Pauuchekiva* (Martinez).

The Western and Desert Cahuilla made seasonal pilgrimages into the mountains to escape the summer heat, to hunt, and to gather foodstuffs. Sites of seasonal occupation have been located all over the San Jacinto and Santa Rosa mountains (except the highest peaks), and archaeologists are finding more every year.

At most of the seasonal village locations, bedrock and portable mortars, metates, and manos have been found, indicating that food processing occurred there. Pictographs, probably Mountain Cahuilla in origin, have been located near Hemet Lake, in the Garner

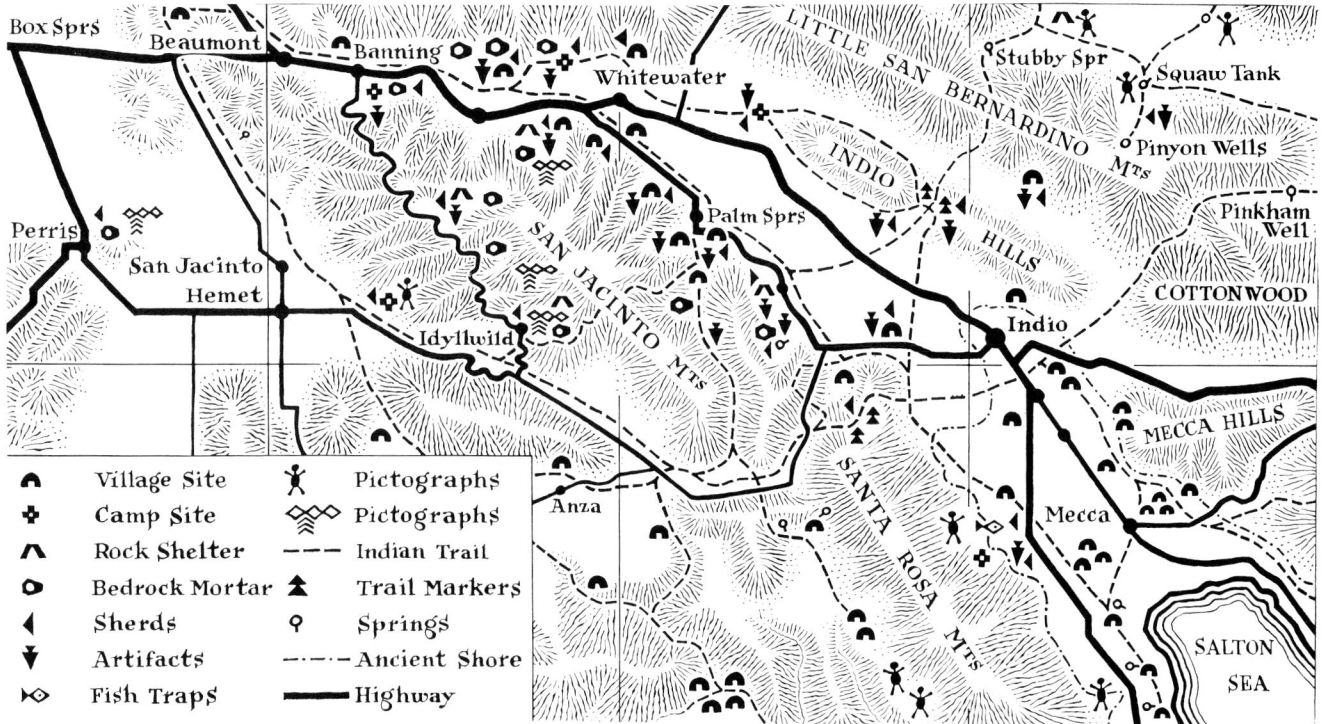

A map showing Cahuilla sites and trails in the San Jacinto and Santa Rosa mountains and in the adjacent valleys. — HARRY C. JAMES

Valley, and in Strawberry Valley. A boulder with intriguing pictographs was found in Fern Valley around the turn of the century. Zigzagging and parallel lines, diamonds, and chevrons are painted on the boulder, probably associated with girls' puberty rites. During ceremonies, the girls would paint similar designs on their faces and nearby rocks.[8]

The seemingly inhospitable environment which constituted the territory of the Cahuilla would seem unlikely to yield much in the way of edible food. Yet, the Cahuilla were masters at recognizing and utilizing the meager vegetation of their homeland. Mesquite, screwbean, yucca, desert agave (century plant), and acorns were primary food sources. When the weather warmed in the higher elevations, they would gather manzanita berries, pine nuts, sage, chia, and elderberries.

Some of these and other plants were used for medicinal purposes. Creosote bush was brewed into a tea and used to treat ailments from colds and chest congestion to stomach cramps. In a poultice form, it helped prevent infection and promoted healing of sores and wounds.

The Cahuilla were skillful hunters of both large and small game animals. Large mammals such as deer, antelope, and sometimes mountain sheep were hunted by adult males. Smaller game such as rabbits, squirrels, and rodents were stalked by both men and boys. Birds, particularly quail, were also important parts of the Cahuilla diet.

A typical Cahuilla village consisted of several types of structures. A ceremonial house, or *kishumnawat,* centrally located, was the largest building. This circular structure was sometimes as large as fifty feet in diameter. In it was kept the *maiswut,* or sacred bundle, consisting of sacred objects wrapped in a reed mat. A sweathouse, or *hovachat,* used primarily by men, was often located near a water source. A family residence, made of reeds, branches, and brush, was known as a *kish.*[9]

The social structure of the Cahuilla consisted of two main groups, or moieties, the Wildcats and the Coyotes. Every person belonged to one of these moieties. A Cahuilla child was considered a member of the group to whom his or her father belonged. The Wildcats were said to be descendents of one of the creator beings known as *Mukat*; the Coyotes were believed to be descendents of the other creator being, *Temayawut.* Individuals who married had to belong to opposite moieties. The two main groups were further broken down into the clans.

Membership in a clan was also determined by the father's relationship. Children belonged to the clan of their father. Each clan claimed its own territory and control over the natural resources within it. The clans

An Indian grinding rock in Strawberry Valley. 13 mortar holes reveal this as a primary food processing location.
— NELL EMERSON ZIEGLER

Over fifty mortar holes, many of which have been filled by blowing sand, indicate this site in Garner Valley was used as a food processing location. Using stone pestles, acorns, nuts, and seeds were ground into meal inside these holes.

This view from the inside of the rock shelter pictured on the opposite page shows mortar holes in front of the cave where food was processed. A short distance away runs a stream where fresh water was available.

The Fern Valley pictograph is one of the best preserved works of prehistoric Indian rock art to be found in the San Jacinto Mountains.

This is a view looking into a large Indian rock shelter. Its depth and protective overhang shielded its occupants from the elements.

Mortar with pestle in place outside of a rock shelter near Alvin Meadows.

would often mark their territorial boundaries with petroglyphs, designs carved into boulders or rock outcroppings. Some areas with plentiful foodstuffs, such as Pinyon Flat, or warm springs, such as *Paui* in the Cahuilla Valley and *Sec he* (Agua Caliente) in Palm Springs, were open to joint use by several clans.

As with all Native Americans, spiritual beliefs and rituals played a major role in Cahuilla life. There were rites of passage for adolescents, ceremonies for marriage, death and burial, and other special occasions. These ceremonies were presided over by the clan leader, known as the *net*.

The greatest of these ceremonies was the *nukil*. Held every year or two, the *nukil* honored the memories of those who had died since the last ceremony had been performed. It lasted seven days and was attended by many different clans. The purpose of the ceremony was two-fold: to help the souls of the deceased to arrive safely in the afterlife, and to terminate the period of mourning for the departed. The coming together of many different clans for the *nukil* also provided an opportunity for trade and for arrangement of marriages.

Marriages were arranged by the parents, sometimes when the couple to be married were still young children. Usually, however, the boy was in his late teens and the girl in her early teens. As with many cultures, the marriage process from initial negotiations to the actual ceremony itself entailed the giving and receiving of gifts. Marriages were therefore economic as well as social alliances between clans.[10]

The Cahuilla held many places as sacred, especially mountain tops or high rock outcroppings. San Jacinto Peak, Tahquitz Peak, and Lily Rock in the San Jacintos, and Toro Peak and Santa Rosa Mountain in the Santa Rosas, are examples. These high points were believed to be places where sacred beings dwelled or touched down when they visited the earth.

Tahquitz Peak in particular and the high San Jacintos in general were believed to be the dwelling place of *Tahquitz*, variously spelled *Tauquish*, *Ta co wits*, or *Taqwis*, the much feared supernatural being associated with meteors, earthquakes, thunder and lightning, and other natural phenomenon. He was thought to possess demonic power and brought harm to people who ventured too close to his mountain stronghold. Tahquitz was feared because he not only could kill people, but also destroy their spirits. Legends of Tahquitz's evil deeds abound, not only among the Cahuilla but among native people throughout Southern California.[11]

One such legend describes the abduction of the son of a Soboba hunter who was guarding a kill his father had made in the San Jacinto Mountains. Tahquitz tried to persuade forest animals to kill the boy, but they refused. Tahquitz then returned the boy to his people, but cautioned him not to tell of this experience for four or five days or he would die. The boy complied and waited five days to tell his story. Tahquitz really meant four or five years, and the next day the boy was found dead.[12]

Another legend tells of the kidnapping by Tahquitz of an Agua Caliente girl whose beauty enamored him. He took her to his mountain cave near Tahquitz Peak, where he forced other captives to act as her servants. He forced her to join him in eating the souls of many people. This continued for several years, but the girl was so unhappy that Tahquitz finally returned her to her people. He made her promise not to tell what had happened until three years had passed. But the villagers badgered her until, after only one year, she revealed to them her experiences as Tahquitz's captive. She was found dead the next morning – another victim of Tahquitz's evil

The famous *Aqua Caliente* at Palm Springs, known to the Cahuillas as *Sec he*. This was a desert Indian gathering place from hundreds of years before the white man's arrival. Pictured here is the first bath house, built in 1874 and razed in 1914. Presently the location of the Spa Hotel.
— PALM SPRINGS HISTORICAL SOCIETY

This boulder located inside a rock shelter has apparently been intentionally pitted by rock carving tools. It is the only known pitted petroglyph known to exist in the San Jacintos.

Desert Cahuilla *kish*. These homes, made of reeds, branches and brush, were located at village sites.
— GEORGE WHARTON JAMES

An olla found by Forest Service personnel after a fire.

Two Edward Curtis photographs of Cahuilla women, taken in the 1920s. The picture on the left shows a woman carrying a basket on her head in Palm Canyon. The right picture is a profile of a young Desert Cahuilla woman.
— SOUTHWEST MUSEUM (both)

powers.[13]

There are many other tales which attest to the demonic nature of Tahquitz. Even today, some believe in his evil power. Earthquakes are said to be Tahquitz stamping about in his mountain cave or throwing huge boulders at his trapped victims.

The population of the Cahuilla before European contact is not known. Archaeologists have estimated that it may have ranged from 3,600 up to a high of 10,000. Around 6,000 is probably a safe guess. Unlike some of the coastal peoples, the Cahuilla population was not decimated by the arrival of the Spanish and their culture remained intact. Their desert and mountain homeland, away from the mission settlements, effectively protected them. The Cahuilla remained relatively intact as a people during the Mexican rancho era, although many of them worked on the great ranchos and were influenced by Californio culture. Sadly, the lot of these native peoples would dramatically decline after California became part of the United States. Encroachment, loss of lands, disease, and culture shock took their inevitable toll, as we shall see in the chapter *Ordeal of A People*.

NOTES

1. Robert Heizer, "Introduction," *Handbook of the North American Indians, Vol. 8, California* (Washington, D.C.: Smithsonian Institution, 1978), p. 3.
2. Richard L. Carrico, et al, *Cultural Resource Overview: San Bernardino National Forest*, prepared under United States Forest Service Contract No. 53-9JA9-0-219 by Westec Services, Inc., San Diego, 1982, p. 4-5.
3. Martin A. Baumhoff, "Environmental Background," *Handbook... Vol. 8, California*, p. 27.
4. *Ibid.*, p. 28.
5. Lowell John Bean and Lisa Bourgeault, *The Cahuilla* (New York: Chelsea House Publishers, 1989), p. 13.
6. Lowell John Bean, Sylvia Brakke Vane, Jackson Young, *The Cahuilla Landscape: The Santa Rosa and San Jacinto Mountains* (Menlo Park: Ballena Press, 1991), p. 5.
7. William Duncan Strong, *Aboriginal Society in Southern California* (Banning: Malki Museum Press, 1972, reprint of 1929 edition), p. 36.
8. Lowell John Bean, et al, *Native American Places in San Bernardino National Forest* (Menlo Park: Cultural Systems Research, Inc., 1981, done by contract with U.S. Forest Service), p. 187-188.
9. Harry C. James, *The Cahuilla Indians* (Los Angeles: Westernlore Press, 1960), p. 42-45.
10. Lowell John Bean, *Mukat's People: The Cahuilla Indians of Southern California* (Berkeley: U. of California Press, 1972), p. 91-92; and Strong, p. 169-172.
11. Almost every book about the Cahuillas mentions the Tahquitz legend. For other cultural groups' fears of Tahquitz, see Philip Stedman Sparkman, *The Culture of The Luiseño Indians* Ramona: Acoma Books, 1971, reprint of 1908 study), p. 220-221; and Bernice Eastman Johnston, *California's Gabrielino Indians* (Los Angeles: Southwest Museum, 1962), p. 21.
12. Chief Francisco Patencio, as told to Margaret Boynton, *Stories and Legends of The Palm Springs Indians* (Los Angeles: Times-Mirror Press, 1943), p. 44-45; and James, p. 82-84.
13. Lucile Hooper, *The Cahuilla Indians* (Ramona: Ballena Press, 1972, reprint of 1920 study), p. 364-365.

Captain Juan Bautista de Anza led two of the most famous overland expeditions in California history. The first, in 1774, was to establish a route between Sonora and California. The second, in 1775-76, brought colonists for the founding of San Francisco. The Anza party is here drawn by Walter Francis. — THE BANCROFT LIBRARY

3

SPANISH EXPLORERS, MISSION RANCHOS AND MEXICAN LAND GRANTS

Early in the year 1772 Captain Pedro Fages of the Catalonian Volunteers, military *comandante* of Spanish California, led a small force of *soldados de cuera* (leather jacket soldiers) eastward from San Diego in pursuit of deserters. The party reached the desert, then turned northwestward into Borrego Valley, ascended Coyote Canyon, and skirted the San Jacintos via an undetermined route. Fages and his soldiers were almost certainly the first Europeans to approach the San Jacinto Mountains.

Fages tells us of his journey in a brief *nota*, or addendum, to a report he wrote on an exploration of the northern San Joaquin Valley a year later:

> Last year, coming from San Diego in pursuit of deserters, I went and struck the plain fifty leagues toward the east. Lack of water forced us into the sierra, but when we were parallel with the mission of San Gabriel we went about fifteen leagues to strike the plain again; and we went along the plain toward the north, keeping close to the sierra, on account of water, travelling for about twenty-five leagues, until we reached the pass of Buena Vista. Most of these twenty-five leagues we were passing through groves of date palms, the land both to the east and the south having more and more palm groves. But the country appeared to be very short of water. We saw many smokes all along the plain.
> Royal Presidio of San Carlos at Monterey, Nov. 27, 1773
>
> [signed]   DON PEDRO FAGES (Rubric)[1]

Captain Fages' brief *nota* gives too few details to pinpoint his route, so how can we assume that he traversed the San Jacintos? Evidence that he ascended Coyote Canyon is provided in the diaries of the Anza Expedition that used this route two years later. Horse tracks were seen in the canyon, and native Indians told the Anza party that soldiers had passed this way before.[2]

The late Herbert Eugene Bolton, master historian of the Spanish borderlands, determined that Fages crossed the coast range from San Diego to the desert by one of several possible routes, then turned north into Borrego Valley. Borrego tilts northward to a pronounced cleft in the mountains, obvious to any explorer. The cleft is Coyote Creek, which divides the San Ysidro and Santa Rosa mountains. Not only does Coyote Creek provide ample water and pasture, it also offers a direct route across the mountains via either Cahuilla (Anza) Valley and Bautista Canyon, or Vandeventer Flat and either Garner Valley or Palm Canyon. We must use conjecture here, as Fages' *nota* gives us no hint of his route until he is "parallel" with San Gabriel Mission. Coyote Canyon divides into three branches at what is known as the "Turkey Tracks." The right branch heading north is Horse Canyon, which leads to Vandeventer Flat on the present Santa Rosa Indian Reservation. The middle branch is Nance Canyon, which leads northwest toward Anza Valley. Tule Canyon, the third branch, heads west into the mountain ridge south of Terwilliger Valley. Two years after the Fages expedition, Anza took the ridge between Nance and Tule canyons, as we shall see. But there is no reason to assume that Fages did. Travelling up Coyote Canyon today to the Turkey Tracks, Horse Canyon, the largest of the three branches, appears to be a feasible route. If Fages took this fork he would have crossed the mountains either via Garner Valley and the South Fork of the San Jacinto River into the San Jacinto Valley, or via Palm Canyon to the desert. If he took the latter course, Fages would have been the first non-Indian through San Gorgonio Pass. But again, this is all conjecture.

Once past the San Jacintos, Fages turned northwest and crossed the low hills – San Timoteo, Reche and Box Springs canyons are all possibilities – into the San Bernardino Valley, now "parallel," as he writes, with San Gabriel Mission. Rather than visiting the mission, he continued northwest over Cajon Pass, returning to the "plain" (desert), then skirted the southern edge of

31

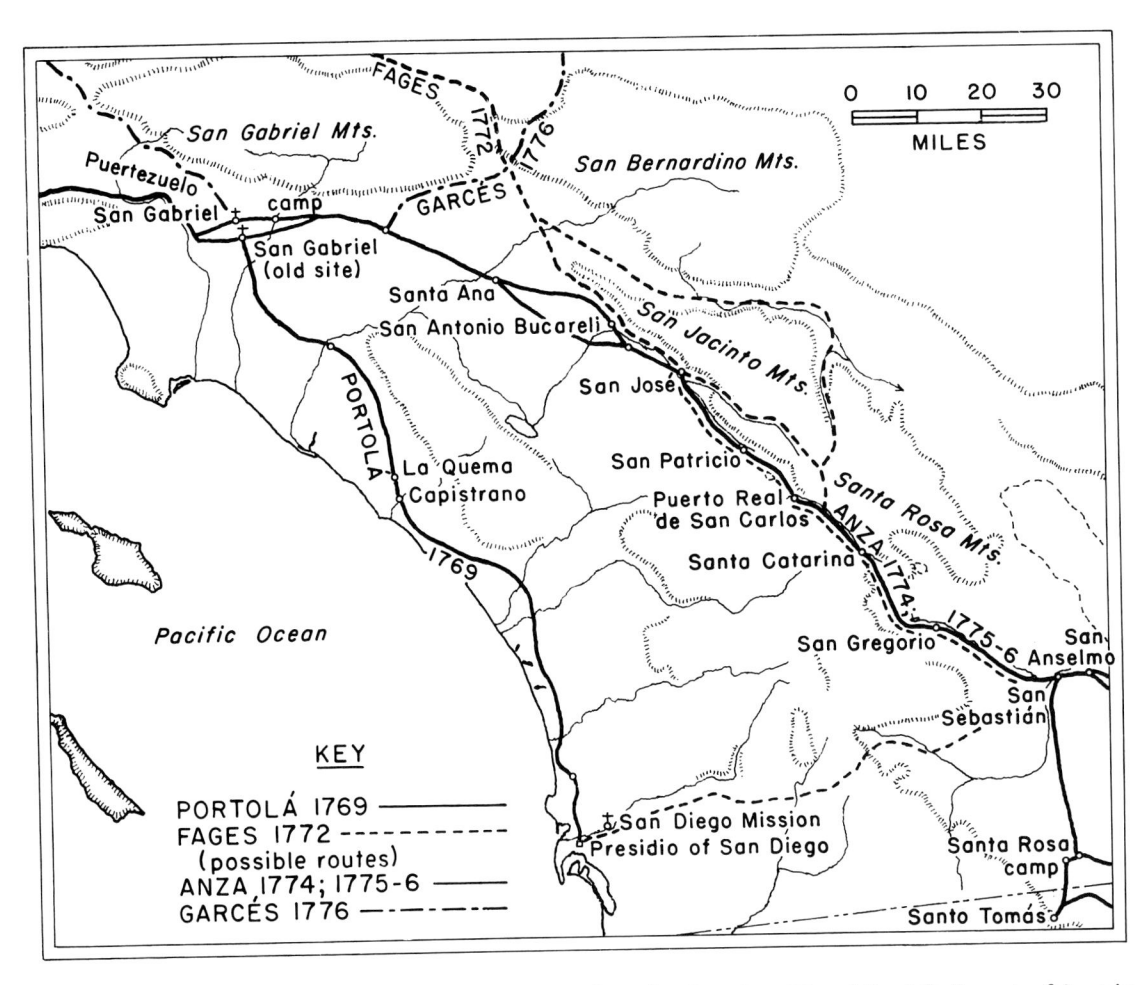

Map showing the possible routes across the San Jacintos by Pedro Fages in 1772, and the definite route of Anza in 1774 and 1775-76. — LARRY JONES

Antelope Valley to what he called the Pass of Buena Vista (Tejon Pass). Bolton believes the "date palms" he mentions were Joshua Trees, numerous in the high desert beyond Cajon Pass. From Buena Vista Pass, Fages dropped into the southern end of the San Joaquin Valley and then crossed the mountains west to Mission San Luis Obispo, completing one of the truly remarkable explorations of early California.[3]

We know much more about the life and character of Pedro Fages, European discoverer of the San Jacintos, than we know about his 1772 *jornada*. Fages was born in Guisona, in the Spanish province of Catalonia, in 1734. He began his lifelong military career in 1762 and served in a Spanish campaign against Portugal. In 1767 he joined the Catalonian Volunteers, an elite military unit, and was dispatched to Mexico. After two years of campaigning against Indians in Sonora, he was assigned to the Portolá expedition to California. He reached San Diego on the packet *San Carlos* before Portolá's overland party, and joined the latter on its famous journey to Monterey in 1769-1770. He served as military *comandante* of California from 1770 to 1774 and led several significant explorations of southern California, San Francisco Bay and the San Joaquin delta.

Pedro Fages had both positive and negative qualities. He was a bold leader and expert trail blazer and explorer. His courage and devotion to duty were exemplary. On the debit side, Fages was accused of being a brutal disciplinarian, subject to violent outbursts of temper, arrogance and unyielding demeanor. His tour of duty as military commander in California was marred by frequent disputes with Father Junipero Serra and other Franciscan missionaries. Ultimately, this friction led to his recall to Mexico in 1774.

He wrote an incisive historical and natural account of California while awaiting reassignment in Mexico City. Even today, this document is a valuable source of information to historians.

Fages' military leadership capabilities led to his promotion to Lieutenant Colonel and his campaigns against the Apaches on the Sonora frontier in the years 1777 to 1781. In the latter year he led a punitive expedition, only partially successful, against the Yumas of the lower Colorado River, in retribution for the bloody Yuma revolt in which Father Garcés was martyred.

Fages returned to California as governor from 1782 to 1791. Again, friction with the Franciscans marred his otherwise successful term of office. Giving him almost as much trouble was his insufferable wife Eulalia de Callis, who did not like California and threatened to leave him on several occasions. Fages retired to Mexico City in 1791 and died there in late 1794.[4]

Fortunately, we know far more about the two Anza expeditions that crossed the San Jacinto Mountains in 1774 and 1775-1776, thanks to detailed diaries by not only Anza himself, but also Franciscan padres Garcés and Diaz on the first expedition and Font on the second. In a brilliant *tour-de-force*, Herbert Eugene Bolton followed Anza's trail by car, horseback, and on foot, identifying the precise route and day to day campsites. Bolton published the fully annotated diaries in his classic five-volume *Anza's California Expeditions*.[5]

Juan Bautista de Anza was born at the Presidio de Fronteras, a few miles south of present-day Douglas, Arizona, in either 1735 or 1736. Both his grandfather and father were distinguished frontier soldiers, and young Anza continued the family tradition. He became an accomplished frontier fighter, participating in many campaigns against the Apaches and other Indian peoples who resented the Spanish presence.

Viceroy Antonio Maria Bucareli y Ursua, encouraged by the successful establishment of five new missions, granted Captain Anza's request to find an overland route to Alta California. Anza, leading a party of 34 persons, including twenty soldiers and two padres, set out from the Presidio of Tubac, near today's Tucson, Arizona, on January 8, 1774. He followed Father Kino's trail to the Colorado and crossed the river with the guidance of friendly Yuma Indians. The party painfully traversed the arid wasteland of the lower Colorado Desert, dipping into what is now Baja California, then trudged north along the foot of the *Sierra Madre de California*.

Of inestimatable help to Anza was an Indian from Mission San Gabriel who knew Spanish and some of the native languages. He was Sebastian Tarabal. Anza called him *El Peregrino* (The Wanderer). The mysterious *El Peregrino* – one of those shadowy characters in history who seem to come from nowhere, shine briefly, then fade into obscurity – guided the Anza party over the route he had taken the previous year when fleeing from San Gabriel to the Colorado River. Without him, Anza's task would have been far more daunting.

On March 10, 1774 the party reached a watering place at the junction of Carrizo Creek and San Felipe Wash. Sebastian recognized the marshy area as the point where the route turned into the mountains. A thankful Anza named it *San Sebastian* in El Peregrino's honor. (It is now Harper's Well, located a few miles east of Anza-Borrego State Park.)

The party then turned west and followed the rocky bed of San Felipe Creek into the broad Borrego Valley. Ahead lay Coyote Creek and the pathway over the mountains promised by Sebastian. Anza recounted his joy:

Juan Bautista de Anza

> Monday, March 14 – A little before daylight we set forth toward the north, and having traveled about six leagues... arrived at a spring or fountain of the finest water, which runs for about two leagues, having many willows... At its head we halted for the night, and to the place I gave the name *Santa Catharina*. Here was found much grass and other green plants, as well as wild vines and trees, which announce to us an improvement in the country from here forward. [6]

They had conquered the desert.

Plentiful water and forage nourished Anza's men and horses as they ascended Coyote Creek. They encountered numerous Indians, who by their jerking gyrations and loud chatter seemed to resent the Spanish presence. Anza called them *Jecuiches*; They were probably Cahuilla, as we call them today. After six leagues, the party came to the forks of Nance and Tule canyons. Until then the grade had been easy. Now, they struggled up the ridge between these two tributaries to a campsite just below a boulder-strewn gap on the mountain crest.

Next day, Anza climbed to the gap and marveled at the scene before him:

> "Right here there is a pass which I named the Royal Pass of San Carlos. From it are seen most beautiful green and flower-strewn prairies, and snow-covered mountains with pines, oaks, and other trees which grow in cold countries. Likewise here the waters divide, some flowing this way toward the Gulf and others toward the Philippine Ocean. Moreover, it is now proved that the sierra in which we are traveling connects with the sierras of lower California. In the course of the journey made today we have seen an improvement in the country in every way and have concluded from its moisture that it may be suitable for seasonal crops and the planting of fruit trees, and that there are pastures sufficient for maintaining cattle."[7]

Anza had arrived at the edge of Cahuilla Valley, dotted with oaks and pines, with the snow-capped San

La Puerta – The Gateway. Anza's "Royal Pass of San Carlos," where he emerged from Coyote Canyon onto the Cahuilla Plains. This view is looking southeast from the top of the pass; Anza's party emerged from behind the trees on the far right. This picture was taken about 1925, when La Puerta was part of the Fred Clark Ranch.
— BUD CLARK

Looking northwest across the Cahuilla Plains (Anza Valley) from the rocks above La Puerta, as it appears today. Anza came from the left, along the tree line, to emerge in the high basin.

Jacintos looming high to the right. A short march took them through the valley, where they camped by a small lake (now dry) which Anza named *Laguna de Principe*. Next day, a storm delayed their departure:

> "Because it had rained and snowed during the night and part of this morning, we were not able to set forth until ten o'clock in the forenoon. We then started, marching northwest and north-northwest, through the valley which lies between two ranges. [Cahuilla Mountain to their left, Thomas Mountain to the right.] We followed it until it narrowed between several other hills, at the foot of which we halted for the night, having traveled three leagues. From these hills there is seen a very pretty little valley which within itself contains water and trees in abundance. We called it *San Patricio*." [8]

Anza's *San Patricio* is today Tripp Flats, located near the head of Bautista Canyon. The following day they descended the long canyon to the San Jacinto Valley, which they named *San José*, or *Saint Joseph*. Anza was entranced with the view:

> "Through this beautiful valley, to which we gave the name San José, runs a good-sized river, on whose banks are large, shady groves. Likewise in the mountains where the river forms there are seen pines, oaks and various other trees. All its plain is full of flowers, fertile pastures, and other vegetation useful for the raising of cattle...as many as one might wish." [9]

The snowy San Jacinto Mountains loomed as a lofty backdrop. Father Garcés, traveling with Anza, called them *la gran Sierra Nevada*. He picked up some metal-bearing rocks in the valley, which suggested to him that the mountains might contain valuable minerals. [10]

The Anza party then followed the San Jacinto Valley northwestward, passing *Playa San Antonio de Bucareli,* "several leagues in circumference and as full of white geese as of water." [11] This was San Jacinto Lake, usually dry, near today's Lakeview.

Anza and his weary party hurried on to Mission San Gabriel, then on to Monterey. They had opened a land route from northwestern Mexico to California, one they hoped would be used for years to come.

Anza repeated the overland march in 1775-1776, this time bringing a colonization party of 240, including 29 women, bound for San Francisco Bay, where Spain's most northernly outpost was to be established. Accompanying Anza this time was Father Pedro Font, one of the master diarists of Spanish California.

Again, the party, now much larger, crossed Borrego Valley and ascended Coyote Creek to Cahuilla Valley. Father Font noticed the restless Indians, who he called *Los Danzantes* (The Dancers):

> The Indians came out of their grottos as if they were angry, motioning to us with the hand that we must not go forward, talking in jargon with great rapidity, slapping their thighs, jumping like wild goats and with similar movements for which reason they have been called the Dancers. [12]

Father Font eloquently described the view from the top of the pass:

> From the Pass of San Carlos, as if the scenery of the theatre were changed, one beholds the *Sierra Madre de California* totally different – green and leafy, with good grass and trees...one sees to the north-northwest and northwest the same *Sierra Madre*, very high and white with snow. [13]

Mission San Luis Rey de Francia, founded by the Franciscans in 1798. From this mission, expeditions were undertaken into the interior country to find ranch sites. Rancho San Jacinto was the furthermost cattle ranch of San Luis Rey, founded sometime between 1816 and 1821.

Father Antonio Peyri, the first *padre* of San Luis Rey Mission. Under Fray Peyri's direction, Rancho San Jacinto was founded.

Reaching the Valley of *San José* (San Jacinto Valley), Font, like Garcés before him, was impressed by the high *Sierra Nevada* (Snowy Range) to the right. *Sierra Nevada* was the name the Spanish used for the San Jacintos, and *Sierra Madre de California* for the coast ranges in general.

The Anza overland trail, opened with such promise in 1774, was closed permanently after the Yuma Massacre of 1781, when two small Spanish missions along the lower Colorado River were destroyed and Father Garcés murdered. Not for forty years would another overland route from Sonora to California be forged, this time via Coachella Valley and San Gorgonio Pass. Coyote Canyon, Cahuilla Valley and Bautista Canyon were once again left to native peoples.

On June 13, 1798, alongside the San Luis Rey River, four miles from the sea, Mission San Luis Rey de Francia was founded. Fray Antonio Peyri came down from San Luis Obispo to head the new Franciscan mission.

It was not long until the padres began exploring the back country. Pine timbers were cut and hauled down from Palomar Mountain on ox-pulled *carretas*. An *asistencia* at San Antonio de Pala, eighteen miles inland from San Luis Rey, was founded in 1816.

San Luis Rey soon became one of the leading missions in livestock production. Herds of cattle and horses grazed on the valley's rich grasslands. Eight mission ranchos were established well inland.

Rancho San Jacinto, furthermost cattle ranch of Mission San Luis Rey, was founded sometime between 1816 and 1821. The circumstances of its founding and exact date are unknown. The name honored the Silesian-born Dominican Saint Hyacinth (*San Jacinto* in Spanish), whose feast day is August 16. As happens so often in trying to trace early California history, few references to the isolated rancho have been uncovered in mission documents.

The first mention of Rancho San Jacinto is found in an 1821 diary of Father José Sanchez, who with Father Mariano Payéras and two soldiers, journeyed from San Diego to San Gabriel looking for suitable mission sites. On September 24, 1821 the two padres set out from Temecula Rancho at daybreak, traveling north-northeast. Father Sanchez writes,

> "Proceeding in the same direction we stopped at *Jaguara*, so called by the natives, but by our people *San Jacinto*. This is the rancho for the cattle of San Luis Rey, distant from Temecula about eleven or twelve leagues.... The soil is very good, but on reaching San Jacinto, its lands, though used for pasture, proved to be of little value on account of the alkaki. From this little elevation where the *enramada* (arbor) is situated, north to south, there are springs. The arroyo which runs from here east to south is covered with alamos for about two leagues. In front of the *enramada*, toward the northeast, is a spring of tepid water. Not far away is fine timber. [14]

So we have the first description of the San Jacinto Valley and the timber on the mountains since Anza, and the earliest documented use of the place name *San Jacinto*.

The eight ranchos of Mission San Luis Rey – Pala, Las Flores, Santa Margarita, San Juan, San Marcos, Temecula, San Jacinto, and Agua Caliente – were said to produce annually by the late 1820s "27,000 head of cattle, 26,100 sheep, 1,300 goats, 300 pigs, 1,950 horses and 180 mules."[15] In one year, Ranchos Temecula and San Jacinto were reported to have produced 20,000 hides for the mission.[16]

A visitor to Rancho San Jacinto in the 1820s and '30s would have seen herds of cattle and horses grazing on the broad plain and drinking from the abundant waters that flowed from the mountains. If the day was hot, many of the animals could be seen resting under the streamside alamos and willows. Atop a low hill in the central valley, just above the springs, was an adobe structure known as *Casa Loma* (Hill House). Here lived the rancho *jefe* (chief) and his Mexican *vaqueros* (cow-

An early view across Rancho San Jacinto Viejo, looking southwest from near Gilman Hot Springs. Mission cattle roamed these plains during the 1820s and early 1830s.

boys). The Indian cowhands lived in grass huts near the river. A few hundred yards away, above the southwest bank of the San Jacinto River, was the *Corral de Pilares* (Corral of the basin or bowl), a four acre enclosure bounded by an adobe wall, that the *vaqueros* and their Indian helpers used for branding cattle at round-up time.[17]

We know that the Spaniards and their livestock used water that emitted from the San Jacinto Mountains and probably took timber from the lower slopes to use as roof beams in rancho buildings. But did they ever penetrate into the heart of the range? No evidence indicates that they ever entered the high country. We can only hazard a guess that cattle might have occasionally roamed up the San Jacinto River into the mountains, and that *vaqueros* went after them.

Across the mountains to the north was another mission cattle ranch. This was *San Gorgonio,* in the pass of the same name, the easternmost rancho of Mission San Gabriel. Like Rancho San Jacinto, just when and under what circumstances it was established are unknown. It was undoubtedly named for St. Gorgonius, an early Christian martyr, whose feast day is March 9. The earliest mention of Rancho San Gorgonio is contained in the records of the Romero-Estudillo Expedition of 1823. The purpose of this expedition was to reopen a land route between Mission San Gabriel, via San Gorgonio Pass, to Sonora. José Maria Estudillo's diary entry of December 25, 1823 states that after leaving Rancho San Bernardino, "We continued east until...we arrived at the last rancho, called *San Gorgonio,* and in the venacular, *Piatopa.*"[18] *Piatopa* was probably an aboriginal village near the mouth of Banning Water Canyon, just north of today's Banning.

There is some evidence that the Spaniards were aware of the San Gorgonio Pass several years before the Romero-Estudillo Expedition passed through it. The mysterious *Jornada del Sal* (Journey for the Salt), when a caravan of *carretas* annually traveled from San Gabriel through San Gorgonio Pass to recover salt from the Salton Sink, supposedly took place first around 1815 and continued for at least a decade.[19]

Romero and Estudillo were obliged to turn back on their first attempt. On January 18, 1824 they camped at *Agua Caliente* (today's Palm Springs). That night they thwarted an Indian attempt to steal the expedition's horses, but were unable to capture the thieves, who "were able to flee through the crags of the sierra under cover of darkness." The Indians escaped into the San Jacinto Mountains, and the soldiers hesitated to pursue them up the craggy canyons.

Next day, the expedition continued northwest until they arrived at "a little spring at the foot of the sierra." Here, Estudillo writes, "We encountered some cowboys from the Rancho of San Gorgonio who came driving cattle from *Agua Caliente* to the above rancho. Immediately they killed two cattle for the troop."[20]

So we know that mission cattle from Rancho San Gorgonio were driven as far as the Palm Springs area – probably to Palm, Andreas, Tahquitz and Chino canyons – to drink from the creeks that tumbled down from the precipitous northwest slope of the San Jacintos, and that Indians, probably Cahuillas, occasionally raided the herds from hideouts in the mountain fastness.

California became part of Mexico when allegiance to the latter was sworn in Monterey on April 11, 1822. The missions began their slow decline, as did the great mission ranchos. The era drew to a rapid close with the enactment by the Mexican government of the Secularization Act of 1833. No longer were the Franciscan padres masters of the vast mission lands or the cattle that roamed them. They were now limited to caring for the spiritual needs of the mission parishers. The mission lands, it was directed, were to be divided among Indian neophytes and Mexican settlers.

Livestock dwindled at many of the ex-mission ranchos, and Rancho San Jacinto was no exception. According to one source, twenty thousand head of cattle were slaughtered at Rancho San Jacinto shortly after it was divested from Mission San Luis Rey, and the hides were sold to American trading vessels.[21]

On August 9, 1842, José Antonio Estudillo, son of José Maria Estudillo and *mayordomo* of the secularized Mission San Luis Rey, filed an application for a grant of four square leagues of Rancho San Jacinto "with the understanding that it is absolutely vacant, the *mayordomo* of that establishment, five *manadas* (herds) of mare which was all that was on said place [having departed], being fearful of the incursions of the Indians."[22] Governor pro tem Manuel Jimeno, being assured that only three Christian Indians lived there and appreciative of Estudillo's service as mission *mayordomo*, awarded land "to the extent of eight square leagues, a little more or less" to Estudillo on December 21, 1842. One of the conditions of the grant was that Estudillo "shall not in any manner prejudice the Indians who are established on said land." Estudillo was also required to "pay the value of the house and corral that are on said place" – *Casa Loma* and the *Corral de Pilares*.[23] As long as he lived, Don Estudillo respected the rights and well-being of his rancho Indians.

When Estudillo's son-in-law Miguel de Pedrorena petitioned Governor Pio Pico for a grant of the "surplus land" of Rancho San Jacinto in 1845, he submitted a *diseño* (map) showing the rancho in two parts. The eastern portion belonging to Estudillo was labeled *San Jacinto Viejo* (Old San Jacinto), and the western half, which he wanted, labelled *San Jacinto Nuevo* (New San Jacinto). Pedrorena also asked for the *Potrero de San Jacinto* (Pasture of San Jacinto) in the hills to the northeast. Estudillo, who had originally petitioned for only the eastern four square leagues of the ex-mission rancho, offered no objection. Governor Pico granted Pedrorena the land he wanted under the name of *San Jacinto Nuevo y Potrero* on January 14, 1846. Strangely, no mention was made of the size of the grant in square leagues as was customary, only that it was "of the extent as shown by the map including the Potrero of San Jacinto."[24]

Within a few years, large herds of cattle were once again grazing in the San Jacinto Valley and drinking from the mountain streams.

The former San Gabriel Mission rancho of San Gorgonio became the subject of a prolonged dispute. In early 1843, James "Santiago" Johnson, an Englishman who had become a Mexican citizen, petitioned Governor Manuel Micheltorena for a square league of land adjoining and partially overlapping the ex-mission rancho. Johnson claimed that he needed the land because he "owned some stock and had no place to keep same." Micheltorena granted Johnson "the tract of land situated between San Jacinto and San Gorgonio, and on

José Maria Estudillo (1772-1830), born in Andalucia, Spain, came to California in 1795. He was the patriarch of the prominent Estudillo family of Spanish and Mexican California. The senior Estudillo participated with José Romero in the earliest known Spanish expedition through San Gorgonio Pass in 1823. His son, José Antonio Estudillo (1805-1852) was granted Rancho San Jacinto Viejo in 1842. – SAN DIEGO HISTORICAL SOCIETY

the north by San Timoteo and Yucaipa, of the extent of one square league, a little more or less," on March 22, 1843.[25] It was named *San Jacinto y San Gorgonio*.

Johnson apparently never settled on the land nor grazed his cattle there. Despite his stated need for the grant, he sold it a year later to Louis Rubidoux, a French-Canadian fur trapper who came from New Mexico to California in 1843. (Rubidoux also bought a half interest in Rancho Jurupa, near present day Riverside.)

Most of old Rancho Gorgonio remained unclaimed, which was probably one reason that Powell "Paulino" Weaver took over the old adobe, built during mission ranch days, and made it his home. He grazed his cattle in San Gorgonio Pass. Weaver was an American fur trapper who came to California in 1831 and became a Mexican citizen. His Mexican citizenship qualified him for a land grant. In 1845 Weaver, along with his friend Isaac Williams of Rancho Chino, petitioned Governor Pio Pico for a grant of "the place of San Gorgonio...which is vacant...[and] place there four or five thousand head of cattle." They also promised to maintain an armed force of nine or ten men for defense against marauding Indians. Weaver and Williams fur-

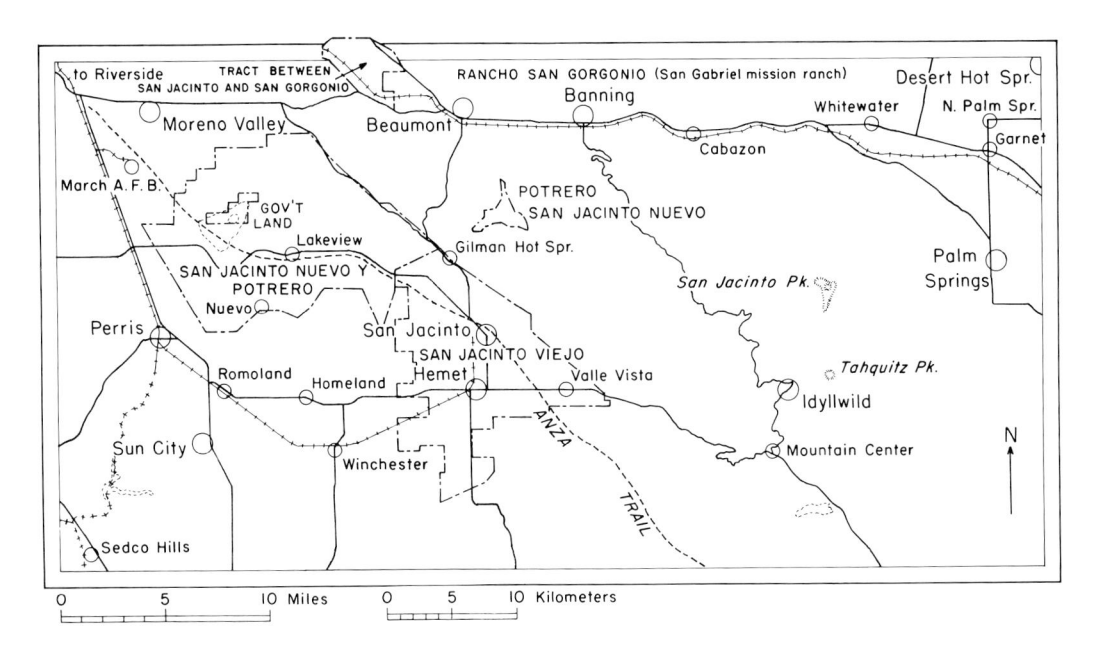

Map showing the locations of Spanish and Mexican ranchos in the San Jacinto and San Gorgonio Pass areas.
— LARRY JONES

ther stated that Santiago Johnson, grantee of *San Jacinto y San Gorgonio,* "lost all right thereto, first because he never occupied it nor made any improvement thereon; Secondly because he sold it to one who did not either make any improvements and who withdrew from this Country and until now has not returned after an absence of one year and a half."[26]

Governor Pico never issued the grant, probably because the ownership was unsettled. Nevertheless, Paulino Weaver continued to live there and run his cattle through the pass.

So as the era of Mexican California drew to a close, there were three land grant ranchos and one "squatter" rancho nestled in the valleys below the San Jacinto Mountains. Cattle roamed below the foothills and quenched their thirst in the mountain streams. But the San Jacinto high country was still the domain of the Cahuillas. There is no evidence to indicate that the Spaniards or their Mexican Californio successors ever penetrated the mountain fastness.

Mexican California came to an end with the American conquest of 1846-1847 and the signing of the Treaty of Guadulupe-Hidalgo on February 2, 1848. With the coming of the Anglos, the San Jacinto Mountains would receive more attention. Soon they would be explored, grazed, mined, deforested in places, penetrated by roads, and built upon to a degree few in the 1840s could have imagined.

NOTES

1. Herbert Eugene Bolton, "In The South San Joaquin Ahead of Garces," *CHSQ,* Oct. 1931.
2. Bolton, *Anza's California Expeditions* (Berkeley, 1930), Vol. II, p. 338, 343.
3. Bolton, "In The South San Joaquin Ahead of Garces."
4. Joseph P. Sanchez, *Spanish Bluecoats: The Catalonian Volunteers in Northwestern New Spain, 1767-1810* (Albuquerque, 1990), p. 58-70.
5. See footnote 2.
6. *Anza,* II, p. 86-87. A Spanish league was supposedly the distance a horseback party traveled in one hour. The distance varied greatly from 2 to 2½ miles in mountain terrain to 5 or 6 miles on level ground.
6. *Ibid.,* p. 92-93.
8. *Ibid.,* p. 91.
9. *Ibid.,* p. 92-93.
10. *Ibid.,* p. 345.
11. *Ibid.,* p. 93-94.
12. Bolton, *Font's Complete Diary* (Berkeley, 1933), p. 148.
13. *Ibid.,* p. 160.
14. Zephyrin Engelhardt, *San Luis Rey Mission* (San Francisco, 1921), p. 45.
15. Tom Hudson, *Three Paths Along The River: The Heritage of the Valley of the San Luis Rey* (Palm Desert, 1964), p. 207.
16. Benjamin Mayes, *Pioneer Notes,* ed. by Margaret Wolcott (Palm Desert, 1929), p. 141.
17. Jane Davies Gunther, *Riverside County, California, Place Names: Their Origins and Their Stories* (Riverside, 1984), p. 102.
18. Lowell John Bean and William Mason, *Diaries and Accounts of The Romero Expeditions in Arizona and California, 1823-1826* (Palm Springs, 1962), p. 35.
19. Francis J. Johnston, "San Gorgonio Pass: Forgotten Route of the Californios?" *Journal of The West,* Jan. 1969, p. 127.
20. Bean and Mason, p. 48.
21. Hudson, p. 209. The writers feel this figure is too high; Possibly three or four thousand head seems more realistic.
22. Gunther, p. 468.
23. *Ibid.*
24. *Ibid.,* p. 466-467.
25. *Ibid.,* p. 471.
26. *Ibid.,* p. 459.

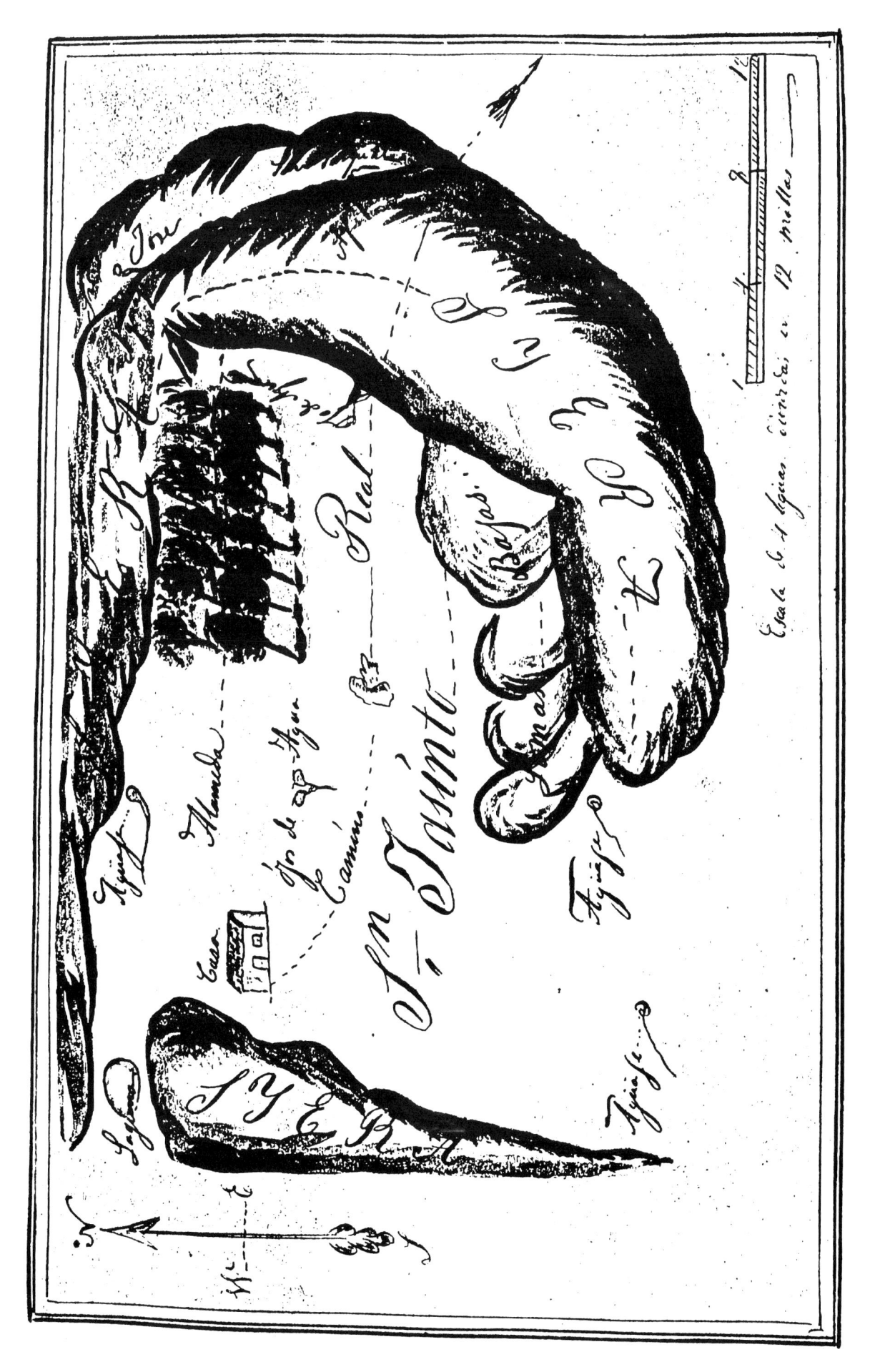

Diseño of Rancho San Jacinto Viejo, as filed by the Estudillo heirs in 1852. – RIVERSIDE CITY AND COUNTY LIBRARY

Government surveyors at Tahquitz Canyon Falls, 1906. — PALM SPRINGS HISTORICAL SOCIETY

4

GOVERNMENT EXPLORERS AND MAP MAKERS

Most of the maps drawn during the Mexican California period were *diseños,* simple drawings showing land grant features and boundaries. These *diseños,* were rough, imprecise sketches that defined the land pictured as bounded by a particular tree, a stream or a hill. If mountains were shown at all, they were simply labelled *cerro* (hill) or *sierra* (range) on most of these drawings.

With the American conquest and the rapid influx of people in response to the gold rush, the old maps and *diseños* proved hopelessly inadequate. The exploring, surveying and mapping of California became a paramount necessity.

The first general survey in Southern California was undertaken by Army Lieutenant Edward O.C. Ord in 1849. Ord's "Topographical Sketch of the Los Angeles Plains and Vicinity" accurately mapped the streets of Los Angeles but simply sketched in the surrounding valleys and mountains. His map shows San Gorgonio Pass as *San Gorgona* and San Jacinto Peak as *San Ygnacio Mt.*[1] Where Ord got the name *San Ygnacio* for the mountain is a mystery.

The earliest recorded use of the name *San Jacinto* for the mountains is found in U.S. Deputy Surveyor Henry Washington's field notes for February 9, 1853, in which he refers to the "San Jacinto Range."[2] Colonel Washington was conducting the first scientific survey of Southern California. He set up his initial point on San Bernardino Peak in 1852, where he established a base line and meridian for his survey.

Also in the year 1853 came the Pacific Railroad Survey, an effort by the Army's Corps of Topographical Engineers, directed by Secretary of War Jefferson Davis and approved by Congress, to find possible routes for a transcontinental railway. Six cross-country railroad routes were proposed for study.

A Pacific Railroad Survey party under Lieutenant Robert Stockton Williamson explored possible routes through Central and Southern California. In November 1853 the Army surveyors charted a course through San Gorgonio Pass. Looking at the high mountains on both sides, Williamson wrote:

> The high mountain of San Bernardino is the highest in the coast range. Its height is not known with accuracy but approaches 9,000 feet. Southeast of this is the peak of San Gorgonio, nearly as high. These two mountains, whose peaks are 30 miles apart, approach each other at their base, and the open pass between is known as the pass of San Gorgonio.[3]

The Williamson party thus labelled today's San Jacinto Peak as "San Gorgonio," an error that was not laid completely to rest for many years.

The Survey's geologist, William P. Blake, marveled at the mountain from Coachella Valley:

> "San Gorgonio [San Jacinto] is the highest peak, and is probably 7,000 feet in elevation....The crest of this chain is much broken, and the sky outline, as seen from the Colorado Desert, is peculiarly sharp and rugged, simulating the teeth of a saw, thus deserving the expressive word 'sierra'."[4]

The mistake was corrected two years later, in 1855, when Lieutenant John G. Parke's Pacific Railroad Survey party passed through the area. Dr. Thomas Antisell, expedition geologist, called the mountain "San Jacinto."[5]

However, Williamson's error caused confusion among map makers for more than three decades. The 1865 Gird map, the Hancock map of 1867, and the 1868 Mitchell map all showed San Jacinto Peak as "San Gorgonio." As late as 1888, the Rand McNally map of Southern California still called the San Jacinto range the "San Gorgonio Mountains."[6]

The next government party to investigate Southern California was Josiah Dwight Whitney's California Geological Survey. William H. Brewer, a young botanist just out of Yale University's prestigious Sheffield Scientific School, was appointed by Whitney to examine Southern California and its little known mountains in 1860. Brewer briefly visited the San Gabriel and Santa Ana mountains but only viewed the San Jacintos from

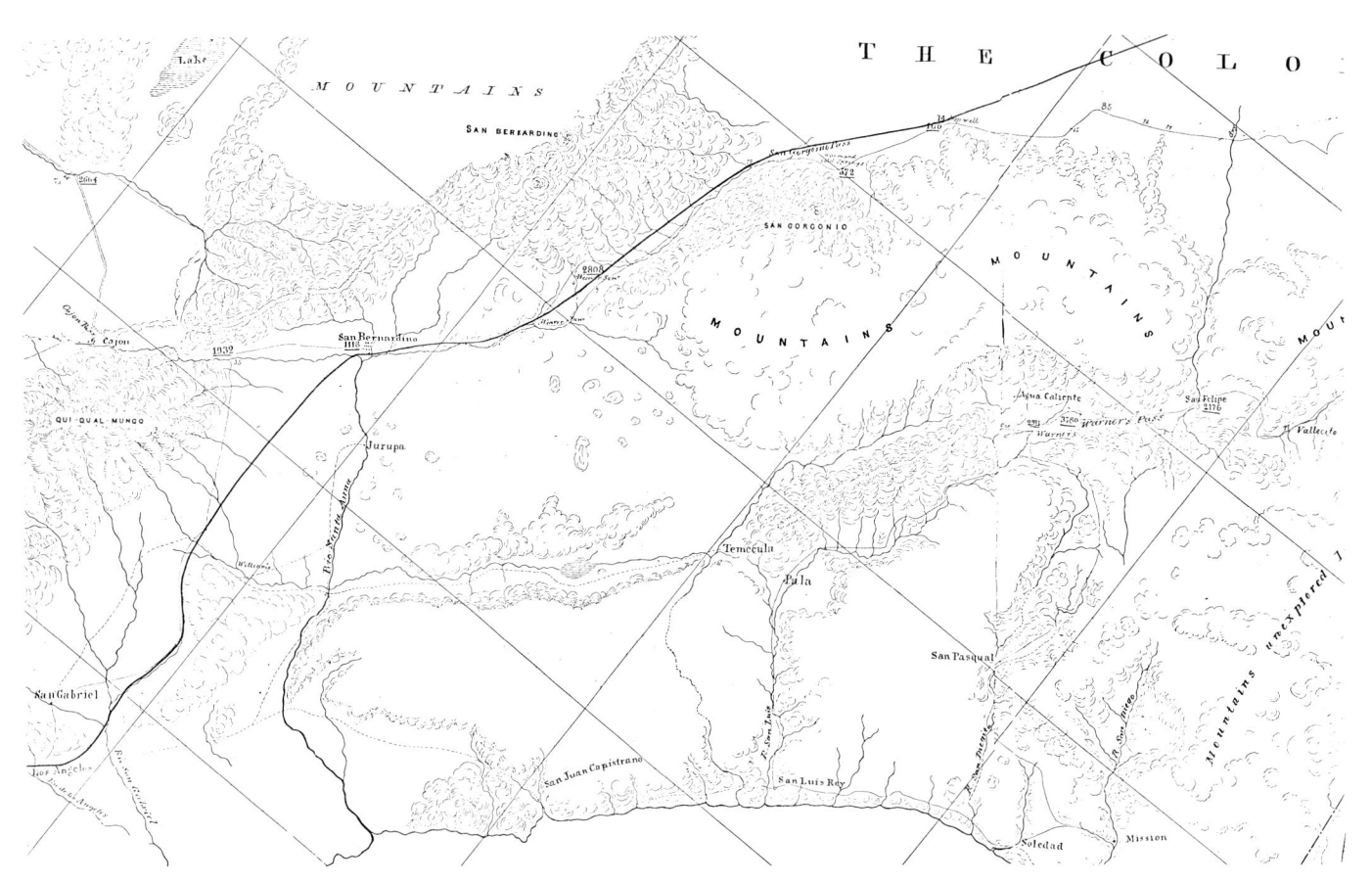

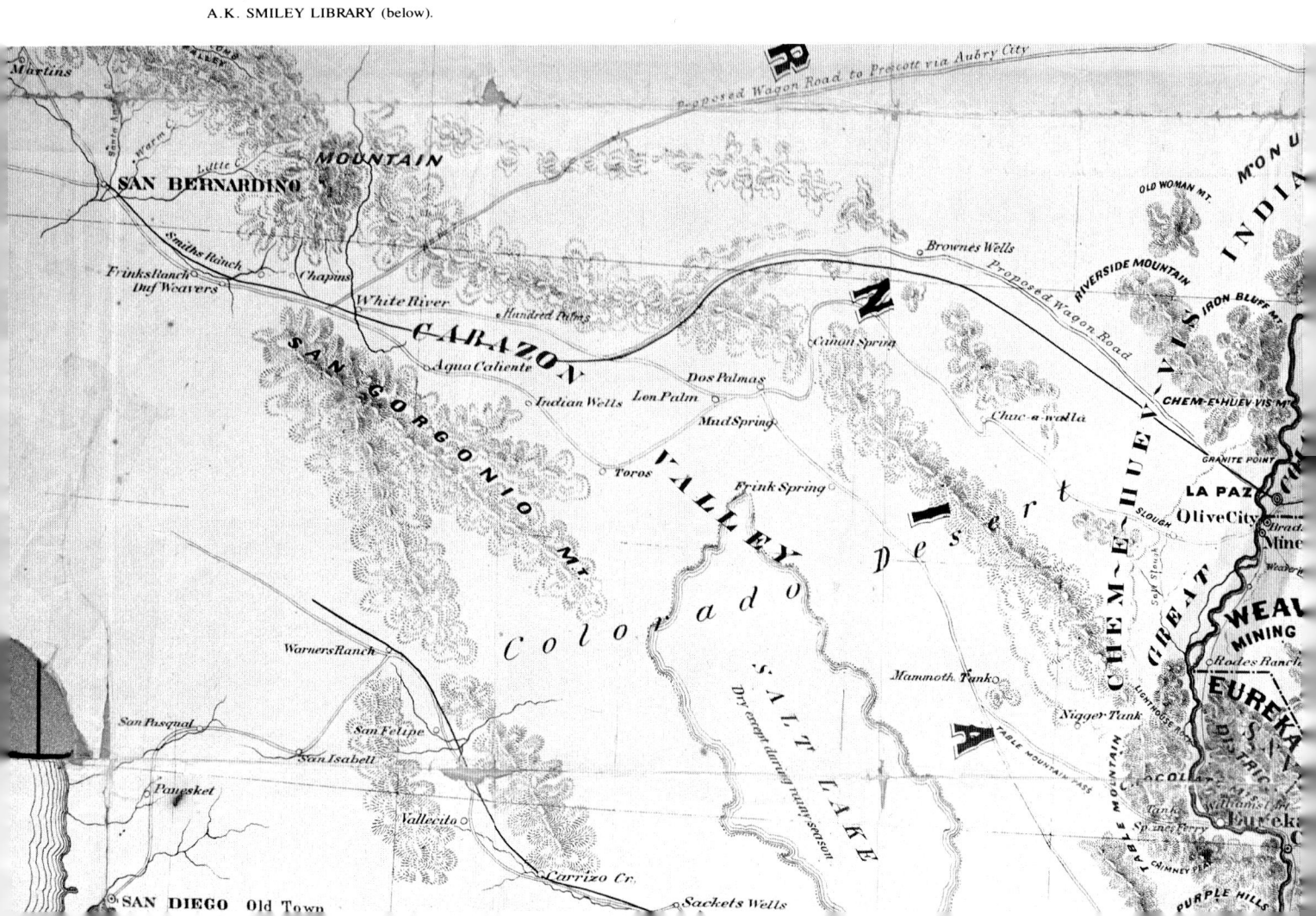

Lt. Robert S. Williamson's Pacific Railroad Survey party travelled through San Gorgonio Pass is 1853. Williamson's 1855 map shows San Jacinto Peak as "San Gorgonio," an error that persisted on some maps into the 1880s. The dark line on the map is the proposed railroad route. The Gird Map of 1865, pictured below, shows the San Jacinto and Santa Rosa mountains as "San Gorgonio Mt." — HENRY E. HUNTINGTON LIBRARY (above), A.K. SMILEY LIBRARY (below).

Williamson's Pacific Railroad Survey party passing through San Gorgonio Pass in 1853. Paulino Weaver's house is amid the trees to the right. The mountain in the background, San Jacinto, was called "San Gorgonio" by Williamson. — HENRY E. HUNTINGTON LIBRARY

Lt. George M. Wheeler directed the U.S. Army's Wheeler Survey, an ambitious project to map the United States west of the 100th Meridian, in the years 1871 to 1879. Wheeler Survey parties explored the desert side of the San Jacintos in 1876 and climbed San Jacinto Peak in 1878. — HENRY E. HUNTINGTON LIBRARY

afar. Professor Whitney, in his geological report of 1865, wrote, "The whole region to the southeast and around San Jacinto is entirely unexplored, as far as we can learn."[7] The professor was apparently unaware of the Pacific Railway Survey's explorations but did get the name "San Jacinto" correct.

Next on the scene was the U.S. Army's Wheeler Survey, an ambitious project to map the United States west of the 100th Meridian under the direction of Lieutenant George Montague Wheeler, undertaken between 1871 and 1878.

A Wheeler Survey party under Lieutenant Eric Bergland made a cursory exploration of the San Jacintos in 1876. The party approached the mountains via the Coachella Valley and San Gorgonio Pass. Oscar Loew, expedition geologist, was impressed with the granitic nature of the range:

> The San Jacinto Mountains, the most southern range of California, consists chiefly of granite, well exhibited in the precipitous faces turned toward the east. It is of dense structure, hard, and a splendid building stone, resembling closely the New England granite. [8]

Loew collected minerals from the San Jacintos, including garnets, tourmaline and titanite. He predicted – wrongly, as it turned out – that mining would become a major economic enterprise in the mountains.

A Wheeler Survey topographical party climbed San Jacinto Peak in 1878 and used it for a primary triangulation point. They calculated the elevation at 10,987.3 feet above sea level. They were guided to the top by Charles Thomas, rancher in the Hemet (Garner) Valley. Their exact route from the Thomas Ranch is unknown; they probably followed the cattle trail through Strawberry Valley and up the Devil's Slide to Tahquitz Valley, the stock path used for summer grazing. The Wheeler Survey was first to use the name "San Jacinto Peak," rather than San Jacinto Mountain or Mount San Jacinto, and were the first government party to penetrate the San Jacinto high country.[9]

To the Wheeler Survey, the San Jacinto range extended south almost to the Mexican border and included the San Jacintos proper, the Santa Rosas, and the small, isolated ranges east of today's Anza-Borrego State Park such as the Fish Creek and Coyote mountains.

Wheeler was not alone in considering the Santa Rosa Mountains as part of the San Jacintos. An 1889 San Diego County map shows the entire mountain chain from San Gorgonio Pass to Anza-Borrego as the San Jacinto Mountains. The U.S. Geological Survey's John S. Brown, in a 1918 decision, stated that the San Jacinto range consisted of the San Jacinto Mountains to the north and the Santa Rosa Mountains to the south, with Palm Canyon dividing the two parts.[10]

As more and more settlers began to locate homes and ranches in the mountains, township surveys to determine land ownership became necessary. In 1875 the Department of the Interior contracted U.S. Deputy Surveyor M. G. Wheeler (no relation to Lieutenant George M. Wheeler of the Army survey) to chart the San Jacinto Mountains. Wheeler started near Valle Vista in the summer of 1875 and worked his way eastward into the mountains. His field notes referred to the lower slopes as "worthless, unfit for cultivation, and destitute of timber." Along the creeks he noted the growth of cottonwoods, sycamores, and oaks. Wheeler was more impressed by open pine forests and grassy meadows, good for grazing in the areas of Garner and Strawberry valleys. He included very few place names on his map, labeling areas "mountain valley," "brush," "timber slope," and the like. Wheeler found much of the higher country "inaccessible" or "unsurveyable."

43

The Wheeler Survey map showing the San Jacintos was never completed, as the survey was absorbed into the United States Geological Survey in 1879. This 1876 Wheeler Survey map marks San Jacinto Peak. Notice Hall's Camp, where ties for the Southern Pacific Railroad, then under construction through San Gorgonio Pass, were cut. Notice also that the railroad, at the time the map was completed, had been built to a point just east of San Gorgonio Pass. — HENRY E. HUNTINGTON LIBRARY

Because M. G. Wheeler's 1875-1876 survey was incomplete, the Department of the Interior sent William Minto and George Sandow to resurvey the San Jacinto Mountains in 1879. They extended their mapping into the higher regions but still found much of the rugged terrain "unsurveyable."

These early surveyors erected stone cairns as boundary markers and set up oak or manzanita posts, or used a convenient tree, as boundary corners. These original markers were long neglected and forgotten as modern, more accurate land surveys superceded them, using metal bench marks embedded in rock. More than a century later, some of these original markers – trees, posts, and boulder cairns – have been located by the Forest Service.

It was the United States Geological Survey that finally produced first rate topographical maps of the San Jacinto Mountains (and all of the United States). The U.S.G.S. was established on March 3, 1879 by act of Congress and superceded all of the other federal surveys. The agency was placed under the Department of the Interior and charged with "classification of public lands, and examination of the geological structure, mineral resources, and products of the national domains."[11] Clarence King was its first director (1879-1881), but it was the U.S.G.S.' second director, John Wesley Powell (1881-1894), who persuaded Congress to expand the agency's responsibilities to include detailed topographic mapping of the United States and its territories. Under the third director, Charles D. Walcott (1894-1907), the topographical mapping program began.

The U.S.G.S. topographical survey, under the guidance of chief topographer Henry Gannett, brought a degree of excellence to map making far surpassing previous surveys. Among the improvements was the use of contour lines rather than the old hachures (hash marks) to indicate elevation.

Under the supervision of regional topographer R. U. Goode, a corps of young, willing and able surveyors set out to map California and its mountains. U.S.G.S. topographical parties, lugging 60-pound plane tables, theodolites (mountain transits) and various other instruments, struggled up chaparral-clad slopes and craggy ridges to set up triangulation stations atop the higher peaks. They worked for weeks on end, weather not withstanding, to map every stream, every meadow and every mountain wrinkle.[12] The resultant topographical maps, most of which appeared in the years 1901 to 1906, were splendid examples of the cartographer's skill. At last, there were accurate maps of the mountains.

The triangulation surveys to map the San Jacinto Mountains took place during the years 1897 and 1898 under the direction of topographers Edmund Taylor Perkins, Jr. and Albert H. Sylvester. Perkins, with several hired assistants, mapped the high terrain around San Jacinto Peak, while Sylvester did the lower regions. They were supplied by a weekly pack train from the town of San Jacinto.[13] The first U.S.G.S. San Jacinto Peak quadrangle map, based on the surveys, appeared in 1901. (Its scale was 1:125,000.)

Perkins supplied many of the place names in use today.

The summit was labeled San Jacinto Peak, rather than Mount San Jacinto or San Jacinto Mountain, and was calculated to be 10,805 feet above sea level – only a foot less than today's accepted elevation of 10,804 feet, and Perkins did not have the precise instruments now in use.

Two of the women in Perkins' life grace summits south of the main peak. Marion Mountain he named for Marion Kelly of White Cloud, Michigan, a young school teacher employed at the Morongo Indian Reservation. Perkins met her when she was camped with friends in Strawberry Valley. The story goes that Miss Kelly fell deeply in love with Perkins, who was described as tall and good-looking, but he kept putting her off by saying he was married to his work. But he did think enough of the young woman to place her name on the mountain. Another young lady was in Perkins' mind, too, one he had met previously while surveying in northern California. She was Jean Waters of Plumas County, California. He put her name on the neighboring summit – Jean Peak. Marion was destined to be disappointed. Jean was more fortunate; she and Edmund Perkins were married in 1903.[14]

Cornell Peak, a needle-like summit above Tamarack Valley, Perkins named for Cornell University, alma mater of geologist Robert T. Hill. The story here is that Hill was camping with Perkins near Round Valley when the former looked up and exclaimed, "That peak looks like the campanile tower at Cornell," or words to that effect. Perkins then placed it on the map.

Folly Peak, San Jacinto's sister summit to the northwest, was said to have named when a disoriented climber ascended it instead of San Jacinto Peak, then fell and injured himself as he tried to hurry over to the main summit.

Antsell Rock was supposedly named for an artist who Perkins met at Keen Camp. The artist's name was Antsell and the mountain he was painting was this craggy knob to the east, so Perkins then and there put "Antsell Rock" on his survey map.[15]

Hemet Valley (today's Garner Valley) appears on this first U.S. Geological Survey topographical map of the area, and therein lies a mystery. What is the derivation of the name *Hemet*? The earliest use of the place name found by these writers appears in the *San Diego Union* of August 16, 1879, where it is spelled *Hemmett* Valley. The "Hemmett Valley Stock Rancho of Chas. H. Thomas" appears in Elliott's *History of San Bernardino and San Diego Counties*, published in 1883. San Diego County records reveal two separate water claims to "Hemmett Valley" and "Hermit Valley" filed in December 1885. Subsequent water claims spelled the valley Hematt, Hemat, Hemett, and finally Hemet.

The early township surveys of the area, undertaken by Deputy Surveyors M. G. Wheeler in 1875 and William Minto in 1879, merely refer to it as a "large valley." The official San Diego County map, as late as 1889, labels it "Mt. Valley."

The earliest spelling of the place name was *Hemmett* Valley, and herein lies a clue. *Hemmett* is a Swedish word meaning place of home or homestead. The late Hemet historian Clarence Swift believed that two Swedes, probably prospectors, briefly made their home in the mountain valley sometime in the 1860s or '70s. No solid evidence supports this theory, but it makes good sense.

There are also stories that the name had an Indian derivation. Various writers have suggested it came from a legendary Indian maiden named *Hemica; Jemet,* said to mean acorn valley; or *Hemet,* a supposed Indian word meaning box valley. None of these fanciful names even remotely resemble any words used by the Cahuilla, who once occupied the valley. Serious historians discount these tales as pure fiction.

All we can be certain of is that the name, first spelled *Hemmett*, appears as early as 1879, that the Lake Hemet Water Company used the name in 1885, that the town of Hemet took its name from the lake in 1886, and that Hemet Valley became known as Thomas Valley shortly after 1900 and finally Garner Valley in 1947.

Another U.S. Geological Survey study of the San Jacintos was undertaken just as Perkins and Sylvester were completing their mapping. This was John B. Leiberg's 1898 reconnaissance of the four Southern California forest reserves as mandated by Congress.

Government surveyors, circa 1875. The instrument on the tripod is a theodolite, or mountain transit, used for mapping. This particular picture shows a Hayden Survey party in Colorado. The Wheeler Survey used similar equipment to map the San Jacintos.
– SMITHSONIAN INSTITUTION

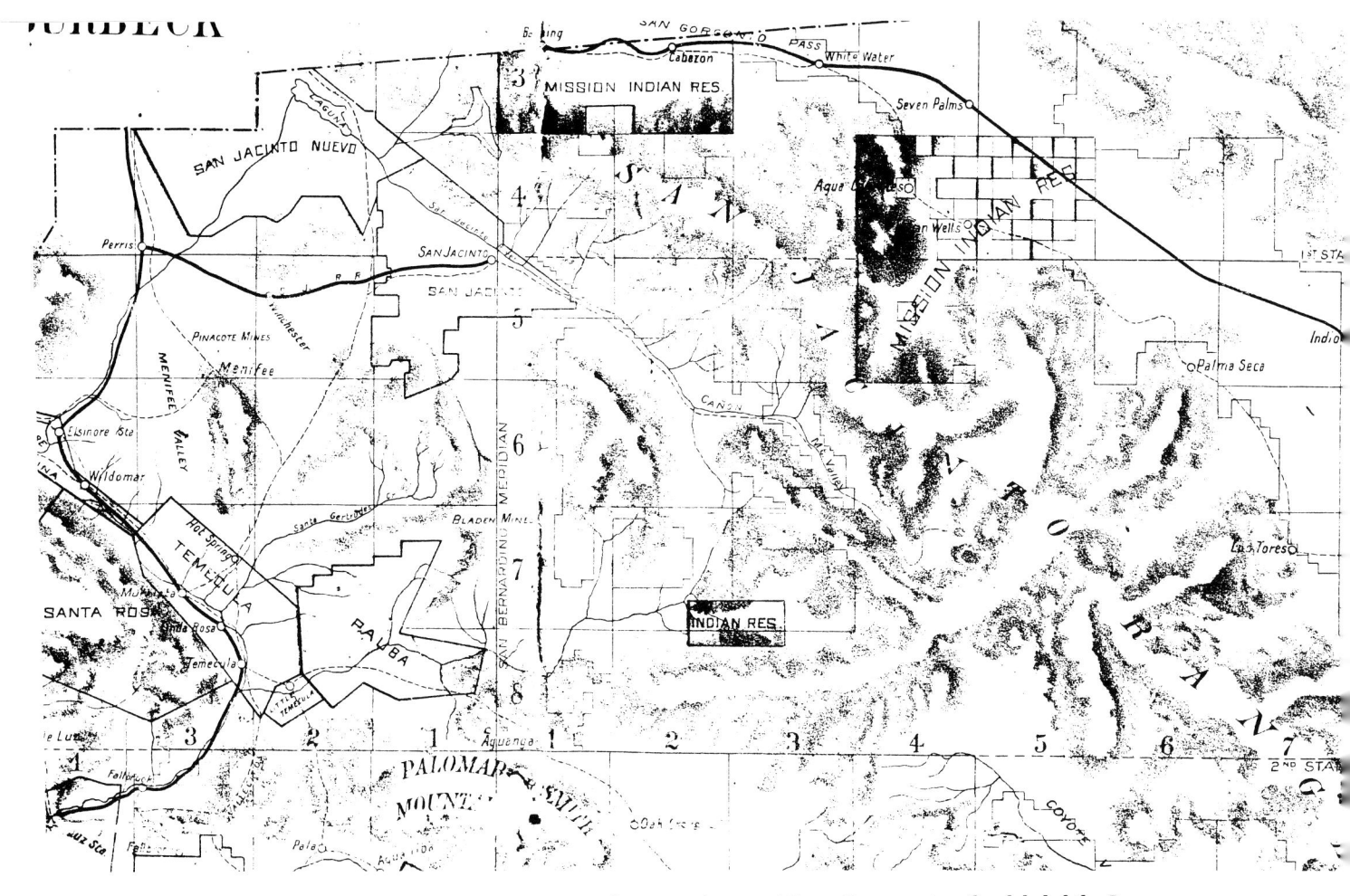

The official San Diego County Map of 1889. The San Jacintos and Santa Rosas are together labeled the San Jacinto Range. – RIVERSIDE CITY AND COUNTY LIBRARY

Leiberg's report on the new San Jacinto Forest Reserve (established in 1897) mapped the forest and chaparral regions and indicated where logging had occurred. Leiberg was critical of damage done to the forest by unrestricted timber cutting and cattle grazing. Interestingly, he divided the San Jacinto Mountains into three sections: The San Jacinto Range, the Toro Range (Santa Rosas), and the Coahuilla Mesa region (Anza Valley and Cahuilla Mountain).[17]

The derivation of the name *Santa Rosa Mountains* is also a mystery. They were apparently named for the Santa Rosa band of Cahuilla Indians, but who first referred to these people by that name, or who gave the name "Santa Rosa" to the old Cahuilla village in Rockhouse Canyon, is unknown. *Santa Rosa Mountains* first appears on the U.S. Geological Survey's Indio topographical quadrangle, surveyed in 1901 and published in 1904. Since then, the name has been universally used.[18]

Topographical remapping by the U.S.G.S. has been undertaken at twenty to thirty year intervals since the original 1897-1898 and 1901 surveys.

After World War II, new technologies were developed, the most important being aerial surveying. The San Jacintos were mapped again, this time using aerial photography. A new 15-minute series, scale 1:62,500, was completed in the years 1957 to 1959. The four quadrangles in this series that cover the San Jacinto Mountains proper are Idyllwild, Palm Springs, Hemet and Banning. Even before the 15-minute maps were completed, the U.S.G.S. began work on a much finer detailed 7.5 minute series with a scale of 1:24,000. First to appear was the Lake Fulmor quadrangle in 1956. The San Jacinto Peak quadrangle became available in 1981.

Today, no mountain range in the world is better mapped than the San Jacintos – a far cry from the vague *diseños* of the last century. Even new techniques, using laser beams reflected off space satellites, promise to bring future maps even closer to that elusive goal of absolute accuracy, a precision undreamed of a few decades ago.

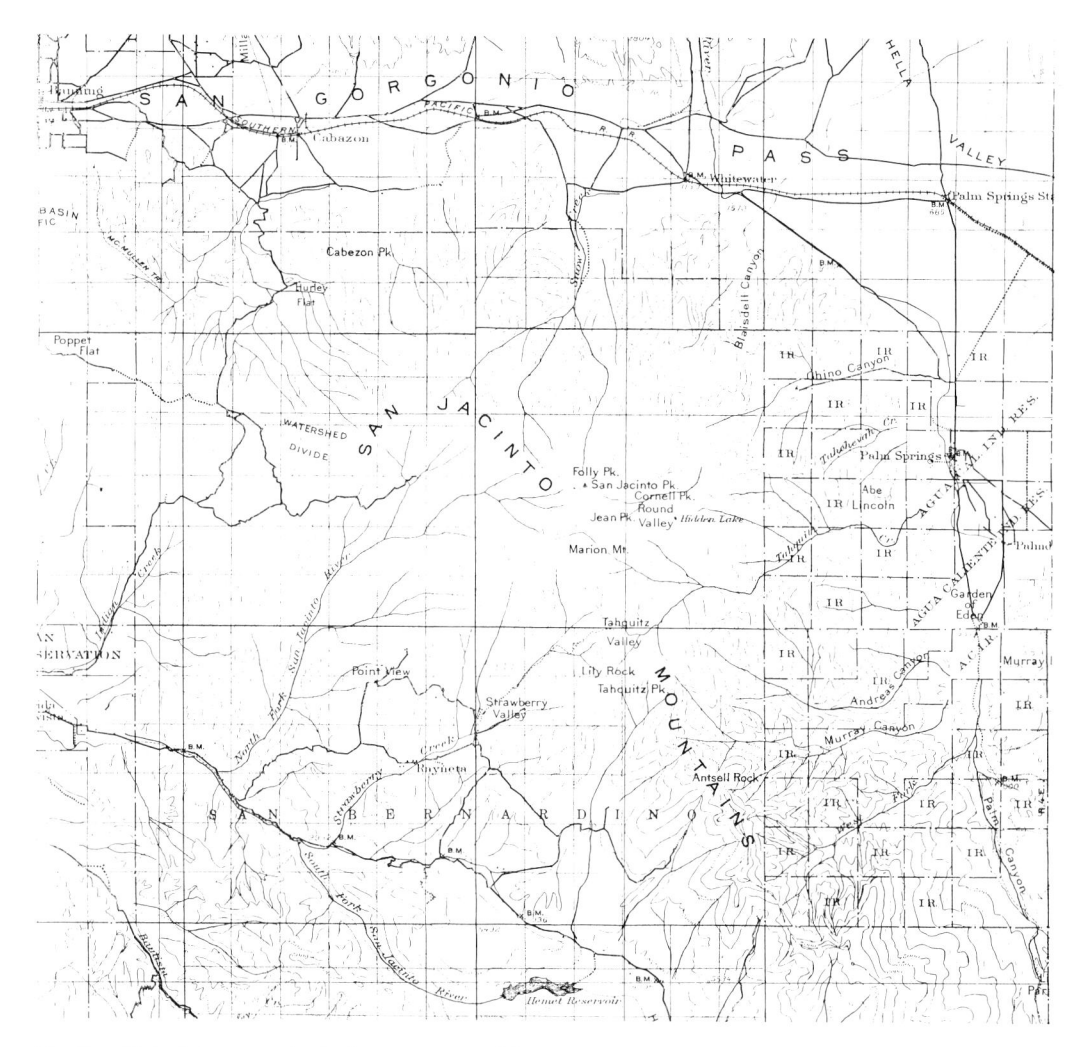

The first United States Geological Survey map of the San Jacinto Quadrangle, issued in 1901. The mapping was done in 1898-1899 by topographers Edmund Taylor Perkins and Albert Sylvester. For the first time, place names such as Folly Pk., Jean Pk., Marion Mt., Lily Rock, and Antsell Rock appear. The U.S.G.S. brought a new standard to map making. — UNITED STATES GEOLOGICAL SURVEY

NOTES

1. E.O.C. Ord, "Topographical Sketch of the Los Angeles Plains and Vicinity, August 1849," *Report of the Secretary of War, Executive Document 47*, 31st Congress, 1st Session; cited in W. W. Robinson, *Maps of Los Angeles* (Los Angeles, 1960).
2. Jane Davies Gunther, *Riverside County, California, Place Names: Their Origin and Their Stories* (Riverside, 1984), p. 464.
3. Lt. R. S. Williamson, *Reports of Explorations and Surveys to Ascertain The Most Practical and Economical Route for A Railroad from The Mississippi River to The Pacific Ocean*, Vol. V (Washington, D.C., 1857), Pt. 1, p. 36.
4. *Ibid.*, Pt. II, p. 138.
5. Lt. John G. Parke, *Ibid.*, Vol. VII, p. 87.
6. Gunther, p. 464.
7. J. D. Whitney, *Geological Survey of California, Vol, I, Geology* (Sacramento, 1865), p. 178.
8. Lt. George M. Wheeler, *Annual Report on the Geographical Surveys West of the One Hundredth Meridian...* (Washington, D.C., 1876), Appendix JJ, p. 173.
9. Wheeler, *Annual Report...1878*, Appendix OO, p. 3103.
10. Gunther, p. 465. The San Jacinto Mountains were part of San Diego County until 1893, when they were included in the newly-formed Riverside County.
11. Mary C. Rabbitt, *A Brief History of The U.S. Geological Survey* (Washington, D.C., 1980), p. 3.
12. Interview with Donald McLain, Altadena, July 1, 1971 and March 19, 1977. McLain (1887-1981) worked for the U.S.G.S. as an apprentice topographer in the early 1900s and knew Perkins. Later he made maps for the Forest Service, U.S. Army, and Security First National Bank.
13. McLain interview.
14. McLain interview. For an outline biography of Edmund Taylor Perkins, see *Who's Who in America*, Vol. 8, 1914-15, p. 1838.
15. McLain supplied these stories on Cornell Peak, Folly Peak and Antsell Rock based on conversations with Taylor. Another story told by Lee Emerson, son of Idyllwild Inn owner Claudius Lee Emerson, goes that Albert Sylvestor, Perkins' U.S.G.S. associate during the 1897-98 mapping of the San Jacinto Mountains, named Marion, Jean, Lily and Folly peaks for his four daughters. Sylvestor reportedly told this to Lee Emerson during his visit to the Idyllwild Inn about 1918. See *Idyllwild Town Crier*, July 28, 1950.
16. Gunther, p. 229-230, discusses the various facts and fictions regarding the name *Hemet*.
17. John B. Leiberg, "San Jacinto Forest Reserve," *19th Annual Report of The U.S. Geological Survey, 1897-98* (Washington, D.C., 1899), Part 5, p. 351-256; and *20th Annual Report..., 1898-99* (Washington, D.C., 1900), Part 5, p. 455-478.
18. Gunther, p. 482.

Charles Thomas (1836-1917), pioneer rancher in the Hemet (Garner) Valley. – LAURA SWIFT

5

CHARLES THOMAS AND HIS RANCH

Charles Thomas and his friend Tom Casey sat back on their saddles, weary from a long day's journey. Accompanied by some friendly Cahuilla Indians, they had started from Thomas' Temecula ranch and, following Indian trails, had ridden hour after hour through brushy hill country, winding their way northeastward toward the high mountains on the skyline. Continuing on after a brief rest, they rounded a hillside and suddenly gazed upon a broad, verdant valley spotted with pines and backdropped with craggy ridges. Thomas and his friend were enthralled with the valley's primeval beauty, known only to the Cahuillas.

Thomas had reached his *nirvana,* his promised land. He would build a ranch and spend almost forty years here. The beautiful mountain basin nestled on the southwestern flank of the San Jacintos became known as Hemet Valley, then Thomas Valley, and finally Garner Valley as it is known today.

Charles Thomas had led an adventurous life. He was born in Chenango County, upstate New York, on October 1, 1836. Orphaned at an early age, he was raised on the farm of his maternal grandparents. The urge for adventure seized him early in life. Tales of the gold rush inspired Thomas to take ship for California. The schooner *Tecumseh,* with young Charles aboard, rounded Cape Horn and reached San Francisco in November 1849. He was barely thirteen years of age when he and a companion set off for the goldfields of the Mother Lode.

Thomas prospected with marginal success for six months, according to one source, or for two years, according to another. Then, once again gripped by the spirit of adventure, he joined William Walker's filibustering expedition to Mexico. The invasion failed, and Walker and his men returned to the United States where they were arrested and charged with violating Mexican neutrality. The filibusters were acquited and released in 1854. Thomas left the group and went to Half Moon Bay, where he managed the Pescadoro Ranch for a year.

Ever restless, Charles Thomas prospected along northern California's Trinity River for a year, then left for the Arizona mines. He apparently had better luck there, as he filed several claims. In 1858 he sold his Arizona claims and moved to Southern California, where he would live the rest of his life. Thomas was said to have been one of six prospectors who discovered the much ballyhooed Temescal tin mines near today's Corona. He mined there for two years.

1861 was a watershed year in Thomas' life. He married Genoveva Bardico (or Badillo), member of a prominent Santa Barbara family, on May 14th. That same year he sold his part interest in the Temescal mines to Los Angeles businessman and land owner Abel Stearns, and moved with his bride to Temecula. Here Charles and Genoveva settled on a ranch and commenced raising a family. Eventually they would produce twelve children, nine of whom lived to adulthood – Adeliza, Fannie, Joseph, Charles, Victoria, Lulu, James, George and Emma. On their Temecula ranch, Thomas grazed cattle and operated a flour mill, his wanderlust spirit finally tempered somewhat by family responsibilities.[1]

Although much has been written about Charles Thomas, there are surprising variances over some of the major events of his life.

How did he discover Hemet (Garner) Valley, and how did he gain ownership of his land there?

A story often told goes that Thomas befriended some starving Indians and gave them flour from his Temecula ranch mill. In appreciation, the Indians led him to the high mountain basin and offered him land in exchange for cattle.[2] Another version deletes the "starving Indians" and says that Thomas, after hearing about good summer grazing land in the San Jacinto Mountains, hired some Indians to guide him there. Still another story, told in Thomas' obituary (*Hemet News,* April 6, 1917), goes that "Through a party of prospectors he learned of the mountain valley and decided to put his cattle there. He entered the valley in the fall of the year 1861." In any event he discovered the basin and drove

The Thomas' original ranch house, built in the late 1860s. This view, showing the porch and rear storage addition added in later years, was taken in the 1890s. Contrary to what someone has written on the picture, *Ramona* was not written here. – BUD CLARK

Charles and Genoveva Thomas, sitting in front of their ranchhouse, circa 1890. – LESTER REED

his cattle there sometime after that. We know that California suffered through a devastating drought during the years 1862 to 1865 and that cattlemen, to save their starving and thirst-crazed herds, drove them into the mountains.[3]

A discrepancy also surrounds the number of cattle Thomas gave the Cahuillas in exchange for the mountain valley. A figure long quoted was 22 head, but according to Victoria Brooke Thomas, daughter of Charles and Genoveva born in 1867, it was 200 head. Mrs. Brooke, interviewed by Idyllwild's editor-historian Ernest Maxwell in 1961, two years before her death, further stated that "the cattle were divided among the Indians at Cahuilla (Anza) Valley where most of them lived. Most of the older ones living in the village where we built the ranch house decided to remain. My father built *ramadas* (brush shacks) for them." The Cahuilla leaders, according to Mrs. Brooke, accepted Thomas' offer on the condition that the Indians living there could remain, and Thomas, always considering himself a friend of the native peoples, honored the bargain.[4]

Thomas gained the right to occupy and graze the mountain basin, but his payment of cattle to the Indians did not constitute legal title as required by federal law. Riverside County historian Jane Davies Gunther, after a diligent search of records in the San Diego County Recorder's Office (The San Jacintos were part of San Diego County until Riverside County was formed in 1893), discovered that Charles Thomas acquired his property through several means. Some he got by filing homestead claims. Most he purchased at one time or another from the United States Land Office, the Southern Pacific Railroad, and other mountain settlers. His land patents were variously in his name, in Genoveva's name, or in the names of this two oldest sons.[5]

The size of the Thomas Ranch varied greatly over the years, from an original 480 acres to 1,700 acres, and at one time almost 8,000 acres. During the 1880s, before Thomas began selling off parcels of land around Lake Hemet and Strawberry Valley, the ranch took in all of Garner Valley and upper Strawberry Creek as far as today's Idyllwild. His biggest property crisis came in 1876, when the Southern Pacific Railroad, in keeping with a generous subsidy provided by Congress allowing the railroad to claim alternate "checkboard" sections for twenty miles on both sides of their right-of-way, appropriated some of the land Thomas thought was his. He was obliged to buy it back from the Southern Pacific.[6]

Thomas' first house on his mountain ranch was a crude log cabin built on the northwestern edge of the valley near where the Garner Ranch house stands today. He drove cattle up from his Temecula ranch and hired Cahuilla cowboys to tend the herds.

Thomas went out of his way to gain the friendship of the native peoples. Besides allowing the older Indians to remain in their *ramadas* on the ranch and hiring many of the younger ones, he paid the Cahuillas a yearly rent to graze his herds on their lands. When the Indians occasionally butchered a cow to satisfy their hunger, Thomas looked the other way. Although living squarely in the middle of Cahuilla ancestral lands, Charles Thomas lived in peace and friendship with them.

To provide access to his mountain ranch, Thomas built a rough wagon road up from Anza Valley, over which he hauled supplies and drove his fattened cattle to market in Temecula. Later, after the railroad reached

The Thomas Ranch, circa 1895. At one time the ranch covered almost all of Garner Valley and extended northwestward into Strawberry Valley. — TOM CORE

San Jacinto in 1888, Thomas' cattle were driven over Keen Camp Divide and down Dry Creek and the San Jacinto River to loading pens at the railhead.

Contrary to what some have written, Thomas did not bring his family to live at his mountain ranch for a number of years. Charles and Genoveva, with children arriving every year or so, continued to live at their Temecula ranch, with Charles making periodic trips to the mountains to oversee his herds and construct more substantial corrals and ranch buildings. Daughter Victoria was born in Temecula in 1867, so it was some time after that date that they all moved to their new mountain home.

The Thomas Ranch rapidly took shape as one of the premier mountain ranches in Southern California. A spacious ranch house with wide verandas, several guest cabins, a white-fenced barn and corral all gave the ranch an elegant look.

The real charm of the ranch was the close-knit Thomas family. Charles and Genoveva were devoted parents, and their nine children willingly took part in ranch activity. Also part of the family were a black girl known as "Pickie" and Tony Martinez, a Hispanic-Indian boy, orphans whom the Thomas' raised as their own.

The Thomas hospitality to visitors was legendary. The author George Wharton James visited the ranch around the turn of the century and wrote, "What a difference it makes when one is tired and hungry to feel that there is a glad welcome ahead, where willing hands will administer to his comfort and cheerful voices and happy smiles make him feel at home. This is the Thomas Ranch! Many a traveler can tell of the warm-hearted hospitality of this whole family, from father to youngest son, from mother to youngest daughter."[7] Helen Hunt Jackson stayed there for a few days while studying the plight of the California Indians in the 1880s. Victoria Brooke remembered that both Ramona Lubo and her husband Juan Diego, immortalized by Jackson's *Ramona,* worked on the ranch, Juan Diego as a sheep shearer. John Muir paid a visit in 1896.

By the mid-1880s there were thousands of head of cattle and a few flocks of sheep roaming the Thomas Valley. Dozens of Indian cowboys tended the herds, corraled and branded them at round-up time, and guarded the animals from wild grizzlies.

Grizzly bears were a constant threat to livestock until well into the '90s. The *San Diego Union* (August 15, 1880) carries an account of a bear hunt by Thomas and Judge Brunson, a friend. Not far from the ranch they came across an 800-pound grizzly, which after a short chase they were able to dispatch.

> "As to which killed or hit the bear first, neither Charley nor the Judge can determine, as both fired together. Charley, however, claims that he was the first to 'go up and kick him' – the bear, not the Judge – 'just to see if the critter was dead.' Bruin had been depredating on stock in the neighborhood, having killed three or four animals before receiving the Judge's subpoena to show cause, etc., etc., why a permanent injunction should not be placed upon such beastly proceedings.

The great bears seldom molested humans. One notable exception was the mauling of a man named Herkey, or Hurkey, a wood cutter working at the Thomas Ranch. The story goes that Herkey's dog chased two grizzly cubs up a tree. The enraged mother charged the woodcutter as he was drinking from a creek, severely injuring him. Herkey was able to struggle back to the ranch house, where he died a few days later. Herkey Creek immortalizes the incident today.

Thomas was no ordinary stock raiser. He reached out for the best breeds he could find, travelling as far as Texas on cattle buying trips. He is credited with bringing the first head of Shorthorns to San Diego County. One observer wrote that his herd of Durham cattle "will compare favorably with any to be found on the Pacific Coast."[8] He also had a prize herd of Angus.

The *Riverside Press and Horticulturalist* (July 29, 1893) reported that Thomas "imported from Kentucky the first thoroughbred stock ever brought to Southern California, and today he owns probably the best herds of thoroughbred horses and cattle in the state."

It was the breeding, training and racing of fine thoroughbred horses that brought real notoriety to Charles Thomas and his ranch. Thomas laid out a race track just south of the barn and corrals and trained his thoroughbreds there. He was quoted as saying that "a good track for a young horse is the same as a school for children. They need a good education."[9] Elias J. "Lucky" Baldwin, who loved racehorses as Thomas did, was a frequent visitor. Baldwin and Thomas became partners in developing a stable of horses that entered races across the country. Son Joe Thomas was for a time Thomas' principle jockey. He is said to have won $50,000 in one race at San Jose. Thomas' racehorse *Pescadore* beat the state record for three-year-olds.

The *Press and Horticulturalist* (July 29, 1893) stated that "This season Mr. Thomas took three of his best young horses East and at St. Louis one of them, *Charley T,* had the best average among 1,800 two-year-olds. So good was his record that Mr. Thomas was offered $8,000 for him, which he refused, holding the colt at $10,000. He is now at Chicago, where he is entered in the big races."

After more than three decades at their mountain home, growing old, and with their children now grown and drifting away, Charles and Genoveva considered leaving the ranch. A deal to sell all their mountain property to Englishman Harold Kenworthy in 1898 fell through after Kenworthy lost most of his fortune on an ill-conceived mining venture.

Their next sale went through. On December 28, 1905 San Bernardino stockman Robert F. Garner paid Thomas $30,000 for the ranch property, then amounting to 1,700 acres.[10]

There was a persistent story that Thomas lost his ranch to pay gambling debts, although Victoria Thomas Brooke, last surviving child of Charles and Genoveva, insisted this was not true. Jack Garner, present ranch owner, tells a different tale: "Thomas had the idea that he could train his racehorses at his mountain ranch and that this would make them run faster at lower elevations, but this was not true. He lost a lot of money finding this out."[11]

Robert Garner allowed the Thomas family one year

Charles Thomas standing on his front porch, circa 1898.
— DAVID SCHERMAN

to sell off their stock and vacate the ranch. Garner took possession on January 1, 1907, and the long saga of the Garner Ranch began (covered in the next chapter).

Charles and Genoveva moved to Redlands, where Thomas operated a livery stable for four years. He died in Ocean Park, near Santa Monica, at the home of one of his daughters, on March 31, 1917.[12] Genoveva Thomas died in 1925. Victoria Thomas Brooke, last of Charles and Genoveva's children, lived to be 95; she passed away in 1963.

NOTES

1. The early years of Thomas' life have been gleened largely from the following sources: Lewis Publishing Company, *An Illustrated History of Southern California* (Chicago, 1890), p. 369-370; J.M. Guinn, *A History of California and An Extended History of Its Southern Coast Counties* (Los Angeles, 1907), Vol, II, p. 1841-1843; Wallace W. Elliott, *History of San Bernardino and San Diego Counties,* Introduction by Harry W. Lawton (Riverside, 1965; reprint of 1883 edition), p. 72; Hemet-San Jacinto Genealogical Society, *San Jacinto Valley, Past and Present* (Hemet, 1989), p. 447; Victoria Thomas Brooke (daughter), interviewed by Ernest Maxwell, Idyllwild *Town Crier,* Dec. 1 and 8, 1961; and Clarence Swift of Hemet, interviewed May 20, 1972.
2. Ernest Maxwell, *Town Crier,* April 28, 1972.
3. Robert Glass Cleland, *The Cattle on a Thousand Hills* (San Marino, 1951), p. 131.
4. Victoria Brooke interview, *Town Crier,* Dec. 1, 1961. See also Ernest Maxwell, *Pictorial History of the San Jacinto Mountains* (Idyllwild, 1988), p. 25-26.
5. Jane Davies Gunther, *Riverside County, California, Place Names: Their Origins and Their Stories* (Riverside, 1984), p. 543.
6. *Hemet-San Jacinto Genealogical Society,* p. 447.
7. George Wharton James, *The Wonders of The Colorado Desert* (Boston, 1906), Vol. II, p. 464-465.
8. Guinn, Vol. II, p. 1842.
9. Hemet-San Jacinto Genealogical Society, p. 447.
10. Redlands *Citrograph,* Dec. 30, 1905; see also Gunther, p. 543.
11. Jack Garner interview, Garner Ranch, August 18, 1992.
12. Redlands *Daily Facts,* March 31, 1917; *Hemet News,* April 6, 1917.

The Thomas family in front of their bunkhouse, circa 1896. Charles Thomas is standing in the middle, with wife Genoveva sitting next to him on the left. Victoria Thomas is standing fifth from left. The rest are other Thomas children and ranch employees. — RAMONA BOWL MUSEUM

Roping a calf in the Thomas Ranch corral.   — DAVID SCHERMAN

Roping calves at the Garner Ranch, ca. 1940. – JACK GARNER

6
CATTLE AND SHEEP

Cattlemen and sheep herders have all too often been considered romantic but secondary figures in the mountain drama. In reality, animal grazing, which included not only cattle and sheep but also horses, oxen, goats and swine, were more important commercially in the Western mountains than the better known lumbering and mining activities.[1] This was certainly true in the San Jacintos. As late as 1912, Riverside County historian Elmer Holmes wrote that the cattle business was the leading industry of the mountains and "plays no small part in the wealth of the County."[2]

There was livestock grazing in the San Jacinto Valley long before it became important in the mountains. José Antonio Estudillo, grantee of sprawling *Rancho San Jacinto Viejo,* and later his sons, oversaw herds as large as 6,000 to 7,000 head of cattle, 1,500 horses, and an undetermined number of sheep.[3] Livestock roamed the unfenced plains and quenched their thirst from the streams and springs that emitted from the mountains, tended by scores of Hispanic and Indian *vaqueros*. Animals grazed freely over what are now the cities of Hemet and San Jacinto. Before the 1880s, "One could not walk safely because of the great herds of wild Mexican cattle that roamed in thousands over the level plains."[4]

The annual roundup came in late spring and was a special occasion on Estudillo's ranch. *Vaqueros* lassoed, corraled and branded the cattle and horses, while skillful Cahuilla sheep shearers scissored the heavy winter coat from the flocks they tended. When roping, corraling, branding and sheering were completed, the Estudillos put on a lively *fandango* and barbeque. The fattest cattle, set aside for market, were driven to the slaughter house in San Bernardino or Los Angeles, sometimes as far as San Francisco.[5]

In the early days of *Rancho San Jacinto Viejo,* desert Indian raiders made forays into the valley and made off with scores of cattle and horses. Salvador Estudillo remembered, "To prevent these robberies, Señor Estudillo maintained a large force of men, who, ostensibly *rancheros,* were in reality fighting men, armed and equipped to stand off the Indians and protect the property of the *patron*."[6]

The great Southern California drought of 1862-1865 eventually forced the Estudillos to drive their herds into the mountains, but not at first. Salvador Estudillo recalled that "As late as 1863, when all other parts of the State suffered from a dry season, this valley had plenty of feed and in it ranged at will 7,000 head of stock."[7] It was not until the third dry year in a row, 1864, that the drought seriously affected the San Jacinto Valley. "Cattle died by the herd in dry creek beds and on the parched earth....Cowboys burned spines from cactus so the cattle could gain some moisture and nourishment from the plants."[8] Salvation was found in the San Jacinto Mountains. Estudillo cattle and horses were driven up Indian trails as far as Strawberry Valley, possible farther, where the grass was still green and there was a trickle of life-saving moisture in the streambeds.

The Estudillos recovered from the drought and large herds once again roamed the plains. But, eventually, they could not survive financial burdens, particularly in paying San Diego County taxes. They were land rich but cash poor. In the late 1860s they began selling portions of their vast rancho "whenever the family strong box ran short of funds."[9]

One of the early buyers was Francisco Pico, nephew of the last Mexican governor of California, Pio Pico. In 1868 he bought 4,500 acres around *Casa Loma,* the old mission hilltop adobe site, and built his home there. Pico cattle grazed on his ranch during the winter and in the mountains during the summer dry season.

Most of the white settlers who bought portions of *Rancho San Jacinto Viejo* were more interested in agriculture than livestock grazing. By the mid-1870s, Anglo names were becoming dominant in the valley – Kennedy, Webster, Tripp, Van Leuven, Tyler, to name a few. Grainfields and fruit orchards, protected from wandering cattle by wooden rail fences and barbed wire, sprang up almost overnight across the San Jacinto Valley. The *San Diego Union* (February 19, 1874) reported that there were fifty to seventy-five settlers in the valley by that date. The *Union* further stated that "The San Jacinto Valley offers peculiar inducements to settlement. There is a large quantity of Government land in and near

Francisco Pico, nephew of the last Mexican governor of California, Pio Pico, purchased 4,500 acres of Rancho San Jacinto from the Estudillo family in 1868. Pico grazed his cattle on his valley ranch during winter and drove them to summer pasture in the mountains. – LAURA SWIFT

The Francisco Pico ranch house atop Casa Loma hill in the north-central San Jacinto Valley. This was the site of the old mission rancho adobe, built about 1821.
– LAURA SWIFT

the valley, of the best character. Water can be had anywhere by digging from ten to fifteen feet, and Mr. Kennedy (one of the old settlers) informs us that the water of the San Jacinto Valley is as pure and soft as rain water.... The soil is capable of producing splendid crops. Mr. Kennedy has threshed fifty bushels to the acre, and has had as large a yield as sixty bushels of barley to the acre."

The community of "Old" San Jacinto began when Proco Akimo, a Russian immigrant via the Aleutian Islands and San Francisco, set up a small trading post at what is now the corner of Hewitt and Evans streets, stocked it with basic goods, and opened for business in either 1868 or 1869. In April 1869 a crude one-room schoolhouse opened to an enrollment of eight students; by 1878 there were one hundred and six. The San Jacinto post office opened its doors on July 27, 1870, with Francisco Estudillo as first postmaster. A small wooden courthouse was erected in 1877 or 1878; J. B. Kennedy was first Justice of the Peace. He was succeeded by Samuel V. Tripp in 1882.

It was the purchase of 10,000 acres of Rancho San Jacinto Viejo by the San Jacinto Land Association, a consortium of Los Angeles and San Bernardino businessmen, in 1882 that heralded boom days for the valley and, at the same time, spelled the demise of open range grazing. The town of "New" San Jacinto, just north of the old community, was born in 1883, although not incorporated until 1888, the same year the California Southern Railroad reached the valley. Livestock raising in the valley continued, but now it was confined to small farms and played second fiddle to vast agricultural enterprises nourished by irrigation projects.

As the era of the open range drew to a close in the San Jacinto Valley, livestock grazing became a major economic activity in the mountain basins. Already mentioned was Charles Thomas, who was tending large herds in Thomas (Garner) Valley as early as 1867. Joining Thomas in adjacent mountain flats and valleys were a number of other cattlemen and their families. The names of Tripp, Arnaiz, Hamilton, Wellman and Reed are almost legendary in the annals of the mountain saga. No history of the San Jacintos would be complete without their stories.

Samuel V. Tripp (1830-1895) came across the plains to California at the tail end of the 1849 gold rush. After an unsuccessful fling at mining, Tripp moved to Los Angeles, became a stone and brick mason, and married his first wife Rose Ann Ramsey. Samuel Tripp worked at a variety of occupations during his life – mason, store keeper, freighter and farmer. He and his wife had three sons – Shasta, Ozro and William – before Rose Anne died in 1869. Tripp and his boys came to the San Jacinto Valley about 1871 and settled in what later became Valle Vista. He was elected Justice of the Peace for the San Jacinto area, in which capacity he presided at the trial of Sam Temple for the murder of an Indian named Juan Diego, immortalized in Helen Hunt Jackson's novel *Ramona*. Tripp was portrayed as "Judge Wells" in the novel.

The San Jacinto Valley, looking east from Little Lake reservoir, ca. 1890. Irrigation turned the valley from a grazing to an agricultural economy. The days when cattle roamed the open range were over by the early 1880s.
— LAURA SWIFT

Samuel V. Tripp (1830-1895) and his sons Shasta, Ozro and William came to the San Jacinto Valley about 1871. A few years later the family homesteaded Tripp Flats, at the head of Bautista Canyon. Samuel Tripp gained notoriety as justice of the peace for the San Jacinto Township, when he presided over the trial of Sam Temple, killer of the Indian Juan Diego, in 1883. — CHARLES VAN FLEET

The story goes that Samuel Tripp's son Ozro, sometime in the late 1870s, journeyed up Bautista Canyon and discovered the little basin at its head that became Tripp Flats. Samuel then went up and filed homestead claims of 160 acres each in the name of himself and his three sons (the patents were received in the years 1890 to 1898). While father Samuel remained in the San Jacinto Valley, sons Shasta and Will Tripp moved to the family homestead at Tripp Flats with 400 head of cattle. It was not long until Tripp cattle were ranging over the Cahuilla (Anza) Valley and up into Thomas Valley. The Tripp brothers also filed on some land along Morris Creek, east of the Thomas Ranch, where they grazed cattle and grew potatoes. The place became known as "Potato Ranch."

By 1900 the Tripps, now multiplied by a third generation, were supplying beef cattle to markets in San Jacinto, Hemet and San Bernardino.[10]

Manuel Arnaiz, born in San Francisco in 1856, grew up on the huge Miller and Lux Ranch near Bakersfield, where he herded sheep and learned the cattle business. He moved to San Bernardino, where he met and married Dolores Garduna, descendent of the Verdugo family of Mexican California, in 1883. The newly-weds lived first in Yucaipa, where they produced four children – Clara, Eugene, Daisy and Fanny. After taking up a homestead near Kenworthy, on the edge of Garner Valley, Dolores gave birth to four more children – Daniel, Edward, Ernest and Henry. Manual Arnaiz and his sons raised cattle on their Kenworthy ranch and winter grazed the animals in the Pinyon Flat and upper Palm Canyon areas. Some of the cattle became separated from the Arnaiz herds in the rugged, brushy country around Pinyon Flat and the Santa Rosa Mountains and turned wild. These "bronco cattle," as the cowboys called them, roamed the mountainous area for many years.

There was much intermarriage among the cattle raising families of the San Jacintos. Clara Arnaiz, oldest daughter of Manuel and Dolores, married Frank Wellman in 1897. Sisters Fanny and Daisy Arnaiz wed brothers John and Antonio Contreras in 1906.

After Manuel Arnaiz died in 1925, his youngest son Henry continued to manage the Arnaiz herds. His home was a cabin near the south end of Garner Valley, just north of the road down to Anza, known as "Nigger Jim Grade" in the early days.[11]

"Nigger Jim" was James "Uncle Jim" Hamilton, born in Ohio in 1822. Hamilton was of racially mixed stock. He came west in 1847 via Mormon wagon trains, lived with Sioux Indians for a year, and finally reached San Bernardino in the early 1850s. He built a hotel in San Diego, then filed for a homestead near Rancho San Felipe in the San Diego back country. When he discovered his homestead claim invalid, because it was on land claimed by a Mexican grant, he moved north and filed a new claim in the Vail Lake area between Aguanga and Temecula. The 1870 census listed Hamilton as black, a widower, living with his four children. Again, his homestead claim was disallowed

The Tripp family at their homestead on Tripp Flats, 1893. Samuel Tripp sits in the middle holding his grandson Arthur. — CHARLES VAN FLEET

Shasta Tripp and his wife Viola. Shasta and his brother Will lived on Tripp Flats and became cattlemen in the early 1880s. — LESTER REED

Wedding photo of William and Alice Tripp, July 21, 1883. — LESTER REED

Old Cahuilla School at Tripp Flats, 1896. Left to right are Willie, Rose and Mary Tripp, Fanny Parks, Arthur, Charles, Edith and Lily Tripp, and teacher Miss Hartley. — HEMET MUSEUM

Roy Tripp, son of Will and Alice Tripp, was shot and killed in the hills north of Terwilliger Valley by Al Heller in 1916. — LESTER REED

Branding time at the Tripp corral, circa 1896.
— LAURA SWIFT

James Hamilton (1822-1897), part African-American, was the first non-Indian settler in the Cahuilla (Anza) Valley area, arriving about 1873. His ranch was at the eastern edge of the valley. Bible-toting "Uncle Jim" was highly respected and loved. His sons and grandsons continued as cattlemen in the Anza and Garner valley country.
— DOLORES ARNAIZ

for being within the boundaries of Rancho Pauba, so the Hamiltons were obliged to move again. This time they relocated successfully on 160 acres at the southeastern edge of Cahuilla Valley, east of present-day Anza.

By the mid-1870s, Bible-toting "Uncle Jim" Hamilton and his sons had built a good-sized stock ranch. Their cattle ranged across the Cahuilla Valley to Hog Lake, west of Thomas Mountain. They also filed on land near Kenworthy in the Thomas Valley. Here the Hamilton cattle, mixed in with the Thomas, Tripp and Arnaiz herds, grazed on the rich summer verdure.

Tragedy struck the Hamilton family in 1895, when son Frank was gunned down in a saloon fight in San Jacinto. "Uncle Jim," highly respected by most who knew him, died in 1897. He is remembered on today's maps by Hamilton Creek.

The two remaining sons of Jim Hamilton, Joe and Henry, carried on their father's cattle business. Both were skilled cowboys, and the Hamilton cattle grew into a sizeable herd. Joe Hamilton lived in Kenworthy, while Henry stayed in the Cahuilla Valley. Continuing in the Hamilton cattle tradition were Joe's two sons by his marriage to Clara Arnaiz, Lincoln and Frank, the latter called "Gummy." Lincoln Hamilton later bought a large ranch in the Anza Valley, where he herded cattle and grew alfalfa, wheat, and barley.[12] He died in 1976, ending a century of the Hamilton cowboy saga.

Frank Wellman, who along with Sam Temple shared a dubious reputation for violence and drunkenness, was born in Iowa in 1858. Little is known about his life until he arived in Strawberry Valley around 1885, where he went to work hauling wagonloads of lumber from Scherman's sawmill down to San Jacinto. Later he built a cabin near the southeast end of Thomas Valley and became a cowboy, driving cattle for Thomas and other ranchers up the notorious "Devil's Slide" to summer pasture in Tahquitz Valley, high in the mountains. He built a log cabin along Willow Creek. In 1895 Wellman filed for a homestead in "Strawberry Valley and north of Tackwish Valley," but the patent was never issued, probably because the high country was included in the new San Jacinto Forest Reserve, set aside by President Grover Cleveland in 1897.

Frank Wellman married Clara Arnaiz, daughter of Kenworthy cattleman Manuel Arnaiz, in August 1897. The marriage raised some eyebrows because Wellman was 39 and his bride only 13. Two children, Mary born in 1898, Jim in 1901, resulted from the union. Wellman had a violent temper and was a heavy drinker, a combination that boded ill and brought about one of the most shocking tragedies in the mountain history. In August 1901, an angry and drunken Frank Wellman assaulted his young wife. Fearing for her own life and her two babies, Clara shot and killed her husband. She was exonerated by the coroner's jury.

The widowed Clara, only 17 with two small children to raise, remained in Kenworthy. In 1902 she married Joe Hamilton. Joe and Clara Hamilton raised four of their own children, along with the two Wellman offspring. It was a loving family, Jim Wellman remembered, and he grew quite close to his stepfather.

Frank Hamilton, son of "Uncle Jim," was shot and killed by Charles Marshall in old town San Jacinto in 1895.
— LESTER REED

Roundup time at Joe Hamilton's ranch near Kenworthy. — LAURA SWIFT

Jim Wellman became a successful cattleman, his herds ranging far and wide over the southern San Jacintos and the desert slopes of the Santa Rosas. Lion Spring, Cedar Spring, Eagle Spring, Mad Woman Spring, Bullseye Rock and Hells Kitchen were all places frequented by Wellman cattle and named by Jim himself. Mad Woman Spring, above Palm Canyon, was so named after two wives of cowboys camped there got in a violent argument. Hells Kitchen, a rocky and brush-choked basin just east of the Desert Divide, was so named because some of Wellman's cattle went down there to feed and Jim had "a hell of a time" getting them out.[13]

Jim Wellman was also a superb big game hunter. His 101 Ranch in Morris Canyon was filled with trophies from hunting expeditions to Canada, Alaska, Mexico and Africa. He claimed to have personally trapped and shot 35 mountain lions in the San Jacinto Mountains alone. He died in 1979. He son Bud Wellman still lives in the Morris Canyon area.

The largest of all cattle operations in the San Jacintos was the Garner Ranch, which, at its height in the 1950s, contained some 9,500 acres and sprawled over most of Garner Valley. The 85-year saga of the Garner Ranch began in 1907, when Robert Franklin Garner took possession from Charles Thomas.

The Garner family has a long history of stock raising, both cattle and horses. Moses B. Garner, Jr., Robert's father, was born in Kentucky in 1828. He was the son of Moses Baumgarner who, shortly after his arrival from Germany, changed his name to Moses Baum Garner, then to Moses B. Garner. The family moved to southern Illinois in the 1830s and became successful farmers.

Tragically, both of the elder Garners were struck down by the great cholera plague of 1851.

Moses B. Garner, Jr. raised horses on his Springfield, Illinois ranch and, at times, was a Pony Express rider, deputy sheriff and finally county sheriff, the position he was holding when he married Hannah Hulda Heard in 1850. In 1861 Moses Garner sold his Illinois property and, with Hannah and their five children, headed west for Virginia City, Montana. Moses, entrepreneur that he was, successfully mined gold and managed a hotel, but the severe Montana winter inflamed his rheumatism and caused the Garners to head for Southern California in 1864. The family traveled by covered wagon via the Salt Lake-Los Angeles Trail and settled in San Bernardino.

Moses Garner quickly became a leading citizen of San Bernardino. He opened a meat market and then a restaurant, and prospered in the real estate business. Always interested in the breeding and racing of thoroughbred horses, Moses operated a large stable and built a race track. He found time to be a bank vice president and served as a San Bernardino County supervisor between 1885 and 1889. Moses and Hannah Garner produced ten children during their life together.

The oldest of the ten offspring was Robert Franklin Garner, born in 1862. Robert inherited the business acumen of his father and quickly rose to prominence. He started out as a butcher, then took over management of his father's meat market, built a packing house, and finally began buying up property and range land for his own growing herds of cattle. At one time or another, Robert Garner owned the Los Flores Ranch in Summit Valley, the Whitewater Ranch near Banning, and various grazing lands in the San Bernardino and San Jacinto

Joe Hamilton family, circa 1908. Left to right are Clara Arnaiz Hamilton with baby "Gummy," her daughter Mary Wellman, Joe Hamilton, with Arnaiz sisters Daisy and Fanny standing behind. — BILL JENNINGS

Manuel Arnaiz family, circa 1887. Manuel (1856-1925) sits on left with son Eugene on lap. Daughter Clara stands in front of Dolores Garduna Arnaiz, Manuel's wife. To the right are Dolores' sister Manuela Quintana and her husband Gregorio Quintana. The Arnaiz cattle ranch was just southeast of Kenworthy. — DOLORES ARNAIZ

Joe Hamilton ranch near Kenworthy, Garner Valley, ca. 1908. — LESTER REED

Gathering at Arnaiz Ranch, ca. 1920. Adults left to right are, unknown, Frank Hamilton, Joe Hamilton, Santana Flores, Daniel Arnaiz, Edward Arnaiz, Clara Hamilton (behind), Guy Exon, Charles Van Deventer.
— FANNY CONTRERAS

Kenworthy School, 1908. L to R, back row: Mary Wellman, Minta Schneider, Clara Hamilton holding Gummy, Sophie Scherman holding Vincent, Henry Hamilton, Joe Hamilton. L to R, front row: Adolph Scherman, Kathryn Scherman, Lincoln Hamilton, Henry Arnaiz, Lucy Hamilton, Dan Arnaiz, Joe Scherman, Jim Wellman, Ed Arnaiz. – DAVID SCHERMAN

Jim Wellman (1901-1979) in center, flanked by Cahuilla cowboys Calistro Tortes (left) and Frank Alveras (right). Picture taken during roundup on Santa Rosa Reservation, ca. 1940. – DAVID SCHERMAN

Cahuilla cowboys roping calves in the Anza Valley, ca. 1910. — CHARLES VAN FLEET

Ernest Arnaiz (1898-1975) represented the quintessential cowboy. He spent his life tending cattle, working at his father Manuel Arnaiz's Kenworthy ranch until the latter's death in 1925, cowboying for Jim Wellman and other mountain cattlemen, employed at a feedlot in the Coachella Valley, and other cattle related jobs.
— DOLORES ARNAIZ

Old cattle cabin at Asbestos Spring near Pinyon Flat, ca. 1925. — BILL JENNINGS

Arnaiz corral at Pinyon Flat, Santa Rosa Mountains behind. — BILL JENNINGS

Moses and Hannah Garner and their ten children, ca. 1890. Robert F. Garner is standing second to right. Robert Garner started out working for his father as a butcher in San Bernardino. Later he bought and developed cattle ranches in San Bernardino and Riverside counties. He purchased the Thomas Ranch in Garner Valley in 1905.
— JACK GARNER

valleys. It was said that he was "second only to the Santa Fe Railroad in paying taxes in San Bernardino County."[14]

Robert Garner, always looking for more ranch land, was enroute to San Diego in late 1905 to buy the Temecula Ranch. When he arrived with checkbook in hand, he found that a man named Walter Vail had beaten him to it. Still looking for a ranch or grazing land to buy, Garner learned that Charles Thomas was trying to sell his cattle ranch in the San Jacintos. Although whether or not Thomas lost money on horses is a matter of dispute, there was no question that he was in hock to the bank. Garner purchased Thomas' note from the bank, then negotiated with the latter over terms. Agreement was reached on December 28, 1905: Garner would pay $30,000 for 1,700 acres remaining of the Thomas Ranch, and allow Thomas and his family until January 1, 1907 to sell off their stock and vacate the place.[15]

Robert Garner proceeded to make his Garner Ranch one of the largest and most profitable stock ranches in Southern California. Cattle by the hundreds were brought in to nourish themselves on the rich grasses of the mountain valley; within a few years there were over 1,500 head. Adjacent grazing lands were bought. Garner leased the 5,000-acre Hancock Johnston Ranch, between Herkey Creek and Keen Camp, and bought it outright in 1912, bringing the total Garner Ranch holdings to more than 9,500 acres. The *Hemet News* (May 9, 1913) reported that "The Garner stock farm...is one of the largest in Southern California, and thousands of head of cattle graze on the green pastures afforded by this level stretch of grassland hidden between the towering mountains."

George Law, writing in 1923, described how the Garner system operated: "Mr. Garner so manages as to have on hand the smallest aggregate of stock during the winter. Thus, in the fall, he markets his fat stock; and not until the spring does he import an equal number from the ranges of Arizona, Utah or New Mexico, to fill their places. But at no time does he overstock his ranges. The two hazards that are commonly the nemesis of stockment – cattle that will not fatten, and discouraged pasture grasses – he avoids by carrying slightly less than the capacity of his ranges, and by pasturing his meadows in sections, allowing each ample time to rest and recuperate. So thoroughly and systematically is this scheme carried out that it is always possible to wade knee-deep in certain of the pastures on the Garner Ranch at any time of the year."[16]

Garner cattle not only grazed on the ranch lands, but on government lease lands in the surrounding mountains. The cattle were driven "over most of Mt. San Jacinto, ranging from the ranch over the grassy slopes and meadows around Tahquitz Lodge to Strawberry Valley and Idyllwild ten miles away. Even up to the Alpine cienegas around Tahquitz Peak, at an elevation of

Four generations of Garners: L to R, Robert Garner, Sr. (1862-1930), Hanna Garner (1835-1940), Jack Garner (1919-present), Robert Garner Jr. (1896-1945)
– JACK GARNER

Garner Ranch cattle near Hemet Lake.
– IDYLLWILD LIBRARY

8,000 feet, the cattle are sometimes driven for a few months in the heart of summer."[17] To reach the high country meadows, Garner's cowboys drove the herd over the old Thomas trail to Fern Valley, then, twenty-five at a time, up the steep Devil's Slide trail. After several weeks of grazing on the tall grasses of Tahquitz, Reed, and Skunk Cabbage meadows, the fattened cattle were driven through "The Hole in the Wall" between Tahquitz and Red Tahquitz peaks and down the slightly less steep Herkey Creek trail. Jack Garner remembers that these high mountain drives continued as late as 1930, after which the San Jacinto Primitive Area was proclaimed and cattle were no longer welcomed.[18]

Desert cattle from the Whitewater Ranch, or from as far away as New Mexico, were assembled each spring at the Beaumont holding pens adjacent to the Southern Pacific Railroad Station. Garner Ranch cowboys – many of them of Cahuilla Indian or mixed Mexican-Indian blood – would then drive the hungry animals down Lamb Canyon to the Pico Ranch in the San Jacinto Valley, across the valley to holding pens at the railroad station in San Jacinto, and finally up Keen Camp Road and over Keen Summit to the Garner Ranch.

Robert F. Garner business ad, 1902. – JACK GARNER

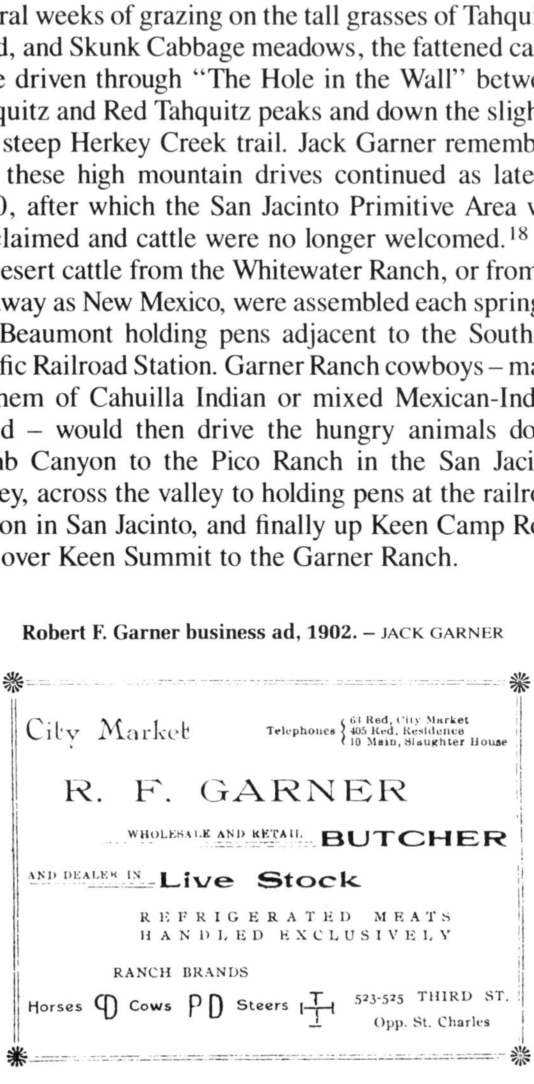

```
City Market      Telephones { 61 Red, City Market
                              405 Red, Residence
                              10 Main, Slaughter House

     R. F. GARNER
     WHOLESALE AND RETAIL  BUTCHER

AND DEALER IN  Live Stock
       REFRIGERATED MEATS
       HANDLED EXCLUSIVELY

         RANCH BRANDS
Horses  ⊕   Cows  ℗   Steers  ⊤   523-525 THIRD ST.
                                  Opp. St. Charles
```

After a summer of feasting on the lush verdure of the mountain valleys, the fat Garner cattle chosen for market were driven back down Keen Camp Road to the Santa Fe loading pens in San Jacinto or all the way to the Southern Pacific loading pens in Beaumont. After being weighed and sold to buyers, the doomed, unknowing animals were shipped to slaughterhouses as far away as San Francisco.

For many years, these cattle drives were led by old Santana, the trusty Cahuilla Indian who was long the Garners' chief cowboy. Other Garner cowboys in the early days were Dan Arnaiz, Gib Miller, Adolfo Jauro and Joe John. Adolfo and Joe John were cousins. They lived on the Soboba Indian Reservation, cowboyed as a pair, and worked for the Garners until they died.

After Robert Garner Sr. died in 1930, Robert Jr. took over the ranch helm, and he was succeeded at his passing in 1945 by son Jack Garner. Jack Garner is still head "honcho" today, ably assisted by daughter Meg and a small, trustworthy staff.

The story of the Garner Ranch would not be complete without mention of Horace Magee and Jozee Salinas, members of the ranch community for half a century and cherished by the Garners as family members.

Horace Magee, born about 1880 in Temecula, was half Indian, quarter Mexican and quarter Irish. His dark skin branded him as an Indian in the eyes of many whites. He came to work on the Garners' Santa Rosa Ranch near Temecula as a young man and was credited with helping to save Robert Jr.'s life by guiding a doctor to the ranch during a violent rainstorm.

Horace Magee's life was abruptly altered by what happened in a Temecula pool hall on Christmas Eve, 1907. According to contemporary accounts, an intoxicated Magee was acting in a loud and abrasive manner in

Horace Magee, part of the Garner Ranch family from 1920 until his death in 1963. He overcame a Temecula poolhall killing and twelve years in state prison to become a model ranchhand for the Garners. — JACK GARNER

Jozee Salinas came to the Garner Ranch as a cook in 1931 and stayed 54 years. She ran the ranch household and helped to manage ranch affairs. — JACK GARNER

the crowded pool hall when Constable Preston V. Swanguen told him to quiet down. Magee pulled out a revolver and fired three shots into Swanguen, killing him instantly. He then turned the gun on Louis "Peter" Escallier, a French cowboy, and killed him with one shot. John Jackson, a Santa Fe brakeman present at the scene, knocked Magee to the floor with a billiard cue, grabbed the assailant's gun and beat him unconscious, fracturing Magee's skull in the process. Jackson, the only witness to testify at the preliminary hearing in Riverside, claimed the shooting came "without provocation" but did say that Escallier had earlier "burned the accused with a lighted cigar."[19]

The Garners tell a far different story of what happened that fateful Christmas Eve. According to their version, Magee was being taunted by a group of unruly white cowboys, who resented the presence of a half-breed in their midst. All, including Magee, had been drinking heavily. What happened next "couldn't be printed in Hustler magazine," said former lawman Hollis C. Hollis of Hemet. It was so crude and abusive that anyone would have been enraged beyond rationality, he said.[20] The most painful outrage was when Magee, his pants pulled down, was spread-eagled on a pool table and a lighted cigar shoved up his anus. Watching these humiliations was Constable Swanguen, who allegedly made no attempt to stop the laughing and jeering white mob. Angry, in great pain, totally humiliated, Magee left the pool hall and returned a short time later with a gun, shooting the constable and his tormentor to death before being beaten unconscious with a pool cue and his own revolver.

Magee was tried and convicted of first degree murder and sentenced to a life term in state prison. The judge did not invoke the death penalty because he ruled that Magee's action was partly caused by liquor illegally given him at a "blind pig," as an unlicensed saloon was called in those days.

Horace Magee spent the next twelve years of his life in prison. By all accounts he was a model prisoner who spent much of his time making beautifully woven belts and lariats. He was often visited by Robert Garner, who never forgot Magee's part in saving his son's life.

At the urging of the Garners, Magee was paroled to the custody of Robert Jr. in 1920. He went to work as a cowboy on the Garners' Los Flores Ranch north of San Bernardino, and then on the Garner Ranch in the San Jacintos. Here he remained the rest of his long life, leaving the mountains only to help on cattle drives or on cattle buying trips. For many years he was the Garners' lead cowboy. On January 2, 1931, California Governor C. C. Young formally commuted Magee's life sentence, calling the latter's act "a crime of passion."

All of those years, Horace Magee was a gentle person of few words who commanded respect. He never lost his temper, Jack Garner remembers. When advancing years slowed his work as a cowboy, Magee remained at the ranch as a member of the Garner family. "We loved him so much," said Jack Garner.

Horace Magee died on March 26, 1963, at the Garner Ranch while his cousin Jozee Salinas was cutting his hair. His wish was that his body go to Loma Linda University for medical research. "I've never been to a funeral in my life," he told Jack Garner, "and I certainly don't want to go to my own." His wish was carried out.

Jozee Salinas was born in 1916 in San Jacinto, the first of ten children. Being the oldest, she helped her mother tend her siblings and cooked for the family. The Depression hit the Salinas family hard, causing the older children to seek outside work. Jozee's brother Joe found work as a cowboy at the Garner Ranch. He returned home one day in December 1933 and told his sister that the Garners were looking for a part-time cook. Next day 17 year-old Jozee accompanied her brother to the ranch and took the job. She stayed 52 years — the rest of her life.

Garner Ranch cattle. – ROY MURPHY

Winter at the Garner Ranch. – MEG GARNER

Jozee Salinas became far more than just a Garner Ranch cook. She cleaned house, tended the garden, and served as barber for the cowboys. It was not long until she ran the ranch household. She became a skillfull horseback rider and cowhand, and learned how to drive cattle, deliver new-born calves and innoculate them. As the years passed, she assumed many responsibilities of ranch management and became a beloved member of the Garner family. Jozee Salinas died in 1985 and was deeply mourned by everyone at the ranch. There will never be another like her.

Untold thousands of people world-wide may not realize it, but they are familiar with the Garner Ranch setting. Dozens of films, mostly Westerns, have been shot at the ranch in the past sixty years. Such familiar cowboy actors as Gene Autry, Hopalong Cassidy and Tom Mix were once commonly seen there. Tim Holt and Richard "Chico" Martin did about eight movies on the ranch. Robert Mitchum and "Wild Bill" Elliott worked there on several films. Many episodes for the popular TV shows "Bonanza" and "The Virginian" were filmed on the ranch grounds.

The decline of the Garner Ranch as a cattle spread began in the late 1960s, when the subdivision craze hit Southern California. Sections of land in Garner Valley were lopped off and developed as housing tracts. The biggest land deals occurred in 1968, when 2,500 acres of the ranch were sold for subdivision, and in 1974, when 2,000 acres were sold. The Forest Service bought or traded for some 2,500 acres of the Garner Ranch by 1991.

A smaller Garner Ranch of about 2,500 acres, centered around the old Thomas home in the upper valley, remains, still owned by the Garner family. Jack Garner's daughter Meg lives there in the original Thomas ranch house, now extensively remodeled. About 600 head of cattle roam the ranch and surrounding lease lands today.[21]

And there were many other cattlemen whose herds once extensively grazed the San Jacintos, the Santa Rosas, and the adjacent hills and valleys. Unfortunately, we can give them only brief mention, to keep this book within manageable size. (A fat volume of many hundreds of pages could be written on cattle ranching in the mountains.)

Asa and Naoma Reed, with sons William, John, and Quitman and two daughters, drove a herd of cattle from Texas to Southern California in 1867. In Temecula, they were told of a mountain meadow, unoccupied at the time, that was a good place to graze cattle. Asa Reed and his oldest son William filed homestead claims in what became known as Reed Valley, close under the western ramparts of Cahuilla Mountain. Here 75 year-old Asa and his closeknit family planted crops and raised cattle. It was not long until the Reeds had one of the largest herds in the mountain area and supplied beef to markets as far away as San Bernardino and Riverside. Son Quitman Reed married into the Tripp family, and in the late 1880s bought 640 acres near Sage to use as a cattle range. He named it Mud Springs Ranch because there was a muddy seepage of water near the center of the grazing area. Three generations of Reeds continued to graze cattle in the rich grasslands below Cahuilla Mountain.[22]

Jacob and Almira Terwilliger and their four children, New York Quakers, came west in 1875 and first settled at the foot of Hall's Grade in San Gorgonio Pass. In 1883 they homesteaded 160 acres at the southern end of the Cahuilla Plains (Anza Valley). Here they built a home, farmed, and raised livestock. Today the area is called Terwilliger Valley, in honor of the first white settlers there.

The brothers Fred and Frank Clark arrived in San Jacinto from Kansas in 1886. They worked at odd jobs around town for several years, but at heart they were cowboys. They learned of cattle grazing opportunities

Jacob and Elmira Terwilliger (two on the right) were the first white settlers in Terwilliger Valley, arriving in 1883. On the left is Anna Terwilliger Clark (daughter) and Pearl (granddaughter). The man in the middle is Fred Hopkins, Cahuilla storekeeper and first justice of the peace for the small community. – BUD CLARK

on the Cahuilla Plains and came up to investigate in 1890. Both of them stayed the rest of their lives. Fred Clark bought land at the southeast edge of Terwilliger Valley from Pesqual Powett in 1891 and built an adobe home. His ranch house was right above *La Puerta,* the doorway to Coyote Canyon and the Borrego Desert, Anza's old "Royal Pass of San Carlos." Frank Clark homesteaded six miles west in what became known as Durasno Valley. Fred remained a bachelor; Frank married Annie Terwilliger and raised two children, Bud and Lola. The Clark brothers quickly became the premier cattlemen in Terwilliger Valley. In winter they drove their herds down to Borrego Valley and Clark Dry Lake (see *The Santa Rosas*).

Bud Clark, son of Frank and Anna born in 1902, recalled that "From the time I was old enough to ride a horse I helped Dad with the cattle. In the fall, Dad and I would drive the herd from Durasno Valley down Coyote Canyon to Borrego Valley, where we had 80 acres and a cabin. I would often stay there alone as a teenager, tending the cattle."[23]

Frank Clark continued as a cattlemen until his death in 1937. His brother Fred, after many years as a cattleman, turned to raising and selling horses.

Art and Violet Cary bought the La Puerta Ranch from Fred Clark in 1938. They built a new ranch house in 1942 and have lived there ever since. The Carys named their spread the VA Ranch (the V for Violet, the A for Art).

William and Mary Webster and their large family settled at the head of the San Jacinto Valley in 1877, where they planted fruit trees and tended cattle. Son David Webster built what was long known as the Webster Trail up the North Fork of the San Jacinto River to Fern Basin. Via this steep pathway, the Websters and other valley cattlemen drove their herds to summer pasture.

Hancock Johnston, son of Confederate General Albert Sidney Johnston, raised Angus cattle and thoroughbred horses at his 1400-acre Big Springs Ranch on the south side of the San Jacinto Valley in the 1880s and early 1890s. Johnston bought 7,800 acres from the Southern Pacific Railroad in 1886 and developed his Johnston Mountain Stock Ranch between Lou Crane's place (later Keen Camp) and the Thomas Ranch. His southern hospitality was legendary, as many a guest to his mountain stock ranch would attest. (Two of his guests in 1888 were Edward Mayberry and William Whittier, who would soon build Hemet Dam.) Johnston Flat honors his name today.

Myron M. Omstott moved from Chino to upper Herkey Creek, buying land from the Southern Pacific, in the late 1880s. Omstott cattle ranged from Herkey Creek to May Valley. In summer, he drove his herd to the head of Herkey Creek and through the "Hole in the Wall" to pasture in Tahquitz Valley. He died sitting in front of his fireplace in 1908, and his heirs sold the ranch to Will Tripp. Tripp ran cattle and operated a sawmill along Herkey Creek. In 1918 he sold the ranch to Tom Fleming, a teamster from Los Angeles and a part owner

Frank Clark and his son Vernal "Bud" Clark, pistols drawn. Frank Clark was a rancher in the Durasno Valley and the first constable of Babtiste (Anza). Bud Clark was appointed a county deputy sheriff when he reached 21. This picture, circa 1919. – BUD CLARK

Fred Clark standing before the Anza Monument on his La Puerta Ranch, circa 1930. – BUD CLARK

of the Colton Cement Company. The Fleming Ranch has been a fixture since then.

There were the brothers Sam and Dick Meeks, who lived in the San Jacinto Valley and drove cattle up the original Devil's Slide to summer pasture in Tahquitz Meadow. They are said to have built the first cabin there.

George Spitler built a ranch at the head of today's Fobes Creek, northeast of Garner Valley, in the 1880s, only to find he was on land claimed by Charles Thomas. Thomas forced him out, then gave the ranch to Fred Blake to settle a loan. Blake in turn sold the land to Ray Fobes in 1918, who turned it into a working cattle ranch. He sold out to Clayton Record in the 1940s. Fobes Canyon, Fobes Spring, and Spitler Peak honor these early settlers.

At the other end of the San Jacintos, above San Gorgonio Pass, William H. "Hack" Hurley ran cattle on what is today's Poppett Flat as early as 1878. Around 1883 he moved over to another mountain flat four miles east and lived there as a squatter for many years. Today the mountain basin is known as Hurley Flats.

English-born Robert Poppett and his large family bought Hack Hurley's old homestead in 1887 and settled there. The Poppetts, unlike other mountain cattlemen, produced dairy rather than beef cattle. "Poppett's Ranch Butter," as well as other milk products, sold well in San Jacinto, Hemet and Banning markets. The family left in 1905, but the name Poppett Flats remains on today's maps.

Westernmost of all, and the only one of the mountain ranches that dates from Mexican California times, was the Potrero Ranch, nestled in a shallow valley surrounded by hills south of Beaumont. The 9,300-acre *Potrero* (meadow) was originally part of the vast *Rancho San Jacinto Nuevo y Potrero* (48,861 acres) granted by Mexican governor Pio Pico to Miguel de Pedrorena in 1846. It was acquired by José Antonio Aguirre around 1850. Joseph Wolfskill, son of Los Angeles land-owner William Wolfskill, paid Aguirre "a small consideration for taxes" and came into possession in 1862. For many decades the Wolfskill family owned Potrero Ranch, but the Aguirres were hired to run it – José Antonio Aguirre first, then his son Miguel, and finally his grandson Martin Aguirre. The Aguirres lived in the old adobe

Fred Clark's adobe ranch house at La Puerta, ca. 1906. Fred is standing in the doorway, David Elsworth sitting. – BUD CLARK

Mexican Longhorn cattle in Cahuilla Valley, circa 1910. It required a skillful cowboy to round up these unruly animals. Some escaped into the brushy fastness of upper Palm Canyon and became wild "bronco cattle."
— BUD CLARK

Cahuilla cowboys from the Santa Rosa Reservation were skillful handlers of the lariat. L to R are Ignacio Guanche, Alex Tortes, and Mariano Tortes.
— DAVID SCHERMAN

ranch house and tended the orchard, the vineyard and the cattle that roamed far and wide over the gentle hill country that forms the northwestern end of the San Jacinto Mountains. The Wolfskill-Aguirre partnership did not end until 1940, when Potrero Ranch was sold to Forrest Stanton.[24]

Some of the best cowboys who tended herds in the San Jacinto and Santa Rosa mountain country were Cahuilla Indians. The six Costo brothers, the Lubo, Lugo, and Casseros brothers, Calistro, Alex, and Mariano Tortes, Augustine Apapas and his son Pio, Ignacio Guanche, Frank Alveras, Leo Arenas, Celso Serrano – these are some of the names that are legendary among the old-time mountain cattlemen. The Cahuilla cowpunchers were not only skillful at herding cattle through the rugged mountain and canyon country, they were masters at roundup time. Their skill with the long rawhide *reata* was unexcelled, according to Lester Reed who watched them as a boy. Reed remembered how, at full speed on horseback, the Indian cowboys gracefully tossed the looped *reata* over a running calf's head and drew it tight around the animal's neck, bringing the frightened calf to a quick halt.[25]

Cahuilla cattle thrived on the meadow grasses of the Santa Rosa Reservation. "I know of no better meadows of their size anywhere than those belonging to the Cahuilla Indians," wrote Reed, " Some of the best beef I ever sold were fattened in meadows leased from the Indians."[26]

Roundup time was a special occasion among the mountain ranchers, a scene never forgotten by any who witnessed it. First the cattle, many of them scattered widely through the brushy, rock-ribbed back country, had to be located and herded together. Some of the wild Mexican cattle were most difficult to round up, and often had to be roped and dragged, one by one, to the corral. Particularly hard to round up were the Arnaiz cattle, who ranged widely from upper Palm Canyon across Pinyon Flats into the Santa Rosa Mountains.

Once the unruly animals were finally corraled, each owner picked out his branded cattle and the young unbranded calves that followed their mothers. The frightened, bawling calves were roped, tied down, and branded, usually on the rump, with a hot iron.

The annual roundup at the Reed's Mud Springs Ranch was a time for festivity. Families from the surrounding country would be invited to a picnic and barbeque, put on right after the cowboys had roped and branded the animals. "I remember one time when there were 45 people there on horseback, and counting the women and children who went in spring wagons and buckboard, there was a total number of 71. The cattle were first rounded up on one of the flats, the animals parted out that were not to be branded or vaccinated, and then those we wanted were driven to a big round corral made from willow poles. Each animal that was to be branded or vaccinated was roped by the head in the corral, then led outside to be roped by the hind feet. Some of the old boys in those days were really good at catching both feet," wrote Lester Reed.[27]

A mountain cattle drive was a dramatic sight to any who witnessed one. Cowboys on horseback, bedecked with Stetson hats and bandana scarfs, wearing leather chaps and toting lariats, yelling profanities, with herd

Ignacio Guanche, one of the best of the Indian cowboys, in the San Jacinto Mountains, ca. 1925.
— DAVID SCHERMAN

John Tortes, Ignacio Guanche, Calistro Tortes, Frank Lugo, and Rafael Tortes were expert cattlemen and horse wranglers on the Santa Rosa Reservation. Ca, 1925.
— DAVID SCHERMAN

dogs snapping at hoofs, forced the unwilling, bawling, snorting, stomping animals along a dusty stock trail. Every few hours the cowboys and their unruly herd stopped to rest. Occasionally a renegade steer or cow darted into the forest or brush, to be quickly cornered and forced back by the ever-watchful cattlemen. Seldom did the cowboys lose an animal, and the herd eventually arrived intact at the chosen destination, whether it be ranch corral, mountain meadow, or loading pen.

The biggest problem the cowboys sometimes faced on a cattle drive was a stampede. The cattle were easily spooked by a loud noise, such as gunfire, or occasionally in the early days, by the sudden appearance of a bear or other wild animal. The terrified cattle would then dart off in all directions, often not stopping for miles. The round-up of the stampeded herd could take hours, days or even weeks. James and George Thomas of the Thomas Ranch suffered the embarrassment of their herd, being driven to Riverside, stampeding just as they entered the city. The cowboys, aided by Riverside police, had to hunt down the animals on city streets and in back yards.[28]

Perhaps the most spectacular cattle drive of all was when Frank Wellman drove livestock up the old "Devil's Slide" trail from Strawberry Valley to Tahquitz Meadow, high under the mountain crest, in the 1880s and '90s. The Devil's Slide trail today is a gradual uphill stroll, certainly undeserving of its notorious name. But in Wellman's day it was quite different. No switchbacks then, just right up the mountainside over loose boulders and fallen limbs, through thorny chaparral thickets to the crest, about a quarter-mile south of the trail's present crossing at Saddle Junction. Many a cow and even a few cowboys took a bone-breaking spill on this treacherous slope, and anyone who knew the Devil's Slide then always remembered it. From the crest, the cattle path led gently downward to the rich meadow grasses of Tahquitz Creek's headwaters, where the cattle feasted for several weeks. Cowboys tending the herds there stayed in the Meeks' cabin. From the mountain valley of Tahquitz Creek, Wellman built another trail over the low ridge into Willow Creek. Near its headwaters he erected a log cabin. From here, he forged a rough cattle trail over a higher ridge, passing just below the spring

Castro Tortes, known as "Chihuahua," and old-time Santa Rosa cowboy. — LESTER REED

Martin Aguirre (center) was the last in line of the Aguirres who ran the Potrero Ranch for decades.
— LAURA SWIFT

The Hancock Johnston Ranch, Johnston Flat near Keen Camp, ca. 1890. – LAURA SWIFT

known today as Wellman's Cienega, to Round and Tamarack valleys, close under the buttress of San Jacinto Peak.[29] (There are no tamaracks in Tamarack Valley. Early cattlemen called the lodgepole pines tamaracks.)

The cattle nourished themselves on the verdant grasses of the high meadows all summer, tended by white cowboys. It has been said that the Cahuilla cowboys, fearful of the mythical demon *Tahquitz* who supposedly lived in the high mountains, would not go up the Devil's Slide. As reported in the *San Jacinto Register* (July 20, 1893), "They [the Indians] cannot be persuaded to herd cattle there, and white men have to do it."

A danger to the livestock, all over the San Jacintos, came from grizzly bears, who were numerous in the mountains in the early days. Several of the huge beasts developed a taste for raw beef and preyed on the herds almost nightly on some occasions. Few humans were mauled. The only known death was that of a woodcutter on the Thomas Ranch named Herkey (mentioned in the previous chapter), who was attacked by an enraged mother grizzly after his dogs had chased her cubs up a tree. But because of their attacks on livestock, cattlemen hunted, trapped and poisoned the beasts until they were completely exterminated. Rancher Quitman Reed told his son about "old-time cowboys roping some of them in the Thomas Valley when they would be found out in the meadows feeding. Those old bears were known to be rather rough and rugged when on the end of a rope, but so were some of the old cowboys of that day – rough and rugged."[30] Reed built a log bear trap and captured two grizzlies, one of them seven feet long and weighing more than 1,400 pounds.[31] The last grizzly bear in these mountains, known as "Clubfoot" because of a bear-trap injury, was killed in Thomas Valley around 1890.

Hancock Johnston and his family, ca. 1890. Hancock was the son of Confederate General Albert Sidney Johnston. He operated the Big Springs Ranch in the San Jacinto Valley and the Johnston Mountain Stock Ranch on Johnston Flat in the 1880s and early 1890s. – LAURA SWIFT

Mountain lions were always a danger to the herds, particularly to young, helpless calves. But these crafty cats were much harder to kill than the grizzlies. Wary of humans, they stayed out of sight, suddenly pouncing on a calf or sheep and disappearing with their doomed prey before the cowboy or sheep herder had a chance to act. The lions had to be tenaciously hunted in their rocky citadels, a time consuming job few cattlemen had the time or patience to do. Jim Wellman, as mentioned earlier, claimed 35 of the big cats during his years as a cattleman. When the mountain lion menace began to seriously deplete the livestock, ranchers hired Cahuilla hunters to track them down.[32]

Sheep herding was never as extensive in the San Jacintos as it was in other Southern California ranges. Most of the sheep in this area were tended by Cahuillas on the Santa Rosa and Soboba reservations. Cahuilla sheep shearers, the best in the business, were annually hired by white sheep owners in the San Jacinto Valley at shearing time. Helen Hunt Jackson admiringly watched the skillful Cahuillas at work when she visited the valley in 1882. She began her famous novel *Ramona* with the sentences, "It was sheep-shearing time in Southern California." Later in the book, she describes "Forms, dusty black against fiery sky, were coming down the valley. It was the band of Indian shearers."[33]

John and Fanny Arnaiz Contreras, 1918. The Contreras were among the first to homestead in the central Anza Valley in 1910. – FANNY CONTRERAS

The Contreras Ranch, Anza Valley, circa 1919. – FANNY CONTRERAS

When sheep herders from outside tried to drive their flocks into Cahuilla Valley in the 1890s, they received a rude reception from the cattlemen. Quitman Reed recalled that "the sheep were rounded up, and along with herders, started on the way back to where they came from."[34] There was good reason for the ranchers' hostility. Sheep, called "hoofed locusts" by John Muir, were vociferous eaters. They turned meadows to dust, nibbling every blade of grass, every seedling, every young bud. Cattlemen in the San Jacintos held the upper hand; they would not allow the high mountain pastures to be decimated by the "woolly lawn mowers."

The slow decline of the cattle industry in the San Jacinto Mountains began after the establishment of the San Jacinto Forest Reserve in 1897. Grazing was regulated on public lands; a fee structure was initiated in 1910 – 35¢ was charged for each cow grazing on federal forest land and 40¢ for each horse. Private lands were not affected, but much of the old high country summer range was. Another reason was economic; beef prices fell drastically in the 1920s and cattlemen found it increasingly difficult to return a profit.

The major factor in the decline of mountain cattle raising was a relentless reduction in land available for grazing. Resorts, a rush of homestead claims, and residential subdivisions sprang up where cattle once freely roamed: Strawberry Valley first, then Cahuilla Valley, Garner Valley, and Pinyon Flats, to name major encroachments on the open range. Cattlemen themselves, anxious to "cash in" on inflated land prices, sold out to developers.[35]

The story of the Cahuilla Plains (Anza Valley) is a case in point. Fanny Contreras, who moved there with her husband John in 1910, remembers how it was: "This was Indian country, a sprawling valley of rolling sagebrush land backing up to foothills and taller mountains on three sides, a treeless wilderness – ever changing, yet ever the same."[36] In 1909 the valley, having been surveyed, was opened to homesteading. Fanny and John filed on 160 acres of "Grade A sagebrush and red shank." They bought a little miner's shack at Kenworthy

Joseph G. and Sophie Scherman with daughter Minta. The Schermans homesteaded in Anza Valley in 1910. – DAVID SCHERMAN

Cutting alfalfa at the Joe Scherman Ranch, Anza Valley, 1919. The three boys in the center are (L to R) Joe S., Vincent, and Adolph Scherman. – DAVID SCHERMAN

The Scherman barn was used as a schoolhouse at Babtiste (Anza) from 1911 until the Hamilton School was opened in 1914. David Scherman, grandson of Joe G. Scherman, stands to the right.

for fifteen dollars, tore it down, hauled the lumber to their new homestead and reassembled it. This little cabin became their first ranch home. They cleared land and planted grain and a vegetable garden, and tended their small herd of cattle.

"Our first winter in that little shack was a challenge," Fanny recalled. "The roof, a checkerboard of cracks and holes through which the sun and stars shone, kept us busy. When it rained we weren't much better off than if we would have been outside, and when it snowed we fought a losing battle sweeping it off the roof before it fell through. But we lived in that one room through two winters. In 1912, when the big influx of settlers began coming into the valley, we were in pretty good shape. By then we had a well and much more cleared land. It was slow, however, for ever foot of land had to be cleared by hand. We had grain to sell, and made four hundred dollars that year. That was a lot of money in those days and it made it possible for us to improve our home and prove up on our homestead. It was in 1913 that we received our Grant Deed, signed by President Woodrow Wilson."[37]

John and Fanny Contreras soon had many neighbors as a rush of homestead claims were filed in the years 1909 through 1913. A. W. "Gus" Whisnand and Joe G. Scherman each filed for the alloted 160 acres each homesteader was allowed in 1909. Some fifty other filed during the ensuing four years. The new community took the name of Babtiste. Scherman's barn served as a temporary schoolhouse until the Hamilton School opened in 1914; the first teacher in the barn was Eula De Vana. Mail delivery was a problem. "We could pick it up at Aguanga or at Keen Camp," remembered Fanny Contreras. "There was a post office at Cahuilla, on the reservation, but the Indians didn't like the idea of the white men getting their mail there. So in 1913 a post office was established in the home of Will Shaney in Babtiste."[38] The name of the growing community was changed from Babtiste to Bautista in 1924 and to Anza on September 16, 1926. The days when the vast, sage-covered Cahuilla Plains were open range for Hamilton and Tripp cattle were a thing of the past.

The era of the hard-riding cowboy and his bawling herd has gone the way of the lumberman and the miner in the San Jacintos – only a faint echo of what once reverberated through forest and meadow. The story is the same throughout much of rural California. Ranch lands have attained greater value to the developer and home builder. Cattlemen now play second fiddle to the hundreds who make their homes in the mountains and the thousands of annual visitors. Cattle ranching in the San Jacintos in now a minor economic enterprise at best. The last roundup is over.

The old Hamilton School, Anza, as it looks today. An Anza Trail marker is on the boulder in the foreground.

The first class at the Hamilton School, Anza, opened in the fall of 1914. This student body photograph was taken on May 17, 1915. Left to right are, back row: Theresa Daschner, Mildred Evans, Elizabeth Shaney, Katherine Scherman, Martha Johnston, Reta Cooper, Lola Clark Bailey; middle row: Margaret Cort, Adolph Scherman, Helen Carroll, Vincent Scherman; front row: Harold Cooper, Arthur Carroll, Richard Daschner, Joseph Scherman, Walter Daschner, Vernal "Bud" Clark. – BUD CLARK

NOTES

1. Samuel P. Hayes, *Conservation and The Gospel of Efficiency* (Harvard U., 1959), p. 49.
2. Elmer Wallace Holmes, *History of Riverside County, California* (Los Angeles, 1912), p. 249.
3. Lewis Publishing Company, *An Illustrated History of Southern California* (Chicago, 1890), p. 169-170.
4. Holmes, p. 226.
5. Lewis, p. 169-170.
6. Salvador Estudillo interview, *San Jacinto Register,* July 24, 1902. See also Robert Glass Cleland, *The Cattle on a Thousand Hills* (San Marino, 1951), p. 68.
7. Estudillo interview.
8. Idyllwild *Town Crier,* April 21, 1961.
9. Hemet-San Jacinto Genealogical Society, *San Jacinto Valley, Past and Present* (Hemet, 1989), p. 16.
10. Lester Reed, *Old-Timers of Southeastern California* (Redlands, 1967), p. 95-131; Jane Davies Gunther, *Riverside County, California, Place Names: Their Origins and Their Stories* (Riverside, 1984), p. 549; and Lewis, p. 347.
11. Reed, p. 227-231; Hemet-San Jacinto Genealogical Society, p. 173-174; author interview with Charles Van Fleet, San Jacinto, 1971.
12. Reed, p. 207-221; Gunther, p. 222-223.
13. Reed, p. 214-216; Gunther, p. 566-567; Idyllwild *Town Crier,* May 24, 1957; Charles Van Fleet interview, 1971; Jim Wellman interview, 101 Ranch, 1971.
14. Jack Garner interview, Garner Ranch, August 18, 1992. See also undated newspaper clippings in Garner family possession.
15. Jack Garner; *Redlands Citrograph,* December 30, 1905.
16. George Law, "Fattening Desert Steers on Mountain Meadows," *Hemet News,* February 9, 1923.
17. *Ibid.*
18. Jack Garner.
19. *Hemet News,* Dec. 27, 1907; *Riverside Daily Press,* Dec. 27, 1907; *San Jacinto Register,* Jan. 2, 1908.
20. *Riverside Press-Enterprise,* April 12, 1977. Magee's side of the story is derived primarily from Jack Garner interview.
21. Jack Garner.
22. Reed, p. 255-284; Gunther, p. 422-423.
23. Bud Clark interview, San Jacinto, January 28, 1993.
24. The short biographical sketches are derived from a variety of sources, the most important being Gunther, Hemet-San Jacinto Genealogical Society, and interviews with Charles Van Fleet (1971), Clarence Swift (1972), and David Scherman (1991). For Poppet Flats and Potrero Ranch, see Garfield M. Quimby, "History of the Potrero Ranch and Its Neighbors," *SBCMA Quarterly,* Winter 1975.
25. Reed, p. 3.
26. *Ibid.,* p. 1.
27. *Ibid.,* p. 284.
28. *Ibid.,* p. 224.
29. Charles Van Fleet, Jim Wellman interviews, 1971.
30. Reed, p. 224.
31. *Ibid.,* p. 268.
32. Jim Wellman.
33. Helen Hunt Jackson, *Ramona* (Boston: Roberts Brothers, 1884), p. 1, 63.
34. Reed, p. 267.
35. Don Bauer interview, 1984. Bauer was District Ranger at Idyllwild in the early 1950s and Supervisor of San Bernardino National Forest from 1958 to 1974.
36. Quoted from Frank M. Woolley, "Twentieth Century Pioneer," *High Country,* No. 45, Summer 1978, p. 32.
37. *Ibid.,* p. 32-33; Fanny Contreras interview, Hemet, March 10, 1992.
38. *Ibid.,* p. 34; Fanny Contreras interview.

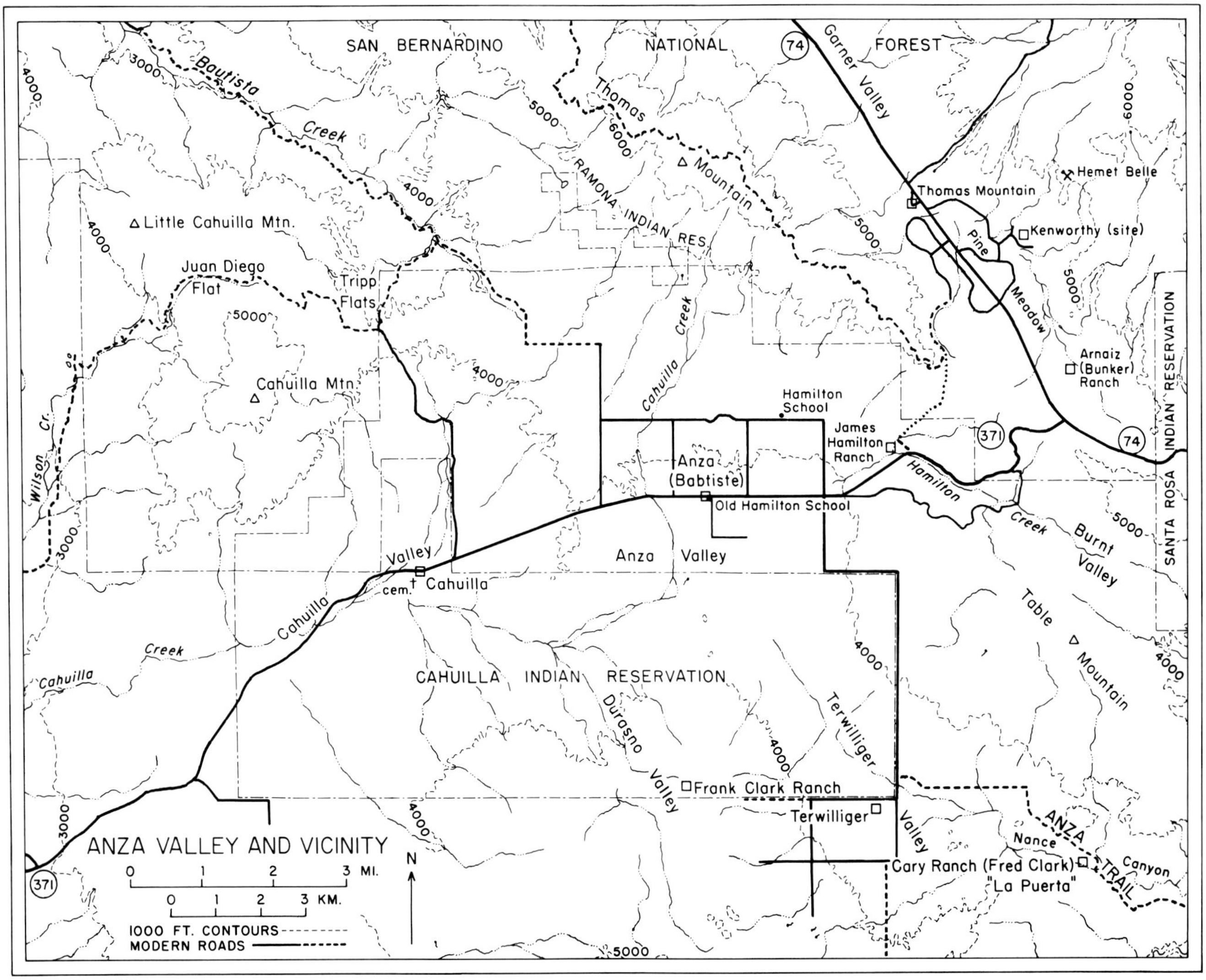

LAURENCE JONES

7

KENWORTHY

In the aftermath of the California Gold Rush, prospectors scurried all over the mountains and deserts of the West, seeking mineral riches. They did not neglect Southern California. Placer gold deposits were discovered on the East Fork of the San Gabriel River in 1854, in Bear Valley in 1855, and in Holcomb Valley in 1860.

Just when gold seekers entered the San Jacinto Mountains is unknown. It is difficult to pin down a date since prospectors, working singly or in pairs, drifted from place to place, receiving little attention unless they made a strike.

The earliest mention of discoveries in the San Jacintos is found in a dispatch to the *Los Angeles Star* (August 4, 1860) from its San Bernardino correspondent, which stated "Rich diggings have been discovered in the San Jacinto Mountains, twenty-five miles south east of this place." It is very possible the discoveries were in the hills above Garner Valley. Charles Thomas, who located in the mountain valley in 1861, was reportedly told about the place by some miners who had prospected there.

The strike evidently did not pan out, for it was ten years before Los Angeles newspapers again mentioned mineral discoveries in the San Jacintos. A very intriguing article in the *Star* (July 6, 1870), quoting a San Bernardino newspaper, hinted that secret mines had existed in the mountains for some time:

> The *Guardian* of the 2d brings intelligence of the discovery of new gold and silver mines. Gold was discovered about forty miles in a south-east direction from the city [San Bernardino]. The Old Padre silver mine has also been discovered in the mountains.... A party has been formed to prospect for the mine.... Charlie Clusker struck upon a well-defined trail leading into the mountains, which he followed, and soon came upon a road, well graded and built of large stones, evidently with care, which following, brought him to the Old Jesuit Mine. Here at last was the mystery solved... Years ago, men had been extensively engaged in mining. The remains of an old shaft was found, partly filled in, but showing marks of the pick and gad. The party at once proceeded to clear away the rubbish, and soon obtained quite a lot of the ore, which is rich enough to satisfy the heart of the most repacious miner – assaying from $600 to $1000 per ton. The mine has been called the Jesuit, and another, close by, the Old Padre. Steps were at once taken to reap the reward of their perserverance and this week a company was formed, the district named the San Jacinto Mining District, a mining code of laws formed, and preliminary steps taken to energetically work the lodes.

Who were the original miners who had worked the *Jesuit* and *Old Padre* mines years earlier? Just where in the mountain were they located? Could they be secret mines dating back to mission or rancho days? No one knows. This is the stuff of which legends are made.

The *San Bernardino Guardian* (July 16, 1870) mentioned these mystery mines and other new discoveries:

> In the San Jacinto range, Mr. Stamps has discovered and is working with arrastras a vein that yields from $100 per ton of ore. Also in this range are the famed Jesuit and Old Padre silver veins, that bid fair to enrich every one possessing an interest in them.

Four years later, the *Guardian* (March 28, 1874) reported, "A number of San Diegans are at present in the Bladen mining district in the San Jacinto mountains." A week later the San Bernardino newspaper (April 6, 1874) quoted the *San Diego Union's* story on the new discoveries:

> From parties who arrived yesterday from the Bladen Mining District... we learn the most sanguine expectations of the miners. On the original discovery Mr. Bladen has sunk a shaft to the depth of forty feet, which discloses a gradually widening vein of ore.... Six specimens of ore, assayed in San Francisco, show from $80 to $100 per ton. The ledge has been distinctly traced for seven miles.... A large number of people are on the ground and considerable excitement prevails.... It is the general opinion that an exceedingly rich and extensive mineral district is being opened in the San Jacinto mountains.

The Bladen gold mines were discovered and worked by Andrew Bladen, a former farmer and blacksmith from Tennessee, from 1874 into the 1890s. They were located on the western slope of Cahuilla Mountain, above today's community of Sage. The mines were only

Just when mining began in the San Jacintos is unknown, possible as early as 1869.

a marginal success, and were abandoned after Bladen died.[1]

Most of the gold mining activity in the San Jacintos since the 1870s has taken place along a low-grade auriferous belt that runs along the southeastern edge of Garner Valley from Quinn Flat to Bull Canyon. The year mining began in these rocky foothills is not known – possibly as early as 1860. The earliest name associated with mining in the area is a Mr. Stamps who, as previously mentioned, was prospecting in the San Jacintos as early as 1870. Stamps' name is mentioned several times during the 1870s, but nowhere is there any indication of the precise location of his mining activities. The *Los Angeles Herald* (November 23, 1879) states that "Messrs. Stamps and Geiger, who have been prospecting near the San Jacinto mountains, returned yesterday. They report the discovery of a sixteen-inch lode twenty-four feet below the surface. Gold in paying quantities is in sight." Seven years later we are at last given a location for Stamps' activities. In the San Diego County Recorders Office, Mining Claims, Book 1, there is a filing for the "Hemet Lode" by C. F. Stamps Jr., P. N. Stamps, Theodore Slatey, and T. A. Darling, dated December 8, 1886. The Hemet Lode's location was in the hills above Quinn Flat.

Pacific Nestor Stamps and Charles Fox Stamps Jr. were apparently brothers, the sons of a raisin grape grower from the town of Orange. Both were printers by trade but seem to have spent a good deal of time prospecting in the San Jacintos. Truman A. Darling had been Anaheim's Southern Pacific agent at one time, and was also involved in various mining ventures throughout the Santa Ana Mountains. The identity of Theodore Slatey remains unclear. The Stamps and their associates must be given credit for the earliest known gold discoveries in the Garner Valley area.[2]

The activity at the Stamps' Hemet Lode mine brought in other prospectors to the area. John Quinn was working a mine as early as 1887, possibly before that. Quinn Flat honors his name today.

Here, in the boulder strewn hills that border the southern half of the Garner Valley, occurred one of the greatest frauds ever to take place in a Southern California mining region. Associated with this colossal fraud were the names Eames Chilson and Lewis Hansen.

Richard W. Chilson and his son Eames Emil Chilson started the development of their Hemet Belle Mine in 1887. The Chilsons' gold prospect was located on the south ridge of Butterfly Mountain, some 200 feet above Pipe Creek. The Chilsons put in a pipeline from a nearby spring (hence the name Pipe Creek) to run a 5-stamp mill and proceeded to excavate several tunnels. By 1890 Eames Chilson, who seems to have taken over the active operation of the mine from his father, was apparently enjoying some success. An old story, probably apocryphal, goes that "When he went to San Jacinto he lit cigars with $10 bills." The *San Jacinto Register* (May 25, 1893) optimistically reported, "The mine is valued by its present owners at $85,000. There is over three hundred tons of ore in the 'dump' that will average $25 of free gold to the ton.... The outlook for the 'Hemet Belle' is very promising and the prospects are that it will bring double in a few years what is asked for it now."

The apparent success of Chilson's Hemet Belle encouraged others to check out gold prospects in the Garner Valley area. Three who came in 1895 were Lewis Hansen, Ira Harmon and William Vaughn, who laid claim to their "Litte Lily" Mine just north of the Hemet Belle. Hanson bought out his partners in 1896 and became sole owner. He had an assay done which he claimed showed rich gold deposits averaging more than $100 per ton.

Little is known of Lewis Hansen other than the information he wrote on his voter registration form in the Strawberry precinct on July 7, 1896: He gave his age as 39, his occupation miner, height 5'8", place of birth Denmark, naturalized October 24, 1885 in Oakland, and post office address San Jacinto.[3] How he happened to venture into the San Jacinto Mountains and later be involved in a swindle that would relieve an English investor of his fortune are unknown. There is also a question as to why he gave his address on legal papers as Pasadena, Los Angeles or San Francisco when he was in truth living all that time in the town of San Jacinto or at Kenworthy.

The year 1896 saw many hopeful prospectors arrive. The Hemet Mining District, also called the Tahquitz Mining District, was organized. The *Riverside Press* (August 8, 1896) reported, "There are about 50 men in the camp.... Every ledge so far uncovered is rich in free gold and sulphurets. Assays recently made indicate that the ore is exceptionally high grade."

Lewis Hansen was busy expanding his holdings. He laid claim to 100 inches of water "for mining and milling purposes " and filed on several new mining claims, including what he called the Adventure and the Minnehaha mines.

On December 10, 1896 Hansen made his big move.

The Kenworthy Mill, at the upper end of town and just below the gold mines, 1897. The mill operated for less than a year; gold was not present in paying quantities in the San Jacintos. — LELA LOCKWOOD NOBLE

He sold all his claims, which had cost him next to nothing, to the newly formed Corona Mining and Milling Company, "a copartnership, principal place of business, Pasadena," for $120,000.[4] Two days later, on December 12, 1896, a Certificate of Copartnership was signed and notorized, giving the location as "Kenworthy in the County of Riverside" and listing the partners as Lewis Hansen, San Francisco; Harold Kenworthy, San Gabriel; George Coffin, Pasadena; Edwin Stearns, Pasadena; and Robert Furlong, Pasadena. Kenworthy, as it later turned out, was the major shareholder and thus had the mining camp named for him.[5]

The *Riverside Press* (December 29, 1896) took notice of this unusual business deal, saying "the consideration" [$120,000] in the transfer of the mining properties from Hansen to the Corona Mining and Milling Company "is the biggest price ever paid in this county."

Harold Kenworthy was a wealthy Englishman, born in London, whose annual income was said to be in the neighborhood of 50,000 English pounds – a considerable sum in those days. He and his wife Cara had come to America several years earlier and were living in San Gabriel when, for reasons known only to Kenworthy, he decided, or was persuaded, to invest in mining properties. The story goes that he was brought to the Tahquitz Mining District and shown the extremely high assay reports on mines owned by Eames Chilson and Lewis Hansen. The assays, performed at the mining camp, were apparently fully accepted by Kenworthy, whereas a more prudent investor would have demanded additional proof of the mines' value.

Lewis Hansen was named general manager of the Corona Mining and Milling company and began spending generous sums – mainly Kenworthy's money – on new equipment and building materials. Expensive machinery was purchased and hauled to the mining camp, including all the parts for an electric cyanide plant with a capacity for processing 100 tons of ore per day, and a portable sawmill powered by a gasoline engine. Redwood lumber from northern California was brought in to build the town of Kenworthy. The company intended to spend $45,000 on improvements and had 22 men at work early in 1897.[6]

In March 1897, two of the original five partners, George Coffin and Edwin Stearns, apparently uneasy over the vast sums being spent by the company and the paultry amounts of gold being recovered, backed out of the partnership, selling their combined one-sixth interest to Lewis Hansen for $20,000, exactly what they invested in the first place. Hansen then sold another one-twelfth interest to Kenworthy, which meant he only gave the two ex-partners $10,000 of his own funds. Kenworthy had now spent more than $50,000 – perhaps as high as $80,000 – and was soon to spend even more.[7]

The town of Kenworthy sprang up almost overnight, financed largely by Harold Kenworthy's generosity. The centerpiece was the two-story Corona Hotel, with accommodations for more than sixty persons. Cabins

Eames Chilson cabin, Kenworthy, 1897. Chilson is in the light shirt, leaning against the building. He owned the "Hemet Belle," one of the few mines in the San Jacintos that was worked for many years. — LELA LOCKWOOD NOBLE

The two-story Corona Hotel in Kenworthy was built to accommodate 60 persons. After the collapse of the Kenworthy mining boom, it lay abandoned, finally to be torn down and the lumber transferred to Keen Camp in 1901. — LELA LOCKWOOD NOBLE

Charles W. Lockwood's general store, Kenworthy, 1897.
— LELA LOCKWOOD NOBLE

Charles Lockwood and his wife Emma at Kenworthy, 1898. The Lockwoods ran the general store there from 1897 to 1899. — LELA LOCKWOOD NOBLE

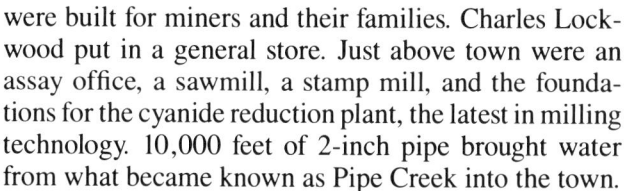

were built for miners and their families. Charles Lockwood put in a general store. Just above town were an assay office, a sawmill, a stamp mill, and the foundations for the cyanide reduction plant, the latest in milling technology. 10,000 feet of 2-inch pipe brought water from what became known as Pipe Creek into the town.

The *San Jacinto Register* (May 13, 1897) announced that "Mr. Harold Kenworthy, a wealthy Englishman who has great interest in the mines, was at the Lockwood hotel last week, with his wife and three servants and a string of valuable horses. Mr. Kenworthy has an income, we understand, of $60,000 per annum and consequently can afford to spend a few thousand in the development of these rich ledges and we feel confident that he and his associates will reap a rich reward. The prospects are that the Tahquitz Mining District will be one of the most prosperous in the state."

In the summer of 1897 a still-optimistic Harold Kenworthy built a house in his mining town, into which he and his wife Cara moved. He also built stables for his horses. He continued buying mining claims throughout 1897, apparently spending large sums on "mines" such as the "Little German," "Little Lily," "Lucky Boy," "Little Girl," "Golden Belle," "C.C.," and "Lily Quartz" – claims that later proved worthless. Money seemed to be no barrier to his dreams of becoming a mining magnate. He also took out an option to buy the nearby Thomas Ranch for $34,000.

A leading citizen of the new mining community was Charles W. Lockwood, proprietor of the C. W. Lockwood General Merchandise Store. He had come to the town of San Jacinto in 1885, where his parents, Thomas and Lorinda Fay Lockwood, owned the Lockwood Hotel. Charles was attracted by the promise of the Tahquitz mines and filed two mining claims in 1896. The following year he moved, with his wife Emma and young daughter Lela, to Kenworthy, where they lived for a while in a large tent. His widowed mother Lorinda

Fay advanced him funds to build his general store. The Lockwood store dealt primarily in staple items such as flour, bacon, coffee and dairy products bought from Thomas Ranch.[9]

Enough people were living in and around Kenworthy by the summer of 1897 for a post office to be established in the store, and Charles Lockwood was appointed the first – and only – postmaster. In 1899 the Kenworthy School was established. Charles Lockwood was appointed school trustee by Riverside County Superintendent Edward Hyatt. Hyatt informed Lockwood that the school would receive $400 to handle expenses the first year, with $300 of that going for the teacher's salary. Hyatt wrote that "$25 would buy all the books, paper, pencils, chalk, etc., for the year, probably."[10] Since there were only eight students that first term, the paultry appropriation was apparently sufficient.

Meantime, Lorinda Fay Lockwood, Charles' mother, was bitten with "the gold bug." She began buying mining claims and an interest in the Corona Mining and Milling Company, and spent much of her time in Kenworthy with her son and his family.

Lela Lockwood Noble remembered the good times she experienced as a child in Kenworthy. The noise and excitement of the mines, the pounding stamps at the mill, the high-pitched whine of the sawmill, the scores of people shuffling through town and into her father's store, all of this was heady stuff for a young girl. She fondly remembered the children she played with, particularly the Arnaiz youngsters. Most fun of all, "The Kenworthys had horses and on Sundays there were races and fancy riding."[11]

Fanny Arnaiz Contreras, who also lived there as a child, recalled the friendliness and generosity of Harold and Cara Kenworthy, how they sent gifts of fruit to the Arnaiz family, how they put on special entertainments on weekends – horse races, greased pig contests, a "fox hunt" where a single rider – the "fox" – would ride

John Quinn cabin on Quinn Flat, near Kenworthy, ca. 1898.
— LAURA SWIFT

Kenworthy School, ca. 1910. The Schoolhouse, erected in 1899, lasted into the 1920s – longer than any other building at Kenworthy. — NELL EMERSON ZIEGLER

ahead of the "hunters," who were children, dropping bits of paper to mark his trail.[12]

Despite the happy scenes in town and the rosy predictions in the newspapers, all was not well with the Corona Mining and Milling Company. The Tahquitz mines were producing only a fraction of the gold the early assays had foretold, and some of the claims the company paid dearly for were producing no gold at all. Expenses were far surpassing income. Wages went unpaid and work stopped at the new cyanide reducing plant. General manager Hansen was obliged to borrow $2,000 from Kenworthy as early as March 1897. The shrewd Hansen soon realized – or maybe knew all along – that there were only piddling amounts of gold in the hills and quietly dumped all or most of his shares in the company. In January 1898 he sold his five-twelfth interest to Lorinda Fay Lockwood. When original copartner Robert Furlong sold his one-sixth interest to an apparently unworried Harold Kenworthy in February 1898, the collapsing Corona Mining and Milling Company was totally in the hands of Kenworthy and the aged Mrs. Lockwood.

The questions arise as to how Harold Kenworthy, about to lose a fortune, could have been so gullible and unaware of what was happening, and how he got "suckered" in the first place. He was obviously far too trusting of the inflated claims of owners anxious to sell. He was totally unaware of the "tricks" often played in the mining business. A recurrent story told down through the years was that the Tahquitz mines were "salted," resulting in the high assays that fooled Kenworthy and other investors. Long-time mountain resident Lincoln Hamilton recalled years later that salting mines was a regular procedure. "All you did was load up a shotgun with gold dust, fire it into the rock, and you had a mine for sale."[13] Lela Lockwood Noble insisted it was common knowledge that the mines were salted to fool investors. "How a mine could be salted and the deception covered for so long is hard to understand," she mused.[14] That these mining claims could be assayed so high and produce next to nothing makes it almost certain, to these writers, that the ore was altered.

Some have blamed Emil Chilson for salting the several claims he sold to Kenworthy, but recent scholarship on the part of Riverside County historian Jane Davies Gunther fingers Lewis Hansen as the main culprit.[15] Hansen was the only partner in the Corona Mining and Milling Company who came out ahead. He sold his original, highly inflated, mining claims to the newly-formed company for the huge sum of $120,000. Then, as a co-partner, he sold a one-twelfth interest to Kenworthy for $10,000 and later assigned his remaining five-twelfth share to the elderly Mrs. Lockwood for an undisclosed sum. Even allowing for up to $50,000 Hansen may have paid for his original shares, he came out with a tidy profit – probably squirreled away in some Los Angeles or San Francisco bank.

After the Corona Company's collapse, Lewis Hansen continued his dubious mining career, filing claims on several other mines in the area, but "never found another Harold Kenworthy to sell them to."[16]

Harold Kenworthy must have been devastated when he discovered, early in 1898, that he had been massively swindled. On May 28, 1898 he sold to one J. R. Newberry for TEN DOLLARS all his rights, title and interest in the now defunct Corona Mining and Milling Company, including "the mill, assay office and store room, bunk house, powder magazine, cook house, barn and carriage shed, blacksmith shop, hotel, sawmill, water works, cottage, barn and corral, pipe lines situate and being erected," along with an inventory listed every single item, no matter how small, in every building.[17]

Harold and Cara Kenworthy then quietly left, hopefully wiser from their experience. They were last heard from in British Columbia, when Harold deeded his unfulfilled option on the Thomas Ranch back to the

82

Site of Corona Hotel as it looks today (1992).

Abandoned mining claim, 1897. The San Jacintos were full of worthless or near-worthless gold claims.

Thomases for the sum of five dollars on November 20, 1900.[18]

The abandoned Corona company property and Kenworthy townsite went through several years in litigation involving Lorinda Fay Lockwood and several litigants, one as far away as Paris, France. In the end, Mrs. Lockwood paid $175 for the hotel property, and $1,500 for all the mines and equipment. The case was closed as of May 1, 1901.[19] The hotel was torn down by Charles Lockwood and the lumber was sold to Keen Camp resort a few miles away.

The town of Kenworthy did not completely disappear. Several families, including the Arnaizs and Joe Hamilton, continued to live there. The one-room Kenworthy School continued to educate children from all over Garner Valley for a decade. Nothing remains at the Kenworthy site today; the present Kenworthy Ranger Station is about a mile northwest of the abandoned ghost town.

Despite the Kenworthy fraud, a number of gold mines continued to be worked in the Garner Valley area. Emil Chilson worked his Hemet Belle Mine until about 1912. Later that year, Irving Carl and a man named Hernandez leased the Hemet Belle and filed on several other claims about a mile east of Kenworthy. They organized the Gold Beauty Mining and Milling Company and put in a 5-stamp mill. The *Hemet News* (September 13, 1912) reported, "Of the many claims which have been developed, the old Hemet Belle mine is the richest, the ore averaging at least $20 in gold to the ton.... An aerial tramway over 2,000 feet in length carries the ore from the shaft to the stamp mill, located in the valley below. Here the ore is crushed to a pulp and is then transferred through the washing process, and the gold is finally scraped off into bags." Next month, the newspaper (October 4, 1912) stated that Carl and Hernandez were planning to install a cyanide plant at their mines. "Mr. Carl has with him a chunk of gold, the product of 24 hours run, which would easily make five 20-dollar gold pieces.... He believes that even better ore exists and that the company will be milling ore which will run over $300 to the ton." Such was not to be. The Hemet Belle, never more than a marginal success, was not mentioned again for two years. The *Hemet News* (January 16, 1914) reported that Thomas Post and Hugh Goff were starting work on the Hemet Belle, and then stated the stark truth: "There are a number of gold mines in the mountains, but very few have ore which will justify development." Nevertheless, prospectors have continued intermittently to work the old Hemet Belle, the last one being D. C. Mayne in the 1960s.

In Bull Canyon, near the southern end of the San Jacintos, was the El Toro Mine, first filed upon by José Antonio Estudillo and Manuel Arnaiz in 1893. There was never much ore found there, although it was worked from time to time for several years. Bull Canyon takes its name from the El Toro (the Bull) claim.

William and Rebecca Penrod filed on the Golden Belle Mine in 1896, located in the canyon immediately west of Bull Canyon. They built a cabin and were still living there in 1910 when U.S. Deputy Surveyor George Pearson noted their presence and gave their name to the canyon.

Near the head of Penrod Canyon and extending to the next gully west was the Gold Shot Mine, filed on by Carl and Albert Christiansen in 1918. They dug a 70-foot tunnel and erected a 15-stamp mill near the mouth of

Asbestos Spring, near Pinyon Flat. Asbestos was mined here from 1880 into the early 1900s. Miners who drank too much from this spring were said to have "a ghastly pallor."
– BILL JENNINGS

Penrod Canyon. The next small gully to the northwest is now named Gold Shot Creek.

There have been hundreds of other mining claims filed in the region, none of them amounting to anything. It has taken years of hard work and thousands of dollars to prove that gold is simply not present in paying quantities in the San Jacinto Mountains.

Although gold recovery in the San Jacintos has been pretty much a bust, other minerals have been successfully mined.

The Garnet Queen Mine on the northwest slope of Santa Rosa Mountain was discovered and developed by Ellsworth Patrick Steward in 1897. Despite the name which suggests gemstones, the Garnet Queen was a tungsten mine. The tungsten ore was recovered from two long open cuts on the mountainside. The mine changed hands over the years and met with varying success. The *California Journal of Mines and Geology* for October 1941 reported a small concentration plant had been installed with an operating capacity of ten tons per day. Other patented tungsten mines in the Santa Rosas were the Indian, the Phoenix, the Pigeon Creek, the Burnt Cow and the Ribbonwood, none of them profitable.[20]

Asbestos, a fire-resistant mineral, was in great demand by industry during the latter part of the 19th century. The world's first commercial asbestos mine had been opened in Quebec only in 1878, so when the black material was discovered on the north side of Pinyon Flat, above Palm Canyon in 1880, excitement ensued. By 1888, the John D. Hoff Asbestos Company of San Diego was actively recovering the mineral and transporting it down the mountain by burro-back.[21] This method of moving the ore out proved inadequate, so after the mines changed ownership in the early 1890s, a wagon road was built. The *Riverside Press* (December 7, 1896) reported that one F. M. Casner "had completed the building of a road, eight miles in length, to the great asbestos mines of that section [Pinyon Flat] which is the property of the Pacific Asbestos Company of Los Angeles. Mr. Casner has the contract of mining and hauling to the San Jacinto depot, a distance of 40 miles, 80 tons per year. He formerly used burros, but by the new road he can drive [wagons] right to the mines." The "Asbestos Road" went from Pinyon Flat westward to the southern edge of Garner Valley, then down "Nigger Jim Grade" to Cahuilla Valley, thence northwest down Bautista Canyon to the railroad depot in San Jacinto. The railroad then shipped the material to Los Angeles, where it was used in the manufacture of boilers and cooking utensils. The asbestos mines continued in operation for many years. The *California Journal of Mines and Geology* (July 1945) reported that 800 tons of the material were being mined and shipped to Los Angeles, where the asbestos was used in the manufacture of automobile batteries, by 1930. The *Journal* listed two asbestos mines north of Pinyon Flat – the Dunn Mine owned by Elmer E. Dunn, and the Percival Mine, owned by Jim Wellman and Jack Harris. Today, Asbestos Mountain and Asbestos Spring commemorate this industrial mining venture.

Asbestos Spring, below the west slope of Asbestos Mountain, was used by the early miners for drinking water. The *Riverside Press* (November 24, 1894) commented on the toxic effects of drinking from "the arsenic spring known to all the ranchers of the mountains in that region. Its use generally blanches the faces of the workmen to a ghastly pallor, and produces peculiar effects in other ways upon the human frame." The long-term deadly effects of asbestos on humans was, of course, unknown at that time. One wonders how many of the asbestos miners later died from lung disease.

Semi-precious gems in the form of tourmaline were also mined in the San Jacintos. "Uncle Jim" Hamilton discovered tourmaline on the south end of Thomas Mountain in 1872. He picked up a few gems and showed them around but it was not until 1893 that serious mining efforts were made. In that year, both the Columbia Gem Mine and the San Jacinto Gem Mine were opened on Thomas Mountain, and some of the finest tourmaline crystals in the world were recovered. It was reported that more than a bushel of fine gems was recovered that first year, including a beautiful red and green crystal eight inches long that was purchased by Harvard University. Another fine specimen was bought by the American Museum of Natural History in New York.

The tourmaline excitement drew quite a number of prospectors to the Thomas Mountain region. The *Riverside Press* (January 12, 1897) reported that a tourmaline mine owned by "Messrs. Jackson and Whiting in the Tahquitz district" was recovering some valuable gems. "Two specimens just taken out measured 1½ by 2½ inches each and are valued at about $400 each, as they are very valuable for ring settings, pins, etc. The color of these stones vary from a dark green to a deep amethyst. This is the only mine in the United States outside of Maine.... The largest tourmaline stone ever found in the world was taken out of this mine by Mr. Chilson and placed on exhibition at the World's Fair, where it took the premium. It was afterwards sold to an Englishman for $500."

In 1902 more tourmaline gems were discovered on Cahuilla Mountain by Bert Simmons. His Fano Gem Mine became notable for the sparkling blue, aquamarine and green tourmaline crystals it produced.[22]

So it was the unlikely combination of tourmaline and asbestos that highlighted mining in the San Jacinto Mountains and made small contributions to the region's economy. Gold was never a real factor here, although it certainly produced a colossal story of fraud.

NOTES

1 Jane Davies Gunther, *Riverside County, California, Place Names: Their Origins and Their Stories* (Riverside, 1984), p. 57; Charles Van Fleet interview, San Jacinto, 1971.
2 Information on Pacific Nester Stamps, Charles Fox Stamps Jr., and Truman A. Darling comes from Orange County historians Phil Brigandi and Jim Sleeper.
3 Gunther, p. 262.
4 *Ibid.*, p. 263. Gunther searched through Riverside County records to root out the details on this complicated mining enterprise.
5 *Ibid.*
6 John B. Brumgardt, "Tea, Crumpets, and San Jacinto Gold: The Short-Lived Town of Kenworthy, California, 1897-1900," *Pacifice Historian*, Fall 1976, p. 279.
7 Gunther, p. 264.
8 Brumgardt, p. 282.
9 Lela Lockwood Noble interview, San Jacinto, March 10, 1973.
10 Brumgardt, p. 281.
11 Lockwood interview.
12 Fanny Arnaiz Contreras, quoted in Brumgardt, p. 283.
13 *Idyllwild Town Crier*, April 12, 1963.
14 Lockwood interview.
15 Gunther, p. 263-268.
16 *Ibid.*, p. 268.
17 *Ibid.*, p. 266.
18 *Ibid.*, p. 267-268.
19 *Ibid.*, p. 267.
20 The *Reports of The State Mineralogist*, later the *California Journal of Mines and Geology*, and still more recently *California Geology*, contain a wealth of information on state mining activities. See the annual *Reports* for 1917 and 1932, and the *Journals* of October 1941 and July 1945 for mining in Riverside County.
21 Gunther, p. 33-34.
22 *Report of The State Mineralogist*, 1917, p. 574; *California Journal of Mines and Geology*, July 1945, p. 165.

A dry washer was used to recover small smounts of gold in the San Jacintos and Santa Rosas. – PALM SPRINGS VILLAGER

Oxen team hauling lumber wagon in Strawberry Valley, ca. 1890. — DAVID SCHERMAN

8

FELLING THE MOUNTAIN FOREST

It is difficult to visualize today, looking at Idyllwild and its tall pines, that barely a century ago the mountain valley was a logging camp. Whole sections of once magnificent forest were reduced to stumps, with shattered limbs and wood debris scattered about. Furrows criss-crossed the devastated landscape, the result of mammoth logs being dragged to the sawmills. The mountain serenity was broken by a cacophony of sounds – the sharp crack of the axe, the whang of the whipsaw, the crash of falling trees, the profanity of tough woodsmen. Loudest of all was the screech of the sawmill machinery as huge logs were sliced into lumber.

For some thirty years, from 1875 until shortly after century's turn, timber cutting was a major economic enterprise in the San Jacinto Mountains. Rich stands of sugar pine, Jeffrey and ponderosa pine, and incense cedar were harvested in a forest belt that extended some nine miles along the lush seaward flank of the range, from Hall Canyon southeast through Fuller Mill Creek, Pine Cove, Strawberry Valley, Saunders Meadow, and all the way down to the Keen Camp area. When the lumbermen were through, most of the great ancient forest trees were gone, replaced over the years by second-growth forest we see today.

Colonel Milton Sanders Hall was first to commercially tap the forest. Colonel Hall, a tall, dark man who sported a black beard and had a keen sense of humor, was a promoter and grading contractor who was commissioned by the Southern Pacific Railroad to grade its right-of-way from Spadra (Pomona) through San Gorgonio Pass to Indian Wells (Indio). He was also contracted to supply the railroad with 300,000 wooden ties and wood for locomotive fuel.

Colonel Hall set to work without delay. By June 1875, his hard-working grading gangs were through San Timoteo Canyon and approaching San Gorgonio Pass. While his grading crews were busy, Hall rode into the San Jacinto Mountains and located fine timber on the northwest slope. To gain access to this timber, Hall and several investors organized the San Jacinto Wagon Road Company with financial backing from the Temple and Workman Bank of Los Angeles. The Los Angeles and Independence Railroad's construction superintendent, E. Y. Buchanan, supervised the building of the precipitous, zigzagging roadway that climbed from what came to be known as Hall City (south of today's Cabezon) up to Hurley Flat, then contoured and climbed over the ridge to the millsite, near today's Lake Fulmor.[1] It was called the San Jacinto Wagon Road, but most referred to it as Hall's Grade. The 14-mile hairpinning roadway was said to have cost Hall $30,000. To help pay expenses, Hall made it a toll road, charging 50¢ per wagon, 10¢ per horseback rider, but with screeching lumber wagons careening downhill all hours of the day, it is doubtful he had many customers.

Even before the road was completed, Colonel Hall had a crew in the mountains cutting timber. His first portable sawmill was set up in the pines near today's Vista Grande, but after a few weeks he moved his timber cutting operation over the ridge to Hall Canyon. Here he erected a small water powered mill along the creek, amid a magnificent forest of sugar and ponderosa pines. One observer described the trees as "the best yet seen in California, some measuring 250 feet in height and others not branching for a distance of 100 feet above the ground."[2]

Hall's lumbering venture was closely watched in Los Angeles. The *Los Angeles Star* (October 30, 1875) reported,

> Mr. M. S. Hall, President of the San Jacinto Wagon Road, informed us that he had shipped an engine and two boilers for another sawmill with a capacity of 100,000 feet of lumber per day, and the machinery for a planing, shingle and lath mill,... In addition to the above, the company will erect a turbine wheel sawmill with a view of utilizing the fine water power they possess. When this is completed, three powerful mills will be at work on the splendid forests of sugar pine, fir and other timber over which the company will have control. There is enough in sight to supply the wants of this section for a long

87

Axemen felling a tree in Strawberry Valley, circa 1886. — CHARLES VAN FLEET

time, and the full inauguration of the great enterprise of which Mr. Hall is the head cannot fail to cheapen the cost of lumber in this and adjoining communities.

Hall's plans were grandiose. He would not only supply the Southern Pacific with all the ties and fuel wood they wanted, but would also provide lumber for all of Southern California. He informed Dr. William Edgar, a rancher in San Gorgonio Pass, that he would sell San Jacinto sugar pine for $15 per thousand feet, half the prevailing market price in San Bernardino.[3]

Within two weeks after Buchanan – now a full partner in the enterprise – completed the San Jacinto Wagon Road, Hall's teamsters were hauling machinery up the steep grade to what became known as Hall's Camp in the basin of today's upper Hall Creek. The place was a beehive of activity. Woodcutters were felling the great trees faster than the two sawmills could cut them into lumber. By mid-December 1875, 400,000 feet of sugar pine had been felled.[4]

The most difficult task was hauling the cut lumber down Hall's Grade to Hall City. Banning historian Tom Hughes tells how it was done:

> This was rather a daredevil job, for besides the regular brakes and roughlocks they had to tie logs and trees on behind loads to drag in the dirt and thus keep the loads off the rumps of the horses. Yet even then there were accidents. At least two men lost their lives on the downward trip, and several teams and wagons were dashed to destruction.[5]

On return trips up the mountain, the eight-horse wagons were loaded with food and supplies for the loggers and mill hands. Hall's Camp became a miniature mountain city, with two sawmills, a bunkhouse and grub shack, a small store, and numerous tents.

Hall City, nestled at the foot of the mountains south of today's Cabezon, became a bustling little community. There was a hotel, a restaurant, a general store, a large boarding house for Hall's railroad graders, lumbermen and teamsters, two saloons, a blacksmith shop, a Chinese laundry, and a dance hall that became, for a time, the social center of the entire San Gorgonio Pass area. Colonel Hall constructed a spacious home for himself and his family.[6]

The *San Bernardino Daily Times* (December 7, 1875), expressing the prejudices of the day, reported the population of Hall City as "over one hundred souls and two Chinamen." The newspaper also exclaimed,

> Here are daily reproduced the scenes that have met the gaze of the old California pioneers. Prairie schooners, with long teams of mules constantly arriving and departing on their trips to and from the timber regions, blasts being set off at all hours of the day and hurling masses of rock in fearful torrents down the mountainside, and occasionally an old-time song by a full chorus in the evening brings back the 'Days of old, the days of gold, and the days of '49'.

But all was not well with Colonel Hall's lumbering enterprise. Economic hard times in Los Angeles caused a run on the Temple and Workman Bank, and Hall was abruptly cut off from funds. He was deeply in debt well before he could start turning a profit. The *San Bernardino Daily Times* (November 26, 1875) stated that "Parties from Hall's Camp do not report very favorably about matters at the mill on the San Jacinto. Many of the hands employed have left because their wages were not paid and the checks given them in lieu of money have been dishonored." Next day the newspaper reported a rumor that "the workmen on the San Jacinto Mountains, including teamsters, mill hands and others, have quit work, and hold possession of the property there in security of debts due them.... It is said that the strike is universal, but one man opposing it."

Timber cutting stopped while Hall frantically tried to renew financing. The *Daily Times* (February 7, 1876) stated that "Colonel Hall assures us that he intends to pay every dollar he owes with interest, and will not allow anybody to lose through him."

But such did not happen. With the complete collapse of the Temple and Workman Bank in early 1876, Hall's mountain lumbering venture was mortally wounded. The Colonel himself was said to have lost $100,000 of his own money, and most of his workers left unpaid.

Hall evidently found some money, for he dismantled one of his mountain sawmills and hauled the machinery down Hall's Grade and over to the mouth of Snow Creek's west fork, under San Jacinto's precipitous north face. Here, at the bottom of a dizzy skidway, the mill was set up to await logs that never reached it. They either jumped track or broke into splinters as they careened down from the heights.[7] The mill was later taken across San Gorgonio Pass to Banning Water Canyon, where it played its final role in another flume failure.

Hall's Camp, the remaining sawmill there, the San Jacinto Wagon Road and all related properties were taken over by the court assignees of the Temple and Workman Bank and sold at a fraction of their original cost to a trio of Sacramento businessmen named Bartholomew, Gilbert and Moore in May 1876. A new steam sawmill was hauled up and installed at Hall's Camp. By September 1876 lumbering had resumed and within two months 250,000 ties for the Southern Pacific Railroad had been produced.[8] Excess lumber was shipped to Colton and San Gabriel. As before, hauling the lumber down Hall's old grade proved the most difficult part of the enterprise. The new owners embarked on the construction of a giant flume to float the cut boards from sawmill to Cabezon, but only four miles of this projected 14-mile flume were ever completed.

The *San Bernardino Daily Times,* as late as February 24, 1877, reported that "The San Jacinto lumber mills are being run to their full capacity on railroad contracts." But lumbering in "Little Strawberry Valley," as Hall's Camp was sometimes called, ceased soon afterwards. The financial burden was too much. By then, the Southern Pacific had crossed the desert to Yuma and bridged the Colorado River into Arizona, and no longer needed ties from the San Jacinto timberlands.

In February 1879 the new steam-powered sawmill put in by Batholomew, Gilbert and Moore was disassembled and hauled to the San Bernardino Mountains. The *San Bernardino Daily Times* (February 11, 1879) informed readers that "The sawmill formerly on the San Jacinto mountain has been removed to this town [San Bernardino] enroute to the La Praix mill on the mountain.... The machinery weighs over 70,000 pounds."

The remaining sawmill at Hall's Camp, a small water-powered one, was appropriated – apparently after being abandoned – by a man named Fuller in 1878 or 1879. He dismantled the mill and dragged the machinery over the ridge to the next canyon east. Little is known about Fuller, not even his first name. There are stories that he had previously run one of Hall's sawmills. He has been immortalized in the names *Fuller Mill Creek* and *Fuller Ridge*.

The Fuller Mill was operated intermittently by several different timber cutters. Sometime in the 1880s, a very rough logging road was built from the San Jacinto Valley up Indian Creek and across the slopes to the sawmill. By this route lumber was hauled down to San Jacinto. The *San Jacinto Register* (October 20, 1892) reported that "The Russ Lumber and Mill Co. have purchased the 'cut' of J. A. Brown at the old Fuller mill, which amounts to nearly a quarter of a million feet of pine lumber of all kinds. They are having it hauled at the rate of 40,000 feet a week. Six six-horse teams are engaged in the hauling." The Fuller Mill was operating as late as 1895, when it was briefly mentioned in the *Riverside Press* (February 23, 1895).

Colonel Milton Sanders Hall, who started it all, is remembered in the name *Hall Canyon*. Hall City has long since disappeared, but the scars of the old Hall's Grade, criss-crossed by a road built in the 1920s, can still be seen on the mountainside above Cabezon. Colonel Hall remained in the San Gorgonio Pass area until 1893, doing some farming and working on the great Banning Water Canyon flume built by the San Gorgonio Fluming Company. This also ended as a costly failure. He died at his daughter's home in Monrovia around 1915.[9]

Even before the demise of Hall's Camp, timber cutting was going on in Strawberry Valley, seven miles to the southeast. Just who started cutting trees and when are unknowns. First mention of plans to build a sawmill in Strawberry Valley is found in the *Los Angeles Star* (February 16, 1872): Richard Garrett, living there at the time, informed the newspaper that he "contemplates building a mill at an early day to manufacture lumber." Stories tell of a water-powered sawmill operating in Strawberry Valley by the mid-1870s, possibly run by two men named Bradley and Stafford. The *San Bernardino Daily Times* (February 24, 1877) reported, "There is a new sawmill in Big Strawberry Valley which is intended to supply the San Jacinto country."

Lumbering began in earnest in Strawberry Valley in the late 1870s. The *San Diego Union* (May 7, 1879) stated that "The mills on the San Jacinto mountain are running out from three to four thousand feet of lumber each day. Not enough to meet the home demand."

Amasa Saunders (1830-1902) operated a sawmill in Strawberry Valley from 1880 to 1886. – LAURA SWIFT

Amasa and Jane Saunders' home, on the right, ca. 1886. It was located where the Idyllwild School is today.
– LAURA SWIFT

Three names stand out among the timber cutters who worked in the valley and adjacent areas during the "great lumbering era" from 1879 to 1906: Amasa Saunders, Anton Scherman, and George Hannahs.

Amasa Saunders, born in Maine in 1830, was a lumberman in his native state before sailing around Cape Horn to California in 1852. He spent four years in the Mother Lode gold fields before moving to San Mateo County, where he re-entered the lumbering business and married Jane Phillips. A few years later Saunders moved north to Mendocino County, where he ran a sawmill until 1879. In that year he and his family moved to Riverside, where he bought ten acres for growing oranges.

Amasa Saunders was primarily a lumberman, despite his dabbles in mining and the orange culture. He arrived in Strawberry Valley in 1880 and purchased a sawmill – possibly the one built several years earlier by Bradley and Stafford. The water-powered mill was unique in its appearance. A spectacular overhead flume led from Strawberry Creek to a mammoth waterwheel which, using a system of gears, turned the circular saw.

Saunders wanted to cut more timber than his water-powered saw allowed, so sometime in late 1884 or early 1885 he turned to steam power. A correspondent for the *San Diego Union* (April 21, 1885) reported that "recently Mr. Saunders has put in a steam engine of seventy horse power and can now do more work than before." Five days later (April 26, 1885) the *Union* correspondent described the operation: "The steam from the engine is puffing and screaching and the saw is whizzing through great pine logs six feet in diameter. How it hums and buzzes when it comes upon a big old pine knot... The boys jerk off the broad boards as a child turns the leaves of the spelling book.... There you have 2,000 feet of lumber from that one big log.... Mr. Saunders is the proprietor of the region round about, and he takes pleasure in showing every courtesy for those who visit this mountain fastness." Saunders logged the rich stands of pine and cedar on both sides of Strawberry Creek. "Bull teams," each with ten oxen pulling a heavy wagon, carted the lumber down Crawford's toll road to San Jacinto. Cedar boards were sent to a Chicago factory which manufactured chests and closet linings.

Saunders bought 120 acres of forested land in the vicinity of present-day Pine Cove in 1884 and received title in 1890. Ironically, he was unsuccessful in gaining title to the timber and grass land east of Strawberry Valley that now bears his name – Saunders Meadow.

Amasa Saunders ran his Strawberry Valley sawmill for at least six years, possibly longer. In 1886 he built a large house for his family in San Jacinto. Always looking for new opportunities, he and a partner bought and ran a 13,000 acre dairy ranch in Baja California. After a few years he returned to spend his final days in San Jacinto, where he died in 1902.[10]

Next on the scene was Anton Scherman, a giant of a man, born in Wurttemberg, Germany in 1845. He learned the engineer and machinist trade in his native land, then emigrated to the United States in 1863. From Chicago, he crossed the plains to Idaho, where he spent two years as an engineer in a quartz mill. He came to California in 1866, worked in the placer mines and sawmills of Calaveras County, then moved to San Francisco where he was employed as a machinist in manufacturing shops and as an engineer for a distillery. He

The Saunders mill pond, Strawberry Valley, ca. 1884.
— SAN JACINTO MUSEUM

Anton Scherman (1845-1910), a German immigrant, operated sawmills in Strawberry Valley, Fern Valley, Dutch Flat, Logan Creek, and Stone Creek during the years from 1879(?) to 1902. — DAVID SCHERMAN

married Catherine Schumacher, also a native of Germany, in 1868, and from this union were born three sons and two daughters. Family life failed to slow him down, and in 1871 he prospected for eight months in Arizona.[11]

Anton Scherman was a very skilled engineer, machinist, miner and sawmill operator when he finally reached Southern California in 1872. He climbed up into the timber-rich San Bernardino Mountains and, in partnership with John Metcalf, set up the Prairie Flats Sawmill. After Metcalf was shot to death by a disgruntled employee, Scherman built his own mill on Strawberry Flat, near today's community of Twin Peaks. He cut timber there until 1879.

In 1881 silver was discovered at Calico in the Mojave Desert, causing a stampede of eager prospectors to descend upon the desert mining camp. Anton Scherman went out there, too, and erected the first quartz mill in Calico. A year later he sold the mill to John Daggett, later lieutenant governor of California.

Just when Anton Scherman came to Strawberry Valley is uncertain. David Scherman, Anton's great-grandson who has collected all he can find on his family history, believes it was 1879. Other sources say it was several years later. His first mill site was a mile upstream from Saunders' mill, in what is today called Fern Valley. He dismantled his sawmill in the San Bernardino Mountains and hauled it, part by part, to Strawberry Valley. Grandson Joe Scherman recalled that "It took him three months to cart everything over here. He came up the old toll road, and it took him a couple of weeks just to get the steam boiler up the hill."[12] Joe said that Sam Temple, the man who shot Juan Diego and gained infamy as Jim Farrar in *Ramona*, tried to prevent Scherman from coming to the valley. "He claimed he owned the property my grandfather bought from a Mrs. Hemstreet. Grandfather just rode up to where Temple was sitting in the road with his rifle and told him, 'Sam, get the hell out of the way.' Sam did."[13]

Scherman's big steam-powered sawmill was soon cutting 25,000 board feet per day and shipping it down Crawford's toll road to the San Jacinto Valley. The *San Jacinto Register* (April 26, 1888) reported that the Scherman mill was "pushed to full capacity, and still cannot supply the demand."

Transporting the lumber from the mountain sawmills to the valley was a painstaking operation. David Scherman describes how it was done: "My grandfather used wagons with six-horse teams to bring cut lumber down the grade to San Jacinto Valley. They used wheel lock skid brakes on the back wheels to slow down the wagon on steep grades. These wheel locks were a strip of iron with sides that the wagon wheels were driven up on; a chain connected the skid with the bottom of the wagon to keep the brake in place and stop the wheel from turning. On very steep grades they would stop to cut a tree and chain it to the wagon so it would drag behind, thereby slowing the loaded wagon to a crawl."[14]

Among Scherman's teamsters were the unruly Sam Temple, evidently forgiven for his transgression, and Frank Wellman. By the early 1890s, the teamsters were steering eight-horse teams, rather than oxen teams, down the mountain with their loads. The strong but slow oxen were used primarily to drag the cut trees to the mill.

The toll was high on Crawford's road – 75¢ per wagon, plus 10¢ per horse – and Scherman didn't like it. Joe Scherman related that his grandfather "couldn't see

Scherman moved his lumbering operation at least seven times during his 23 years on the mountain. The photo above is believed to be the first Scherman Mill in Fern Valley. Below is the Scherman Saunders Meadow Mill in 1882. — DAVID SCHERMAN

Oxen hauling a huge log to the Scherman Mill in Strawberry Valley. Theodore P. Lukens took this picture while studying forest destruction in 1898. — HENRY E. HUNTINGTON LIBRARY

why one man should own the road, so he agitated to get this area out of San Diego County."[15]

Scherman moved his sawmill at least seven times, possibly more, during his twenty-three years of cutting timber in the San Jacintos. From his first location in Fern Valley, he apparently moved to Saunders Meadow; a photograph dated 1884 shows his mill there. In March 1889 he joined with George Hannahs and two others to form the Strawberry Valley Lumber Company. The new company purchased 1,300 acres in the Dutch Flat-Pine Cove area, northwest of Strawberry Valley. Although Scherman was a partner in the company, he apparently continued cutting on his own. He moved his sawmill to Dutch Flat, a mile above Strawberry Valley. Dutch Flat took its name from Scherman's German (Deutsch) ancestry.

Cutting went on at a fast pace. To feed his insatiable lumber machine, Scherman's loggers cut trees not only around Dutch Flat, but also northwestward over the ridge. Scherman moved his sawmill over to Logan Creek, just northwest of today's Pine Cove, then another two miles northeast to Stone Creek.

Anton Scherman, ever the entrepreneur, opened a lumber yard in South San Jacinto in 1888. Then he not only produced lumber, but he also sold it retail to the public. He must have tired of double duty, for he sold the lumber yard to Martin Meier in 1892. Meier ran it for many years, relying on Scherman's sawmills for lumber. Wood not destined for the lumber yard went to the San Jacinto Box Company, incorporated in 1889. Thousands of orange crates were manufactured there from lumber supplied by Scherman and George Hannahs. The *San Jacinto Register* (October 10, 1889) reported that Scherman and the Strawberry Valley Lumber Company, then run by Hannahs, "have shipped in the past month, nine cars of boxes from their mills in the San Jacinto mountains, and have orders on hand for ten more carloads to be shipped this month."

George B. Hannahs soon became Scherman's main competitor in the mountain lumber business. Hannahs built his first sawmill on upper Dutch Flat, a short distance above the Scherman mill. While fully engaged in lumbering, he moved with his family into Strawberry Valley and founded the community of Rayneta. (See *Strawberry Valley, Idyllwild and Keen Camp*).

Hannahs was born in Michigan in 1856, the son of a Michigan senator of the same name. The young Hannahs received a good education and became a successful businessman in Chicago, Illinois. Around 1887 he moved to California, where he managed a box factory in Coronado for eight months.[16] Through the influence of San Jacinto businessman Harry Ashenfelter, a family friend, he became a partner in the Strawberry Valley Lumber Company in 1889. The *San Jacinto Register* (March 7, 1889) portrayed Hannahs as "a man of push and energy and [who] works with a determination to make a success at whatever he undertakes." In ensuing years, as it will be seen, he certainly lived up to this description.

In 1895 Hannahs, along with San Jacinto busi-

The Scherman Sawmill on lower Dutch Flat, a mile north of Strawberry Valley. Scherman operated his mill on Dutch Flat during most of the 1890s, longer here than at any other location. Dutch Flat, corrupted from "Deutsch Flat" by a map-maker, honors the pioneer German-born lumberman. — CHARLES VAN FLEET

David Scherman, great-grandson of Anton Scherman, pointing out the location of the Scherman Dutch Flat Sawmill, 1992.

Ox team hauling cut logs to the Scherman Sawmill, ca. 1890. The young man in the middle is Anton Scherman, Jr. — DAVID SCHERMAN

Hauling a new boiler up to Scherman's Dutch Flat Mill, 1894. — CHARLES VAN FLEET

The Scherman Sawmill, location undetermined, possibly near Keen Camp, ca. 1902. Anton Scherman left for Germany that year and turned the logging operation over to his three sons — Anton Jr., Joe G., and Henry.
— SAN JACINTO MUSEUM

Cut lumber was hauled from the Scherman Mill to San Jacinto by four, six, and eight-horse teams. Accidents were common on the steep downgrade. — SAN JACINTO MUSEUM (left), CHARLES VAN FLEET (right)

Sam Temple (seated) and Frank Wellman were employed as teamsters by Anton Scherman, hauling lumber from Strawberry Valley down the steep mountain grade to San Jacinto. Temple attained notoriety as the killer of Juan Diego in 1883, immortalized in Helen Hunt Jackson's *Ramona*. Wellman worked at various times as a teamster and a cattleman. Wellmans Cienega is named for him.
— SAN JACINTO MUSEUM

Scherman lumber wagon enroute to San Jacinto, ca. 1890.
— DAVID SCHERMAN

The San Jacinto Box Factory turned lumber from the Scherman and Hannahs mountain sawmills into citrus crates. — CHARLES VAN FLEET

95

A Dolbeer "Donkey" Engine was purchased by Anton Scherman in 1897 and installed at his Stone Creek Sawmill, shown here. — DAVID SCHERMAN

The Martin Meier Lumberyard at the south end of San Jacinto was founded by Anton Scherman in 1888, sold to Martin Meier in 1892. Meier ran it for many years, relying on Scherman's sawmills for lumber. — DAVID SCHERMAN

nessmen Fred Hards and Homer Daggett, formed the Native Lumber Company. Hannahs was named manager of the company and was always its guiding force. By 1896 the company's Dutch Flat mill was running at full capacity and was a major source of lumber for orange boxes. The *Riverside Press* (September 21, 1896) reported that "The sawmill of the Native Lumber Company... is working on an order for 60,000 orange boxes, to be delivered to a Riverside firm."

A problem faced by both Scherman and Hannahs was that, by the mid-1890s, Strawberry Valley was becoming a well populated resort community. With a general store and post office, three resorts, and many cabins and tents clustered in the heart of the mountain valley, lumbering was no longer welcomed there.

Another factor mitigating the expansion of timber cutting in the mountains was a growing chorus of criticism. President Grover Cleveland, acting on the recommendation of the National Forest Commission, established the San Jacinto Forest Reserve in 1897, although it was some time before forestry officials would effectively curb tree cutting on public lands. Much of the San Jacinto forest belt was in private ownership, however, and was not affected by Cleveland's action.

Several turn-of-the-century visitors decried the destruction of the forests. Prolific writer George Wharton James, recounting a horseback trip into the San Jacintos in 1902, described his distaste of the deforested landscape:

> Soon we pass a lumber camp, one of those relentless slaughterhouses of trees that have taken years to grow, and that ruthlessly denude the mountain slopes of their rich clothing of pines, firs, and spruces. We recognize the need of lumber, but we are bitterly opposed to the present methods of cutting it which take no thought for the morrow, stripping vast areas and never planting a seed for the future.[17]

Also in 1902, University of California botanist Harvey Monroe Hall studied the San Jacinto mountain forests and wrote:

> The worst enemy the forests have has been, not the forest fire, but the sawmill. Many a pine-clad slope has been stripped of its best trees in order that they might be converted into lumber.... In the vicinity of Strawberry Valley about 4000 acres have been lumbered over and perhaps 2500 acres lying in the basin just south of Fullers Ridge.[18]

Despite the complaints, lumbering continued outside of Strawberry Valley. While George Hannahs' Native Lumber Company continued operating at Dutch Flat, Scherman hauled his machinery back over to Fern Valley, a mile above the resorts. His loggers hardly paused for breath. The *Redlands Citrograph* (September 18, 1897) stated that "600,000 feet have been cut and hauled down the mountain since the mill started."

Around 1900 Scherman purchased a Dolbeer "donkey" engine to drag the cut logs to the lumber wagons. A correspondent from the *Riverside Press and Horticulturist* (September 21, 1900) described Scherman's operation: "A half day was passed near the new saw mill watching the men saw down the trees. It was a thrilling sight to see a giant pine fall to the ground with a tremendous crash,... The workings of the donkey engine was fascinating as it pulled the logs by means of a long wire cable to the place where they were loaded on the wagon and then drawn by ten oxen to the mill."

The first of the disasters that jolted large scale commercial lumbering in the San Jacintos occurred in August 1901, when the Native Lumber Company's sawmill was completely destroyed by fire. Hannahs rebuilt on a lesser scale, but in 1907 sold most of his timberlands to Arthur Gregory, Redlands fruit packer. The *San Jacinto Register* (February 14, 1907) stated that "A sawmill and box factory will be built, and the forest will be stripped of everything that can be made into box shooks." But Gregory never built his sawmill nor stripped the forest; he was too busy developing the Crestline area in the San Bernardino Mountains.

In 1902 Anton Scherman turned his sawmill over to

Anton Jr., Joe G., and Henry Scherman operated the Scherman Sawmill after their father left for Germany in 1902. This picture shows the work crew at the Scherman Mill near Keen Camp, ca. 1903. — DAVID SCHERMAN

The last location of the Scherman Mill was near Herkey Creek, from 1904 to 1906. The mill burned to the ground in the latter year, ending two and a half decades of Scherman lumbering on the mountain.
— CHARLES VAN FLEET

The Native Lumber Company's sawmill on upper Dutch Flat, run by George Hannahs, ca. 1896.
— CHARLES VAN FLEET

sons Anton Jr., Joe and Henry, and left, with his second wife Anna, for six years to his native Germany. The Scherman brothers moved the sawmill down to Johnston Flat, just east of Keen Camp, then over to Herkey Creek, cutting timber from May Valley as far east as Apple Canyon. But like George Hannahs' sawmill, the Scherman mill was destroyed by fire in 1906. The *San Jacinto Register* (May 17, 1906) fully described the conflagration: "A member of the crew was awakened about 11 p.m. by the brilliant light of the burning mill, and he immediately aroused the rest of the crew. Everything possible was done to check the flames but to no avail. The mill burned to the ground in a miraculously short time.... Sparks from the engine was the only cause that could be assigned for the fire."

Anton Scherman returned from Germany in 1908, but never returned to lumbering. Instead, ever the entrepreneur, the 63-year old Scherman bought an interest in a Los Angeles paper mill. His end came in 1910, when he fell off the machinery and broke his back, dying a few days later.

William B. Tripp bought the Onstott Ranch after Myron Onstott's death in 1908 and erected a sawmill just west of Herkey Creek, using the machinery of the burned Scherman mill. Tripp logged the forest from just east of Keen Camp to the edge of Garner Valley from 1908 until 1918. His teamsters hauled the lumber down the Keen Camp Road to Hemet.

The last major lumbering operation in the San Jacintos was undertaken in Dark Canyon, a tributary of the San Jacinto River's North Fork, about eight miles northwest of Idyllwild. The San Jacinto Lumber and Box Company, incorporated in 1908, built a citrus box factory in San Jacinto and a sawmill in upper Dark Canyon, about a half mile above the present Banning-Idyllwild Highway. Hiram Roach operated the company's Dark Canyon mill from 1908 to 1922.

By 1912, the Dark Canyon sawmill was running at full capacity, and lumber was being hauled down by

The William Tripp Sawmill at Herkey Creek, ca. 1917. Tripp salvaged the machinery from the burnt Scherman Mill and cut the forest from near Keen Camp eastward as far as Apple Canyon during the years 1908 to 1918.
— LAURA SWIFT

wagon, many loads per day, to feed the insatiable appetite of the box factory in San Jacinto. So much lumber was being produced that the company was able to sell thousands of board feet to outside concerns. The *Hemet News* (November 14, 1913) reported that "The biggest sale of lumber ever consumated in San Jacinto was made this week by the San Jacinto Box and Lumber Company to the Brookings Lumber Company.... The Company has sold 500,000 feet of lumber, which will be shipped at once. It will require over 100 carload shipments to fill the order. Teamsters will commence hauling at once.... Hauling lumber down the mountain is a dangerous business and during the past few years several teamsters have met death on the steep grades."

Fire, the nemesis of all mountain lumbering operations, destroyed the Dark Canyon sawmill in August 1914. The mill, 500,000 feet of lumber, and 4,160 acres of surrounding forest were lost. The *Hemet News* (August 21, 1914) reported that "The heaviest loss falls on H. S. Roach, lessee of the mill. All of the cut lumber and saw logs belonging to him, and the 500,000 feet of lumber ready for market is estimated as being worth $10 per thousand, or $50,000, which is a total loss." To add to Roach's woes, the Forest Service filed suit against him for $4,775 in damages for national forest timber burned.

The Dark Canyon sawmill was rebuilt, but Hiram Roach's misfortunes continued. In 1916 he lost a leg in an accident at the mill. The *Hemet News* (October 6, 1916) described what happened: "Mr. Roach's leg was cut off above the ankle when he slipped and fell on the big revolving saw in the mill. Mr. Roach was attempting to repair the machinery near the saw when in some manner he lost his balance, falling upon the saw.... Roach was rushed down the mountain to his home in San Jacinto, where two hours later he was given medical aid. He was weak from loss of blood... but is doing nicely now, and there is little doubt that he will live, although he will be a cripple for life." Amazingly, Roach was back at work at the sawmill six weeks later, with a pegleg.[19]

In 1922 the Dark Canyon sawmill was leased by Henry Guernsey of the San Bernardino Lumber and Box Company. The *Idyllwild Breezes* (July 28, 1922) stated that Guernsey was "now sawing 16,000 feet of lumber a day. While the mill has been in disuse for a number of years, the machinery is of the best and as things are running very smoothly, Mr. Guernsey expects to maintain a capacity run of 20,000 feet of lumber a day. The lumber will be used for box shooks, the box factory being located at San Bernardino."

During the 1920s, C. L. Emerson's Idyllwild Lumber Company ran a small sawmill in Idyllwild to produce lumber for the building boom there.

There was a flurry of timber cutting in the Idyllwild area during the post-World War II building boom. Ernest Maxwell, Idyllwild's leading citizen and historian, remembers the short lumbering frenzy:

> There were sawmills in town and loggers were cutting willy-nilly. Lumber was so valuable that everybody who could get his hands on a chain saw was butchering the forest.
>
> "There were no rules, just cut, cut, cut. There were some beautiful 300-foot sugar pines going down. At the rate things were going, I saw that the place was being denuded and I helped start an Izaak Walton League chapter here to fight the trend. Our main thrust followed the Forest Service policy that said the environment or wildlife habitat came first.[20]

Environmental safeguards in effect today prevent any such "willy-nilly" forest destruction from occurring. Selective logging has taken place in the San Jacinto Mountains in recent years, often a clean-up effort after a

Hiram Roach cut timber in Dark Canyon from 1908 until about 1920. This was the last major lumbering operation in the San Jacinto Mountains. — SAN JACINTO MUSEUM

C. L. Emerson's Idyllwild Lumber Company produced lumber for the Idyllwild building boom of the 1920s. — DAVID WENDELKEN

forest fire. But the days of the axe and whipsaw-brandishing woodsman, the chugging and screeching sawmill, and the heavy lumber wagon pulled by bawling oxen are gone forever.

Cut timber being hauled to Emerson's sawmill in Idyllwild, 1921. Gus Whisnand is driving the four-horse team; Joe Scherman is standing directly behind him. — A. W. WHISNAND

NOTES

1. Henry E. McAdams, "Early History of the San Gorgonio Pass, Gateway to California," unpublished MA thesis, University of Southern California, 1955, p. 276-292. Available at Riverside City and County Library. See also Jane Davies Gunther, *Riverside County, California, Place Names: Their Origins and Their Stories* (Riverside, 1984), p. 219-222; and Tom Hughes, *History of Banning and San Gorgonio Pass* (Banning, n.d., ca. 1938), p. 15, 17-18, 157-158.
2. McAdams, p. 278.
3. *Ibid.*, p. 278.
4. *Ibid.*, p. 279; Gunther, p. 220.
5. Hughes, p. 157.
6. *San Bernardino Daily Times,* December 7, 1878; Gunther, p. 220.
7. Hughes, p. 17-18.
8. McAdams, p. 290.
9. Hughes, p. 158.
10. Amasa Saunders background gleaned from Gunther, p. 489; Lewis Publishing Company, *An Illustrated History of Southern California* (Chicago, 1890), p. 135; Hemet-San Jacinto Genealogical Society; and *San Jacinto Register,* January 23, 1902 (obituary).
11. Lewis, p. 369; David Scherman interview, Yucaipa, 1991.
12. Joe Scherman interview, *Idyllwild Town Crier,* April 12, 1963.
13. *Ibid.*
14. David Scherman interview, Yucaipa, November 16, 1992. Anton Scherman was David's great grandfather.
15. Joe Scherman interview, *Idyllwild Town Crier,* May 14, 1965.
16. *San Jacinto Register,* March 7, 1889.
17. George Wharton James, *The Wonders of The Colorado Desert* (Boston, 1906), p. 464.
18. Harvey Monroe Hall, "A Botanical Survey of San Jacinto Mountain," *University of California Publications in Botany,* Vol. 1, June 7, 1902, p. 25-26.
19. *Idyllwild Town Crier,* May 14, 1965; *Hemet News,* August 21, 1914; November 30, 1917.
20. Herb Pasik, "Mr. Idyllwild," *Westways,* November 1985.

Artist Henry Sandham's impression of the killing of Alessandro (Juan Diego) by Jim Farrar (Sam Temple), March 24, 1883. – RAMONA PAGEANT ASSOCIATION

9

ORDEAL OF A PEOPLE

The Cahuilla Indians were fortunate in one respect. Their culture survived basically intact into the 1860s, thanks to their relative isolation from Spanish, Mexican Californio and Anglo settlements. The Cahuilla of the mid-19th century probably numbered around 2,500 to 3,000 people, living mostly in the San Jacinto and Santa Rosa mountains, the San Gorgonio Pass area and the Coachella Valley.[1] Many of them were already acquainted with the Californios and the Anglos, working as ranch hands or being utilized as guards to protect the ranchos from desert Indian raiders.

However, the relentless advance of white civilization eventually engulfed the Cahuilla as it had the coastal Indians a half century earlier. The result was the loss of most of their ancestral lands, much of their culture, and, too often, death at the hands of the white man or his diseases. California has no sadder chapter in its history than the demise of its Native Americans.

Upon encountering the land-hungry whites, Native Americans had only three options – to resist, to withdraw, to cooperate. None of these options could insure their survival as an independent people.[2]

Many of the Cahuilla tried cooperation. Chief Cabezon (Big Head) and his Desert Cahuilla followers moved into San Gorgonio Pass to help guard against desert renegades. The greatest of 19th century Cahuilla chieftains, Juan Antonio, brought his Mountain Cahuilla people to Rancho San Bernardino in 1843 or 1844, hired by the sons of Antonio Maria Lugo to protect the sprawling rancho and its great herds of cattle and horses from hostile desert Paiutes and Mojaves. Juan Antonio became a valuable friend and ally of the whites.

Little is known about Juan Antonio's background. He was a Mountain Cahuilla, probably born in the Anza Valley area sometime around 1783. His family name was said to be *Costo,* his clan *Coos-woot-na.* He is said to have been appointed *Capitan* of the Rancho San Jacinto Indians by the padres of Mission San Luis Rey, possibly as early as the 1820s. By the 1840s Juan Antonio was recognized by many – perhaps most – of the Cahuilla clans as their revered leader. He was always accompanied by a loyal "honor guard" of ten to twelve young Cahuilla warriors. According to Los Angeles judge Benjamin Hayes, who had occasion to meet him, Juan Antonio "was accorded more absolute respect and deference by his people than we show to the president of the United States."[3] Hayes described him as being "very stout, scarcely five feet four inches tall – short and thick – wirey even in old age, and with an aspect about the eyes, nose and brow that came nearer to that of the African Lion than I ever have seen in another human face."[4] He had a firm will and dispensed quick justice – often death – to Indians accused of serious crimes. Although he got along well with white men, he never accepted their religion; he adhered to his native spiritual beliefs to the end of his life.

Juan Antonio and his well-armed Mountain Cahuilla loyally protected Rancho San Bernardino until the Lugos sold it to Mormon colonists in 1851. He then moved his people into San Timoteo Canyon, where they continued to guard against hostile incursions. Juan Antonio's penchant for dispensing quick justice sometimes got him in trouble with American authorities. In 1851 he tracked down, cornered, and killed all eleven members of the outlaw John Irving gang, rather than turning them over for trial as prescribed by U.S. law. Benjamin Wilson, mayor of Los Angeles, wrote that Indians "ought never to be allowed to meddle with the punishment of whites for public offenses."[5]

Perhaps Juan Antonio's most valuable service to the white man came during the Garra Revolt of 1851. Antonio Garra, chief of the Cupeño Indians in the Warner Ranch area of San Diego County, was very unhappy about the taxes his people were being forced to pay and concerned about the increasing number of immigrants and new settlers passing through Cupeño territory. To stop the incursion of whites, Garra chose the path of resistance. He actively sought an armed uprising of Indian peoples from the Colorado River to the San Joaquin Valley, but was able to persuade only

Pablo Costo, grandson of the great Mountain Cahuilla chief Juan Antonio, was said to bear a striking resemblence to his grandfather. — HARRY C. JAMES

Chief Cabezon (Big Head), Desert Cahuilla, brought his people to San Gorgonio Pass to guard white settlements against desert Indian raiders. — HARRY C. JAMES

the Quechans of the lower Colorado and the Los Coyotes band of Cahuilla to join him. Rumors of a widespread Indian uprising so alarmed the whites that a state militia, under General Joshua Bean, was called to arms in the summer of 1851. The Mormons of San Bernardino fortified their town. Captain Samuel Heintzelman led a small detachment of U.S. Cavalry from San Diego to the Colorado River and back.

The Garra Revolt began on the night of November 21, 1851, when Francisco Nocate of the Los Coyotes band of Cahuilla led an attack on Warner's Ranch. Jonathan Warner, forewarned of the raid by some loyal Cupeño, managed to escape, but four whites were killed, Warner's home was looted and burned, and his cattle were driven off.

Upon learning of the attack, the army, the militia, and hastily organized volunteer groups converged on Warner's Ranch. Garra, unable to gain the support of the nearby Luiseño, fled to Coyote Canyon. Desperate for Indian support, the Cupeño chief agreed to meet with Juan Antonio. But instead of joining with the renegade chief, Juan Antonio and his twenty-five Cahuilla seized Garra and his family, escorted them back to San Timoteo Canyon, and turned them over to General Bean. With Antonio Garra's capture, his followers dispersed and the revolt was doomed.[6]

The final battle of the Garra Revolt took place in Coyote Canyon on December 20th. Army Captain Samuel Heintzelman and a detachment of 46 soldiers and volunteers were riding into the canyon when they were attacked by the rebel Cahuilla chief Chapuli and his Los Coyotes band. In a short engagement, Chapuli and eight of his followers were killed, and the surviving Cahuilla retreated into the Santa Rosas. Heintzelman set the Indian village afire, then after a short excursion around the southern end of the Santa Rosas looking for the Indians who had fled, advanced up Coyote Canyon on the old Anza Trail to Cahuilla Valley. Here he met with Juan Bautista, chief of the the Powki village Cahuilla, who professed his loyalty to the whites.[7] (Bautista Canyon honors this Cahuilla chieftain today.)

The battle in Coyote Canyon marked the end of organized Indian resistance in the region. Four Indian sub-chiefs allegedly involved in the Warner Ranch raid were executed by Captain Heintzelman in Coyote Canyon on Christmas Day, 1851. The chiefs were forced to dig their own graves and a firing squad of twenty "put them in it." In January 1852 Antonio Garra and several of his followers were tried, found guilty, and sentenced to death. Garra was proud to the end. "Gentlemen, I ask your pardon for all my offenses and expect yours in return," the *San Diego Herald* (January 17, 1852) reported him as saying. Blindfolded, kneeling at the head of his grave, the bold Cupeño chief was shot to death by a ten-man firing squad. Cooperation with the whites or withdrawal from ancestral lands appeared to be the only options left for Native Americans in Southern California.

The whites were anxious for peace, also. The settlers, ranchers, cattlemen and prospectors now swarming into the Southern California back country wanted the Indian situation solved, one way or another. Some advocated

A Cahuilla couple on the Cahuilla Reservation, circa 1900. The Cahuilla village of *Paui* has been occupied continuously since about 1874. – SOUTHWEST MUSEUM

forcing the native peoples off their lands and killing them if they resisted. Cooler heads did not always prevail.

Even before the Garra Revolt, Congress made an attempt to solve the California Indian problem. In September 1850, the appointment of three Indian Commissioners was authorized with instructions to make treaties with the various native tribes. $50,000 was appropriated for expenses. The commissioners appointed were Redick McKee of Virginia, George W. Barbour of Kentucky, and Oliver M. Wozencraft of Louisiana – none of whom had any experience in dealing with California Indians. The three commissioners met in San Francisco in January 1851 and divided the state into three districts – McKee would negotiate Indian treaties in the north, Wozencraft in the central part of the state, and Barbour in the south. The commissioners quickly realized that they faced a difficult task. The California native peoples were divided into dozens of small tribal groups with no sense of unity. (Garra tried to unify and failed.) A great number of treaties would have to be negotiated. Adding to the problem, whites were generally scornful toward the native peoples and looked with disdain on the commissioners' efforts. Barbour resigned in frustration in the fall of 1851 and Wozencraft took over his duties in the south.

Spurred by the crisis atmosphere caused by the Garra Revolt, Wozencraft hurried to the white community of Temecula and issued a call for all Cahuilla and Luiseño chiefs to join him for treaty-making purposes. The Luiseño chieftains quickly appeared, but the Cahuilla were reluctant to join the talks. The reason was animosity between the two Indian groups that went back to the so-called Temecula Massacre of 1847, when Juan Antonio and his Cahuilla warriors had slaughtered upwards of fifty Luiseños. Wozencraft insisted that the Cahuilla attend the conference and threatened punishment if they didn't. Reluctantly, Juan Antonio, accompanied by his body-guards and other Cahuilla chiefs including Juan Bautista, rode into Temecula to the sullen glare of the assembled Luiseños.

The Treaty of Temecula, signed by the Luiseño and Cahuilla chiefs on January 5, 1852, was generous to the native people. The Indians acknowledged that the United States was "the sole and absolute sovereign" of all the territory ceded to it by treaty with Mexico, agreed to accept "the exclusive jurisdiction, authority and protection of the United States," and promised to "refrain from the commission of all acts of hostility and aggression" against U.S. citizens. The Indians were to live in peace among themselves and conform to and be governed by the laws and regulations of the Indian Bureau.

In return for agreement on these terms, a vast territory was "set apart forever for the sole use and occupancy" of the Cahuilla, Luiseño and Serrano. This huge Indian reservation was to encompass all of the San Jacinto and "San Gorgonio" mountains, the desert country immediately to the east, the Cahuilla Valley and mountains, and the hill country west almost to Pauma and Temecula. In addition, the Indians were promised "livestock, clothing, supplies, agricultural implements, schools and instructors."[8]

The Treaty of Temecula, along with seventeen other treaties negotiated with 140 Indian tribal groups and clans all over California, would have granted native peoples more than 11,700 square miles of interior lands. When the treaties were made known, a storm of protest arose among white settlers. The howls of protest echoed in the chambers of the California Legislature, which debated the treaties in March 1852. Some legislators objected to Indian rights to any California land. Governor John McDougal advocated moving all the California Indians to an arid desert area bordering Mexico, where he said they could fend for themselves. Only J. J. Warner, owner of Warner Ranch and state senator from San Diego County, stood up in favor of the treaties. Not unexpectedly, the state legislature instructed California's two senators to oppose the treaties in Washington. The U.S. Senate rejected all the California Indian treaties in June 1852.

The rejection of the treaties left the California Indians sullen and dejected, more exposed than ever to ruthless exploitation by incoming whites. The Cahuilla were particularly resentful, as many of them had considered themselves friends of the white man. Other than a few attempts to steal livestock from Paulino Weaver's ranch in San Gorgonio Pass and from ranches near Temecula, the Cahuilla remained peaceful. Some withdrew into the mountains, where they were relatively free of white pressure.

Juan Antonio was bitterly disappointed. A rumor spread that he contemplated joining the Colorado River tribes and stirring up another revolt, but he remained loyal to the whites – at least outwardly – to the end of his life. The old chief refused to leave San Timoteo Canyon, despite the encroachment of more and more white settlers. In 1856, with increasing numbers of trespassers on his peoples' lands, Juan Antonio complained to an army officer:

> The Americans are now squatting here, and taking away my land, wood, and water. The man [Paulino] Weaver living at San Gorgonio has our animals killed whenever they go there. We have not land enough to plant; my people are poor and hungry; they want something from the government. Some Americans tell us that we must go away to the mountains to live; other Americans tell us that we must all live together on some land. We do not understand it and we do not like it.[9]

Despite a progression of superintendents and agents appointed by Congress and the Indian Bureau during the 1850s and '60s, the plight of the California Indians continued to worsen. Edward F. Beale, made Superintendent of Indian Affairs for California in 1852, proposed a series of reservations guarded by military posts on which Indians would be taught agriculture and basic trades. Beale set up the San Sebastian Reservation in the Tejon Pass area in late 1853, but was removed from office before he could establish any more. Beale's agent for the southern district, Benjamin Wilson, wrote a long, sympathetic report on the Indians of Southern California, and called for a large reservation, extending from the mountains to the Colorado River, on which the Tulareño, Cahuilla, Luiseño and Dieguiño would be taught the rudiments of white civilization and turned into productive members of society.[10] None of this came to pass. Beale's successor, Thomas J. Henley, proposed three reservations in the eastern desert – one of them outside California – to which all the state's Indians would eventually be moved, in order to "rid the state of this class of population."[11] Such extremist sentiment for eliminating the California Indian was, sadly, all too prevalent.

A smallpox epidemic swept through Southern California in 1863, and it was particularly deadly to the Indians. Among its victims was Juan Antonio. The old chief was succeeded by his long-time lieutenant Manuel Largo, who led most of the survivors back to the San Jacinto Valley, where they had once worked for Spanish padres on the vast mission rancho. Others scattered among the Cahuilla of San Gorgonio Pass or the desert beyond. Whites quickly occupied San Timoteo Canyon.

Chief Cabezon's people in the Pass area suffered poor crops as incoming white settlers laid claim to water rights. This was to be expected, as the Indians, without legal title to the land and unfamiliar with federal or state laws, were left with little recourse other than submission or withdrawal. Many of the Pass Cahuilla drifted away to desert villages farther south, such as Agua Caliente (Palm Springs), Torres and Martinez. Some joined the Mountain Cahuilla.

The Mountain Cahuilla, long thought secure because of their relative isolation, found their ancestral domains relentlessly shrinking. First to feel pressure from encroaching whites were Cahuilla living in the San Jacinto Valley. The Estudillo family began selling off sections of their vast Rancho San Jacinto Viejo in 1868, and by the early 1870s the valley had some fifty settlers. Friction was inevitable. Lands the native people once roamed freely were fenced off, and water from the San Jacinto River and several springs was diverted to the settlers' fields, depriving the Indians of water for their own small crop lands. Cahuilla, desperate for food, began stealing and butchering cattle belonging to valley ranchers. There were confrontations, and several Indians were arrested. Settlers called for the government to remove the Cahuilla from the San Jacinto Valley. The *San Diego Union* (July 3, 1873) voiced the white complaints:

> In time past these Indians were tractable, and were easily managed by the rancheros, but within the last two or three years they have acted badly, stealing and killing stock from time to time, and continually annoying the settlers.... It is preposterous to suppose that four or five hundred Indians will be allowed to exclude from such a magnificent area of land a community of tax-paying citizens. The Government having opened these lands to preemption and invited settlement upon them, is bound to guarantee possession to the settlers, and to protect them in that possession.

One of the last basket makers of the Santa Rosa Indian Lupe Guanche Olveras with one of her work ba[skets] Circa 1920 Aunt of Art Guanche

VERIFIED BY Arthur Louis Guanche

Lupe Guanche Olveras was one of the most skillful basket makers on the Santa Rosa Reservation. Here she finishes a basket, ca. 1920. Below are a selection of Cahuilla star and rattlesnake baskets, examples that reveal the skill of the Cahuilla craftswomen. — DAVID SCHERMAN (above), SOUTHWEST MUSEUM (below).

Manuel Largo, chief of the valley Cahuilla, was blamed for the Indians' "obstinacy." The *Union*, while decrying his stubborn refusal to move his people out of the valley, praised him as an outstanding leader:

> Largo is a remarkably intelligent Indian, and feels the dignity of his position fully. He is in fact a monarch in that part of the country and his word is law among the Indians, and his mandates are executed without question. He considers himself the owner of the land occupied by his band, and declares that he means to hold possession.

Resisting white settlement in the rich agricultural and grazing lands of the San Jacinto Valley was like trying to hold back the ocean tide. As more settlers arrived, fenced off more land, and took more water, pressures to remove the Cahuilla increased. The *San Diego Union* (September 11, 1873) again voiced white sentiments:

> We have in recent issues of The Union spoken of the difficulties that have arisen in the San Jacinto Valley, in the northern part of the county.... Here a very large number of Indians have lived for many years, and they regard the land as their own, and already resist its settlement by a white population. Of course, we cannot but pity the ignorant Indians, but at the same time we must not permit them to keep back the development of the material interests of our county. The land is for the people who can cultivate it and become producers, adding to the prosperity of the commonwealth, and the Indians must go.

His people hemmed in, unable to make a living in their traditional ways, reduced to performing menial labor for white settlers, Chief Largo moved his band up to the ancient village site of *Paui,* on the west side of Cahuilla (Anza) Valley, in 1874. Now only the Soboba remained in the San Jacinto Valley, and their time of tribulation was soon to come.

It is interesting to note that not one white settler in the San Jacinto Valley was ever physically harmed by Manuel Largo's Cahuilla. With the exception of a single incident in April 1872, when lawmen attempted to arrest an Indian named José Murat for stealing a cow, no shots were fired. The crime of Largo's people was that they "annoyed" the settlers by remaining on the land, using precious water, and occasionally butchering cattle when they were hungry.

Cahuilla Valley proved no safe haven for Largo's people. Even here, in the ancestral heartland of the Mountain Cahuilla, the people were not protected from white encroachment. By the late 1870s, this isolated mountain basin felt the trod of cattle herds, owned by ranchers like the Hamiltons, the Parks, and the Tripps. Charles Thomas and his family occupied the nearby Hemet (Garner) Valley. (Thomas looked the other way when the Indians occasionally butchered a cow and never, in his many years as a rancher, was molested by the neighboring Cahuilla.) Only in the Santa Rosas – Rockhouse Canyon, Old Nicolas Canyon, Horse Canyon – were the Mountain Cahuilla still free from land-hungry settlers.

A tired but still proud Manuel Largo relinquished his position as chief of the Mountain Cahuilla in 1877. The *Union* (July 12, 1877), no friend of the Indians, praised the old chief: "Manuel Largo, old and almost blind, lives in the upper part of the valley, at the 'Peach Tree.' He is well known to the older settlers, and has aided many times in catching horse thieves who have from time to time preyed on the people in that section of the country. He is an excellent old man and is deservedly respected. His authority over his tribe was absolute, and it was ably and justly used." He was succeeded by Fernando Lugo.

Ironically, it was Ulysses S. Grant, considered one of our worst presidents, who brought a degree of concern and honesty to the federal administration of Indian affairs. President Grant and his first Commissioner of Indian Affairs, Ely S. Parker, himself a Seneca Indian, were motivated to acting largely by the Indian Wars on the Great Plains. The Grant administration's new "Peace Policy" was designed to help Native Americans enter the mainstream of American life and eventually become productive citizens. The Indian was to be nurtured and educated "in the ways of social and economic life in civilized American society." The first step on this road to assimilation would be the reservation system, where native peoples would be governed by honest Indian agents and protected from white incursions.[12]

This ideal, of course, was never realized, but a start was made. A new Board of Indian Commissioners was established by Congress in 1869, with ten members appointed by the President. Major General J. B. McIntosh became Superintendent of Indian Affairs in California. McIntosh made a tour of Southern California in 1870 and found the condition of the Mission Indians pitiable, the Cahuilla only slightly better off. (From this time on, the Cahuilla were usually included in the Mission Indian category, although most of them had little contact with the Spanish missions.) He recommended the setting aside of several reservations. Per his recommendation, the San Pascual Agency was established for the Luiseño Indians in 1870, but opposition from white settlers in San Diego County was so violent that the agency was abolished the following year.[13]

John G. Ames was appointed special agent to investigate the condition of the Mission Indians in 1873. The Ames Report, favoring many small reservations in or near areas where the Indians were living, received much attention. Ames was succeeded as special agent by Charles A. Wetmore. The latter's 1875 report urged that small tracts be appropriated or purchased by the federal government and held in trust for the native peoples. The Ames and Wetmore reports were given favorable attention by newspapers and resulted in President Grant's decision to take action in behalf of the Mission Indians.[14]

By executive order on December 26, 1875, President Grant set aside nine small reservations in San Diego County for the use and benefit of the Mission Indians.

Helen Hunt Jackson (1830-1885) dedicated the last years of her life to bringing justice to the Native American. She visited the Southern California Mission Indians in 1882 and 1883. Her *Report on The Conditions and Needs of the Mission Indians* (1883) and, even more, her romantic novel *Ramona* (1884) dramatized the plight of the Southern California native peoples.
— RAMONA PAGEANT ASSOCIATION

Abbot Kinney (1850-1920), best remembered as a land developer, shared Mrs. Jackson's concern for the Mission Indians. He accompanied Mrs. Jackson on her 1883 travels through Southern California Indian country.
— RAMONA PAGEANT ASSOCIATION

Those in Cahuilla territory were the Potrero Ajenio (later Morongo), Coahuilla (Cahuilla), and Agua Caliente reservations. On May 20, 1876, again by executive order, additions were made to the Potrero Ajenio and Agua Caliente reservations and six new ones were created. Two of them were Cahuilla – the Torres-Martinez and Cabezones (later Cabezon) reservations. The Coahuilla Reservation, centered around *Paui* in Anza Valley, was the only one set aside for Manuel Largo's Mountain Cahuilla. Four others, located in the San Gorgonio Pass and Coachella Valley areas, were occupied by Desert Cahuilla and Wanakik (Pass) Cahuilla bands.

Unfortunately, these early reservations were unsurveyed, not well protected by law. Federal supervision was almost nonexistent. The native peoples had no legal rights under California law. White settlers continued to encroach on Indian lands and, in many cases, took over control of water sources. Without water, agriculture was impossible on the barren lands left to the Indians. With their ancestral hunting and gathering lands diminishing year by year, with inadequate water resources, the plight of many of the Mission Indians was becoming desperate.

Increasingly, the younger Cahuilla turned to low-paying wage and subsistence jobs, working for white settlers and ranchers. Mountain Cahuilla cowboys tended the herds of Charles Thomas, Manuel Arnaiz, and the Tripp brothers. Some worked on fruit ranches. Cahuilla sheep-shearers became the best in the business, and at sheep shearing time were in great demand all over Southern California. Cahuilla women were employed as domestic help. For many of the older, tradition-bound Cahuilla, such options were not available.

In 1877 a Mission Indian Agency was created by the Indian Bureau to try to improve the condition of the Southern California Indians. J. E. Colburn was appointed Indian Agent with headquarters in San Bernardino. Colburn was succeeded by Reverend S. S. Lawson in 1878. Lawson was sincere in his efforts to aid the native peoples. He met old, white-haired Chief Cabezon at a gathering of the Cahuilla in 1878. Cabezon, last of his generation of Cahuilla chieftains, sadly described the plight of his people:

> When white brother come, we make glad, tell him to hunt and ride. He say, "Give me a little for my own," so we move little way, not hunt there. Then more come. They say move more, and we move again. So many times. Now we are small people, we have little place, but they say move to new place, away from white friends, go from our valley.
> "I know not," he mourned, "I know not."[15]

Onto the scene in 1882 came a remarkable woman with a burning desire to help Native Americans. She would write a novel that would eventually make the plight of the Southern California Indians reverberate in the halls of government and become household knowledge.

Helen Hunt Jackson (1830-1885) was a native of Massachusetts who lived many years in Colorado. Following the tragic deaths of her first husband and two sons, she embarked on a prolific writing career. Magazine articles, travel sketches, stories and poems flowed from her pen, none of them of great literary merit. She would be unread and unknown today if she had not happened to attend a meeting while visiting Boston in

Chief Victoriano and his third wife. Victoriano, leader of the Soboba, died in 1888 at a reported age of 133 years. — LAURA SWIFT

Jose Pedro Lucero and his wife at their Soboba home, ca. 1899. Lucero was the village story teller. — G. W. JAMES

1879, where she heard Chief Standing Bear and his niece Bright Eyes graphically describe the misfortunes of their people, the Ponca Indians of Nebraska. What she heard so shocked her that she dedicated the rest of her life to helping the American Indian.

Mrs. Jackson's first book on the subject, *A Century of Dishonor,* was a strongly worded indictment of the federal government and greedy whites. Upon its publication in 1881, she sent a copy, at her own expense, to every member of Congress. She was shocked and disappointed when her book produced little response and no change in the government's Indian policies.

Late in 1881, Mrs. Jackson was commissioned by *Century Magazine* to write a series of articles on the California missions. She arrived in California in early 1882 and set out to visit each of the decaying mission sites. In San Diego she met Father Anthony Ubach and first learned of the sorry condition of the Mission Indians. With Father Ubach she traveled into the San Diego County back country, visiting San Pascual and Temecula, places where the "robber whites," as she called them, had recently evicted the native peoples. In Temecula she heard of the Soboba Indian School in the San Jacinto Valley, established in 1880 as the first institution of its kind in California. This she insisted she must visit.

Riding into the San Jacinto Valley with Father Ubach, she found a village of 157 Indians and well-kept wheat fields, peach and apricot orchards watered by a network of irrigation ditches from natural springs on the hillside. She visited the aged chief Victoriano and his grandson, acting chief José Jesus Castillo, who spoke for the Soboba. From Miss Mary Sheriff, teacher at the Indian school, she was shocked to learn that the peaceful Soboba, who had lived here for generations tending their fields and orchards and raising sheep, were in danger of eviction.

The original inhabitants of Soboba were Cahuilla. It is easy to understand why they settled there. The Soboba village and fields border the great San Jacinto Fault, and this, geologists tell us, accounts for the hot springs, numerous cold springs and water seepages that grace the landscape. Abundant water made the place a veritable Garden of Eden set amid arid surroundings.

Franciscan padres from Mission San Luis Rey established Rancho San Jacinto as their furthermost cattle ranch sometime between 1816 and 1821. The padres brought with them a good number of San Luis Rey Mission Indians, known as Luiseños, to tend the herds of cattle, horses, and sheep. Later, some Serrano came over from the San Bernardino Valley to work on the great rancho. Many of these native peoples – Cahuilla, Luiseño, Serrano – remained in the San Jacinto Valley after the decline of the mission rancho and made their homes at Soboba, at the far northeastern edge of the valley.

In 1842 Mexican Governor *pro tem* Manuel Jimeno granted Rancho San Jacinto Viejo, encompassing the eastern half of the San Jacinto Valley, to José Antonio Estudillo, with the stipulation that the new owner "shall not in any manner prejudice the Indians who are established on said land." As long as he lived, Don Estudillo

Teacher Mary Sheriff and her students at the Soboba Indian School, ca. 1884. The Soboba School was the first such institution in Southern California, established in 1880. Miss Sheriff first told Helen Hunt Jackson about the threatened eviction of the Soboba from their lands.
— SAN JACINTO MUSEUM

respected the rights and well-being of his rancho Indians, but some of his heirs were not so conscientious.

The problem that caused so much trouble for the Soboba originated with the Land Law of 1851 in which Congress decreed that all claimants to land in California present their claims within a given time to a Board of Land Commissioners. Virtually all of the California native peoples, unfamiliar with United States laws and legal procedures, failed to comply, and subsequently most of them were evicted from their ancestral lands. The Soboba, reassured by Estudillo, believed they were secure.

The situation changed in the 1860s, after José Antonio Estudillo's passing. The many Estudillo heirs were land rich but cash poor. Starting in 1868, the heirs sold various tracts of the great land grant rancho whenever they needed funds. By 1880 most of the rancho lands had been sold.

The initial survey in 1851, confirming the Rancho San Jacinto Viejo grant to Estudillo, did not include Soboba village. But an 1878 survey, patented on January 17, 1880, mistakenly included the village, the cultivated fields, and the water. Law suits among the various white claimants over disputed boundaries ended up in court. By order of Judge W. F. McNealy of San Diego Superior Court, three surveyors were commissioned to remap Rancho San Jacinto Viejo lands. Upon receiving the completed survey in early 1882, Judge McNealy divided up the rancho lands among the white claimants. The Soboba, with no legal claim recognized by the court, received nothing. In the eyes of the court, they were squatters.

Matthew Byrne of San Bernardino was awarded 700 acres on the northeastern side of the San Jacinto Valley, including the Soboba village, the cultivated fields, and all the water. Byrne planned to graze sheep on his lands

Mary Sheriff Fowler (1841-1921) in old age, ca. 1920. Almost alone among the whites, she fought to prevent the removal of the Soboba from their lands. In later years, living in San Jacinto, she enjoyed telling about her friendship with Helen Hunt Jackson and the struggle for Indian rights. — SAN JACINTO MUSEUM

and at first said the Soboba could remain. A few months later he changed his mind and threatened to evict the Indians unless the U.S. Government paid him $30,000 – far more than he had originally paid the Estudillo heirs – for his 700 acres. The Department of the Interior's Indian Bureau refused even to consider Byrnes' demand, so the latter petitioned Judge McNealy in San Diego for an order of eviction against the Soboba. There matters stood when Helen Hunt Jackson left, promising Mary Sheriff that she would do what she could for the friendly Soboba.[16]

Mrs. Jackson continued her tour of Mission Indian settlements all over Southern California, from San Diego to Santa Barbara counties. She met Sierra Madre land developer Abbott Kinney in Los Angeles. Kinney held similar views on the Mission Indian's plight and promised to help her. She then returned to her home in Colorado Springs. Awaiting her was a disturbing letter from Mary Sheriff saying that Byrnes was going ahead with his intention to evict the Soboba.

Helen Hunt Jackson was distressed to the point where she found it difficult to sleep. She fired off letters to Secretary of the Interior Henry Teller and Commissioner of Indian Affairs Hiram Price, pleading for government action on behalf of the Soboba and the Mission Indians in general. She wrote a friend that "there is not

Sam Temple (1842-1909), San Jacinto teamster, shot and killed the Indian Juan Diego after the latter had taken his horse. The killing was immortalized in Helen Hunt Jackson's *Ramona*. — LAURA SWIFT

Ramona Lubo (1850?-1922), widow of Juan Diego, on the Cahuilla Reservation where she lived most of her later life. She was a shy, unassuming person who did not relish the attention focused on her. — CHARLES VAN FLEET

in all the Century of Dishonor, so black a chapter as the story of the Mission Indians... driven off their lands like foxes and wolves."[17] She volunteered to serve as special agent to further investigate the deplorable condition of the native peoples of Southern California.

Teller and Price were sufficiently impressed to recommend her as a special commissioner of Indian affairs in Southern California. President Chester Arthur approved the appointment on July 7, 1882. The following January, at her insistence, Abbot Kinney was appointed her co-commissioner.

Mrs. Jackson hurried back to Southern California in early 1883 and, with her commission partner Kinney, went first to see the Soboba. The situation was bleak. Matthew Byrne had applied to the court in San Diego for an order of eviction against the Soboba, and no one – other than loyal Mary Sheriff – seemed willing to take up their cause. The Soboba village chief told Mrs. Jackson, "If the government says we must go, we must; but we would rather die right here than move."[18] When Mrs. Jackson returned to Los Angeles, she hired, at her own expense, the law firm of Brunson and Wells to defend the Soboba cause. She wrote Miss Sheriff, "I could not bear to go away and leave the matter in such shape.... So I have myself guaranteed to the lawyers a certain sum... to see the case through if a suit of enactment is brought against the village." Later, she persuaded Secretary of the Interior Teller to appoint Brunson and Wells special assistant United States Attorneys to represent the Mission Indians.

Mrs. Jackson was in San Bernardino meeting with Indian Bureau agent S. S. Lawson when a letter arrived from Mary Ticknor, the schoolteacher at the Cahuilla Reservation in Anza Valley. Mrs. Ticknor wrote her about a tragic incident involving a Cahuilla Indian named Juan Diego who had been shot to death by a white man named Sam Temple on March 24, 1883. A few weeks after the murder, Jackson and her party were riding into the San Jacinto Mountains when someone brought up the incident. The driver so strongly defended Temple that she wondered about the type of people living there and determined to find out all she could about the killing. She wrote to Mary Sheriff asking for details.[19] The story has been told in a number of different ways, but the following is Mrs. Jackson's account:

> An incident which has occurred on the boundaries of the Cahuilla Reservation a few weeks before our arrival there is of importance as an illustration of the need of some legal protection for the Indians of Southern California.
>
> ...A Cahuilla Indian named Juan Diego had built for himself a house and cultivated a small patch of ground on a high mountain ledge a few miles north of the village. Here he lived alone with his wife and baby. He had been for some years what the Indians call a 'locoed Indian,' being at times crazy, never dangerous.
>
> ...Juan Diego had been off to find work at sheep-shearing. He came home at night riding a strange horse. His wife exclaimed, 'Why, whose horse is that?' Juan looked at the horse and replied confusedly, 'Where is my horse then?' The woman, much frightened, said, 'You must take that horse right back; they will say you stole it.' Juan replied that he would as soon as he had rested; then threw himself down and fell asleep.
>
> From this sleep he was awakened by the barking of the dogs, and ran out of the house to see what it meant. The woman followed, and was the only witness of what then occurred.
>
> A white man, named Temple, the owner of the horse which Juan had ridden home, rode up, and on seeing Juan poured out a volley of oaths, leveled his gun and shot him dead. After Juan had fallen on the ground Temple rode closer and fired three more shots in the body,... the woman looking on. He then took his horse, which was standing tied in front of the house, and rode away.
>
> The woman, with her baby on her back, ran to the Cahuilla village and told what had happened. This was in the night. At dawn the Indians went over to the place, brought the murdered man's body to the village, and buried it.[20]

Ramona Lubo at Juan Diego's grave on the Cahuilla Reservation, ca. 1890. — RAMONA PAGEANT ASSOCIATION

The remains of the adobe home on Juan Diego Flat, where Juan Diego and Ramona lived before the shooting. This 1905 picture shows what little was left. The heavy rains of 1916 completed the destruction of the adobe. Nothing remains at the site today. — RAMONA PAGEANT ASSOCIATION

Sam Temple, the killer of Juan Diego, hastened back to San Jacinto and reported to Justice of the Peace Samuel V. Tripp that he had just killed a horsethief. Next day, Sunday, March 25th, 1883, Judge Tripp assembled a coroner's jury consisting of William and George Blodgett, William Stice, J. C. Jordan, Frank Wellman, and Will Webster – all white, several of them friends of Sam Temple, none of whom witnessed the killing. Judge Tripp and the jurists rode up to the site of the killing, but found that Juan Diego's body had already been removed and his clothing burned by the Indians. With no body to examine, Tripp dismissed his coroner's jury, then rode down to Cahuilla village. There he saw the body, disfigured with buckshot and bullet wounds, and allowed it to be buried.

Sam Temple's trial began on Monday, March 26, but the case was continued until the following Saturday, March 31, to "allow time for further evidence." Subpoenas were issued for the six white "witnesses," none of whom were present at the killing. Juan's widow was not called, nor were several other Indians who may have witnessed the killing from a distance. Indian testimony against whites had once been illegal in California; although those laws had been changed, it was seldom permitted in practice.

The defendant testified that he shot Juan Diego only after the latter lunged at him with a knife. "I told him to stop," Temple claimed, "As he did not stop I turned the gun upon him and pulled the trigger but don't think I struck him the first shot. He still advanced and I stepped back and shot at him a second time.... I turned the gun and knocked him down and shot him again with my revolver..."[21]

The six witnesses testified that they had gone up to the killing site with Judge Tripp the next day and had viewed footprints, blood on the ground, and a pile of burnt clothing. No one appeared for the prosecution. Judge Tripp accepted Sam Temple's version of the killing and ruled that Juan Diego's death was justifiable homicide. Temple was released.

Ramona Lubo, Juan Diego's widow, interviewed years later by author George Wharton James for his book *Through Ramona's Country* (1909), insisted that her husband had no weapon of any kind when he was shot repeatedly in cold blood by "that wicked man shouting foul oaths." (Ramona Lubo lived in Cahuilla village until her death in 1922. She is buried there, as is Juan Diego, in the Cahuilla cemetery. Her youngest son by Juan Diego died at the age of fourteen. She gave birth to another son, Condino Hopkins, fathered by a white man, around 1887. Condino lived until 1951.)

The killing of Juan Diego – merely another incident of a white man killing an Indian – would have been soon forgotten, had not Helen Hunt Jackson written of it in her Mission Indian report to Congress, and later, fictionalized it, in her romantic novel, *Ramona* (1884).

From the San Jacinto Valley, Mrs. Jackson and Abbot Kinney rode up to the Thomas Ranch, then on to the Cahuilla (Anza) Valley, where they visited the Cahuilla Reservation. They were impressed with the Cahuilla:

> The Cahuilla village, situated here, was one of the most interesting that we visited, and the Indians seemed a clear-headed, more individual and independent people than any other we saw.... The isolation of this village has also tended to keep these Indians self-respecting and independent.... The population of the village numbers from one hundred and fifty to two hundred. The houses are of adobe, thatched with reeds,... These Indians make the greater part of their living by stock-raising. They also send out a sheep-shearing band each year. They have sixteen fields, large and small, under cultivation, and said they would have had many more except for the lack of plows, there being but one plow for the whole village. They raise wheat, barley, corn, squashes, and watermelons.... The women were neatly dressed, the children

Historian Phil Brigandi, curator of the Ramona Bowl Museum, examining the monument at Juan Diego Flat, erected by the Billy Holcomb Chapter of E. Clampus Vitus in 1979. The monument is across the road and about 100 yards southwest from the actual site of Juan Diego's adobe.

especially so, and the faces of all, men, women, and children, had an animation and look of intellectual keenness very uncommon among the Southern California Indians.[22]

From there, Mrs. Jackson and Kinney rode on to visit Warner's Ranch, Santa Ysabel, and other small Indian settlements in the San Diego back country, before returning to Los Angeles. Mrs. Jackson parted with Abbot Kinney and hurried back to Colorado Springs, where she wrote her *Report on The Conditions and Needs of The Mission Indians* in remarkably short time, completing it on July 13, 1883. In the report, she made eleven recommendations, the most important being that the Mission Indian reservations be clearly surveyed and marked and white settlers be prevented from encroaching on them, that more schools be established on the reservations, that agricultural implements be distributed to encourage Indian farming, and that special U.S. attorneys be appointed to safeguard Indian legal rights.

Again, Helen Hunt Jackson was disappointed in the lack of response. Despondent, she cast about for some way to bring the plight of the Mission Indians to America's attention. Could a novel succeed where reports had failed? The idea appealed to her. Soon it dominated her whole being. She wrote to Don Antonio Coronel and his wife, friends she had met in Los Angeles: "I am going to write a novel, in which will be set forth some Indian experiences in a way to move people's hearts. People will read a novel when they will not read serious books. The scenes of the novel will be in Southern California, and I shall introduce enough of Mexicans and Americans to give it variety.[23]

Mrs. Jackson isolated herself in her favorite New York City hotel, The Berkeley, and began writing at a furious pace. Her health was not good: she had a persistent cold and – although she did not yet know it – she was dying of stomach cancer. She wrote almost every day and long into the night for four months.

Sam Temple with his six-horse team pulling two wagons, Hemet, ca. 1898. Temple always claimed he was justified in killing Juan Diego for stealing one of his horses.
— DOROTHY COWPER

Ramona Lubo in later years, ca. 1910. Made famous by Helen Hunt Jackson's novel, Ramona became an object of curiosity visited by hundreds of persons over the years. She did not enjoy the limelight. — LAURA SWIFT

112

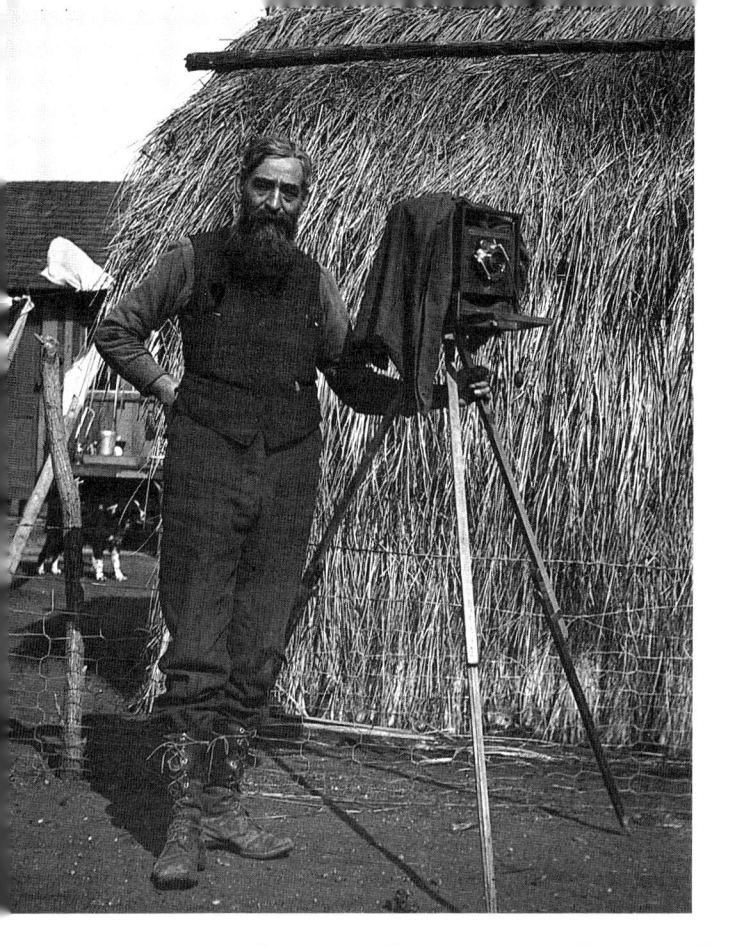

Author George Wharton James visited Ramona Lubo in 1900, bringing along his camera and gramophone. He took her picture and recorded her voice on a wax disk that does not seem to have survived. James wrote about the "real" Ramona story in *Through Ramona's Country* (1909). — SOUTHWEST MUSEUM (both)

She originally planned to title her book *In the Name of the Law*. For some unknown reason she changed the name to *Ramona*. Ever since, writers have speculated on who the real Ramona was: Someone she met at the De Valle's Rancho Camulos? Ramona Wolfe, wife of Temecula store keeper Louis Wolfe? The Indian Ramona Lubo, widow of Juan Diego?

The best interpretation of Ramona of the novel is that of Phil Brigandi, historian and curator of the Ramona Bowl Museum in Hemet:

"In fifteen years of researching the background of the Ramona story, I have come to the conclusion that it is misleading to speak of a 'real' Ramona. You might just as well look for a 'real' Tom Sawyer, or a 'real' Scarlett O'Hara. Yes, it is true, that each of these characters is based on fact. But with Ramona, so many people move quickly from 'based on fact' to 'fact.'…

"Jackson herself had no illusions about what she was doing. On February 20, 1884 she wrote to Abbott Kinney: 'For dramatic purposes I have put the Temecula ejectment *before* the first trouble in San Pasquale. Will anybody be idiot enough to make a point of that? I am not writing history. I hope the story is good.'…

"Too many people still assume that *Ramona* is really 'fact,' not just 'based on fact.' It is a powerful and important myth, but as historians, we owe it to the real people and events Jackson based her story on to not become lost in the *Ramona* myth."[24]

Ramona, completed in March 1884, was a romantic novel centered around two lovers – the handsome Indian Alessandro and the beautiful half Indian, half Scotish Ramona – set in an idyllic, largely mythical Spanish Southern California. The tragic climax of the story takes place in the San Jacinto Mountains and is based on the real-life shooting of Juan Diego by Sam Temple. In the novel, Alessandro takes the place of Juan Diego, but there the resemblance ends: the hero is portrayed as a good-looking, intelligent, romantic, noble Indian, a far cry from the "locoed" Juan Diego who really was (Although Alessandro is eventually driven mad, or "loco."). Ramona of the story, a majestic young woman of Spanish culture, in no way resembles Ramona Lubo, the full-blooded Indian, nor any other candidate for the "real" Ramona. Jim Farrar is Sam Temple and is portrayed rather realistically as a hot-tempered bully. Judge Wells is patterned after Samuel Tripp. Many writers connect the novel's Aunt Ri with Mrs. J. C. Jordan of San Jacinto.

Ramona, first serialized in the *Christian Union*, then published as a book in November 1884, was an instant success, but not in the way Helen Hunt Jackson had envisioned. Critics praised the romance but virtually ignored the Indian reform message she wished to convey. She was deeply disappointed. She did not live to see *Ramona* become a classic and finally be recognized as a poignant drama of white abuse of the Mission Indians.

Ramona Lubo at the San Bernardino Orange Show in 1921, less than a year before her death. Rose Costo, standing beside her, worked for many years for the Ramona Pageant in Hemet.

The Ramona Pageant in Hemet, started by Garnet Holme in 1923, has been an annual attraction ever since. The story portrayed, based on Helen Hunt Jackson's novel, is fiction and bears little resemblence to what actually happened.

Helen Hunt Jackson died of cancer in San Francisco on August 12, 1885.

The ordeal of the Soboba continued to unfold. While working on her Mission Indian report, Mrs. Jackson learned that President Chester Arthur had partially heeded her call to help these embattled Indians. By executive order dated June 19, 1883, the President set aside Indian Canyon and its water rights, a mile east of the village, and the adjacent foothills to the north as the Soboba Reservation, 3,172 acres in all. The President could set aside public land for a reservation but not private land. Soboba village and the major springs, which the Indians needed to water their cultivated lands, were part of Rancho San Jacinto Viejo and belonged, according to court decision, to Matthew Byrne. Since the government refused to meet his terms, he was determined to occupy it.

In November 1883, Byrne was granted his eviction order by the San Diego Superior Court. In a shrewd and heartless move, Byrne waited to serve the eviction papers until sheep-shearing time in the spring of 1884, when most of the Soboba men were away. In the words of Riverside County historian Elmer Holmes, "One beautiful Sunday in April, after this winter of anxiety in Soboba, three men crossed the swollen river and visited every home in the village. They were not welcome visitors, for they brought to each family the order of the court that they must gather up their goods and chattels and leave.... There was mourning in Soboba that day... no comfort to the hearts of the stricken Indians, for the edict of banishment had come to them with paralyzing effect."[25]

It appeared that the Soboba would be removed just as were the Indians of Temecula, San Pascual, and, later, Warner's Ranch. But now came a startling change of fortune in favor of the native people. The Soboba village captain went from house to house, gathering the eviction notices, and is said to have told the families, "Don't grieve so, my people, we have friends among the Americans who are going to help us. Have you forgotten the 'good woman' who is doing so much to save our homes?... Do not give up, but trust the good God still, for I am sure He will see that our village and gardens are not taken from us."[26]

The eviction papers were taken to Los Angeles and given to the law firm of Brunson and Wells, previously engaged by Mrs. Jackson. But the two attorneys were forced to withdraw from the case when the Indian Bureau refused to recompensate them for their considerable expenses. Mrs. Jackson, mortally ill with cancer, made a plea to C. C. Painter of the newly-formed Indian Rights Association. Painter took the case directly to President Chester Arthur, who arranged for the appointment of Shirley C. Ward, son of Mission Indian Agent John S. Ward, as special attorney to represent the Soboba. The Indian Rights Association was obliged to pay Ward's salary and expenses when the Department of the Interior refused to do so.

There was much resentment among whites at Helen Hunt Jackson's "interference" on behalf of the Soboba. The *San Diego Union* (March 23, 1884) supported Byrne's right to evict the Indians as he "is the owner of the land, honestly bought and paid for." The *Union* complained that "It is hardly likely that this view of the case will meet the approval of Mrs. Helen Hunt Jackson, who seems to think that the Government ought to take private property for public use without compensation." Even the local office of the Indian Bureau seemed to take offense at Jackson's intrusion into what they considered their own domain. Mary Sheriff's salary was cut in half, presumably because she had helped Mrs. Jackson. Jackson was enraged when she learned this and promised to make up the difference with her own funds. She wrote an angry letter to Secretary of Interior Teller, who quickly restored Miss Sheriff's full salary.

Shirley Ward succeeded in placing an appeal of the San Diego Superior Court decision before the California Supreme Court. The required appeal deposit of $3,000 was paid by the Indian Rights Association after the Department of the Interior declined to supply any funds. The U.S. Attorney General wrote Ward that he should abandon the Soboba case and "allow execution [of the San Diego Superior Court ruling] to issue."

In the case of *Byrne v. Alas,* Ward argued that the Soboba had the right to remain on their lands based on the original Estudillo grant of 1842 and that the United States was bound by the Treaty of Guadalupe-Hidalgo, under which California became part of the United States, to honor the Spanish and Mexican land grants. He stated that the provision in the Estudillo grant guaranteeing Indian tenure should take precedent over their failure to present their claim to the Land Commission in the prescribed years of 1851 to 1852, and that the patent issued to Byrne in 1882 did not preclude the Soboba right of occupancy.

In a landmark decision rendered on January 31, 1888, the California Supreme Court determined that Byrne held fee-simple title to the land, but held it "subject to the right of the Indians to occupy the same so long as they will." The Soboba right of occupancy was based on the original Rancho San Jacinto Viejo land grant and their "continuous use and occupancy" of the land in question. "Congress did not intend the rights of Indians should be cut off by a failure on their part to present their claims before the Land Commissioners," wrote the justices.[27]

Unfortunately, the California Supreme Court decision in *Byrne v. Alas* was compromised a year later by a United States Supreme Court decision. In *Botiller v. Dominguez* (1889), the high court upheld the supremacy of claims confirmed by the Land Commission as opposed to claims based on provisions of the Treaty of Guadalupe Hidalgo. "The Court is bound to follow the statutory enactments of its own government," the majority decision affirmed.[28] Since Native Americans failed to present their land claims before the Land Commission in the prescribed years, they held no valid title to their lands, even if they could prove continuous use and occupancy going back hundreds of years. Although *Botiller v. Dominguez* was a separate case and did not directly apply to the Soboba, its ramifications affected the Indians for many years. It opened the way for more litigation on the part of Matthew Byrne. Byrne, and later his heirs, the legal owners of the Soboba lands in the eyes of the San Diego Superior court, continued to

A Soboba family, circa 1900. The Soboba were able to hold onto their lands, thanks to efforts by Helen Hunt Jackson and later the Indian Rights Association. Other Southern California Mission Indians were not so fortunate. — LAURA SWIFT

press for eviction and paid taxes on the property until 1902. In 1903 the State of California seized the Byrne property, including the Soboba lands he claimed, for non-payment of taxes. The California Legislature was persuaded to sell the Soboba part of the seized lands to the federal government for $775, the amount of taxes owed. The deed was recorded on September 11, 1911 and, at last, legal title was held in trust for the Soboba.

Even this action did not settle the land controversy and litigation continued as late as 1916, when the Citizens Water Company of San Jacinto unsuccessfully attempted to evict the Soboba and take over their water rights.[29]

The fact that the Soboba survived on their original lands is a tribute to their stubborn determination and the help of Helen Hunt Jackson along with the Indian Rights Association. Their triumph during a sad period when so many other native peoples of Southern California were evicted from their ancestral lands stands as a shining light in a field of darkness.

C. C. Painter and his Indian Rights Association continued to take an interest in the declining fortunes of the Mission Indians. White settlers continued to encroach on Indian lands and evictions were common. In 1887 the Association published a pamphlet entitled *The Present Condition of the Mission Indians of California* which complained about unjust removals and urged government action to protect the reservations.

Pressure from the Indian Rights Association and other reform groups ultimately brought Congressional action. On January 12, 1891 President Benjamin Harrison signed "An Act for the Relief of the Mission Indians." In accordance with the act, a three-man "Commission to the Mission Indians" was appointed and directed to study the problem and recommend changes or additions to the reservation system. Albert Smiley, C. C. Painter, and Joseph Moore were the three commissioners appointed. Because of the hard work and leadership of the first-named, it became known as the Smiley Commission.[30]

Albert Smiley of Redlands and his two fellow commissioners, both Easterners, traveled throughout Southern California investigating the plight of native peoples. They quickly came to understand the handicaps that made solutions to the Indian issue exceedingly difficult: the legal tangles of land claims, poorly conducted surveys, the knotty issue of water rights, indifference on the part of county, state, and federal governments, not to mention the outright hostility of many white settlers on Indian lands. Working their way through this morass of confusion and conflict, the Smiley Commission came up with a final report in December 1891. The commission recommended that between 30 and 33 separate reservations be given government patents, which would be held in trust for 25 years. After that period, the plan was to allot the land in fee simple to individual Indians, in keeping with the assimilation goal of the Dawes Act of 1887.

Among the Cahuilla, the Morongo and Aqua Caliente reservations posed major problems.

The 61,000-acre Agua Caliente Reservation, stretching from the Whitewater River to today's Palm Desert on the northeastern flank of the San Jacintos, was totally "checkerboarded" by the Southern Pacific Railroad. All the odd sections belonged to the S.P., while the even sections, minus some areas taken over by whites, were Indian. Besides this, whites had appropriated water rights to Palm Springs, Tahquitz Canyon, and even Andreas Canyon well within the Cahuilla lands. The Commission worked patiently with Charles Crocker, one of the Southern Pacific's "Big Four," and with some of the white landowners to negotiate some land exchanges and guarantee Indian water rights to Andreas Canyon and part of the flow of Tahquitz Canyon. The Agua Caliente Reservation was reduced to a "manageable" 4,500 acres of even sections with water rights.

The Morongo Reservation, on the north side of San Gorgonio Pass and home to both Serrano and Cahuilla, was equally checkerboarded. "We found the Indians the acknowledged holders of lands they did not want or work, and the whites insisted upon rights to lands that are absolutely essential to the Indians if a reservation is to be established there."[31] In simple terms, the whites had grabbed most of the cultivatable lands and water rights, while the Serrano and Cahuilla were left with mostly arid and unwatered terrain. The Commission did its best to reach a solution: the 88,000-acre reservation was reduced to 14,500 acres of arable land with water rights. The native people were finally able to scratch out a living in relative peace.

The Commissioners found the Cahuilla Reservation in Anza Valley, main home of the Mountain Cahuilla, the most stable of all the Mission Indian reservations and recommended that it "remain as is." The 250 Indians who lived there had a profitable stock raising enterprise, comfortable homes, and a school which was well attended. They were "independent" and "ambitious," and in much demand as outside workers. Many of the men were hired as farm workers, cowboys, and sheep-shearers.

Under the Act for the Relief of the Mission Indians, the Bureau of Indian Affairs set aside two small new reservations for the Mountain Cahuilla in 1891: the 560-acre Ramona Reservation on the northern edge of the Anza Valley close under Thomas Mountain, and the Santa Rosa Reservation of approximately 6,000 acres on the western and southwestern slopes of the Santa Rosa Mountains. Albert Smiley visited the latter and was impressed with the Santa Rosa captain, Ponce Leon, and the cattle grazing there.

Following the Act for the Relief of the Mission Indians and the Smiley Commission report of 1891, federal supervision of the Cahuilla economic, political, and social life became much closer. Reservation life resulted in the altering of many Cahuilla traditions. "These changes resulted from the belief of many non-Indians, and especially Indian agents, that Indian people should be assisted economically, but that Indian culture should be destroyed because it was the complete opposite of what they saw as 'civilization'," wrote anthropologist Lowell John Bean.[32] The Indian Bureau started with the children. Schools were set up on or near the reservations in which young Cahuilla were taught English and discouraged from speaking their own language. They were trained in agriculture, stock raising, and other mostly menial roles. The Government supplied animals and agricultural tools to encourage the Cahuilla to farm and raise livestock.

This "assimilation" goal – to remake Native Americans into productive replicas of white society – was never more evident than in a conference of Mission Indian superintendents held in Temecula in June 1910. Francis A. Swayne, agent for the Cahuilla Reservation in Anza Valley read a paper entitled "How to Secure Better Moral Living Among The Indians." Swayne called for Indians to be taught strict observance of law and adherance to Christian priples, and urged the abolishment of what he called "enemy songs and immoral and degrading chants," which he said were undermining the morals of too many Mission Indians. Amos R. Frank, Mesa Grande Reservation agent, called for the strict suppression of gambling on the reservations and claimed that Indians "feared the law more than they respected it." Soboba Reservation agent Will H. Stanley wanted to supplant Indian fiestas with agricultural fairs to encourage competition among the various reservations to produce the best grains, fruits, and livestock. This, he said, would be of "wonderful benefit to our Mission Indians." All agreed that the Government ban on alcohol use by the Indians would be rigorously enforced.[33]

Economically, the Cahuilla – particularly the Mountain Cahuilla – were better off. There was a growth of farm activity. Crops were planted and orchards cultivated. Livestock raising, both for sustenance and for cash sale, grew. The Cahuilla supplied an important labor pool for local agriculture, fruit ranching, cattle grazing, and, later, for road building.[34]

Culturally and politically, though, a great number of Cahuilla were unhappy under the close supervision of the Indian Bureau agents and resented the latters' attempts to undermine their traditions.

This frustration was reflected in the murder of Will H. Stanley, Indian Agent for the Soboba and Cahuilla reservations, in 1912.

Will Stanley was a teacher, then principal of the Soboba Indian School. In 1907 he was appointed Indian Agent for the Soboba Reservation. When Francis Swayne left the Cahuilla Reservation in 1911, Stanley took over as agent for that reservation, too. He was known as a highly competent, somewhat zealous leader in the struggle to mold Native Americans into competent, productive, morally strong members of society. "Much of the gain in sobriety, industry and morality, which the Soboba Indians are now exhibiting, is due to the competent and energetic work of Mr. Stanley, who was for years an efficient teacher in the day school, and has been their most capable superintendent or agent for the past three years," wrote Riverside County historian Elmer Holmes. "He has secured the agency building for the little town, persuaded the government to develop more water for irrigation and better water for domestic use, and to put in pumping plants. He has also been the most active force of all the agents in crushing out the illicit sale of liquor to the Indians in the villages under his care."[35]

Whereas Stanley was a hero to many whites, he was viewed with a good deal less enthusiasm by the Cahuilla. Many of them chafed under his close supervision and arbitrary manner, and deeply resented his efforts to change their culture. Open hostility was just below the surface.

On May 2, 1912, Will Stanley, accompanied by two Indian policemen, Celso Serrano and John Largo, journeyed from San Jacinto up to the Cahuilla Reservation to settle a dispute over property boundary lines and a proposed roadway. Meeting with Cahuilla leaders in the reservation schoolhouse, Stanley was besieged with a number of other complaints. There was a fear voiced that the government was planning to take away cattle and horses previously given to the Indians, and confiscate the newly-born colts and calves. Resentment flared over Stanley's edict prohibiting what the agent called "weird, unChristian" ceremonials and incantations for healing the sick. Stanley's rigorous policy against Indian liquor use was criticized. If whites could drink, why couldn't they? Underlying all these complaints was the steady encroachment of white settlers; a large section of Anza Valley adjacent to the Cahuilla Reservation had been opened to homesteading in 1909. Many of the older Cahuilla considered these lands belonged to them.

Indian policeman Will Pablo in Andreas Canyon, ca. 1914. Pablo (1859-1935), a Wanakik (Pass) Cahuilla born in Palm Springs, worked for the betterment of his people and was well respected by them. Some Indian lawmen were disliked as "white men's lackeys." Celso Serrano and John Largo, both policemen for the Cahuilla Reservation, were shot by resentful Cahuillas. Today, Indian lawmen represent their own people rather than the Indian Bureau.
— PALM SPRINGS HISTORICAL SOCIETY

The meeting degenerated into a shouting match and several Cahuilla leaders got up and abruptly left the schoolhouse. Stanley and his two Indian policemen went outside and ordered the recalcitrant Cahuilla to return, only to come face to face with a large crowd of angry people.

The exact sequence of what happened next is unclear. According to witnesses who testified later, several angry protesters jumped Indian policeman John Largo and wrestled away his gun. Francisco Lubo, one of the incensed Cahuilla, grabbed the gun and shot Celso Serrano, the other policeman. Then Ambrosio Apapas, leader of the protesting Cahuilla, took the gun from Lubo and fired again at Serrano, chased Stanley back into the schoolhouse where he let loose a fusillade of bullets at the Agent, school teacher Carl Stevens and agricultural advisor Henry Peterson. Will Stanley, mortally wounded with a bullet in the chest, gave the following account just before he died:

> As we came to the door Francisco Lubo shot at Selzo [sic] and Selzo pulled his gun and shot back. I was on the porch and held up my hands and said 'Don't shoot, boys.' Then Ambrosio Apapas shot at Selzo and staggered him. He recovered himself and as Francisco Lubo went to Selzo, Ambrosio Apapas came to me and Mr. Stevens. I held up my hands and told him not to shoot but he leveled the revolver at Mr. Stevens and myself, and we ran. We had no arms. I ran to the left and Mr. Stevens and Mr. Peterson, who was in the schoolhouse, ran toward the school dining room. He pointed his gun at me and I fell across a seat and he shot me. I fell and he took a shot at Mr. Peterson and Mr. Stevens as they went through the door. He ran on through and that was the last I saw of him.[36]

When it was over, Will Stanley lay dying. Celso Serrano was wounded with a bullet in his side. John Largo lay badly beaten by the angry mob. Teacher Carl Stevens was unnerved but intact, suffering only a surface wound where a bullet had grazed his cheek. Henry Peterson had a bullet in his coat.

Will Stanley was rushed down to Hemet and died early the next morning. The others all recovered.

The killing caused a sensation. Ambrosio Apapas and Francisco Lubo were arrested for the murder of Stanley and the attempted murder of Serrano and taken to the Riverside jail. U.S. Marshalls escorted the two accused Cahuilla to the United States District Court in Los Angeles, where they were arraigned for murder and attempted murder. A grand jury was appointed to investigate the shooting incident. Two months later, eight more Cahuilla were indicted as co-conspirators.

The trial was held in the United States District Court in Los Angeles in March 1913. Six of the ten Cahuilla defendants – Ambrosio Apapas, Francisco Lubo, Pio Lubo, Pablino Lubo, Cornello Lubo, and Leonicio Lugo – were found guilty of second degree murder and sentenced to ten years in the federal penitentiary at McNeils Island, Washington.

Francisco Lubo died in prison a year later. The others were paroled after serving four or five years. Ambrosio Apapas, Stanley's killer, was the last to be paroled in 1919.[37]

The bitterness lingered for many years. Many of the Cahuilla involved in the Will Stanley tragedy had strong feelings against some of their own people who worked for the Indian Bureau. Indian policeman John Largo was shot and killed during a confrontation with Francisco Lugo and Felix Tortes on the Cahuilla reservation on March 22, 1921. Several Indians who said they witnessed the killing testified in the ensuing trial that Largo pulled his gun first, so the defendants were acquitted.[38]

It is a simple matter to condemn certain Cahuilla for the killing of Will Stanley and John Largo and the attempted murder of Celso Serrano. The killing of any human being engaged in lawful pursuit is a tragedy. What is not so simple is to be fully aware of the fears and frustrations of a native people under close government supervision, their culture under attack, being encroached upon by white settlers.

The reins of federal control were loosened in the 1920s, and even more so in the '30s. The Indian Citizenship Act, passed by Congress in 1924, at last gave full citizenship to Native Americans. The California Indian Jurisdictional Act of 1928 set up a Court of Claims before which Indians could sue for compensation for lands illegally taken from them.

It was under Franklin D. Roosevelt's "New Deal" administration that most significant changes took place, and it was John Collier, the progressive commissioner of the reorganized Bureau of Indian Affairs from 1933 to 1945, who led the assault on the old federal ways of

The Soboba Festival, 1910. For many years this was an annual event, attended by people from all over the San Jacinto Valley. – RAMONA PAGEANT ASSOCIATION

dealing with the Indian. "The genius of John Collier... was that he saw the bankruptcy of federal Indian policy more clearly than anyone else in his generation. With its emphasis upon the allotment or division of Indian reservations into individually owned parcels of land and the forcible assimilation of Indians into white society, that policy had brought widespread poverty and demoralization to the majority of Indians."[39] As a result of Collier's initiative, Congress passed the Indian Reorganization Act of 1934, which authorized Native Americans to organize their own governmental bodies and form tribal corporations to conduct economic enterprises, provided a revolving loan program to stimulate tribal economic development and, most significantly, put an end to the Dawes Act and its policy of forced assimilation. Throughout his twelve-year administration, "Collier fought to realize a dream in which Indian tribal societies were rebuilt, Indian lands rehabilitated and enlarged, Indian governments reconstituted or created anew, and Indian culture not only preserved but actively promoted."[40] Although John Collier was not always successful in changing idea into reality, and Native Americans have mixed feelings about his administration, an important start was made. No longer would the white man so thoroughly control Indian life.

The Indian Reorganization Act was particularly significant for the Cahuilla. Tribal councils were organized to administer each reservation. The tribal councils, without the unwelcome interference of white Indian agents, determined their own social and cultural agenda. However, these were depression years, and the councils were not so successful in bettering the economic conditions of their people.

The Depression and World War II had strong effects on the Cahuilla. During the economically depressed 1930s, many Cahuilla employed outside the reservation lost their jobs and returned to reservation lands where

Cahuilla *kish*, Cahuilla Reservation, circa 1900. — MALKI MUSEUM

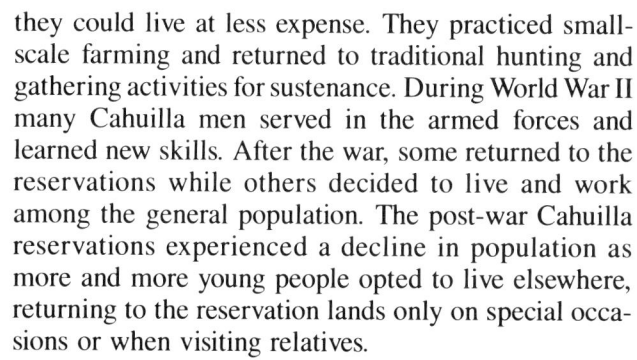

Soboba woman and two children, ca. 1910. — SAN JACINTO MUSEUM

they could live at less expense. They practiced small-scale farming and returned to traditional hunting and gathering activities for sustenance. During World War II many Cahuilla men served in the armed forces and learned new skills. After the war, some returned to the reservations while others decided to live and work among the general population. The post-war Cahuilla reservations experienced a decline in population as more and more young people opted to live elsewhere, returning to the reservation lands only on special occasions or when visiting relatives.

The post-war years saw a divergence in the economic fortunes of the various Cahuilla reservations. The Agua Caliente Band became the wealthiest Indian group in Southern California with their "Golden Checkerboard" of Palm Springs real estate. (Not all the Palm Springs Indians benefited; some still live in poverty.) The Morongo Reservation Indians improved their economic status with bingo and card parlors. Unfortunately, the Mountain Cahuilla were unable to share in the economic benefits of their desert Indian neighbors. A prolonged drought during the 1950s and early '60s curtailed agricultural activities that had expanded right after the war. The cattle business declined as grazing areas outside reservation lands were no longer available.

A significant piece of post-war legislation was Public Law 280, passed by Congress in 1955. Under its provisions, the federal government withdrew almost all of its jurisdiction over Native Americans. Each reservation now elects its own tribal council. The elected council represents the group and acts as a liaison between the reservation and the Bureau of Indian Affairs, other federal, state and county agencies, and private corporations. The tribal council also determines the use of tribally-owned assets and is especially active in providing for federal and state welfare and health care benefits, along with overseeing social and educational programs.[41]

Today, about twenty people reside on the Santa Rosa Reservation, and about thirty live on the Cahuilla Reservation. Total tribal membership for each is about seventy-five, scattered from San Diego to Los Angeles. Although most of the people live elsewhere, respect for their traditions and culture remains strong among younger as well as older Cahuilla.

In the words of distinguished anthropologist and Cahuilla scholar Sylvia Brakke Vane, "Four hundred and fifty years after the arrival of the first Spanish ships on its borders, native Californians take pride in their traditional culture and maintain their ethnic identity while adapting, as do other Californians, to the pressures of a rapidly changing world."[42]

The Cahuilla feel a deep affinity with their ancestral way of life as reflected in their traditions, their culture, their spiritual beliefs, and their craftsmanship — truly significant resources that can enrich the lives of not only Native Americans but all of us.

Pedro Chino, after whom Chino Canyon is named. He lived near the canyon mouth and was reported to be over 100 when he died in 1939. – PALM SPRINGS HISTORICAL SOCIETY

Hot sulphur spring in Chino Canyon, photographed by J. Smeaton Chase in 1915. – PALM SPRINGS HISTORICAL SOCIETY

NOTES

1. Lowell John Bean, *Mukat's People: The Cahuilla Indians of Southern California* (Berkeley, 1972), p. 76-77.
2. George H. Phillips, *Chiefs and Challengers: Indian Resistance and Cooperation in Southern California* (Berkeley, 1975), p. 2.
3. Marjorie Tisdale Wolcott, "The Lugos and Their Indian Ally: How Juan Antonio Aided in the Defense and Development of Rancho San Bernardino," *Touring Topics,* November 1929.
4. Phillips, p. 52. See also Gerald A. Smith, "Juan Antonio: Cahuilla Indian Chief, A Friend of the Whites," *SBCMA Quarterly,* Fall 1960.
5. John Walton Caughey (ed.), *The Indians of Southern California in 1852: The B. D. Wilson Report* (San Marino, 1952), p. 11.
6. There are many written accounts of the Garra uprising. The best is Phillips, p. 76-94.
7. Phillips, p. 92-94.
8. Horace Parker, *The Treaty of Temecula* (Balboa Island, 1967). See also Phillips, p. 119-123.
9. George William Beattie and Helen Pruitt Beattie, *Heritage of The Valley: San Bernardino's First Century* (Oakland, 1951), p. 235.
10. Caughey, p. 1-69.
11. Edward Dale, *The Indians of The Southwest: A Century of Development under The United States* (Norman, Okla., 1971), p. 39-40.
12. William S. McFreely, *Grant: A Biography* (New York, 1981), p. 305-318, discusses Grant's Indian policies.
13. Dale, p. 82.
14. Dale, p. 84-85.
15. Lowell John Bean and Harry Lawton, *The Cahuilla Indians of Southern California* (Banning, 1965), p. 3-4.
16. There are several accounts of the attempted eviction of the Sobobas. See Helen Hunt Jackson, *Report on the Condition and Needs of the Mission Indians* (Colorado Springs, 1883); Elmer Wallace Homes, *History of Riverside County, California* (Los Angeles, 1912), p. 242-244; Valerie Sherer Mathes, *Helen Hunt Jackson and Her Indian Reform Legacy* (Austin, Texas, 1990), p. 48-51, 57-58, 69-71, 87-88; Van H. Garner, *The Broken Ring: The Destruction of the California Indians* (Tucson, 1982), p. 75-81.
17. Mathes, p. 53.
18. Jackson, *Report...*, p. 17.
19. Mathes, p. 58-59, 78.
20. Jackson, *Report...*, p. 19.
21. "People Against Sam Temple," March 31, 1883, Justice Court of San Jacinto township, County of San Diego, State of California; San Diego Historical Society collection. The author is indebted to Phil Brigandi, curator of the Ramona Bowl Museum, Hemet, for this and other documents relating to the Juan Diego killing and the Ramona story.
22. Jackson, *Report...*, p. 18.
23. George Wharton James, *Through Ramona's Country* (Boston, 1909), p. 20.
24. Phil Brigandi to author, December 10, 1992.
25. Holmes, p. 243-244.
26. *Ibid.*, p. 244.
27. Byrne v. Alas et al, Cal. 628 (1888), cited in Donald G. Shananhan, Jr., "Compensation for the Loss of the Aboriginal Lands of the California Indians," *Southern California Quarterly,* Fall 1975.
28. Botiller v. Dominguez, U.S. 238 (1889), cited in Shanahan.
29. *Hemet News,* Nov. 3 and 17, 1916.

Cahuilla Mountain, in the heart of Cahuilla Indian country. Behind the ridge to the right is Juan Diego Flat.
— ROY MURPHY

30 Larry E. Burgess, "Commission to the Mission Indians, 1891," *SBCMA Quarterly,* Spring 1988.
31 *Ibid.,* p. 28.
32 Lowell John Bean, *The Cahuilla* (New York, 1989), p. 93.
33 *Riverside Daily Press,* May 30, 1910; *Hemet News,* June 10, 1910.
34 Florence C. Shipek, "History of Southern California Mission Indians," *Handbook of North American Indians, Vol. 8, California,* ed. by Robert F. Heizer (Washington, D.C., 1978), p. 610-611.
35 Holmes, p. 245.
36 *Hemet News,* May 10, 1912.
37 For details on the Will Stanley killing and subsequent trial, see Riverside Daily Press, May 2, 3, 6, 1912; Hemet News, May 10, 17, July 19, Sept. 20, Dec. 13, 1912, and Jan. 10, March 7, 14, 28, April 4, May 9, 1913; Los Angeles Times, Dec. 18, 1919. There have been more books written on the Cahuilla than any other Southern California native people, but none of them mention the Will Stanley killing. All of these books go into great detail on aboriginal sites and Cahuilla culture, but virtually ignore Cahuilla history since the 1860s.
38 *Hemet News,* March 25, April 1, Nov. 11, 1921.
39 Lawrence C. Kelly, "The Indian Reorganization Act: The Dream and the Reality," *Pacific Historical Review,* August 1975, p. 291.
40 *Ibid.,* p. 292.
41 Lowell J. Bean, "Indians of California: Diverse and Complex Peoples," *California History,* Fall 1992, p. 323.
42 Sylvia Brakke Vane, "California Indians, Historians, and Ethnographers," *Ibid.,* p. 341.

Nattie Costo of the Cahuilla Reservation in 1970, when she was 84 years old. She is holding a storage basket used by her grandmother for acorns, cactus fruit and nuts.
— DOROTHY COWPER

Strawberry Valley, circa 1890. The picture above shows a farm family, names unknown. Notice the cultivated field and farm house in the background. Below are deer hunters returning from the high country with their kill.
— BILL CLARK (above), LAURA SWIFT (below)

10

STRAWBERRY VALLEY, IDYLLWILD AND KEEN CAMP

Richard Garrett called Strawberry Valley a "Garden of Eden" when he first saw it in 1871. To him, it was a paradise on Earth. Down the middle of the valley rushed a sparkling stream, bordered with lush ferns and wild strawberry plants. Looming above was the most spectacular mountain scenery in Southern California: jagged ridges of white granite, dominated by the great citadels of Lily Rock and Tahquitz Peak. Most impressive of all was the magnificent forest of sugar and ponderosa pines, standing "straight as arrows, one hundred to one hundred eighty-five feet in height, with bark five to seven inches thick," as Garrett described them.[1]

Richard Garrett, who said he was from Santa Clara, California, is the earliest name associated with Strawberry Valley. In a letter to the *Los Angeles Star* (December 16, 1871), he mentioned that several families had taken up homestead grants in the valley, all of them happy to be living in this forest paradise.

Whether or not Richard Garrett was the first to build a home here is unknown. It has been written, many years later and with no documentation, that the first settlers arrived in 1865, and that a school house was built here as early as 1871.

An unnamed party of Riverside men, heading for San Jacinto Peak, passed through Strawberry Valley in 1874 and, in a letter published in the *San Diego Union* (September 17, 1874) gives us more information: "Two years ago a man named Garrett established himself here intending to erect a water power sawmill. He built a good log house, fenced some land, made a log wagon, and selected a site for his mill and race, but was taken suddenly sick while ascending the mountain and died of heart disease. He lies buried near where his house stood, his name and age on a bar of iron set at his grave and his wagon standing over it. His family soon left and the Indians afterwards burned his house."

Years later, a solitary tombstone was found near the Idyllwild golf course, at the lower end of Strawberry Valley, with the inscription "R. Garrett, 1872."[2]

Apparently Strawberry Valley in the early 1870s was a favorite place to graze sheep. The Riverside party wrote the *Union* (September 17, 1874) that "Messrs. Fryer and Fagan have kept about 3,000 sheep there all summer which are fat and in fine condition. Our party procured part of one, and it was as fine mutton as we ever tasted."

Joseph Crawford's Strawberry Valley Toll Road, which rose from Oak Cliff in the canyon of the San Jacinto River steeply up the mountainside via Chimney Flats and Alvin Meadow, was completed in 1876 (see *Mountain Roads*). Crawford's steep pathway brought in new settlers, timber cutters, and a few vacationists. Samuel Tripp, the judge in the *Ramona* story, lived here a short time, according to historian Lester Reed, and there were "three other families or houses in the area. Sulphur Springs Thompson, as he was later called, lived in the present Fern Valley. Some people by the name of Smith were in the valley. A family by the name of Shehan and Sam Temple, the man who killed Juan Diego, were there at times."[3] Angelo Domenigoni and his sons, a Swiss family living in the San Jacinto Valley, drove cattle up to pasture in Strawberry Valley in the 1880s, possibly earlier. Domenigoni Flat, where the Idyllwild School of Music and the Arts now stands, was homesteaded by Angelo in the early 1880s.

Anton Scherman came up as early as 1879, Amasa Saunders in 1880, both of them lumbermen. The days of patriarchal old-growth forest drew to a close as the timber cutters sawed down the great trees (see *Felling The Mountain Forest*). By 1890 Strawberry Valley had changed markedly in appearance. There were now long stretches of open land spotted with stumps, amid groves

Advertisement for George Hannahs' Camp Idylwilde that appeared in the *San Jacinto Register*, 1891. Hannahs probably deserves credit for first using the name *Idylwilde*.

The Henry House, owned by G. W. Henry, was located near Hannahs' Idylwilde Camp. It catered to visitors only one summer, 1891.

of uncut pines and cedars. A few tents of happy campers nestled under the canopy of the remaining forest and alongside the rushing creek.

1889 was apparently the year that Strawberry Valley really caught on with campers. The toll road was now free and people swarmed up by horse and buggy, particularly when the lowlands sweltered under the hot summer sun. Anton Scherman's Strawberry Valley Lumber Company began charging campers 50¢ per month, "which entitles them to the use of wood and water, and the amusements of the grounds," reported the *San Jacinto Register* (June 20, 1889). The amusements included "a comfortable hotel, a dance hall, several croquet sets, swings, etc."

The *San Jacinto Register* (June 27, 1889) stated that G. B. Hannahs was managing the hotel. George B. Hannahs and his wife Sarah had recently arrived in Strawberry Valley and erected a sawmill on upper Dutch Flat (see *Felling The Mountain Forest*). They apparently joined with a Mrs. M. Mitchell in building the single-story wooden structure they first called the Strawberry Valley Hotel. Mrs. Mitchell was apparently the major owner, for advertisements in the summer of 1890 named her as proprietor and called the resort the Mitchell House.

In the summer of 1890, George and Sarah Hannahs opened their own resort which they called Camp Idylwilde, first mentioned in the *San Jacinto Register* of July 27, 1890.

There have been several conflicting stories about the origin of the name Idyllwild, or Idylwilde as it was first spelled. Laura Rutledge, often given credit for suggesting the name, was not around at the time (She and her husband Charles did not appear in Strawberry Valley until 1901). David Prescott Barrows, an anthropologist who authored a pioneering study of the Cahuilla Indians, claimed that his father, Thomas Barrows, suggested the name in 1891. It seems most likely to these writers that the Hannahs deserve credit for the name; it was they who opened Camp Idylwilde in 1890.

The summer of 1890 saw upwards of 500 campers enjoying the delights of Strawberry Valley. Joining the Mitchell House and Camp Idylwilde that summer was John and Mary Keen's Keen House, located in the lower valley just east of Domenigoni Flat. The Keens owned the three-story Florida Hotel in Valle Vista. Mr. Keen apparently remained below to manage the Florida Hotel, while Mrs. Keen operated the mountain hostelry. The Keen House was described as "a long one-story structure, built for summer use only, comfortable and clean. Mrs. Keen is a born landlady, who makes her guests feel perfectly at home, and who is thoughtful for every comfort. The table is well supplied with good food, well cooked and nicely served."[4] G. D. Allen opened a general store nearby, carrying groceries, clothing, and sporting goods for campers and hunters.

A fourth Strawberry Valley resort opened in the summer of 1891 – G. W. Henry's Henry House, located in "Idylwilde Camp," adjacent to the Hannahs' Camp Idylwilde. The following year the Henry House was sold to Mrs. Mitchell, who in turn apparently sold the property to George Hannahs. The details of the transaction are unclear, but by August 1892 Idylwilde Camp, which apparently encompassed the original Idylwilde resort along with the Mitchell property, was listed in news-

Ho! For Strawberry Valley,

A Noted Health Resort in the Pine Forests of the San Jacinto Mountains.

The MITCHELL HOUSE

IS THE PLACE TO STOP.

THE BEST HOTEL.	THIRTY ROOMS.
BEST OF COOKS.	ELEVATION 6,000 FT.
GOOD SPRING BEDS.	TERMS REASONABLE.
QUANTITIES OF FRUIT AND MILK.	ASTHMA AND CONSUMPTION RELIEVED.
FIRST-CLASS TABLE.	DELIGHTFUL MOUNTAIN SCENERY.

Stage leaves San Jacinto Tuesdays, Thursdays and Saturdays at 6 o'clock a. m., and reaches the hotel in time for dinner.

A Cool Valley Among Pine Trees.

The above sentence describes "Strawberry Valley" exactly. It is located at an elevation of 6,000 feet among the pine forests and running brooks of San Jacinto Mountain. It is the coolest place in Southern California during the summer season. The best place known for pulmonary diseases. Lovers of sport find good hunting, etc. The place to take the latest novel and recuperate in a hammock under towering pines. The hotel to stop at is right in the center of the valley and is known as the "Mitchell House." Good rooms, good beds, appetizing table and the best of service guaranteed.

Mrs. M. Mitchell, jun16 **Proprietor.**

Mrs. M. Mitchell purchased the Henry House in 1892 and the resort became known as the Mitchell House. Mitchell in turn sold the tent hostelry to George Hannahs.

paper advertisements as under "G. B. Hannahs, Proprietor." Besides the hotel accommodations, George Hannahs and his wife Sarah supplied "excellent tents and portable cottages to let, all equipped with beds and clean, fresh bedding, easy chairs and the usual necessities of a sleeping room. He has a store well stocked with canned meats and fruits, fresh fruit, fresh meat, staple groceries, etc., for the convenience of those who camp and do their own cooking."[5] Mail was delivered by stage three times a week.

On March 3, 1893 George Hannahs was named postmaster of the first post office in Strawberry Valley. It was located in his general store in the lower valley, about where the road today crosses Strawberry Creek to ISOMATA. Hannahs named his store and post office *Rayneta,* in honor of his young son Raymond. In a short time the small community around the Hannahs store and post office became known as Rayneta. (George Hannahs was post master of Rayneta, then Idyllwild, at various times until his death in 1931. He was succeeded by his wife Sarah, who was postmistress of Idyllwild until 1937.)

Hannahs was so busy with his lumber business in San Jacinto and his sawmill on Dutch Flat that he was apparently unable to continue managing Idylwilde Camp. In 1895 he sold it to Mrs. Celia Stokes. Mrs. Stokes was a warm hostess and quickly expanded the social activities at her resort, as illustrated in the *San Jacinto Register* (July 25, 1895):

> Idylwilde Camp presented a pretty sight Saturday evening. The new pavilion was lighted by Chinese lanterns and a big bonfire, and all of the campers in the valley thronged to witness the dancing. Hemet, Florida and Webster's Canyon sent in a large delegation and probably two hundred people in

---

STRAWBERRY VALLEY HOTELS

Get Out OF : THE : HEAT!

. . . GO FOR A REST TO . . .

. . Strawberry Valley!

It is situated in the San Jacinto Mountains, only a day's journey from Los Angeles. After leaving the train at San Jacinto, you have only 16 miles of well-graded, picturesque mountain road to travel. A few weeks in these cool, pine-scented surroundings, in the pleasant company of other campers, will prove a healthful and enjoyable pastime. All pulmonary diseases relieved in the bracing air. Try this resort and be satisfied.

THE KEEN HOUSE.

When you arrive at this lovely valley among pine trees at an elevation of 6,900 feet . . .

Enquire for . . . .
. . THE KEEN HOUSE.

It has been successfully managed by Mrs. J. M. Keen for three years. You will find a first-class table and home comforts. It has never been consolidated with any other house with her consent. Terms reasonable. jun23

The Keen House, founded by John and Mary Keen in 1890, was located in lower Strawberry Valley across the creek from Domenigoni Flat.

all participated in, or looked on, at the ball. Good music was furnished by George Engel, violinist, and Will Tinker, organist, and as the floor was in an excellent condition from the plenty of wax, the young people found it a great hardship to stop their merrymaking at twelve o'clock.... At 11:00 a supper of good things was served in the Idylwilde dining-room by the hostess, Mrs. Celia Stokes. Everybody had an enjoyable time and pronounced the ball a grand success. Mr. and Mrs. Stokes added greatly to the enjoyment of the evening by arranging for the good music, refreshments, and the grand bonfire.

Newspapers that summer were full of accounts of social events at the several Strawberry Valley resorts: dances, musical recitals, croquet and tennis matches, candy pulls, and grand bonfires.

During the last two decades of the 19th century, Southern California became a Mecca for thousands suffering from tuberculosis, or "consumption" as it was then called. To accommodate these health seekers, tuberculosis sanitaria were built all over the southern counties, from Santa Barbara to San Diego, much as convalescent hospitals and senior citizen facilities have multiplied in recent years.[6]

Some physicians believed that the clean, cool air and sunshine of the Southern California mountains offered the best cure for consumptives. They prescribed several months of rest in places like Strawberry Valley. As early as 1889, health seekers began to visit the valley. The *San Jacinto Register* (June 23, 1892) reported:

> It has become pretty generally known that the cool, invigorating air of Strawberry Valley is the most beneficial known for diseases of the throat and lung. Physicians, for several years past, have recommmended their consumptive patients to summer in Strawberry. The altitude, 6,000 feet,... has been found to possess just the dry, healing qualities necessary to

The Keen House, ca. 1893. The early resort consisted of a main lodge and housekeeping cabins and tents. One of the attractions of Keen House was Mary Keen's cooking. –
— LAURA SWIFT

The stage from San Jacinto made daily trips up the old Crawford Road during the summer season.
— SAN JACINTO MUSEUM

worn-out lungs. Several hundred invalids sought out Strawberry last season and received untold benefits from the trip.

In the summer of 1899, two prominent Los Angeles physicians – Walter Lindley and F. T. Bicknell – vacationed in the San Jacinto Mountains. While camping in Strawberry Valley, both doctors came up with the idea that here would be a wonderful place for a tuberculosis sanatorium. They hurriedly took up options on some 2,000 acres in the upper part of the valley, then returned to Los Angeles and, with the backing of many prominent physicians, organized the California Health Resort Company. The Company incorporation was completed on April 21, 1900, with ninety stockholders and an initial capital investment of $250,000.[7] The *Riverside Press and Horticulturalist* (May 26, 1900) reported that "The plan is to put the Sanatorium on the upper end of the valley, at what is now Idlewilde."

Dr. Lindley made many trips into the mountains to oversee the construction of a spacious, two-story sanatorium, containing forty rooms. A number of cottages were erected on the grounds, as was a general store, a livery stable, a gymnasium, golf links and a tennis court.

The health resort was named the Idyllwild Sanatorium, probably because it was located on the grounds of George Hannahs' old Idylwilde Camp. It was ready for patients in June 1901, with Ralph A. Lowe as manager and Dr. H. G. McNeill as resident physician.

There is an often repeated story that Mrs. Laura Rutledge first suggested the name Idyllwild when the government decided to locate a post office there. The evidence to back up this story remains inconclusive. As previously mentioned, Idylwilde Camp dates back to 1890, well before the Rutledges appeared on the scene. Idyllwild, spelled the way it is today, first appeared in the *Hemet News* of June 7, 1901, along with the information that Charles Rutledge, hired as bookkeeper for the Sanatorium, had arrived with his family. Three weeks later the newspaper (June 28, 1901) reported that "the name of Rayneta post office will be changed to Idyllwild." There is no mention of who suggested the change. It is entirely possible that it might have been Laura Rutledge's idea, so the Rutledge story cannot be totally discounted. The Rutledge family remained in Idyllwild all summer. The *Hemet News* (September 20, 1901) mentioned that Charles Rutledge, now "resident secretary" of Idyllwild Sanatorium, his wife and daughter made a trip to San Jacinto Peak.[8]

With the growing popularity of Idyllwild as a health resort, it was only natural that valley entrepreneurs would offer stage service up the mountain. In May 1901, the San Jacinto-Idyllwild Transportation Company was incorporated by San Jacinto businessmen, Dr. Lindley of Idyllwild Sanatorium putting up half the capital. The new company reached an agreement with the Santa Fe Railroad for a reduced five dollar round trip fare from Los Angeles to Idyllwild via rail and stage. By June, San Jacinto hotels were filled with people enroute to Idyllwild.

When William Whittier, founder of Hemet and owner of much of the town, learned of this, he was furious. Whittier never did like San Jacinto, ostensibly because the *San Jacinto Register* had criticized his Hemet Land Company and Lake Hemet Water Company. In fact, he ordered his employees not to shop in the neighboring town.

Whittier hurried down from San Francisco and quickly organized the Hemet Livery Stage Company. He purchased horses and stage wagons, hired R. H. Stetson to run the operation, and began his own stage service to Idyllwild.

Whittier's intention was to run the San Jacinto-based rival stage line out of business. Determined – some say

The Keen House in 1898, with an extended line of buildings. Every time the Keens enlarged the resort they would tack on another structure. To the right are John and Mary Keen. This was the most popular resort in Strawberry Valley during the 1890s. — BUD CLARK

The Keen House, ca. 1895. Mary Keen is 2nd from left; Sarah Hannahs, 4th from left; Jane Saunders is on the right. — CHARLES VAN FLEET

Panoramic view of the Keen House and its cabins, ca. 1898. — NELL EMERSON ZIEGLER

Angelo Domenigoni and his family, Swiss immigrants, settled in Winchester in the San Jacinto Valley in the late 1870s. Angelo pastured his dairy cattle in lower Strawberry Valley as early as 1879 and filed on 160 acres there in 1880. Domenigoni Flats honors his name today.
— LAURA SWIFT

Domenigoni Flats, lower Strawberry Valley, ca. 1890.
— SAN JACINTO MUSEUM

ruthless — businessman that he was, this is just what he did. He persuaded the Santa Fe Railroad to offer his Hemet company reduced ticket fares. He offered reduced lodging and meal prices at his Hemet Hotel. He advertised his Idyllwild stage service all over Southern California. He wrote to P. N. Myers, manager of his Hemet enterprises, that "I would like to have the San Jacinto people pull out of the stage business." When he discovered the San Jacinto-Idyllwild Stage was taking a road that crossed his Fairview Ranch property, he erected a locked gate and forbade their trespassing. His knockout blow came when he persuaded Dr. Lindley to pull out of the San Jacinto company. In April 1902 Whittier reached an agreement with Lindley to form the Hemet-Idyllwild Stage Line. He had won, as he usually did in his long career as a businessman. He bought out the nearly bankrupt San Jacinto line, and moved their equipment, stages and horses to Hemet. Over the ensuing years, Hemet, not San Jacinto, was usually the valley base for Idyllwild-bound stages.[9]

For several summers, travelers on the Hemet-Idyllwild Stage were "treated" to a mock hold-up. As the stage reached Chimney Flat on the old road, masked bandits on horseback sped out of the forest, brandished pistols, and forced the wagon to a halt. Amid shreaks and squeals, visitors were relieved of their cash, jewelry or anything else that looked valuable. Of course, this was all part of the fun, and all the "loot" was returned to the guests when they reached the Idyllwild Inn.

Shortly after the turn of the century, automobiles began making the trip to Idyllwild. Credited with being the first was a Locomobile driven up from Hemet on August 11, 1900. Dr. Walter Lindley was the driver. He wrote in the *Southern Practitioner* (October 1900) that his Locomobile made the trip "rapidly and without hesitation," to be greeted in Strawberry Valley with "bonfires and cheers."

Although Strawberry Valley was crowded with summer visitors, the Idyllwild Sanatorium was a failure. The mile-high altitude was too high for invalids, and the

Gus Hemstreet's home in Fern Valley, near the upper end of Strawberry Valley, ca. 1892. Hemstreet and his wife were among the earliest known settlers in Fern Valley, arriving sometime in the 1880s. — SAN JACINTO MUSEUM

The Hard family camped in Strawberry Valley every summer during most of the 1890s. Many families came up to escape the lowland heat. — LAURA SWIFT

George B. Hannahs (1856-1931) has been called "The Father of Idyllwild." Michigan born, he arrived in Strawberry Valley to set up a sawmill on upper Dutch Flat in 1889. A year later he opened Idylwilde Camp, a summer resort. In 1893 he established a store and post office on Domenigoni Flat that he called Rayneta. For many years he was Idyllwild postmaster. – CHARLES VAN FLEET

The Hannahs' store and post office in lower Strawberry Valley. George Hannahs named it *Rayneta*, meaning "Little Ray," after their son. Here Little Ray sits on a burro, attended by his mother Sarah. – LAURA SWIFT

nights were too cold. The drive up over steep, winding, dusty roads limited its appeal to healthseekers. It was said that the Sanatorium hauled its guests "up in buckboards and down in boxes." Furthermore, healthy mountain vacationers failed to appreciate consumptives in their midst and stayed away from the big hotel. The California Health Resort Company steadily lost money.

In July 1903, after only two years administering to consumptives, Idyllwild Sanatorium closed its doors, was remodeled, and reopened as a resort hotel a month later. Its name was changed to the Strawberry Valley Hotel, "The Pleasure Seeker's Paradise," and all persons with lung disease were prohibited. Ralph A. Lowe remained as manager.

Fate was unkind to the big hotel. An early morning fire on April 20, 1904 completely destroyed it. The *Riverside Press and Horticulturalist* (April 22, 1904) described what happened:

> During a furious snowstorm Wednesday morning, Idyllwild, the famous mountain hotel in Strawberry Valley, was burned to the ground. The big hotel building, formerly used as a sanatorium, and one of the cottages were totally destroyed. Ten cottages, the store, bowling alley, electric plant and steam laundry were saved.
>
> The cause of the fire is not known, but it is supposed to have originated in a small room in which were kept a quantity of paints and oils....

> A blinding snowstorm was raging at the time, the wind blowing a gale and piling the snow in deep drifts. To this fact is due the escape of other buildings on the place from destruction....
>
> Within forty minutes of the time the fire was discovered not an upright piece remained of the big building.

The hotel had lasted only three years. The California Health Resort Company immediately announced plans for rebuilding their hotel on a smaller scale. A new single-story structure was completed in time for the 1905 summer season and named The Bungalow.

However, the doctors and other investors who owned the California Health Resort Company grew tired of the constant financial drain. In July 1906 they sold the resort and surrounding property to Frank R. Strong and George W. Dickinson, Los Angeles real estate investors. The new owners incorporated the property as the Idyllwild Mountain Resort Company. Dr. Lindley apparently retained some financial interest in the company; he served as general manager for several years.

Strong and Dickinson extensively renovated the Bungalow and erected more guest cottages. The resort was initially called "Idyllwild Among The Pines," but after a few years it became known simply as "Idyllwild."

Whittier's Hemet-Idyllwild Stage Line, managed by Frank Holloway, brought up guests almost every day during the summer season.

During the next few years, Idyllwild continued to grow not only as a summer resort but as an all-year community. Whereas there had been only ten or twelve private cabins in Strawberry Valley before 1910, by 1914 there were more than fifty. George Hannahs, who owned a thousand acres, subdivided part of his property into two and a half acre lots in 1913. He sold a dozen or so right away. The community of Idyllwild was taking shape.

Dr. Walter Lindley, Los Angeles physician, organized the California Health Resort Company, backed by many prominent physicians, in 1899. Dr. Lindley and his associates erected the two-story Idyllwild Sanatorium for tubercular patients in 1901.

The Idyllwild Sanatorium under construction, 1901.
— DAVID SCHERMAN

Angelo Domenigoni and his sons drove dairy cattle up to their property on Domenigoni Flat and opened the Idyllwild Creamery. They supplied fresh dairy products to the Idyllwild resort, cabin owners and campers.

Meanwhile, John and Mary Keen tried to compete with Idyllwild by enlarging their Keen House near Domenigoni Flat. In 1902 they bought the abandoned Corona Hotel in Kenworthy. They hired Charles Lockwood to disassemble it and haul the lumber over to Strawberry Valley. With Kenworthy lumber, they rebuilt Keen House.

But it was a losing struggle to compete against the nearby Idyllwild Inn. In 1905 Strong and Dickinson's Idyllwild Mountain Resort Company bought the land on which Keen House was located. John and Mary Keen then purchased 160 acres from the Hancock Johnston Ranch and moved their resort, lock, stock, and barrel, down to their new location, a mile east of today's Mountain Center. They built a new lodge and cabins and called it Keen Camp.

Keen Camp became as popular as the old Keen House had been, thanks largely to the gracious hospitality of John and Mary Keen. The relocated resort catered mostly to Hemet and San Jacinto residents coming up to escape the valley's summer heat. The Keen Camp Post Office opened on May 21, 1909, with Mary Keen as first postmaster.

In 1911, after two decades as gracious mountain hosts, the Keens sold their resort to Percy and Anita Walker and retired to Hemet. Mary Keen, 75 years of age, died in February 1917; John Keen, 87, passed away in December 1919.

Percy Walker drowned in Lake Hemet while trying to assist two fishermen whose boat had capsized. This 1912 tragedy placed upon Anita Walker's shoulders all the responsibility of managing Keen Camp. The *Hemet News* (May 9, 1913) stated that "It is creditable to her business acumen that Mrs. Walker met the call so capably." The same newspaper reported the progress made in enlarging the camp:

> "Besides the hotel building proper, eight or ten cottages have been built, and this year a number of log cabins and tent houses have been added. A large dancing pavilion affords entertainment for the young people, and a billiard room, bowling alley, tennis courts and saddle livery gives opportunity for a variety of healthful sports. Good fishing, hunting and trapping are found within a stone's throw. There is no opportunity for the energetic visitor to complain of monotony."

The Hollywood motion picture industry found in Keen Camp and the surrounding area an ideal spot to film movies. In 1914 Cecil B. DeMille and fifteen actors and actresses stayed at Keen Camp while filming scenes for "The Squaw Man." DeMille and the Laskey players also filmed "The Girl of The Golden West" there. DeMille told the *Hemet News* (November 13, 1914) that "Keen Camp is an ideal place for the production of western dramas and especially for 'The Girl of the Golden West,' as the setting is identical to that in which the story is layed."

A fire destroyed the main lodge at Keen Camp in September 1915, but a newer, bigger hotel, with a dining room capacity of 200 people and "the largest ball room in Riverside County," was ready for guests the following spring.

Idyllwild continued to be a magnet for visitors from all over Southern California. Guests from as far away as Santa Barbara, and even a few from the Midwest, signed their names in the hotel's great register. In 1913 C. J. Gilbert and Don Porter, both experienced hotelmen,

The Idyllwild Sanatorium was the first large structure built in Strawberry Valley. It lasted only two years as a medical facility for consumptives. In 1903 it was changed to the Strawberry Valley Hotel and opened to healthy visitors. The magnificent structure burned to the ground during a blizzard in April 1904.
— HENRY E. HUNTINGTON LIBRARY

The fireplace of the Idyllwild Sanatorium, 1901.

The Game and Reading Room of the Sanatorium.

Cottages at Strawberry Valley Hotel, ca. 1903.

The Idyllwild Sanatorium in winter, 1902.

131

The Hemet-Idyllwild Stage Line began daily journeys to the mountain resort in the summer of 1902. The jolting ride up the old Idyllwild Road took a half day. — CHARLES VAN FLEET

A brochure promoting the Idyllwild Sanatorium, 1901. Notice "San Gorgonio Mountains" instead of "San Jacinto Mountains," an error that started with the Pacific Railroad Survey in 1853 and was not put fully to rest until the turn of the century.

The Idyllwild Sanatorium was converted to the Strawberry Valley Hotel in 1903. Consumptives were no longer admitted. The impressive building burned in 1904.

CALIFORNIA'S ALPS
(WITH MAPS AND ILLUSTRATIONS)

THE IDYLLWILD SANATORIUM

(ALTITUDE 5250 FEET)

SAN GORGONIO MOUNTAINS
RIVERSIDE CO., CAL.

By NORMAN BRIDGE, M. D., Los Angeles
Emeritus Professor Medicine, Rush Medical College, University of Chicago

AND

WALTER LINDLEY, M. D., Los Angeles
Professor of Gynecology, Medical College of the University of Southern California
Ex-President of the California State Medical Society 1890

"The value of a hilltop to the fretted soul has been known from all time; there is peace at a great height, hope and strength in a broad panorama." — *Cleveland Moffit in the Century, September, 1901.*

STRAWBERRY VALLEY
"THE PLEASURE SEEKER'S PARADISE"

All Sanatorium features eliminated. No tuberculous people admitted. Idyllwild Hotel transformed into a modern pleasure resort under the new name of "The Strawberry Valley Hotel." Best of accommodations and cool, airy rooms.

Special Low Rates for August and September.

Strawberry Valley Resort and Hotel are one mile above the sea; have pure, cold, spring water and first-class table; afford amusements, delightful tramps and rides in the heart of the San Jacinto Mountains, and every comfort. Those who prefer tent life can rent a tent or take their meals at Strawberry Valley Lodge, or buy provisions at the store and "keep house." Take Santa Fe to Hemet and stage to Strawberry Valley. Complete information and booklet at 211 W. 4th St., or 1414 S. Hope St.
Or by addressing
R. A. LOWE, Mgr. Strawberry Valley Hotel, Idyllwild, Riverside Co., Cal.

A new single-story hotel was constructed on the site of the burned structure and opened for guests in the summer of 1905. It was first called "The Bungalow," but renamed The Idyllwild Inn a year later.

Stages arrive at the Idyllwild Inn, ca. 1906. The resort was purchased by Frank R. Strong and George W. Dickinson, Los Angeles real estate magnates, in 1906.

signed a ten-year lease with owners Strong and Dickinson. Gilbert and Porter renovated the Bungalow, now renamed the Idyllwild Inn, and added more cottages and tent houses to accommodate the increasing number of mountain visitors.

Gilbert and Porter's ten year lease lasted only four years. In November 1917 Strong and Dickinson, retaining 2600 acres for real estate speculation, sold the Idyllwild Inn and 1000 acres surrounding to four San Jacinto businessmen – Claudius Lee Emerson, his brother Albert S. Emerson, Jack Hopkins and L. A. Williams – for a consideration of $100,000. Idyllwild, Incorporated was organized, with Claudius Lee Emerson as president. The Emersons soon bought out Hopkins and Williams, and for twenty-one years Idyllwild Inn was an Emerson family operation, with Claudius Lee in charge.

Claudius Lee Emerson was born in Lodi, California in 1872. He came to San Jacinto in the 1890s and worked at various jobs before entering the banking business. He rose from bank clerk to cashier and finally to manager. In 1900 he married Zelma Schultz and from this union came five children – Marjorie, Nell, and a number of years later Alice, John and Lee.

The Emersons rented a cabin at Dominegoni Flat and spent their summer vacations, starting about 1911, in Strawberry Valley. Daughter Nell recalls those delightful summers in the mountains and particularly remembers the all-day trips by wagon to get there. The family would leave San Jacinto about four in the morning and ride up the canyon of the San Jacinto River to Oak Cliff, where they would rest their team before starting up the steep switchbacks. Then it was up the switchbacks, with the family singing much of the way, to cool, oak-shaded Halfway House. From there the grade eased as they rode through groves of oak and pine, passing Chimney Flat and Alvin Meadow. The children would often ask, "Dad, how much farther?" "It's a whoop and a hollar and a right smart git," he would reply.[10] Those summers in Strawberry Valley were so much fun, Nell remembered. This love of the mountains resulted in the Emersons' decision to buy Idyllwild Inn and the thousand acres adjacent to it in 1917.

Emerson set out to make Idyllwild one of the premier resorts in Southern California. The Inn was modernized and forty new tent cabins were built. The tennis courts were refurbished and a nine-hole golf course replaced the old golf links. Tennis and golf tournaments brought in top players from all over California. Emerson told the *Hemet News* (March 28, 1918) that he "will endeavor to impress upon the people of Southern California the beauty and desirability of the place as an all year around resort.... There will be no closed season at Idyllwild."

To build his "dream community," Emerson donated land to the Boy Scouts, religious groups, and to Riverside County for a public campground. The Riverside Boy Scouts' Camp Emerson opened in 1921. Idyllwild Public Campground, part of it on land given by Emerson, opened the same year. Emerson gave 35 acres to the Southern California Council of Religious Education for a summer leadership training camp in 1924. The Long Beach Boy Scouts' Camp Tahquitz, on land sold by Emerson at a greatly reduced price, opened in 1925. Thirteen acres were donated for the Idyllwild Pines religious school in 1928.

The real estate business in Idyllwild came into its own during the 1920s. Emerson's Idyllwild, Incorporated offered half-acre home sites "at prices far below values placed on similar properties in other mountains." For $350, the buyer would gain possession of a beautiful

Claudius Lee Emerson, his wife Zelda, and daughters Nell and Marjorie, ca. 1915. Emerson, a San Jacinto banker, purchased the Idyllwild Inn in 1917 and ran it as a family enterprise for 21 years. – NELL EMERSON ZIEGLER

The Hole-In-The-Tree was a popular photo spot for many years. The tree was located in lower Strawberry Valley, where the Idyllwild and Keen Camp roads forked. Here Marjorie and Nell Emerson pose, ca. 1912.
– NELL EMERSON ZIEGLER

wooded lot with running water supplied by a new pipeline. The *Idyllwild Breezes,* a weekly summer newspaper that ran from 1919 to 1929, reported in its September 7, 1920 issue: "One hundred and fourteen home sites have been sold in Idyllwild during the past two years. When the present management took hold of Idyllwild they dreamed of... a possible twenty-five for sale, but they never in their most hopeful mood expected to sell one hundred. But that mark has been passed and the demand is growing. Hardly a day passes now without a sale."

Strong and Dickinson, the other big land-holder in Strawberry Valley, began the development of their Fern Valley properties in 1923. Streets were laid out, a water system was put in, and lots were subdivided for summer homes in Fern Valley, about a mile above Idyllwild proper. Walter Wood – the first big name in Idyllwild real estate history – came up to manage Strong and Dickinson's Idyllwild Mountain Park Company, and sold lots under his own agency known as Fern Valley Estates. By the late 1920s, Wood was selling as many home sites as Emerson's Idyllwild, Incorporated. Walter Wood also took the lead in building the club house and golf course in Saunders Meadow as competition for Emerson's Idyllwild Golf Course in Strawberry Valley. In 1929 Wood sold eighteen acres to Christian Endeavor of Los Angeles for their Tahquitz Pines camp in east Fern Valley. Margaret Rentchler came up representing Christian Endeavor in the sale and stayed to become a real estate agent for Fern Valley Properties.

In 1924 a group of Long Beach businessmen bought 800 acres on the ridge northwest of Idyllwild from George Hannahs. They began subdividing what became the community of Pine Cove.

By the late 1920s Idyllwild, Fern Valley and Pine Cove had over 400 homes, ranging from simple wooden

The Emerson's Idyllwild Inn, ca. 1929. – NELL EMERSON ZIEGLER

Getting ready for a trail ride to San Jacinto Peak. The riders assemble in front of the Idyllwild Inn, ca. 1922. Domingo Costo, leader of the trail ride, is the big man with the wide-brimmed hat to the right.
– CHARLES WHISNAND

The Idyllwild swimming pool was just south of the Idyllwild Inn, seen in the background. Today, The Center of Idyllwild stands on the site. — NELL EMERSON ZIEGLER

The Idyllwild Inn tennis courts were the scene of tournaments featuring some of the best players in Southern California. — NELL EMERSON ZIEGLER

cottages to large stone-walled villas. Subdivision and the selling of home sites continued at a rapid pace. Idyllwild's first "Golden Age" was well underway.

Electricity came to Idyllwild in 1923, when the Southern Sierras Power Company put in a 32,000-volt line from the San Jacinto Valley and erected a power substation a block west of Idyllwild Inn.

The social center of Strawberry Valley remained the Idyllwild Inn. The Inn and its recreational facilities was a family endeavor, run by Claudius Lee Emerson and his wife Zelda, with strong support from the five Emerson children. Daughter Alice Emerson Nelson fondly remembered,

> From 1917 to 1938 the Inn and the Idyllwild resort community was a family-oriented enterprise. As we became old enough to enter into activities, we helped in various ways during the summer season. John and Lee worked in the grocery store or behind the desk at the Inn. Nell and I helped Domingo Costo wrangle dudes on the trail or, on occasion, waited tables in the dining room. Marjorie held forth in the coffee shop. Our parents didn't press us into service – we demanded our right to get in on the fun, and we loved every minute of it.
>
> The Inn was at that time the center of social life for all of Idyllwild – home owners and guests alike – and for valley people who came to enjoy the many activities. The large lobby with its big stone fireplace and spacious dance floor, was the scene of parties, home talent theatricals, musicals and masquerade balls....
>
> In summer we danced every night to the music of an orchestra made up of college boys, who doubled in the daytime as porters, coffee-shop workers, life guards and messenger boys.... We danced every night but Sunday. On Sunday night we sang hymns.
>
> It was all fun – at least for the children. The many parties, tennis tournaments, golf tournaments, breakfast rides, moonlight rides, over-night pack trips to San Jacinto Peak, bonfires, etc., were planned for Inn guests but open to all.[11]

The Idyllwild Inn and its surroundings were popular with Hollywood motion picture companies. At least twenty feature films were shot in Strawberry Valley during the 1920s. Cecil B. DeMille, Mary Pickford, Douglas Fairbanks, Charles Laughton and many other Hollywood luminaries were frequent guests at the Idyllwild Inn.

By 1913 the horseless carriage had replaced the horse and buggy in carrying guests up to Idyllwild and Keen Camp. Apparently Whittier, who now spent most of his time in San Francisco managing his enterprises there, no longer cared about running stages from Hemet to Idyllwild. In 1913 L. A. Williams and George Gray bought two 45 horsepower Overland touring cars and opened auto stage service from the Hotel Vosburg in San Jacinto to Idyllwild every day except Sunday. The round trip fare was $5.00. In 1914 and 1915 Max and Perry Green's San Bernardino Mountain Stage Line put two 22-passenger White trucks in service to carry visitors from Hemet to Idyllwild. In 1915 the Williams Brothers Auto Stage Line carried passengers from Hemet to Keen Camp for $3.00. In 1917 the Williams Brothers bought several 6-cylinder Studebaker touring cars for service from Hemet to both Idyllwild and Keen Camp. But the popularity of auto stage service to the mountain resorts declined after 1920, as more and more people drove their own automobiles up the mountain grade.

So much traffic was using the roads to Idyllwild and Keen Camp that Riverside County turned them into control roads in 1921. Autos assembled at the Oak Cliff control station were allowed up the road to Idyllwild every hour and a half; the next hour and a half down traffic used it. Autos went up the Keen Camp road on even hours, and down on odd hours. The controls were in effect until the early 1930s.

Keen Camp, although now overshadowed by Idyllwild, continued to be a summer resort favored by San Jacinto Valley people and movie makers. In 1919 Anita Walker married Robert Elliott, and the two managed the resort together. They renamed it Tahquitz Lodge and added more guest cabins and a swimming pool. The

Idyllwild Pines was founded as an inter-denominational religious training school in 1928. The land was donated by Emerson.

Tahquitz Pines was founded in 1929, when the Fern Valley land was purchased by the Christian Endeavor Union of Los Angeles.

The Riverside County Campground in Idyllwild opened in 1921. Part of the land was donated by Emerson.

Riverside Boy Scouts camped on Emerson property along Strawberry Creek as early as 1919. In 1921 Emerson donated the land to the Scouts, who in appreciation named it Camp Emerson.

Camp Tahquitz of the Long Beach Boy Scouts opened in 1925. The scout camp remained in Idyllwild until 1958, when it was moved to Barton Flats in the San Bernardino Mountains. — CHARLES MILLER

Emerson's Idyllwild Golf Course was in lower Strawberry Valley, just east of Domenigoni Flat.

Real estate agent Walter Wood of Fern Valley Properties built a golf club and course in Saunders Meadow in the late 1920s. The clubhouse pictured above later became the site of Elliott's Desert Sun School.

The auto stage from Hemet reaches Idyllwild Inn, 1927.

These housekeeping tents were a block south of Idyllwild Inn, where Walcott's shopping center is today. — NELL EMERSON ZIEGLER

Claudius Lee and Zelda Emerson on their fiftieth wedding anniversary, 1951. To the left is Claudius' sister, Mary Elizabeth Warner. The Emersons and their children were the beloved hosts of Idyllwild Inn from 1917 to 1938.
— NELL EMERSON ZIEGLER

The Idyllwild Store and Post Office, ca. 1926. The building burned in 1941 and was replaced by the present market. Elmer Horsley was long the proprietor.

Elliotts sold Tahquitz Lodge to S. F. Champion and a group of Los Angeles businessmen in 1924. The new owners turned the resort into a private membership club, freezing out the general public. This proved to be a mistake. The syndicate, headed by Robert Reed, was unable to make mortgage payments and the case ended up in court. Litigation dragged on until 1930, when judgement was rendered in Robert Elliott's favor.[11] (Anita Elliott had died in 1928.) Robert Elliott and Alyce Walker, Anita's daughter by her first marriage, reopened Tahquitz Lodge, but business was never again as good as it was in earlier years, thanks largely to the depression.

The depression years affected Idyllwild, too, but did not keep people away. Youth groups and religious organizations continued to make Idyllwild a summer home away from home. Hundreds of Boy Scouts and a few Girl Scouts enjoyed a week or two at Camp Emerson and Camp Tahquitz. Idyllwild Pines, an interdenominational religious training school, saw new prospective ministers and counselors arrive every two weeks. Tahquitz Pines, bought by the Christian Endeavor Union of Los Angeles in 1929, opened in 1935. Riverside Junior College ran a summer school in Idyllwild, starting in 1932.

New businesses and resorts sprang up. Ernest Benjamin Gray opened his photo and gift shop in 1930. Mr. and Mrs. J. C. Peniwell started Peniwell Camp in 1931. John and Clara Postle opened their Fern Valley Cafe, complete with dining room, store and cabins, in 1934. They raised some eyebrows when they applied for and received a liquor license, much to the disapproval of religious and youth groups. Elmer Horsley took over management of the Idyllwild store and market in 1937. Anna Poates was the popular hostess at Rustic Tavern, starting in the mid-1930s.

Idyllwild Inn remained the central magnet of the mountain community, but business fell off during the

Full electric power came to Idyllwild when the Southern Sierras Power Company station was built behind the Idyllwild Store in 1923. Previously, electricity was supplied by a generator attached to an old steam boiler at Emerson's sawmill. The generator was turned off every night at 10. — NELL EMERSON ZIEGLER

Pine Cove was founded by Long Beach businessmen in 1924. Shown here is Summit Camp, ca. 1932.

Idyllwild was the location for many Hollywood movies during the 1920s and '30s. Stars who stayed at the Idyllwild Inn during filming included Mary Pickford (left), Katherine Hepburn (center), and Paulette Goddard (right). — BOB AND VIRGINIA GRAY

depression years of the 1930s. Emerson had overextended himself when he bought 450 acres around Domenigoni Flat and made plans to build a dam and form a lake there. When his Idyllwild Lake plan fell through, combined with declining business at Idyllwild Inn, Emerson's Idyllwild, Inc. was forced into receivership. Gregory Esgate was appointed to manage Idyllwild Inn in 1936. Claudius Lee and Zelma Emerson, so beloved for their charm and generosity, lost all their Idyllwild holdings and were obliged to leave the mountain community in 1938.

On May 1, 1938, the Idyllwild, Inc. receivers leased Idyllwild Inn and all of its resort facilities to Ruth Curry Burns. Ruth was the widow of Foster Curry of the Yosemite Curry family. After Foster's death she had married Hollywood actor Edmund Burns. Together the two had managed Camp Baldy in the San Gabriel Mountains until its demise in the great flood of March 1938.

Ruth Curry Burns applied to the State Board of Equalization for a permit to sell liquor at Idyllwild Inn. She wanted to open a cocktail bar at the resort, as she had at Camp Baldy.

Mrs. Burns' request for a liquor license ignited a storm of protest among religious leaders and organizations that considered Idyllwild a spiritual and youth haven. Hundreds of letters and telegrams were sent to the State Board of Equalization asking that no liquor license be granted. In response to this storm of protest, the State Board turned down Mrs. Burns' application. Ruth Curry Burns angrily criticized the religious groups, stating that every popular resort in the state served alcoholic drinks, and Idyllwild was behind the times.[13]

Despite the liquor controversy, Ruth and Edmund Burn considerably "livened up" the Idyllwild resort for the summer 1938 season. They instituted a two-week "Forty-Niner Days" celebration, with all kinds of entertainment. Lee Miller and his orchestra, Walter Bean and his hill-billy band, Hollywood singer Len Karpel and dancer Snooky Bishop played to overflow crowds. Chief Sky Eagle, his wife Light Feather and daughter Sunbeam ran an Indian Trading Post and put on a tribal dance to the delight of guests. The Forty-Niner Parade ended the two weeks of festivities.

But the denial of a liquor license continued to grate on Ruth and Edmund Burns. They abruptly gave up the lease in September 1938 and returned to Camp Baldy to rebuild the resort there. Ruth Curry Burns simply could not – or would not – be associated with a resort that couldn't serve alcoholic beverages. The most lively summer in Idyllwild's history ended with a whimper.

With the Burnses gone, Idyllwild, Inc. leased the resort to Gregory Esgate, who had managed Idyllwild Inn for several years previously. Esgate announced that he hoped to regain the "homey atmosphere" of earlier days.[14] Liquor was not compatible with his vision of the ideal family vacation spot.

Other resorts and businesses opened in the Idyllwild area in the late 1930s and early '40s. Mrs. Harry Libby's Westhaven, with guest cabins and a general store, opened at Pine Cove in 1939. In 1940, Stacy's Lodge opened in Fern Valley.

In 1939 Rollin Humber, a real estate manager for Strong and Dickinson in Los Angeles, was sent to Idyllwild to manage the concern's Idyllwild Mountain Park Company office in Fern Valley. He met Margaret Rentchler, who had been at the company's Fern Valley office since 1929, and the two were married in the fall of 1939.[15]

Under Rollin and Margaret Humber, exclusive agents for the Idyllwild Mountain Park Company, Fern Valley

John and Clara Postle's Fern Valley Lodge opened in 1934. It featured a cafe, store, and cabins. Somehow the Postles were able to obtain a liquor license and were first to serve alcoholic beverages legally in Idyllwild.

Ruth Curry Burns leased the Idyllwild Inn from Idyllwild, Inc. in 1938. Her efforts to obtain a liquor license were thwarted by religious and youth group leaders, who wanted Idyllwild to remain a "dry" community. Burns left in a huff at the end of the summer session and returned to Camp Baldy. Here she serves a drink to a friendly burro.

began its remarkable growth from a small adjunct of Idyllwild into a major residential and commercial section of the mountain community.

In Idyllwild proper, Jerry Johnson was the principal agent selling residential and commercial properties. Bob Appleton was handling real estate sales in Pine Cove.

Although most of this development fostered by Johnson, the Humbers, and Appleton had to await the post-World War II years, the pattern was set for Idyllwild's second "Golden Age."

Idyllwild was lively during the war years, catering to servicemen and their families. Officers of General Patton's army, training in the desert, rented houses in the mountain community for their wives and children. On weekends, Patton's men journeyed to Idyllwild in jeeps, trucks, and command cars (for higher officers) to be with their families and enjoy the hospitality of the village. Many private owners opened their homes to the servicemen, and Saturday night dinner dances at the Idyllwild Inn were very popular. Joining Patton's soldiers on weekends were soldiers from Camp Haan near Riverside and airmen from March Air Field and Ryan Air Field in Hemet. On many weekends, Idyllwild resembled a joyful military camp.[16]

Despite the army presence, Idyllwild, Inc. was again forced into receivership and was taken over by bondholders. In 1944, all of Idyllwild, Inc. properties were purchased by Dr. Paul D. Foster, Los Angeles physician. Foster also bought the Fern Valley Cafe from John and Clara Postle and the Rustic Tavern from Mrs. Anna Poates, and 400 homesites that had not been sold. Foster appointed Bud Funk manager of Idyllwild Inn.

Fire took its toll. In January 1941 Horsley's Idyllwild Store burned to the ground. Jerry Johnson rebuilt the market and leased it to Horsley and Clarence Bosworth. Idyllwild reached a low point on May 4, 1945, when the 40-year old Idyllwild Inn was completely destroyed by

The present Idyllwild Market was built in 1941 to replace one that burned. Elmer Horsley and Clarence Bosworth managed the market when this picture was taken in 1945.
— DAVID WENDELKEN

Margaret and Rollin Humber managed Strong and Dickinson's Idyllwild Mountain Park Company office in Fern Valley. Under their leadership Fern Valley began its spectacular growth. They are pictured here shortly after their marriage in 1939. — MARGARET HUMBER

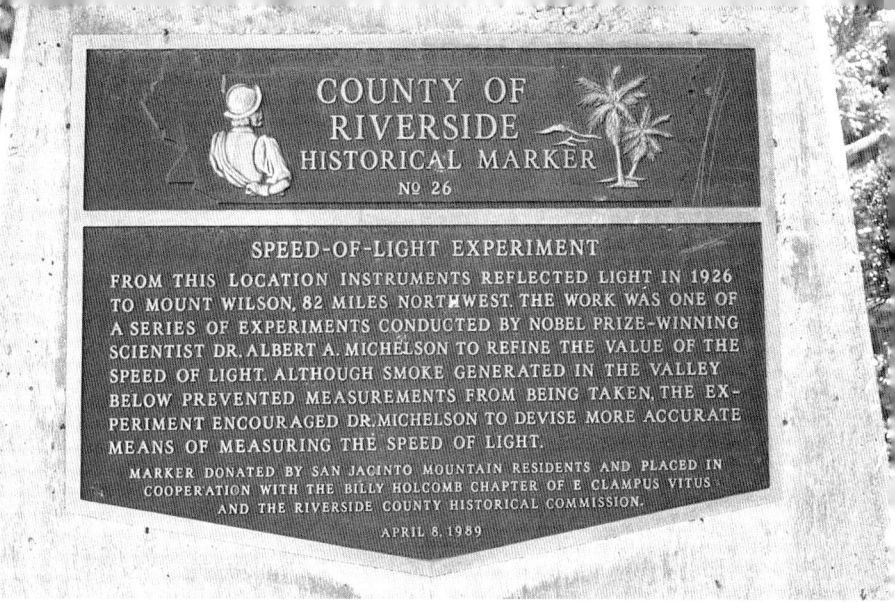

Dr. Albert Michelson conducted speed of light experiments from a ridge above Pine Cove in 1926. The pillar on the left supported a mirror that reflected a light beam from Mt. Wilson, 82 miles away. The historical marker was placed at the site in 1989.

fire.

While Idyllwild catered to servicemen during the war, Keen Camp died. Alyce Walker Murphy was unable to pay the mortgage on Tahquitz Lodge, and the bank foreclosed on the resort in 1942. Just as final arrangements to sell the lodge and cabins were being made, a devastating fire struck. Tahquitz Lodge and several cabins, including the Murphy home, were destroyed in the 1943 blaze. In 1944 the property of old Keen Camp was sold to the Pasadena Young Women's Christian Association. The Y.W.C.A. renamed the resort Tahquitz Meadows and planned to build a summer women's camp after the war.

Better times lay ahead. With war's end, Idyllwild began a period of spectacular growth, a story that will be told in an ensuing chapter.

Idyllwild Inn burned to the ground on May 4, 1945, ending forty years of continuous operation. A new Idyllwild Inn was erected the following year.

NOTES

1. *Los Angeles Star,* December 16, 1871. Richard Garrett, who came to Strawberry Valley sometime before that, sent a series of letters to the newspaper. See also *Star,* February 16, 1872.
2. John Raymond Gabbert, *History of Riverside City and County* (Riverside, 1935), p. 250.
3. Lester Reed, *Old-Timers of Southeastern California* (Redlands, 1967), p. 97.
4. *Riverside Press and Horticulturalist,* July 22, 1893.
5. *San Jacinto Register,* September 15, 1892.
6. John E. Bauer, *The Health Seekers of Southern California, 1870-1900* (San Marino, 1959) covers the whole phenomena of the sanatorium craze.
7. Norman Bridge, M.D. and Walter Lindley, M.D., *The Idyllwild Sanatorium, San Gorgonio* [sic] *Mountains* (Los Angeles, 1901), p. 4. See also Bauer, p 85-86.
8. The Laura Rutledge naming of Idyllwild story is traced back to her obituary in the *Hemet News,* May 14, 1937. Gunther, p. 247, states that the post office name change came on September 26, 1901.
9. Mary E. Whitney, *Fortune Favors The Brave: History of the Lake Hemet Water Company* (San Jacinto, 1982) tells the story of the stage battle waged by Whittier, p. 74-76.
10. Nell Emerson Ziegler interview, Hemet, April 7, 1992.
11. Alice Emerson Nelson, "Memories of Idyllwild, 1917 to 1938," in *Friendliest Valley: Memories of the Hemet-San Jacinto Area,* ed. by Violet Tapper and Nellie Lolmaugh (Hemet, 1975), p. 92-93, 96-97.
12. *Hemet News,* February 15 and 29, 1924, March 28, 1930.
13. *Hemet News,* April 29, June 17 and 24, July 1 and 8, 1938.
14. *Hemet News,* September 16, 1938.
15. Margaret Humber interview, Hemet, April 9, 1992.
16. Mary Sigworth and Virginia Gray interviews, Idyllwild, May 1992.

John and Mary Keen moved their resort from Strawberry Valley down to a meadow a mile east of today's Mountain Center in 1905. They operated Keen Camp until 1911, when they sold the resort to Percy and Anita Walker. After Percy Walker drowned in Lake Hemet, Anita married Robert Elliott in 1919 and built Tahquitz Lodge, the main attraction of Keen Camp. The Lodge was a popular hostelry until its demise by fire in 1943. On the left is Tahquitz Lodge, ca. 1925; to the right is Keen Camp Store.

The dining room and porch of Tahquitz Lodge, Keen Camp, ca. 1930.

Keen Camp School, ca. 1924.

Cattle grazing in the meadow near Keen Camp.

Harry Wendelken (1896-1951) was Idyllwild's first professional photographer. He came to the mountain community in 1921 and was employed at Emerson's lumber mill. Later he worked as an electrician, stone mason, carpenter, and general roustabout. He was Idyllwild's postmaster from 1934 until about 1949. Wendelken's main interest was photography and he chronicled Idyllwild's growth on film for thirty years. He produced hundreds of post cards, which he sold at the Idyllwild Inn and at other shops around town.
— SANDRA SMITH

The Idyllwild post office during the 1930s and '40s was located in the center of town, across North Circle Drive from the Idyllwild Inn. The old post office building today is occupied by the Idyllwild Beauty Shop and Candy Cupboard. — SANDRA SMITH

Idyllwild Inn after a winter storm, ca. 1940

Lou Crane's ranch, built in the 1890's, occupied the Keen Camp site until John and Mary Keen bought it in 1905
— LAURA SWIFT

Fred Alvin sitting in front of his home on the old Idyllwild Control Road, ca. 1912. Alvin Meadow honors his name today. — NELL EMERSON ZIEGLER

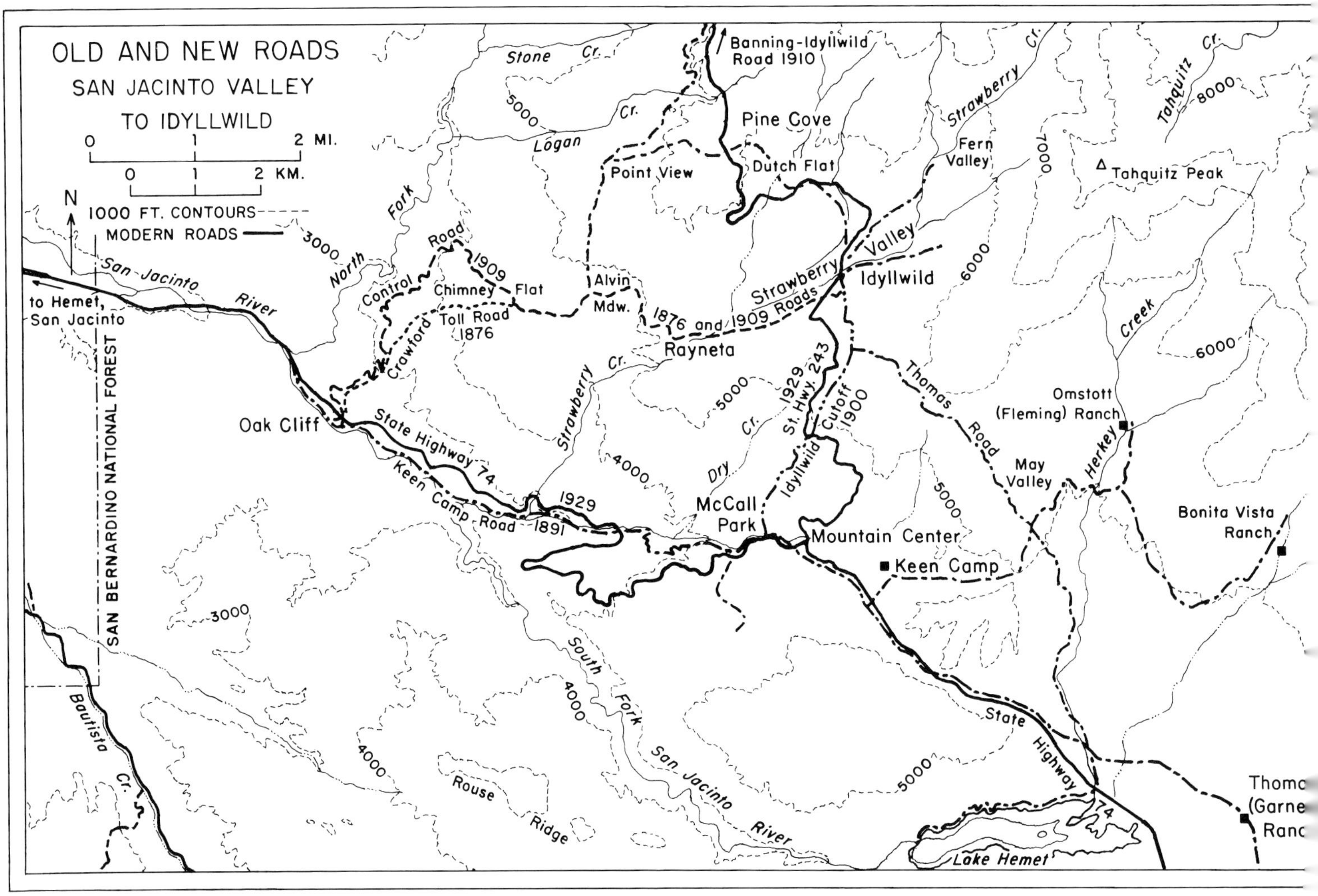
OLD AND NEW ROADS
SAN JACINTO VALLEY
TO IDYLLWILD
0 1 2 MI.
0 1 2 KM.
N
1000 FT. CONTOURS
MODERN ROADS
Stone Cr.
Banning-Idyllwild Road 1910
Pine Cove
Strawberry Cr.
Tahquitz Cr.
8000
5000
Cr.
Logan
Point View
Dutch Flat
Fern Valley
7000
Tahquitz Peak
North Fork
3000
Road
1909
Control
Chimney Flat
Alvin Mdw.
Valley
Strawberry
Idyllwild
6000
San Jacinto River
to Hemet, San Jacinto
Crawford Toll Road 1876
1876 and 1909 Roads
Rayneta
Creek
6000
Strawberry Cr.
1929 St. Hwy. 243
Cutoff 1900
Thomas Road
5000
Omstott (Fleming) Ranch
Oak Cliff
State Highway 74
Dry Cr.
Idyllwild
May Valley
Herkey
Keen Camp Road 1891
4000
1929
McCall Park
5000
Bonita Vista Ranch
Mountain Center
Keen Camp
SAN BERNARDINO NATIONAL FOREST
3000
South Fork
4000
State Highway 74
Bautista Cr.
4000
Rouse Ridge
San Jacinto River
5000
Lake Hemet
Thoma
(Garne
Ranc

11

MOUNTAIN ROADS

Visitors to the San Jacintos before the 1870s were obliged to use a network of foot and horse trails to climb into the mountains. Ancient Indian footpaths went up many of the canyons and criss-crossed the ridges. As early as 1860, possibly earlier, prospectors forged crude pathways into the range. Charles Thomas was said to have followed a miners' trail when he first visited Hemet (Garner) Valley in 1861. The *Los Angeles Star* of July 6, 1870 mentions a good trail and even a road leading to a mystery mine somewhere in the San Jacintos: "Charlie Clusker struck upon a well-defined trail leading into the mountains, which he followed, and soon came upon a road, well graded and built of large stones, evidently with care, which following, brought him to the Old Jesuit Mine." The location of this road is unknown.

It was the need for railroad ties that led to the building of the first known wagon road into the San Jacintos. Colonel Milton Sanders Hall, given a contract to supply wood for the Southern Pacific as it constructed its rail line through San Gorgonio Pass in 1875, hired E. Y. Buchanan to hew a roadway up to the timber stands in the upper reaches of Indian Creek (see *Felling The Mountain Forest*). Hall's San Jacinto Wagon Road, or Hall's Grade as it became known, would have delighted today's ORV enthusiasts . It zigzagged steeply up the lower mountainside from Hall City, near today's Cabezon, up to Hurley Flat. Some grades were in excess of twenty percent. From Hurley Flat it climbed south, then southwest to meet the present Banning-Idyllwild Road near Vista Grande, essentially following today's Hurley Flat Road. How Hall's Grade reached the present Lake Fulmor, site of the sawmill, in unclear; indications are that it followed close to the route of today's highway.

The road was a terror for teamsters from the start. Many a lumber wagon careened down the grade to shattered oblivion. Men and horses were killed in terrible accidents. Hall charged a toll to use his road, but few used it. After the Colonel went bankrupt, the roadway was practically abandoned. At least San Diego County thought so when they declared the road abandoned and made it a free public road in 1879. Peter Shane, who lived near Vista Grade into this century, was named roadmaster. The County's 1879 resolution referred to the terminal of the road as "Little Strawberry Valley," a name that failed to hold.[1] It is Lake Fulmor today.

At the same time Hall's Grade was in operation, another steep roadway was carved up the west slope of the mountains from the San Jacinto plains to Strawberry Valley, today's Idyllwild. This was Joseph Crawford's toll road, built in 1875-76. Crawford, born in New York in 1832, later a resident of Wisconsin and a Union Army veteran, moved to the San Jacinto Valley in 1875. He acquired 240 acres of farm land near Valle Vista, at the extreme east end of the valley, and built a home at Oak Cliff, along the San Jacinto River just inside the mountains. Crawford took notice of the many horseback parties enroute to Strawberry Valley. As an entrepreneur, he decided it would be profitable to build a toll road up to the popular mountain basin. He formed a consortium with Will Webster and two other men named Sayward and Radisell and applied for a franchise from the San Diego County Board of Supervisors.

In September 1875 Crawford and his partners were awarded a 50-year franchise to build and operate a toll road from San Jacinto River Canyon to Strawberry Valley. They set to work at once and, with the help of Indian laborers, had the road finished and open for business by May 1876. The cost was about $3,000. A toll gate, operated by Crawford himself, was set up at Oak Cliff where the road left the canyon and started up the mountainside. Wagons were charged 75¢, horseback riders 10¢ (later raised to 25¢). Crawford apparently bought out his partners; their names were no longer mentioned after the road was completed.

A small wayside community grew at Oak Cliff, also known as Toll Gate, with the toll house, cabins, stable, corral, and a camping area. Vacationers bound for Strawberry Valley often spent the night there to get an early morning start up the toll road.

The remains of Hall's Grade can be seen zigzagging up the mountainside south of Cabezon. The steep roadway was built by Colonel Milton Sanders Hall in 1875. Its purpose was to bring lumber down from Hall's Camp, near today's Lake Fulmor, to the Southern Pacific Railroad then being constructed through San Gorgonio Pass.

Crawford's roadway was known as a "no nonsense" road; it didn't waste any time or extra distance getting to Strawberry Valley. From Oak Cliff, it zigzagged steeply – some grades were said to be as high as 30% – up the ridge just east of the San Jacinto River's North Fork to Halfway Spring, a popular rest stop. From the spring, the grade eased as the road turned east, skirting Chimney Flat and Alvin Meadow, before rounding the slope into lower Strawberry Valley.

W. H. Marquis made the trip in 1877 and many years later wrote about his experiences:

> We started on the afternoon of June 4, 1877. We had a good team of farm horses with a medium-sized wagon in which we placed a tent, provisions, and a few cooking utensils. A saddle horse was led for use in the mountains....
>
> ...we proceeded only as far as the foot of the San Jacinto mountain grade [Oak Cliff] so the team would be fresh for the hard pull in the morning.
>
> We had been talking about the grade and wondering if we were likely to have any trouble making the ascent.... Accosting a man working along a ditch by the roadside, we asked if the grade was steep. He replied, 'Steep? Why, it's so steep that in some places it leans over.' And there was talk about pitches that were seven feet to the rod. This was not at all reassuring, but we had confidence in the ability of the team to make it.
>
> A hasty breakfast eaten by the light of the campfire, the team well rested and fed, the toll paid..., we started. Patterson drove, walking part of the time. Johnson and I walked at the rear of the wagon and it was our business to see that the 'chuckblock,' wedge-shaped, was chucked under the hind wheel whenever the team stopped to rest, even when the brakes were set. Five and a half hours were consumed in making the two and a quarter miles of the steep part of the grade. At length we reached the edge of the virgin forest, where we stopped for lunch...
>
> In the afternoon we drove slowly up into beautiful, peaceful Strawberry Valley. The primeval forest, groves of symmetrical fir trees, clusters of shapely cedars, oaks black and yellow, and great sugar pines, their dropping branches hanging full of long, slender cones, had not then been marred by the destructive hand of man."[2]

With a wagon road through to Strawberry Valley, lumbermen like Amasa Saunders and Anton Scherman were able to haul their cut lumber down the grade to San Jacinto. Scherman objected to paying the toll, which – with his wagons constantly going up and down the road – ate up a good portion of his profits. There are stories that some of Scherman's teamsters, the likes of ornery Sam Temple and Frank Wellman, broke through the toll gate without paying. Scherman petitioned the San Diego County Board of Supervisors to cancel, or buy out, Crawford's 50-year franchise and make the road a free public thoroughfare. In 1888, San Diego County declared Crawford's road "most unsuitable and totally unfit for a toll road" and cancelled his franchise.[3] Although the County made some improvements, this first wagon road to Strawberry Valley remained a steep and difficult route.

The next road from the San Jacinto Valley into the mountains was built by the Hemet Land and Water Company, with some help from San Diego County, in 1891. The initial purpose for this road was to haul cement, machinery and supplies to build Hemet Dam. Edward L. Mayberry planned and directed this project. Although he hired a contractor to build the roadway, it became known first as the Mayberry Road and later as the Keen Camp Road.

The 1891 Mayberry Road, like most mountain roads of the time, was built with manual labor and Fresno Scrapers, the latter being broad plow-like devices pulled by horse teams that scraped dirt and rocks from the mountainside. The route followed the old Crawford

Joseph Crawford (1832-1911), a Union Army veteran, came to the San Jacinto Valley in 1875. With three other men, he built the first wagon road to Strawberry Valley in 1875-76. Crawford's Toll Road had grades as high as 30% and was said to be "so steep that it bent over backwards."
— LAURA SWIFT

A portion of Crawford's Toll Road near Chimney Flat, as it looks today (1992).

Road alongside the San Jacinto River as far as Oak Cliff. Then, instead of zigzagging up the mountainside, it continued up the canyon bottom, past the point where the present State Highway 74 makes its first switchback, and straight ahead up Dry Creek another mile or so. Then it lurched up the south slope in five steep hairpin turns to intersect the present highway just below today's McCall Horse Camp. From there it followed the present route over Keen Camp Summit and down into Garner Valley to the dam site.[4]

Some of the old hairpin turns of the Mayberry Road are visible today, although blanketed with brush. The best place to view the switchbacks is from the observation point at the end of Double View Drive in Idyllwild, where you can look down across the canyon and faintly make out traces of the old roadway, just dimples in the chaparral.

The Mayberry, or Keen Camp Road, gave ready access to Garner Valley. It was a much more direct route than the old wagon road from Temecula via Cahuilla Valley and up the "Nigger Jim Grade" – named for Jim Hamilton who carved out the grade sometime in the 1880s – into the south end of Garner Valley. The new route was used by dam builders, Garner Valley cattlemen, miners, and later by Keen Camp vacationers.

Around 1900, a steep lateral road was constructed from the vicinity of today's McCall Park up around Chalk Hill to Strawberry Valley, making a longer but slightly easier route to the latter. The upper part of this wagon road followed the old Thomas cattle trail from Garner Valley to Strawberry Valley. Vacationers could then make a loop trip, going up via the Crawford Road and down via the McCall cut-off and the Mayberry Road, or *vice versa*.

Construction began in 1908 and was completed in 1909 on a new road from Oak Cliff to Idyllwild. Riverside County, with the help of the Forest Service, completely realigned and regraded the old Crawford Road to give easier access to the mountain resort. This new roadway climbed north from Oak Cliff, weaving back and forth across the earlier road, then continued farther up the slope before turning eastward and rejoining the old route near Chimney Flat. Then it followed a gentle grade over to Strawberry Valley and up to the Idyllwild Inn. This became known as the Idyllwild Road and was the main access route to the resort for twenty years.

So much traffic was using both the Idyllwild and Keen Camp roads that both were placed under controls, starting at Oak Cliff, in 1921. The controls were in force from May until the end of deer hunting season in October, during daylight hours. Up and down traffic moved at hourly intervals on the Keen Camp Road (by then known also as the Switchback Road), and at 90 minute intervals on the Idyllwild grade.

With Idyllwild growing as a mountain community, the need for an all-year, high gear highway from the San

147

Oak Cliff - horses were changed here for the Idyllwild grade.

Oak Cliff station on the San Jacinto River, 6 miles up from Valle Vista. This was where the Crawford Road left the canyon and started up the mountainside to Strawberry Valley. A small wayside community grew here, with Crawford's toll house, cabins, stable, corral, and a camping area.
— SAN JACINTO MUSEUM (left), CHARLES VAN FLEET (right)

Jacinto Valley to the resort became apparent. By 1923, the *Idyllwild Breezes* (September 10) called a proposed high gear road "the biggest thing for Idyllwild that has come up for consideration. A seven per cent mountain grade, less than eight miles in length, would eliminate all the terrors of mountain driving."

After several years in the planning stage, Riverside County and the Federal Government reached agreement on jointly financing the road. Riverside County road crews, assisted by prison labor, started work on the new highway in 1927. The high-gear thoroughfare was completed and opened for public use on May 28, 1929. This 1929 highway followed essentially the route of today's State Highway 74 to Mountain Junction, then up the present route to Idyllwild. The new distance from Hemet to the Idyllwild Inn was 23-1/2 miles, 45 minutes of driving – a great improvement over the 8 to 10 hours once required to negotiate the old Crawford Road.

The *Hemet News* (May 31, 1929), in announcing the highway's opening, stated, "Practically the only danger on the road will come from a tendancy to drive too fast. However, motorists who attempt to establish speed records on the grade will find themselves in difficulty with the law. George Atkins, state motor patrol officer with headquarters in Hemet, will patrol the new road regularly."

In the 1940s the highway was widened and some of the curves were straightened out. More extensive

Lumber wagons descending the old Idyllwild Grade, ca. 1895. — SAN JACINTO MUSEUM

The Owl Stage Line ran daily service from Hemet to Idyllwild, ca. 1898. Fare was 50¢ per passenger.
— CHARLES VAN FLEET

A passenger stage nears Idyllwild on the old grade, ca. 1896.

A buggy and several persons on horseback reach Strawberry Valley, ca. 1898.

improvements were made in the 1960s, but today's drivers, going from Hemet up to Mountain Center and on to Idyllwild, essentially follow the 1929 route.

The old Mayberry Road with its five abrupt switchbacks was abandoned after 1929, its roadbed now barely discernable in the brush. The 1909 Oak Cliff-Idyllwild grade remains open today as an unpaved Forest Service road, open to the public except during fire season. It is still called the Control Road. Four-wheel drive vehicles are recommended for any who wish to drive it.

Another major route to Idyllwild is the Banning-Idyllwild Road, a thoroughfare that took years, interspaced with long delays, to complete in its present form.

Banning and Beaumont businessmen proposed a road from their towns to Strawberry Valley as early as 1900, and a preliminary survey was made in 1902. Riverside County gave its approval and W. F. Mulford was contracted to build the first section as far as Colonel Hall's old lumber camp (today's Lake Fulmor) in 1905.

At first, Hall's Grade, the extremely precipitous wagon road built in 1875, was used to climb into the mountains. After Riverside County surveyor George Pearson studied various alternatives in 1908, a new access was chosen, taking advantage of a rough road built by rancher Ed Poppett in 1885. County road crews, paid 30¢ per hour, along with forty men hired by

The Mayberry or Keen Camp Road, completed in 1891, ascended San Jacinto River Canyon and Dry Creek, with five short switchbacks near the top, to Keen Camp and Lake Hemet. A lateral road from near today's McCall Horse Camp to Idyllwild was built about 1900. This route was much less steep than the old Idyllwild Grade from Oak Cliff.

On the old Keen Camp Road, ca. 1914. Tahquitz Peak can be seen in the background.

A vehicle descending the old Idyllwild Grade in 1913.
— WESTWAYS

the Forest Service at $1.75 per day, went to work, and the road was completed to Idyllwild in September 1910. The road cost $50,000 and was 32 miles in length.

This first Banning-Idyllwild Road went south from Banning, just as the present highway does, then swung west before climbing in a southeastward direction to Poppett Flat. It joined the present Banning-Idyllwild Highway just above the flat, and for the rest of the way followed the present route, except that it had many more curves and contoured much farther into and out of Hall Canyon. The road was unpaved, single lane with occasional turn-outs for passing, and slippery in wet weather because of the clay soil on part of the roadbed. Despite these handicaps, it was well traveled in summer. A Banning-Idyllwild Stage Line was organized by three Banning businessmen in 1911. Errol King and Hays Minor were hired to drive two four-cylinder EMC open touring cars between the Southern Pacific station in Banning and Idyllwild Inn during the summer season.

The completion of the new high-gear highway from Hemet to Idyllwild in 1929 took much traffic away from the narrow Banning-Idyllwild road. Businessmen in Banning, Beaumont, and Idyllwild urged Riverside County to bring the old road up to modern standards. Much of the credit for converting the winding dirt road into a scenic paved highway rests with County Supervisor Robert E. Dillon of Beaumont. With the support of numerous civic leaders and business groups, Dillon was able to persuade his fellow supervisors to authorize a survey to locate a high-gear route between Banning and Idyllwild.

Riverside County surveyor and road commissioner Alex C. Fulmor conducted a survey for the new highway in 1933 and 1934, but construction did not begin for another year. Fulmor's survey and proposed route were criticized as being too expensive during the depression years; some called the planned route "Fulmor's Folly."

Finally, opposition was surmounted, and in June 1935 a crew of county prisoners began work at the Idyllwild end of the road. There were a number of delays when the prison crews were needed elsewhere in the county, but by 1937 work on the highway was progressing steadily. The prison workers were housed first at Keen Camp, then at Vista Grande and finally at the edge of Banning.

World War II brought a halt to work on the new highway. A. C. "Bud" Keith succeeded Fulmor as county road commissioner in 1946, and work resumed on the final five miles of highway from Dark Canyon over Marion ridge to Pine Cove. The new allignment was completed in early 1949 and the highway, with twelve miles still unpaved, was opened to the public. The Forest Service financed the final surfacing of the route the following year.

The new high-gear Banning-Idyllwild Road was finally dedicated on October 14, 1950. It had taken fifteen years to complete (17 if you include Fulmor's survey), and cost Riverside County $1,454,888 and the federal government $175,000.[5]

The California Division of Highways (later Caltrans) took over maintenance in 1953 and named the route State Highway 243. Later it was designated a state scenic highway.

A new high-gear paved highway from the San Jacinto Valley to Mountain Center and on to Idyllwild was completed in 1929. Persons could now drive from Hemet to Idyllwild in an hour or less. Today this is State Highway 74.

Alex C. Fulmor, who had played such a large part in the building of the Banning-Idyllwild Highway, was honored with the naming of Lake Fulmor. The little mountain lake was formed when Fulmor dammed and built the highway across Hall Canyon, rather than contouring into the canyon as the old road did.

The last major thoroughfare to wind its way through the San Jacinto Mountains was the scenic Palms to Pines Highway, joining Coachella Valley with the high country. This desert-to-mountain route was conceived by A. C. Lovekin of Riverside as early as 1919. Lovekin proposed that the road follow the old Rincon Trail up Palm Canyon to Vandeventer Flat, then northwest through Garner Valley to join the Hemet Highway at Keen Camp. County Surveyor A. C. Fulmor surveyed the Rincon route in 1920 and said the entire highway could be built for $80,000 (It eventually cost almost $500,000).

Coachella Valley business leaders, led by by Indio publisher J. Win Wilson, supported a palms to pines highway but called for a Dead Indian Canyon-Pinyon Flat route, much closer to Indio than Palm Canyon.

Several years of political haggling ensued until Palm Springs finally accepted the Dead Indian-Pinyon Flat route. One final obstacle was surmounted when the Santa Rosa Indians agreed to accept $4000, rather than the $8000 they had asked for, to cross reservation land on Vandeventer Flat.

The highway was jointly built by Riverside County and the Federal Government. Riverside County had prison labor on the job as early as 1926, constructing the stretch from Keen Camp down Garner Valley to Vandeventer Flat, a distance of 23 miles. The County also constructed the difficult uphill grade from Dead Indian Canyon (just above today's community of Palm Desert) up to the National Forest boundary below Pinyon Flat. The middle stretch between Pinyon Flat and Vandeventer Flat was built by the Federal Bureau of Public Roads. The entire 36-mile scenic highway was completed on July 23, 1932.

The dedication of the Palms to Pines Highway was held at Keen Camp on June 18, 1932, a month before it was opened for public travel. Over 1,100 persons attended, enjoying a festive barbeque and suffering through a number of long-winded speeches by County and Federal officials and desert businessmen.[6]

Now one could drive from desert palms to mountain pines in less than an hour, enjoy the delights of Keen Camp and Idyllwild, and return by either the Banning-Idyllwild or Hemet highways. The San Jacintos – except for the high mountain wilderness above Idyllwild – had been tamed.

In 1971, Highway 74 – the Palms to Pines route – was officially designated a state scenic highway, the longest in Southern California.

The old way of carving out mountain roads, using manpower and a Fresno scraper. – U.S. FOREST SERVICE

Banning, ca. 1915. Banning businessmen campaigned for a road to Idyllwild as early as 1900. The first Banning-Idyllwild Road, completed in 1910, was a narrow, steep and winding thoroughfare, unpaved.

NOTES

1. Tom Patterson, "Banning-Idyllwild Road is just bits, pieces of earlier roads," *Riverside Press-Enterprise,* June 13, 1971; also Patterson, "New land reserve is historical part of the old Banning-Idyllwild Road," *Press-Enterprise,* September 21, 1980.
2. *Hemet News,* July 22, 1932.
3. *San Jacinto Register,* August 30, 1888.
4. Tom Patterson, "Switchbacks built in 1891 long thought best road to Idyllwild," *Riverside Press-Enterprise,* December 25, 1983; also Patterson, "Idyllwild was uphill no matter what road," *Press-Enterprise,* August 22, 1971.
5. See Patterson, note 1. Other sources on Banning-Idyllwild Road are Tom Hughes, *History of Banning and San Gorgonio Pass* (Banning, n.d., ca. 1938), p. 45; *Redlands Daily Review,* September 9, 1910; *Hemet News,* September 23, 1910; December 29, 1933; July 12, 1935; November 20, 1936; July 12, 1940; *Redlands Daily Facts,* October 16, 1950.
6. *Hemet News,* April 25, 1919; January 8, 1926; April 30, 1926; February 7, 1930; July 25, 1930; January 29, 1932; June 17 and 24, 1932; August 12, 1932.

Fuller Mill Creek Public Campground on the Banning-Idyllwild Road, 1917. The new Banning-Idyllwild Highway took fifteen years to build. It was completed in 1950. — BOB AND VIRGINIA GRAY

Dedication of the Banning-Idyllwild Highway took place on October 14, 1950. Honored guests at the dedication included (left to right) Alex C. Fulmor, Riverside County road commissioner most responsible for building the road; Hollywood actress Jane Powell; and A.C. Keith, Riverside County highway engineer.
— BOB AND VIRGINIA GRAY

Lake Fulmor, along the Banning-Idyllwild Highway, honors the man who built the road. The lake was formed in 1948 when Hall Creek was dammed and the highway built across. — BOB GRAY

Lawlor Lodge on the Banning-Idyllwild Highway was built as a weekend retreat by Los Angeles attorney Oscar Lawlor in 1916.

The Palms to Pines Highway, connecting the desert with the San Jacinto high country, was completed in 1932. It was designated a state scenic highway in 1971.

Hemet Land Company and Lake Hemet Water Company
HEMET, RIVERSIDE COUNTY, CAL.

Photographic View of Lake Hemet. Taken from a point ¼ mile south of Dam. Source of water from which the Hemet Lands are supplied.

DIRECTORS:

W. F. WHITTIER,
San Francisco, President.

E. L. MAYBERRY,
Alhambra, Vice-President.

JAMES B. STETSON,
of Holbrook, Merrill & Stetson,
San Francisco.

J. S. CHAPMAN,
Los Angeles, Attorney.

(Phone 312)

Reduced Rates from Los Angeles to Hemet and return.

7,000 acres of Citrus and Deciduous Fruit Lands. Size of outlying tracts from 5 to 40 acres, indefeasible water-right. Soil inexhaustible and of superior quality; climate unexcelled for pulmonary troubles and rheumatism.

This tract is located in the midst of one of the finest, largest and most fertile valleys of Southern California. For particulars address

HEMET LAND COMPANY,
ROOM 28, BAKER BLOCK, LOS ANGELES, CAL.

Or, E. L. MAYBERRY, Hemet, Riverside County, Cal.

This advertisement for the Hemet Land Company and the Lake Hemet Water Company appeared in *Land of Sunshine* in 1895. William F. Whittier and Edward L. Mayberry poured millions into a successful scheme to build a great mountain reservoir and water distribution system and develop the new community of Hemet in the San Jacinto Valley.

12

LAKE HEMET

William F. Whittier and Edward L. Mayberry shared much in common. Both were born in Maine – Whittier in 1832, Mayberry in 1834, both were successful in their chosen occupations, both achieved success while living in San Francisco, and both loved thoroughbred horses and horse racing. Whittier was a hard-nosed businessman who had made a fortune in the paint and glass business. Mayberry was a civil engineer and builder, who designed and constructed a number of prominent buildings in San Francisco and the Napa Valley. Their friendship developed in the 1860s, undoubtedly promoted by their common love for horses.

Mayberry moved to Southern California in 1876, ostensibly because of poor health, and purchased, a few years later, the 260-acre El Molino Ranch from the Kewen estate, a hilly spread that embraced parts of today's Alhambra and San Marino. Here he indulged in his passion for horse breeding.

It was probably through a mutual interest in horses that Mayberry met Hancock Johnston. Johnston, son of Confederate General Albert Sidney Johnston, bred race horses at his Big Springs Ranch, south of Hemet in the San Jacinto Valley. In March 1886 Johnston had purchased a section of land in the extreme northwestern end of Garner Valley (then known as Hemet Valley) and developed his Hemet Valley Stock Ranch there.

In the summer of 1886, Mayberry visited Johnston at his Big Springs Ranch. Together the two rode up to Johnston's Hemet Valley Stock Ranch and on over to see Charles Thomas, owner of the sprawling Thomas Ranch that occupied most of Garner Valley. The story goes that the threesome – Mayberry, Johnston, and Thomas as guide – went hunting together. They rode over to the rocky gorge at the head of the San Jacinto River's South Fork, where Mayberry immediately recognized the possibilities of constructing a dam to impound irrigation water.

Mayberry was not the first to envision harnessing mountain water for valley use. In 1875 J. H. Hamner and Samuel V. Tripp constructed a mile-long ditch from inside San Jacinto River Canyon to their farm lands at the southeastern edge of the San Jacinto Valley. This became known as the Hamner Ditch, Hamner getting two-thirds of the water, Tripp one-third. William B. Webster bought out Hamner and Tripp in 1881 and took control of the water ditch.

Early settlers in the San Jacinto Valley utilized simple ditches and wells for their water needs. All this changed with the organization of the San Jacinto Land Association in 1882. The Association laid out the new town of San Jacinto and sold town and farm lots by the hundreds. The need for an adequate system of water supply and distribution became acute.

To meet these valley water needs, two competing companies were organized in early 1886. The Fairview Land and Water Company, a joint stock venture of San Jacinto residents, purchased the Hamner Ditch from the widowed Mary Webster and filed for water rights in the South Fork, North Fork and Strawberry Creek, the three main branches of the San Jacinto River. The Lake Hemet Company, with the noted developer Abbot Kinney as president, bought water rights from Luther Wildon and James Crain in San Jacinto River Canyon and took an option to buy land for a proposed reservoir at the head of the South Fork. The Lake Hemet Company spent $6,000 on a survey for a dam and reservoir site.

Both the Fairview and Lake Hemet companies faced obstacles. The former discovered, to their chagrin, that there was not enough water year around from the North Fork and Strawberry Creek to supply their irrigation needs. The South Fork, which did have adequate water, was controlled by the Lake Hemet Company, but the latter did not have the financial resources to buy land and develop the dam, reservoir and conduits needed. Before either of the two companies could further their schemes, a new, well-financed enterprise entered the scene.

Edward Mayberry, after his hunting and scouting trip, hurried home and contacted his friend William Whittier.

155

William F. Whittier (1832-1917) supplied the business acumen to develop the Lake Hemet Reservoir and the town of Hemet. In later years, he divided his time between his San Francisco business ventures and his interests in the San Jacinto Valley. — LAURA SWIFT

Edward L. Mayberry (1834-1902), a civil engineer and builder, supervised the building of Lake Hemet Dam and the water distribution system that allowed the development of Hemet. Mayberry was the visionary of the two; Whittier the hard-headed businessman.

Whittier rushed south from San Francisco and together the two rode up to examine the potential reservoir site. Whittier, a man of great wealth and business acumen, saw the possibilities of not only a mountain reservoir to supply water for the whole eastern end of the San Jacinto Valley, but also land development in the valley itself. He agreed to supply a major share of the capital for such an undertaking.

On January 27, 1887, Whittier and Mayberry, along with Hancock Johnston and Albert Judson, incorporated two enterprises – The Lake Hemet Water Company to build the dam and irrigation works and The Hemet Land Company to buy and develop land in the valley with water supplied by the proposed reservoir. Total capitalization was $2 million, with Whittier and Mayberry providing well over half of that amount.

365 acres for a reservoir site were purchased from Charles Thomas and Hancock Johnston. The dam site itself was bought from the Southern Pacific Company, which had received the land as a federal subsidy for building the railroad through San Gorgonio Pass in 1875. 6,000 acres were purchased in the San Jacinto Valley, including the site for the planned city of Hemet. Agreement was reached with the Fairview Land and Water Company, which gave up most of its water rights in the mountains, including all claims to the South Fork, in return for receiving water at no charge the first year after the dam was built, and at the same rate as Whittier and Mayberry sold water to their own customers after that. The original Lake Hemet Company, in debt, gave up its water rights for a small consideration and disbanded.

Judson, never more than a figurehead, resigned as president in July 1888. Whittier assumed the presidency and ruled the twin companies with an iron hand the remainder of his life. Mayberry was given the title of general manager.[1]

While Whittier concerned himself with the companies' business affairs and the laying out of the new town of Hemet, Mayberry set to work on the dam and irrigation facilities.

First, a wagon road would need to be built from Hemet to the dam site. Whittier and Mayberry went before the San Diego County Board of Supervisors and secured a deal whereby the Lake Hemet Water Company would put up $500 and the County would contribute $700, with the provision that the road would become a public thoroughfare after the dam was built. Mayberry hired contractors Proctor and Marriage to construct the wagon road and grading work began in the fall of 1888. By early 1891, the road was completed and the hauling of cement, equipment and machinery to the dam site began. The Mayberry Road, as it became known (later the Keen Camp Road), was a great improvement over the old Crawford Toll Road, built to Strawberry Valley in 1875-76. It was much more direct, proceeding from Hemet up the San Jacinto River Canyon, then up Dry Creek, before swithbacking up over Keen Camp Summit, and down into Garner Valley (see *Mountain Roads*).

James Dix Schuyler, a prominent engineer who had built the Sweetwater Dam east of San Diego, was hired to design a masonry dam strong enough to hold back the waters of projected mile-long Lake Hemet. Over 100 men were hired, mules and wagons were purchased, and a bunk house, warehouse, cement mixing plant and other buildings were erected near the dam site. Over 11,000 barrels of portland cement were ordered and

The upstream face of Hemet Dam soon after construction, ca. 1895. — LAURA SWIFT

The top of Hemet Dam shortly after completion, ca. 1895. — LAURA SWIFT

shipped from Antwerp, Belgium to San Diego, then carried by rail to the Hemet depot where six-mule teams hauled it up the mountain to the dam site. Trees growing on the reservoir site were cut down. A sawmill was built to cut the downed timber into lumber for buildings and for use in constructing miles of flume in San Jacinto River Canyon and the valley below. Trenches were dug at the head of the gorge and filled with granite and concrete to insure that no water would leak under the dam.

At last, all was ready for dam construction. Mayberry directed operations as the first stone for the dam was laid on June 6, 1891. Mary E. Whitney, in her masterful history of the Lake Hemet Water Company, describes how the giant stones were placed:

> The term stone was relative because each one weighed between five and fifteen tons. The stones were granite, hornblende, and were readily available within four hundred feet of the dam, some lying loose and some embedded in the surrounding bluffs. After a stone was quarried, it was picked up and moved to the dam by one of two sets of eight hundred foot cables, strung across the canyon in opposite directions, fifty feet high, from which great block and tackle chains were hung on carriers. The carriers traveled the cables, drawn back and forth by steam engines perched high on the sides of the bluffs above the dam. The cables were anchored by trees on the bluffs and by an 'A' frame on the dam.
>
> After a stone was fastened to the chains, it was picked up and on a signal suspended in mid-air and rolled upon the cable to a point just outside the dam. Here it was washed by a man with a hose, the stone cleaned of sand and rock powder before it was laid on the dam by a water powered derrick. The power to run the derrick was by a flume. The high point of the water assured pressure for both derricks and the water hose. Each stone, after it was washed, was placed no more than six inches from one laid before and mixed cement was troweled and tamped between each one.[2]

By this method, stone by stone, the great masonry dam began to rise. It was forty-five feet high by January 1892, when a series of mountain storms and a fire in the building holding the rock crusher caused several months delay. Work recommenced in May 1892 and continued uninterrupted until the following January, when heavy rainfall caused the reservoir to fill and water to spill over the entire length of the dam, then 110 feet high. Another long delay to repair flood damage was followed by the construction of a twelve and a half-foot concrete parapet atop the masonry, bringing the height of the dam to 122½ feet, at the time the highest masonry dam in the world. At the same time a notch one foot deep and fifty feet wide was left in the center of the parapet to serve as a spillway. The dam was completed in November 1895 at an estimated cost of $183,712.49, a tribute to the ingenuity and mechanical genius of Edward Mayberry. Behind it was formed Lake Hemet, with a water storage capacity of 10,500 acre feet, enough at the time to fully supply the water needs of the eastern San Jacinto Valley.

Well before the dam was finished, Mayberry was working on a water transmittal system to provide for the domestic and irrigation needs of the Hemet Land Company's properties in the valley. Water was allowed to flow eight miles down South Fork Canyon, where it was diverted into a wooden holding dam near the confluence of Strawberry Creek. From here, a wooden flume carried the water down the main canyon, through a sand removal plant, across two bridges and into a 22-inch riveted iron pipe two miles long. From the end of the pipe the water flowed through an open masonry ditch four miles to a receiving and distributing reservoir in the valley.

Hemet Dam holds back the waters of Lake Hemet. At the time of its completion, it was the highest masonry dam in the world. – BILL JENNINGS

Visitors on Hemet Dam, 1907. The maintenance shed can be seen in the left background.

The construction of the elaborate water storage and distribution system in the San Jacinto Valley, the controversies over who had rights to the water, and the long struggle to make the privately-owned water system a public utility are outside the scope of this history of the mountains and more properly belong in the saga of the San Jacinto Valley. They are superbly covered in Mary Whitney's history of the Lake Hemet Water Company. The attention here will be centered on Lake Hemet.

The 122½-foot high Hemet Dam proved not high enough to hold back flood waters during severe mountain storms. Proof of this came with the great flood of January 1916, when six feet of water poured over the top of the dam and severely damaged the flumes and pipes in the canyon below. To prevent, or at least alleviate, future disasters, a second 12½-foot concrete parapet was built atop the dam, raising its height to 135 feet, in 1923. The canyon flume and pipe systems were rebuilt and strengthened. Water has flowed over the dam on several occasions since the 1916 flood, but damage has been minimal.

The last years of Hemet Dam's builder were marred by ill-health and financial reverses. Mayberry apparently made some bad investments and was obliged to borrow $105,000 from Whittier, using his stock in the Lake Hemet and Hemet Land companies, his El Molino Ranch and his stable of thoroughbred horses as collateral. Mayberry made interest payments but was unable to repay the principal, causing a strain on the long-time friendship of the two men. When Mayberry's wife filed for divorce, an angry Whittier, a strong family man, foreclosed on his partner, taking over all the latter's stock in the two companies, his El Molino Ranch and all his horses. Whittier must have felt some remorse for his actions; he was at Mayberry's bedside when he passed away in 1902.

Whittier, ever the energetic and tenacious businessman, continued in complete control of the Hemet Land and Lake Hemet Water companies. He oversaw the growth of Hemet from its birth in 1892 into the dominant community of the San Jacinto Valley, surpassing its older rival, San Jacinto. He looked on with pride as "his" town incorporated on January 20, 1910. In his later years, he spent most of his time in his San Francisco mansion. William Whittier died in San Francisco on January 26, 1917, aged 85.

Meantime, Lake Hemet was the center of a long controversy over whether or not the public should use the lake for recreational purposes. When the lake was formed, Whittier stocked it with trout from his McCloud Ranch near Mount Shasta. He invited his friends and business associates to fish the lake, but would not allow camping, boating or swimming because they might pollute the domestic water supply. Despite these restrictions, fishermen, boaters and swimmers frequently used the lake and repeatedly had to be chased away by Lake Hemet Water Company guards. A high fence was erected, but this failed to halt the trespassers, many of them guests at nearby Keen Camp.

The impasse over the lake's use continued until 1931, when the Riverside County Board of Supervisors announced that the County would build a road to a

Water flows over the top of Hemet Dam after spring rains, 1906.

Water flows over the spillway of Hemet Dam, ca. 1916.
— NELL EMERSON ZIEGLER

federally-owned one-half mile strip on the lake's north shore, where facilities for camping, boating, fishing and swimming would be put in. The supervisors received a Forest Service recreational permit to use the federal land abutting the lake, despite opposition from the Lake Hemet Company.

Faced with a condemnation suit, the water company agreed to give the County an easement across its lands for a road from the Palms to Pines Highway to the government strip on the north shore, but then refused to sign a deed granting the right-of-way unless the County relinquished all rights to the waters of the lake. Not willing to agree to these terms, the supervisors started condemnation proceedings. Defeated on the road and public campground issues, the Lake Hemet Water Company, determined to prevent anything but shoreline fishing, erected a barbed wire fence fifty feet from the lake's 135-foot contour facing the government strip. The forest Service demanded the fence be removed or it would become the property of the United States.

Finally realizing it could not prevent public camping and boat fishing indefinitely, the Lake Hemet Water Company announced in 1933 that the lake would be open to public use except for swimming. The company would rent boats at fifty cents per hour or $1.50 per person for the day. Thereafter, the water company realized a profit almost every year from its boat rentals. The company reached an agreement with Riverside County and the Forest Service in 1935 whereby a free public campground would be opened on the north shore. In return, no swimming was permitted, and the company was given the exclusive right to rent boats.[4]

In 1949 the water company leased land at the head of the lake to E. W. Hale for the construction of a general store. Lake Hemet was now one of the major recreational attractions in the San Jacinto Mountains.

Another great water project that involved the San Jacinto Mountains was the Metropolitan Water District's thirteen-mile San Jacinto Tunnel, constructed during the years 1933 to 1938. The Metropolitan Water District (MWD) was organized in 1928 for the purpose of bringing water from the Colorado River to Southern California cities and towns who subscribed to the project. A $220 million bond issue was passed in 1931 authorizing what came to be known as the Colorado River Aqueduct. Surveys for possible aqueduct routes were undertaken even before the bond issue was approved. The route chosen went from Parker Dam, to be built on the Colorado River, west across the Colorado Desert and through the Little San Bernardino Mountains, across the head of Coachella Valley to Cabezon. Here the San Jacinto Tunnel, longest in the entire aqueduct, would cut through the mountains. From the west portal, the aqueduct would head west across the San Jacinto and Moreno valleys to Lake Mathews, then north and west into Los Angeles County. The entire aqueduct would be 327 miles long, much of its length across barren desert.[5]

The most difficult section of the entire Colorado River Aqueduct was the thirteen-mile tunnel through the granitic bedrock of the northwestern San Jacintos. Construction of the tunnel began on March 17, 1933. Tunneling began at the East Portal, south of Cabezon, and at the West Portal, two miles north and slightly west

An intake canal, lined with concrete, near the mouth of San Jacinto River Canyon, ca. 1910. An elaborate water distribution system was designed by Mayberry.

Boaters on Lake Hemet, ca. 1899. The Lake Hemet Water Company discouraged use of the lake by vacationers until 1933. — LAURA SWIFT

of San Jacinto. Verticle shafts were drilled on both sides of the mountain ridge: the Cabezon Shaft and the Potrero Shaft. Inclined adits were blasted through on both sides of the mountain. Progress was so slow that a third inclined shaft – the Lawrence Adit high on the central ridge – was drilled in 1936.

From both portals and via the shafts and adits, the horseshoe-shaped tunnel, 16 feet in diameter, gradually took shape in the bowels of the mountain. Huge drill carriages, mounted on narrow-gauge rails, did most of the work. J. L. Burkholder, assistant general manager of project, described how it was done:

> Typical drill carriages provided two decks from which the drillers, by use of swivelled arms and columns, supported at the front end of the carriage, spaced and directed drill holes to conform to adopted blasting rounds. From five to eleven drills were thus mounted as required by the rock conditions to drill 25 to 80 holes. The pipe framework of the carriage was used for delivery of air and water to facilitate speedy connections to each drill. The old screw-fed type drills were not used; instead, automatic feed and pneumatic drills were standard equipment because they gave the advantage of constant pressure on the bit, thus permitting maximum drilling speed.
>
> Blasting was done with 40 to 60 per cent gelatin powder (using 1¼ X 12-in. cartridges in distinctive red wrappings) of which an average of 2.7 lb. per cu. yd. of solid rock was used. Some rock required as much as 7 lb. per cu. yd. The powder was detonated electrically from a 440-volt circuit used exclusively for this purpose.[6]

After each blast, a mucking crew moved in to remove the detritus. Crawler mounted shovels lifted the blasted rock and deposited it into muck cars, which were then pulled out of the tunnel by small electric locomotives. Conveyor belts lifted the detritus out of the inclined adits.

Delays were frequent. Whereas desert tunnels encountered almost no water leakage, the San Jacinto Tunnel was literally drenched with underground water that poured from cracks in the highly-faulted granite. Special hydraulic pumps, working 24 hours a day, had to be installed until the steel and concrete lining of the tunnel could shut off the flow. The cost overrun was high, not only because of the special measures required to stop the leakage, but also to settle lawsuits filed against the MWD for damage to the San Jacinto Valley watershed. Wells ran dry, the water diverted from its natural flow into the tunnel. (Water leakage continued to be a problem even after the tunnel was completed and lined with concrete.)

There were delays caused by unexpected rock structure, as drilling crews encountered both solid granite and highly fractured rock that easily crumbled, causing some cave-ins. Several men lost their lives in blasting accidents and cave-ins. A workers' strike in 1936 held up the project for several weeks.

The great San Jacinto Tunnel was finally blasted all the way through in November 1938. But it was not until October 14, 1939 that the concrete lining was completed and the tunnel ready to carry Colorado River water to Southern California cities. It was one of the great engineering achievements of the 1930s.

As Hemet and San Jacinto grew in population, the Lake Hemet Water Company was increasingly hard-pressed to supply their water needs. Negotiations with the Metropolitan Water District took place, and in 1949 the MWD agreed to accept the valley communities as members, in return for the dropping of law suits over water loss through continued tunnel leakage. The Eastern Municipal Water District was formed and approved by San Jacinto voters in 1950, and the new district immediately joined the MWD. In Hemet, voters approved the formation of the Lake Hemet Municipal Water District in 1954. The following year the new

The MWD San Jacinto Water Tunnel was finally blasted through in November 1938. Here, workers from both ends celebrate the completion. – METROPOLITAN WATER DISTRICT

The San Jacinto Valley outlet of the 13-mile tunnel under construction, 1938. – METROPOLITAN WATER DISTRICT

publicly-owned water district bought out the old Lake Hemet Water Company, ending sixty years of private management. Lake Hemet and its dam now belong to the Lake Hemet Municipal Water District.

Perhaps the saddest story in the saga of the Metropolitan Water District's San Jacinto Tunnel was the damage caused to the Soboba Indian Reservation. Underground water flow was so disturbed by the tunnel constuction that virtually every spring and well on the Soboba Reservation dried completely or was reduced to a trickle. Orchards died and farmland lay fallow for lack of water. Many of the reservation Indians were obliged to haul water from San Jacinto for domestic use. The Metropolitan Water District was unresponsive to Soboba pleas to restore the lost water, and the dispute ended up in a morass of litigation that continued for years. The Soboba refused an MWD offer of $30,000 in damages, and resisted a government attempt to annex them to the Eastern Municipal Water District of San Jacinto with good cause: they would have to pay for water they once owned outright. Several bills to ease the Soboba water plight failed passage in Congress. It was not until 1978 – forty years after their natural water supply had been nearly destroyed – that the Soboba finally had their water supply restored. A new water system was installed, funded by a $554,000 grant from the Department of Health, Education and Welfare's Indian Health Service and $121,060 from the Department of Commerce's Economic Development Administration.[7]

NOTES

1. Mary E. Whitney, *Fortune Favors The Brave: A History of The Lake Hemet Water Company* (San Jacinto, 1982) gives a superb account of Whittier and Mayberry's role in the water development of the San Jacinto Valley. See also Whitney, "William Franklin Whittier," *California Historical Courier,* September 1986. The Hemet-San Jacinto Genealogical Society's *Hemet and San Jacinto, Past and Present* (Hemet, 1989) gives biographical sketches of both men.
2. Whitney, *Fortune...*, p. 31-32.
3. *Ibid.*, p. 33-34.
4. Whitney, *Fortune...*covers the Hemet Lake recreational controversy on p. 198-200 and 205-206.
5. Charles A. Bissell (ed.), *The Metropolitan Water District of Southern California: History and First Annual Report* (Los Angeles, 1939), best covers the building of the Colorado River Aqueduct. For the San Jacinto Tunnel, see p. 102-103, 159, 164-173.
6. *The Great Aqueduct: The Story of The Planning and Building of The Colorado River Aqueduct* (Metropolitan Water District of Southern California, 1941), p. 35.
7. Van H. Garner, *The Broken Ring: The Destruction of the California Indians* (Tucson, Arizona, 1982), p. 82-95; Gunther, p. 503.

Northwest from the sky island of the Santa Roses. – ROY MURPHY

13

THE SANTA ROSAS

South from the Palms to Pines Highway, the Santa Rosas rise as a sky island out of the desert foothills. Reaching elevations in excess of 8,000 feet at Toro Peak and Santa Rosa Mountain, the high mountain backbone supports a rich forest of Jeffrey and ponderosa pine, white fir and incense cedar. A multitude of springs seep cold water down the slopes to the thirsty terrain below. In summer, when the surrounding desert country swelters under the burning sun, this green oasis in the sky is cool and refreshing.

There are really two Santa Rosas. South and east from the lofty Santa Rosa Mountain-Toro Peak backbone, the range is lower and shows the strong influence of the desert. Here on the slopes and benches above four thousand feet, pinyon pine and California juniper are supreme, covering endless miles of mountainous terrain. On the north flank of the range is an ocean of chaparral, primarily shaggy-barked, red shank (also called ribbonwood). In the desert foothills and canyons to the east, west and south, lower Sonoran vegetation takes over – tall and spindly ocotillo, yucca, chamise, barrel and cholla cacti, and waxy-green creosote. In some of the watered canyons are small oases of *Washingtonia filifera*, magnificent fan palms. Except for the high backbone of Santa Rosa Mountain and Toro Peak, the Santa Rosas are primarily a desert range.

The desert Santa Rosas are the home of the largest herd of bighorn sheep in California, estimated at more than 500 head. These noble masters of the arid crags live mainly in the eastern and southern parts of the range, rocky regions where man seldom disturbs their habitat. Crucial to their survival are the handful of all-year springs on the desert slopes and canyons. Other large mammals in the Santa Rosas are mule deer and a few stealthy mountain lions.

Like the San Jacintos to the north, the Santa Rosas have long been the home of Cahuilla Indians. Desert Cahuilla villages were in or near the mouth of every major canyon on the eastern slope of the range, above the shoreline of ancient Lake Cahuilla (today's Salton Sea). Mountain Cahuilla villages were located in Coyote, Horse, Nicholas, and Rockhouse canyons, tucked in the southwestern foothills of the Santa Rosas, and on high benches on the northwestern slopes. The Santa Rosas supplied these hardy peoples with the necessities of life – acorns, pinyon nuts, mesquite, agave, yucca fibers, wild game, water. Indian footpaths crisscrossed the range, traveling from spring to spring. In summer, whole villages would migrate from the desert and foothill areas into the mountains to gather food, hunt, and escape from the searing heat.[1]

The high Santa Rosas were apparently both revered and feared by the Cahuilla. 8070-foot Santa Rosa Mountain was considered a hallowed and sacred place, but the nearby summit of Toro Peak (8716′) was apparently avoided; there are stories that this highest mountain in the Santa Rosas was taboo, the dwelling place of evil spirits.[2]

Today, about twenty families, mostly Cahuilla, live on the 11,090-acre Santa Rosa Indian Reservation, located on an oak and pinyon-shaded bench northwest of the main mountain backbone, on both sides of the Palms to Pines Highway. This reservation, established in 1907, is sometimes called "New" Santa Rosa to distinguish it from two "Old" Santa Rosa villages, one in Rockhouse Canyon, the other on a 6000-foot bench close under the south face of Santa Rosa Mountain.

The Old Santa Rosa in Rockhouse Canyon dates back to prehistoric times. All that remains today are the foundations of three rock dwellings, located in the upper canyon, above Cottonwood Spring. The Cahuilla got their water from this spring and from seepages at the head of the valley, at the foot of the mountain wall rising to Toro Peak and Alta Seca Bench. George Wharton James, the prolific writer and wanderer of the Southwestern deserts, descended the old Indian trail from Alta Seca Bench into Rockhouse Canyon and described it thusly in *The Wonders of The Colorado Desert* (1906):

> We descend from the mesa into Rock House Canyon and on
> our arrival feel like taking off our hats to our faithful burros.

Toro Peak from Santa Rosa Mountain. – LAURA SWIFT

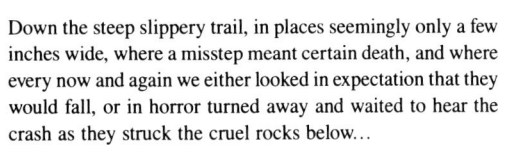

Southeast from Toro's summit. Salton Sea to left; Rabbit Peak on right.

> Down the steep slippery trail, in places seemingly only a few inches wide, where a misstep meant certain death, and where every now and again we either looked in expectation that they would fall, or in horror turned away and waited to hear the crash as they struck the cruel rocks below...
>
> From above, the valley appeared to be smooth. Now we find it to be the rockiest country we were ever in. Hour after hour we wander along over rocks, around rocks, under rocks, never free from them for a single moment. At noon we reach a deserted Indian kish. Where are the owners? We find a collection of ollas partly filled with acorns or water, and there are mortars, pestles, metates, and grinding stones. Outside is a big stone pile or oven, where the squaws have roasted their mescal. This is made from the shoots of the agave, which grows here profusely....
>
> A stone house, the ruins of which we pass, gives this canyon its name, Rock House Canyon. A little brush shack, built close up to a boulder, suggests that the builder had the desire to dwell under the shadow of a 'mighty rock in a weary land.'[3]

Another prolific writer, botanist Charles Francis Saunders, followed James' trail and wrote about Old Santa Rosa in *The Southern Sierras of California* (1923):

> In all the gray expanse was not a sign of water save the one brook murmuring in the willows and alders, no evidence of contemporary human life; but of an ancient life once active here there were abundant vestiges – ruins of rock houses, a parched and broken reservoir, rotted fences and basket granaries, broken pottery, mortars and rubbing-stones, arrow-straighteners, and what not. At the back a trail wound around the mountain to a spring gushing out from beneath two huge alders – a lovely, green, peaceful spot, where we may imagine the Santa Rosa damsels of long ago coming to fill their water-jars and gossip, glad to escape, if it were summer, from the persistant sunshine of their treeless village.
>
> The site of this ancient rancheria afforded an interesting object lesson in how primitive man could live, and live quite well, in an environment where his civilized brother would find existence intolerable.[4]

Archaeologists have identified two old village sites near the head of Rockhouse Canyon, called *Kewel* and *Kolwayakut*. Together, they have been called Old Santa Rosa. Another smaller village site was located at the present rock house ruin near Cottonwood Spring, which no longer flows. On a small mesa above Hidden Spring in lower Rockhouse Canyon was a seasonal village site known as *Ataki*. The rock houses themselves were made of boulders piled about three feet high and roofed with juniper branches and brush.

There is evidence that the Cahuilla lived in Rockhouse Canyon, on and off, until the early years of this century, when most of them moved to reservations, where they had a land base supposedly secure from white encroachment, and better access to jobs and supplies provided by modern society.[5]

The other "Old" Santa Rosa was a Cahuilla summer village site, used when the sweltering heat made the desert sites uncomfortable. Here, close under Santa Rosa Mountain, the people would gather acorns and pine nuts, hunt deer, and – in more recent years – herd cattle and sheep. The remains of an old apple and peach orchard are still there. *Sewiu* is the Cahuilla name for this site. The high mountain bench is still sometimes utilized for animal grazing.

Nicholas Canyon, leading from the head of Rockhouse Canyon up to the villages on the northwest slope, was another place frequented by the Cahuilla. It was named for old Nicolas Guanche, the last of the Guanche family to live there, who died around 1918. The remains of the old Nicolas rock house is on the ridge just southeast of Nicolas Spring, a major water source for Indians traveling from Rockhouse Canyon to the pinyon and juniper country of today's Santa Rosa Reservation.

Pinyon Flat, which extends north from today's Palms to Pines Highway, was used by both Desert and Mountain Cahuilla for gathering and hunting. It was a "common area," apparently never the territory of any one group.[6]

The remains of an Indian rockhouse in Rockhouse Canyon, southern Santa Rosas. — CHARLES VAN FLEET

An olla at Old Santa Rosa, former Cahuilla village site in Rockhouse Canyon. — CHARLES VAN FLEET

Nicolas Guanche (sitting) and Mariano Tortes at the Santa Rosa Indian Reservation, ca. 1915. Old Nicholas Canyon is named for Guanche, who lived in the canyon for many years. — DAVID SCHERMAN

Calistro Tortes' home, known as "The Big House," on the Santa Rosa Reservation. — DOROTHY COWPER

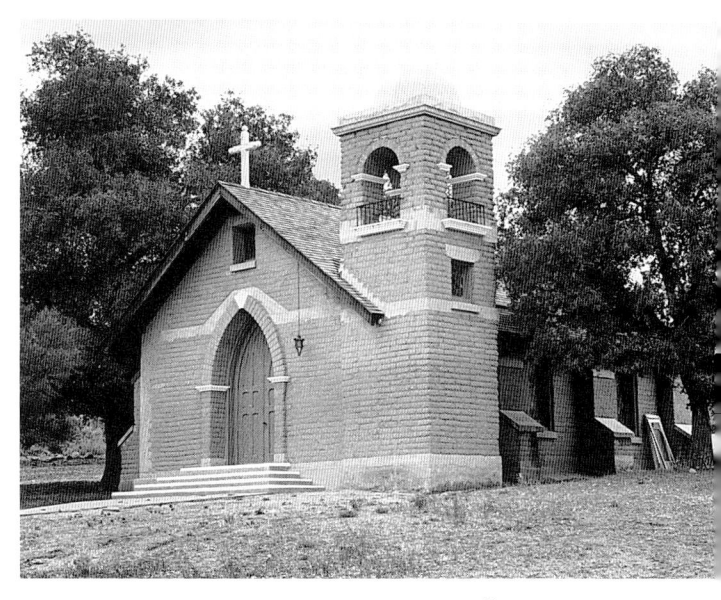

The Catholic Church on the Santa Rosa Indian Reservation.

The entire pinyon and juniper region from Pinyon Flat south through Horsethief Canyon, Cactus Spring and up to Pinyon Alta Flat near Martinez Mountain was utilized by the Cahuilla for gathering and hunting. Cactus Spring was an important summer village site.

Gold seekers were probably the first white men to penetrate the desert ramparts of the Santa Rosas. The earliest white visitor may have been one-legged Thomas "Pegleg" Smith. In 1828 Smith, crossing the desert after a trapping expedition in the Southwest, left the standard route somewhere near the southern end of the Santa Rosas and sought a shortcut to Los Angeles. The story goes that he picked up some black lumps of what he thought might be copper atop "one of three hills." In Los Angeles he showed his rocks to a friend, who suggested he have them assayed. The assayer's report report revealed the lumps to be pure gold coated with black desert varnish. This is where the story becomes hard to believe: Smith had other things to do and ignored the black gold find until many years later, when he began to brag about his discovery during saloon drinking bouts. He reportedly returned to the Santa Rosas in the 1850s but was never able to locate the right spot. Smith spent his remaining years drinking and spinning yarns about his lost gold mine until his death in 1866.[7]

The legend of Pegleg's lost gold mine mushroomed after Smith's death. An endless stream of prospectors have criss-crossed the southern Santa Rosas and the Anza-Borrego desert region searching for it, and some have claimed to have located it. The greatest promoter of the Pegleg legend was desert rat Harry Oliver, who founded the first Pegleg Smith Club in 1916. Oliver built the original Pegleg Smith Monument just south of Coyote Mountain in Borrego Valley, where it still stands today, piled high with rocks.

And there was Fig Tree John, the colorful Cahuilla Indian made famous by Edwin Corle's novel of the same name (Corle made him an Apache in his novel). Old Fig Tree, whose real name was Juanito Razon, was said to have made many of his purchases with gold dust or small gold nuggets, giving rise to the belief that he had a secret gold mine somewhere in the Santa Rosas. He lived above the western shore of the Salton Sea and died in 1927, supposedly at the ripe age of 135. Ever since, prospectors have searched the desert canyons of the Santa Rosas in a vain attempt to find Fig Tree John's lost gold mine.

The lost gold mines of Pegleg Smith and Fig Tree John may be nothing more than elusive fables, but gold in modest amounts has been brought out of the Santa Rosas. Around 1900 Nicholas Swartz made a strike in upper Rockhouse Canyon. He rebuilt one of the old Indian rock houses and lived there for about six years. He reportedly recovered $18,000 in gold for his efforts. Other prospectors have dug out minute amounts of gold from ledges in the Rockhouse Canyon area, but not enough to make their years of searching worthwhile.[8]

Other minerals have been found in the Santa Rosas, but not in quantities enough to make long-term mining

Thomas "Pegleg" Smith's lost gold mine was supposedly located somewhere near the southern end of the Santa Rosas. Pegleg said he found lumps of black varnished gold while crossing the desert enroute to Los Angeles in 1828. He returned many years later but could never relocate the mine. Since then, hundreds of prospectors have vainly sought Pegleg's lost gold. – HENRY E. HUNTINGTON LIBRARY

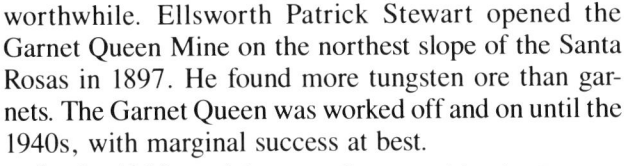

Fig Tree John at his home near the northwestern shore of the Salton Sea, ca. 1918. Legend has it that Fig Tree had a gold mine somewhere in the desert foothills of the Santa Rosas. Nobody has ever been able to locate it, although many have tried. – PALM SPRINGS HISTORICAL SOCIETY

worthwhile. Ellsworth Patrick Stewart opened the Garnet Queen Mine on the northest slope of the Santa Rosas in 1897. He found more tungsten ore than garnets. The Garnet Queen was worked off and on until the 1940s, with marginal success at best.

In the 1930s, calcite was discovered in the Borrego Badlands, at the far southeastern end of the Santa Rosas, by prospectors searching for Pegleg Smith's lost gold. Famed desert artist John Hilton filed a claim on the deposit, but was not able to mine and market it. During World War II, calcite suddenly became valuable because of its double refractive quality, for use in bombsights. A road was built in to the deposits and the calcite was extensively mined. The boom was short-lived, however, as scientists developed a synthetic crystal that could replace the calcite in bombsights.[9]

There are tales of an Indian emerald mine in Rockhouse Canyon, now lost forever under tons of rock deposited by an earthquake.[10]

Despite intensive prospecting over many years, mining has never taken hold in the Santa Rosas – that is, except in the minds of those who believe fantastic fables of lost gold or emerald treasures. If real mineral wealth is there, it has never been found.

Not only prospectors but also cattlemen roamed far and wide over the Santa Rosas, beginning in the 1890s. From his ranch in Garner Valley, Manuel Arnaiz drove his Mexican longhorns all over the northeastern slope of the Santa Rosas, from Pinyon Flat south to Cactus Spring and beyond. The brothers Fred and Frank Clark lived at their ranches just south of Anza Valley but drove their hungry herds to winter pasture in the southern Santa Rosas every year. Their main winter camp was in Borrego Valley, and from there the cattle were herded to Clark Valley, Rattlesnake Spring and Hidden Spring. Clark Dry Lake and Clark Well honor these early cattlemen today. Other oldtime cattlemen who drove their animals into the southern Santa Rosas include the Tripp family, John McCain, and Doc Beatty. One of the last was Jim Wellman who, from his 101 Ranch above Garner Valley, roamed his herds all over the eastern foothills of the range, from the 1920s into the 1950s. A good many of the waterholes in the Santa Rosas were named by cattlemen, particularly by Jim Wellman: Rattlesnake Spring was so named after Doc Beatty tied a live rattlesnake to a tree there as a joke to spook Jim Wellman's horse.[11]

The Cahuilla of the Santa Rosa Reservation were excellent cowboys, too, and pastured their herds on the northern and western slopes of the range. Some friction developed when white cattlemen encroached on Indian lands, particularly in the Vandeventer Flat area. The friction was eased when Vandeventer Flat was included in the Santa Rosa Reservation in 1907, but was not totally resolved until recent years.

Horsethieves may have been active in isolated parts of the Santa Rosas in the early days. Horsethief Creek, which drains into Deep Canyon on the northeast slope of the range, allegedly received its name after rustlers, driving stolen horses from as far away as San Diego, used the cottonwood-lined creek as a hideout and as a place to rebrand the purloined animals, before driving them on to San Bernardino to sell. The story goes that the thieves then stole the horses back and completed the entire procedure in reverse.[12]

Until recent years, only a handful of white settlers sought homes in the desert-tempered Santa Rosas. Some of those who did were colorful characters.

Frank Vandeventer, born in New York about 1824, operated the Agua Caliente stage station on the old Bradshaw Trail to the Colorado River. After the Southern Pacific Railroad came through in 1876, the stage station was closed. Sometime around 1879, Vande-

Looking for the Lost Pegleg Gold Mine, 1948. Eddie Duval (front left) thinks its "off to the south;" Harry Oliver, the Desert Rat (black hat) believes it's to the west, in the San Ysidro Mountains; A.A. "Doc" Beauty (pipe and goatee) is sure it's in the Borrego Badlands to the southeast; John Hilton, desert artist, points north into the Santa Rosas.
— DESERT MAGAZINE

The Clarks' Coyote Canyon cattle camp, ca. 1905. Frank Clark is kneeling at the right, Fred Clark is standing next to his horse, Theodore "Frying Pan" Ebbens is behind the mules to the left. A Cahuilla cowhand tightens the load on one of the mules. The Clarks drove cattle from Anza Valley down Coyote Canyon to Borrego Valley every winter. Clark Dry Lake is named for them. — BUD CLARK

venter followed the old Rincon Trail up Palm Canyon to a pinyon and oak-shaded flat that the Mountain Cahuilla knew as *San we yet*. He built a cabin there and grazed cattle with his Indian wife and two sons, Charlie and Johnny, and the place became known as Vandeventer Flat. Frank Vandeventer died in 1902 and his two sons took over the flat. Charlie Vandeventer, part Indian, part Dutch, dark-skinned with a short Van Dyke beard, was described as "a peculiar man" by other mountain settlers. He had an affinity for practical jokes involving explosives and was an accomplished violinist. According to one story, Charlie blew up a giant live oak right outside the Vandeventer house, leaving him deaf for several weeks. Another time, Charlie was said to have placed some nitro on an anvil in the blacksmith shed and persuaded a friend to hit it with a sledgehammer.

The resulting explosion blew the two boys right out of the shed and sent the sledgehammer through the roof. The boys were shaken but not badly hurt. Charlie's musical activities were not as threatening to life and limb. He taught himself to play the violin and performed at some dances in Anza Valley by fiddling upside down, suspended from the rafters by his knees.[13]

Charlie Vandeventer made his living by doing odd jobs, selling apples and pears from his twelve fruit trees, and leasing Vandeventer Flat to cattlemen for $25 per year. He and his brother John worked as forest rangers on the San Jacinto Forest Reserve for several years. Around 1908 a ranger station was built on the flat.

The Mountain Cahuilla always considered Vandeventer Flat as rightfully belonging to them. Indian graves were on the land. In 1907 the Cahuilla com-

Charlie Vandeventer's cabin on Vandeventer Flat, ca. 1905. The cabin was located on land belonging to the Cahuillas; Charlie and his brother John were forced to leave in 1909.
— CHARLES VAN FLEET

Nightingale store, lunch room and gas station, ca. 1935. Arthur Nightingale and his wife Mae purchased land at the south end of Pinyon Flat and opened their store when the Palms to Pines Highway was completed in 1932.
— LAURA SWIFT

Arthur Nightingale (1896-1967) was the pioneer settler on Pinyon Flat. — PINYON GAZETTE

plained to the Bureau of Indian Affairs that Vandeventer Flat "has been our home and the home of our ancestors," and asked that the land be returned to them. The Department of the Interior agreed and included Vandeventer Flat in the Santa Rosa Indian Reservation in 1907. Charlie and John Vandeventer, after a futile attempt to gain title, moved to Valle Vista about 1909. The Vandeventer Ranger Station remained, a source of friction between the Forest Service and the Santa Rosa Cahuilla, until it was abandoned in 1927.[14]

Theodore "Frying Pan" Ebbens, a German who spoke broken English, came into the Santa Rosas to prospect and stayed in and around the mountains most of his life. He built a crude shelter in a small, spring-fed valley close under the eastern spurs of Toro Peak. Ebbens and his burros were often seen wandering through the northeastern Santa Rosas and down to Palm Springs for supplies. He was living in his little mountain valley when U.S. Geological Survey topographers mapped the Santa Rosas in 1901. They utilized his services as a mountain guide and packer. When the U.S.G.S. Indio Quadrangle map appeared in 1904, Ebbens' name was attached to two of his favorite mountain haunts. Ebbens Valley, east of Toro Peak, and Ebbens Creek, above Palm Desert, immortalize the German mountainman today.[15]

Arthur H. Nightingale, born in North Dakota in 1896, was a mechanic by trade. He also liked to dabble in real estate. After buying land in Borrego Valley, someone told him about the hidden charms of the Santa Rosas. He climbed into the mountains in 1928, and his life was never the same afterwards. Nightingale and his wife Mae purchased three sections high on Santa Rosa Mountain from the Southern Pacific Land Company and, in 1931, built a cabin near Stump Springs. The Palms to Pines Highway was under construction at the time, and this provided a golden opportunity for the enterprising Nightingales. They bought several sections of land at the south end of Pinyon Flat, along the highway route, and contracted with Riverside County to house the highway workers. Arthur Nightingale erected a small village of tenthouses for the workers, and built a pipeline from Stump Spring down the mountainside to provide water. Immediately after the highway was completed in 1932, Arthur and Mae opened their Nightingale Store, long a landmark at Pinyon Flat. In 1933 they started subdividing and selling home lots. To provide lumber for building homes, Arthur Nightingale carved out a steep dirt road up the mountainside to timberline and erected a small gasoline-powered sawmill, the only one in the Santa Rosa Mountains. For many years the Nightingales and their little store, cafe and gas station were beloved fixtures along the scenic highway. Arthur Nightingale died in 1967, survived by his wife Mae, who continued to live on Pinyon Flat for many years.[16]

Three miles up the highway from Pinyon Flat is the small community of Ribbonwood, named for the shaggy, red-barked tree that blankets much of the northern slopes of the Santa Rosas. Ribbonwood was the dream and creation of Wilson Howell, a pioneer rancher in the Coachella Valley. Howell spent much of his spare time exploring the mountains above his desert ranch. About 1927 he moved to this north slope of the Santa Rosas and built a home. He ended up a few years later owning 2000 acres. Howell was no ordinary mountain settler; he set about improving his land by building roads, clearing areas for a small apple orchard and vegetable garden, and erecting a number of log, rock and earthen dams to curtail erosion. When the Palm to Pines Highway came through in 1932, he opened a store and added guest cabins and a picnic area. Wilson Howell's

The Sugar Loaf Cafe, today (1993) owned by Stuart Lince, on the Palms to Pines Highway. The left half of the building is the old Nightingale Store.

Ribbonwood lasted until his death in the early 1960s, after which much of it was subdivided for mountain homes.[17]

Down in the broad wash of Martinez Canyon, which drains much of the eastern Santa Rosas, Jack Miller built a sturdy rock cabin in the early 1920s. Miller was a prospector who spent years in a vain search for gold in the Santa Rosas and nearby desert areas. He found no gold, but plenty of Indian artifacts. To get his "grubstake" for further prospecting trips, he often worked odd jobs for dairymen and local ranchers in the Coachella Valley. In later years, Miller constructed at least two other rock cabins – one near the mouth of Martinez Canyon, another up at the canyon head just below Pinyon Alta Flat. He spent several years clearing a rough road to his main rockhouse halfway up the canyon. After World War II and the advent of four-wheel drive vehicles, vandalism became a problem. Miller's rockhouse was ransacked several times while he was away. In frustration, he placed a cable across his canyon road and posted signs at his cabin warning, "this place is boobytrapped; danger explosives; stay out." Miller sold his Martinez Canyon homestead in the late 1950s and moved to Pinyon Flat, and later to Temecula where he died in the 1970s. In recent years, the Bureau of Land Management determined that the Jack Miller Rockhouse was located on public land, just north of the homestead. In 1990 the BLM restored the rockhouse as an historic monument.[18]

Perhaps the most interesting character who ever inhabited the Santa Rosas was S. A. "Desert Steve" Ragsdale, who bought 560 acres right at the top of Santa Rosa Mountain in 1937. He built a sturdy log cabin on the forested summit, and a spectacular tree ladder to enjoy the view. He posted his mountain property with placards, advising visitors that "Decent folks are welcome; Enjoy but don't destroy."

Desert Steve was a great teller of yarns and a self-proclaimed poet. Born in Kansas in 1888, he came to California in 1908 and became a cotton rancher in the Palo Verde Valley. In 1921 he homesteaded 700 acres along U.S. Highway 60, halfway between Indio and Blythe, and founded the community of Desert Center. For years he operated a service station there. He also founded short-lived desert communities he called Utopia, Cactus City, and Hell – all now bypassed by Interstate 10 and forgotten. He built his cabin on Santa Rosa Mountain, he said, to enjoy some respite from the summer heat.

Randall Henderson, the late editor of *Desert Magazine*, called Ragsdale "a courageous pioneer and the

Jack Miller's Rock House in Martinez Canyon, built in the 1920s, has recently been restored by the BLM.

Desert Steve Ragsdale (1888-1971) at the gravesite he built for himself at Desert Center. He composed his own epitaph. Ragsdale has been called "a courageous pioneer and the world's worst poet." – CHARLES VAN FLEET

world's worst poet." Some of his poetry was indeed dreadful – so bad that many people loved it. Here is a sample he posted outside his Santa Rosa Mountain cabin:

"If hungry then come to our house made of logs.
We will share our beans and also our hog.
But don't shoot our deer or birds, my friend.
If I catch you at it, I'll kick your rear end."

Desert Steve Ragsdale died at Pinyon Flat in 1971. He had asked to be buried on a rocky point above Palen Valley, in the heart of the desert he loved so much. Bureaucratic red tape prevented this, and his remains lie in a Coachella Valley cemetery. True to form, Desert Steve wrote his own epitaph:

DESERT STEVE
Worked like hell to be an honest
    American citizen
Loved his fellow men and served them
Hated booze guzzling
Hated war
Hated dirty deal
Hated damn fool politicians.
• • •
He dug his own grave.
Here are his bones.
I put this damn thing up
Before I kicked off.
Nuff said – Steve.[19]

High on the bouldery flanks of Asbestos Mountain, northeast of Pinyon Flat, Steve and Nina Paul Shumway homesteaded 640 acres in 1932. Here, overlooking the broad expanse of the Coachella Valley, they carved out an eagle's aerie and built a cabin they called "The Tors."

Desert Steve Ragsdale's cabin on the summit of Santa Rosa Mountain, built in 1937. He spent part of his summers here to escape the desert heat.

Ragsdale's tree ladder gave climbers a spectacular view of the surrounding mountains and desert. Notice the woman on top. The ladder has since been removed by the Forest Service. – DOROTHY COWPER

Steve and Nina Paul Shumway, ca. 1939. The Shumways built their dream home on the flank of Asbestos Mountain and explored the surrounding country. Nina Paul Shumway's *Your Desert and Mine* **(1960) has become a desert literary classic.** – DESERT MAGAZINE

The Shumway home high on the side of Asbestos Mountain, 1939. – DESERT MAGAZINE

The small community of Ribbonwood was created by Wilson Howell when the Palms to Pines Highway was completed in 1932. It consisted of a small store, picnic grounds, and several cabins. – DESERT MAGAZINE

Wilson Howell, creator of Ribbonwood, came to this north slope of the Santa Rosas about 1927 and stayed most of his remaining years. – DESERT MAGAZINE

Previously date farmers in the Coachella Valley, the Shumways spent the last half of their lives exploring the California deserts and desert mountains. Nina Paul Shumway was an accomplished writer, whose articles appeared in *Desert Magazine* and various other publications. She will always be remembered for her book *Your Desert and Mine,* a delightful account of wanderings over the Southwestern deserts, the Coachella Valley and the Santa Rosas. In the chapter "Burro-ing in the Santa Rosas," she describes a burro trip up Martinez Canyon, over Pinyon Alta Flat to Horsethief Canyon, a climb of Toro Peak and a descent of the old Indian trail to Rockhouse Canyon and the ruins of Old Santa Rosa. Read how she describes the view from Toro Peak:

> The vast ranges of California, Arizona, Mexico, boiled up like irridescent bubbles on the stupendous shining expanse of desert. Off to the west the Pacific appeared as an argent streak in the heat haze. Only to the north was the far sweep of vision balked by the crags of San Jacinto towering 2000 feet higher than the Bull's horns.[20]

Nina Paul Shumway's book stands alongside George Wharton James' *Wonders of The Colorado Desert* and Charles Francis Saunders' *Southern Sierras of California* as classics of the desert ranges.

High up amid the wind-rustled pines on the north slope of Santa Rosa Mountain lies a water seepage known as Stump Spring. As previously mentioned, Arthur Nightingale built a cabin there in 1931. Around 1950, Max and Elizabeth Lewis of Altadena bought the property from Nightingale, and with the latter's help, rebuilt the cabin into comfortable living quarters. They

The high Santa Rosas, a forested island surrounded by desert. — DESERT MAGAZINE

lugged up a generator to provide electricity for their mountain hideaway, and put in a horse corral with the help of Art Guanche, a friendly Cahuilla from the Santa Rosa Reservation.

Elizabeth Lewis was an accomplished artist and used her Stump Springs cabin as her studio. Working in her mountainside studio, Lewis produced beautiful "dry brush" sketches of weather-contorted pines and "Hiroshiga" trees that were in great demand by art lovers.

A fast-moving forest fire threatened the Lewis' mountain home in July 1954. Elizabeth Lewis and visiting friend Phoebe Sumner, along with the latter's two young sons, fought off the blaze until a Forest Service fire crew arrived, thereby saving the cabin studio.[21]

Max Lewis died in the late 1950s. Elizabeth Lewis remained a few years longer, continuing her much sought-after tree sketches, until selling out in the early 1960s. Since then, a number of owners have used Stump Springs as a weekend getaway, the only inhabitable residence in the high Santa Rosas.

There have been other pioneer cabin builders in the northern Santa Rosas, many of whose names have been forgotten. Most of them shared a common love of this country of pinyon and ribbonwood, between palm and pine, set amid the harsh grandeur of boulder ridges, deep desert canyons, and far reaching vistas.

Subdivision and home building came to the northern Santa Rosas in the 1960s and continues to the present day. Pinyon Pines, Pinyon Crest, Alpine Village, and Spring Crest are now vibrant mountain communities. Several hundred people now live along State Highway 74, from Pinyon Flat eastward to the edge of the Santa Rosa Indian Reservation.

Still, most of the Santa Rosas remain as wild as ever. South from Horsethief Creek and Toro Peak, the desert range is the lonely domain of bighorn sheep, coyotes, and the ubiquitous rattlesnake. Fortunately, much of this untamed desert-mountain vastness is being preserved today.

The 20,160-acre Santa Rosa Wilderness was set aside by the California Wilderness Act of 1984. This Forest

The Stump Springs cabin, perched on the edge of a ridge in the high Santa Rosas, offers one of the most spectacular views of any home in Southern California. It was built by Arthur Nightingale in 1931 and extensively remodeled by Max and Elizabeth Lewis in the 1950s. This and Ragsdale's cabin on Santa Rosa Mountain were the only two private cabins in the high Santa Rosas.
— DOROTHY COWPER

Max Lewis rides into the corral at Stump Springs, ca. 1955. — DOROTHY COWPER

Elizabeth Lewis in her Stump Springs studio. Her India ink "dry brush" sketches of wind-sculpted trees were very much sought after. – DOROTHY COWPER

The gate at the entrance to Stump Springs. Elizabeth Lewis is on the right. – DOROTHY COWPER

Service administered wilderness extends from just south of Pinyon Flat to Pinyon Alta Flat and the head of Martinez Canyon, encompassing all of the Horsethief Creek drainage and the east slope of Santa Rosa Mountain. Access is by foot or horseback only.

Most of the terrain to the east and south of the Santa Rosa Wilderness is administered by the Bureau of Land Management. Today's BLM is far removed from its predecessor, the old General Land Office, whose main duty was disposing of public lands. The present BLM seeks to preserve the lands under its jurisdiction and, in the Santa Rosas, is doing a creditable job in protecting the wildlife, preserving cultural sites such as the Martinez rockhouse, and guarding against illegal human encroachment. Evidences of Native American culture in the Santa Rosas are safeguarded by the Archaeological Resources Protective Act of 1979, making it illegal to disturb Indian artifacts on public lands.

The 14,000-acre Philip L. Boyd Deep Canyon Desert Research Center named in honor of the Palm Springs banker who donated the first 2,000 acres in 1958, was dedicated in 1970. The Deep Canyon facility is part of the University of California's Natural Reserve System and provides for scientific study of the area's unique geology and animal life. Extensive research has been done on the habits of the peninsular bighorn sheep (*Ovis canadensis cremnobates*), which makes its home in the Santa Rosas. University of California scientists, in cooperation with other agencies such as the Forest Service and the California Department of Fish and Game, have made the Deep Canyon Desert Research Center one of the nation's prime facilities for learning about the desert environment.

To top it all off, all the BLM lands in the Santa Rosas were designated a National Scenic Area by the Secretary of the Interior in 1990. The Santa Rosa National Scenic Area, one of only four in the United States, will be administered as a partnership among various agencies, special interest groups, and surrounding communities – the BLM, the California Department of Fish and Game, the Agua Caliente Cahuilla, the Deep Canyon Desert Research Center, the Nature Conservancy, the Palm Springs Desert Museum, the City of Palm Springs – to formulate long-term plans for the preservation and compatible public use of the Santa Rosas. The goal is to protect the unique qualities of this desert mountain range as a buffer from the urban landscape which is engulfing Southern California.

The entrance to Rockhouse Canyon in the southern Santa Rosas.

Santa Rosa Mountains

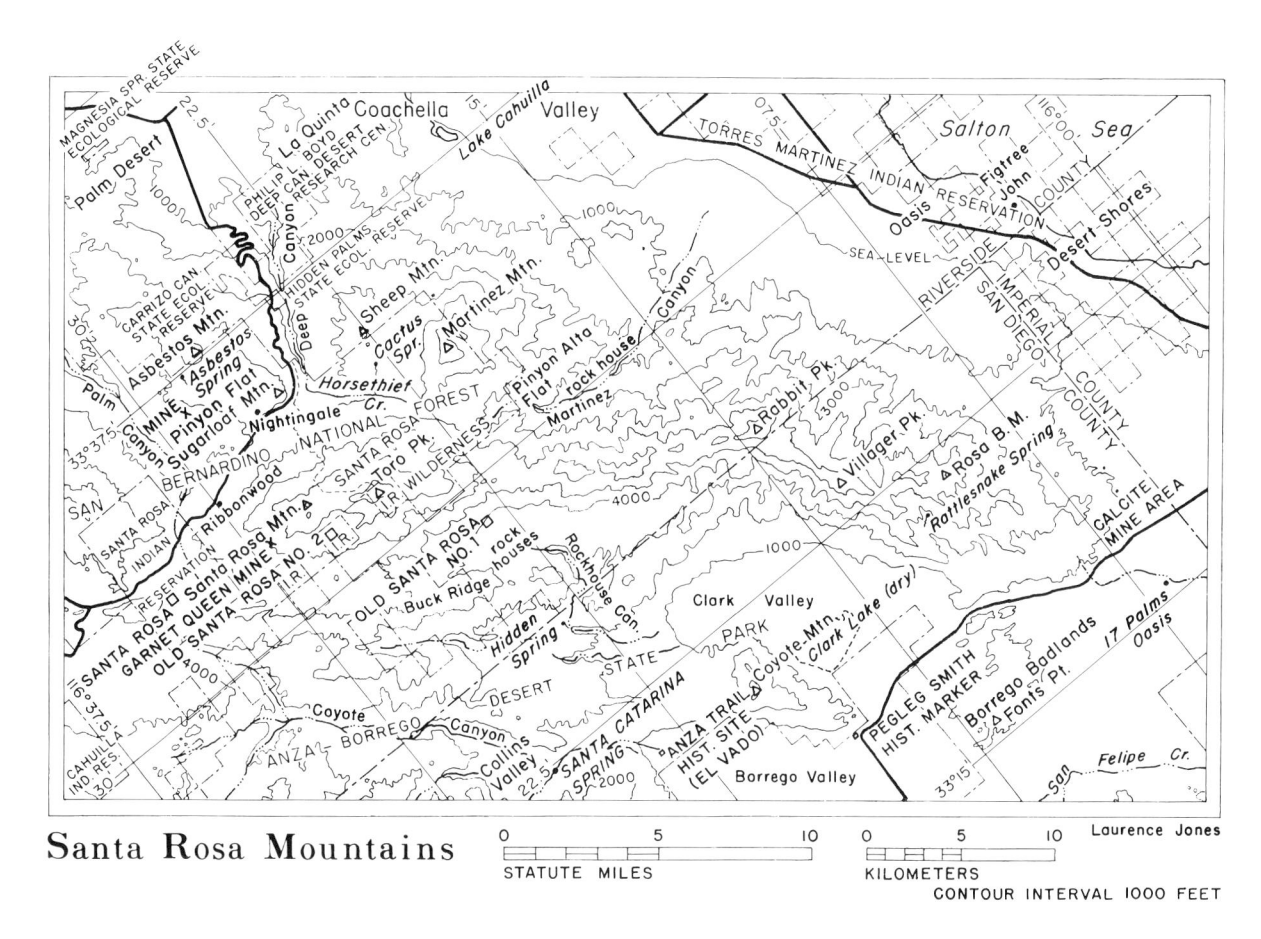

CONTOUR INTERVAL 1000 FEET

NOTES

1. Lowell John Bean, Sylvia Brakke Vane, Jackson Young, *The Cahuilla Landscape: The Santa Rosa and San Jacinto Mountains* (Menlo Park, 1991), p. 5-10.
2. Randall Henderson, "Toro Is Taboo," *Desert Magazine*, July 1938.
3. George Wharton James, *The Wonders of The Colorado Desert* (Boston, 1906), p. 440-441.
4. Charles Francis Saunders, *The Southern Sierras of California* (Boston, 1923), p. 170-171.
5. Bean, Vane, Jackson, p. 6-7.
6. *Ibid.*, p. 75-76.
7. There are many accounts of Pegleg Smith's legendary lost gold mine, and they differ in many details. Perhaps the best is Philip A. Bailey, *Golden Mirages: The Story of the Lost Pegleg Mine, The Legendary Three Gold Buttes, and Yarns of Those Who Know The Desert* (Ramona, 1971), reprint of 1940 edition.
8. Diana Lindsay, *Our Historic Desert: The Story of The Anza-Borrego Desert* (San Diego, 1973), p. 76.
9. Lowell and Diana Lindsey, *The Anza-Borrego Desert Region: A Guidebook to The State Park and the Adjacent Areas* (Berkeley, 1978), p. 119.
10. Lindsay, p. 104-105.
11. Lester Reed, *Old Time Cattlemen and Other Pioneers of the Anza-Borrego Area* (Benson, Arizona, 1977–reprint), p. 35-56; Bonner Blong interview, Idyllwild, February 23, 1992. Blong worked 34 years with the California Department of Fish and Game, much of that time studying bighorn sheep in the Santa Rosas. He became well acquainted with Jim Wellman.
12. *Idyllwild Town Crier*, April 18, 1952; Gunther, p. 244
13. Ernest Maxwell interview with Jim Wellman, Lincoln Hamilton, Henry Arnaiz, and Joe Scherman, in *Idyllwild Town Crier*, April 12, 1963.
14. San Bernardino National Forest Records, FRC 095-59D0543, Box 24, in Federal Records Center, Laguna Niguel. This file is mainly a log of complaints and negotiations between the Forest Service and the Santa Rosa Indians over Vandeventer Flat. It also contains material on cattle use of the Flat by the Arnaiz and Hamilton families.
15. Edmund C. Jaeger, "Saga of Frying Pan Ebbens," *Desert Magazine*, March 1956.
16. Erika Tollinger, "Our Hill," *Pinyon Gazette*, April 1972.
17. Mabel Wilton, "Paradise Above The Palms," *Desert Magazine*, July 1944; V.O. Luckock, "He Face-Lifted A Mountain," *Westways*, October 1954.
18. Bureau of Land Management, California, *Newsbeat*, July 1991; Bonner Blong interview, Idyllwild, February 23, 1992.
19. Bill Jennings, "Desert Steve, The Town Founder," *Desert Magazine*, June 1979. See also Randall Henderson, *On Desert Trails, Today and Yesterday* (Los Angeles, 1961), p. 67-69; and *Desert Magazine*, November 1937 and November 1950.
20. Nina Paul Shumway, *Your Desert and Mine* (Los Angeles, 1960); and Shumway, "Hard Rock Homesteaders; *Desert Magazine*, September 1939; and "Burro-ing in The Santa Rosas," *Desert Magazine*, May 1939.
21. Dorothy "Peg" Cowper interview, September 16, 1992. Cowper lives in South Pasadena and has a mountain home in Pine Cove, near Idyllwild. She is an accomplished naturalist and anthropologist with intimate acquaintance with the San Jacinto and Santa Rosa mountains. "Peg" accompanied the writer up Santa Rosa Mountain and pointed out the historical and natural highlights.

Tahquitz Peak Lookout, ca. 1923 – CHARLES VAN FLEET

14

GUARDIANS OF THE FOREST

People today take our national forests for granted. Most of us understand and appreciate the importance of forest and wildlife preservation. It may be hard to realize that this conservation ethic is relatively new. Slightly more than a century ago, public sentiment was very nearly the opposite.

Nineteenth century pioneers had the attitude that the nation's natural resources were inexhaustible. It was considered "progress" when a local virgin forest was cut down to make way for farms and commercial ventures. Taming the wilderness was the "pioneer thing" to do. Fortunately, toward the end of the nineteenth century, a few far-sighted, conservation-minded individuals boldly stepped forward to try to save the rapidly dwindling woodlands. Congressional legislation followed, but only after a fierce political struggle.

The Forest Reserve Act of March 3, 1891, signed into law by President Benjamin Harrison, was one of the most important pieces of legislation ever to affect the preservation of United States forest lands. This act contained a brief clause that gave the President authority to

> from time to time set apart and reserve, in any State or Territory having public land bearing forests, in any part covered with timber or undergrowth, whether of commercial value or not, as public reservations, and the President shall, by public proclamation, declare the establishment of such reservations and the limits thereof.

Every national forest today owes its existance to this act.[1]

The San Gabriel Timberland Reserve, proclaimed by President Harrison on December 20, 1892, was the first in California. In February 1893, the President created the huge Sierra Forest Reserve, the San Bernardino Forest Reserve, and the small Trabuco Forest Reserve in the Santa Ana Mountains. All four of these California reserves were set aside largely as a result of strong pressure from local civic and agricultural interests, motivated by the need for watershed protection.

Unfortunately, the Forest Reserve Act of 1891 failed to provide for federal administration or policing of the new reserves. There were no forest officers in the field and virtually no laws governing the use of the forests. Local watershed problems were handled long-distance by the Department of the Interior in Washington, D.C., which relied heavily on local officials and water companies to fight fires and report misuse of the forest.

In 1896, the National Academy of Sciences, at the request of Secretary of the Interior Hoke Smith, formed the National Forest Commission. The Commission was charged with inspecting the nation's timbered lands and determining whether or not they should continue to be protected and maintained, and if so what legislation should be introduced toward such protection.[2] Of the Commission's seven members, only one, Gifford Pinchot, was a trained forester. He was a strong supporter of the move to safeguard the forests for wise use.

In the course of its Western travels, the National Forest Commission accompanied by naturalist John Muir, visited the San Jacinto Mountains in September 1896. The party stayed overnight at the Thomas Ranch and examined the forests in and around Strawberry Valley, where extensive logging had taken place.[3]

The lengthy report produced by the National Forest Commission not only recommended protection and maintenance of the established forest reserves, but also called for the creation of two new national parks and thirteen new forest reserves. Among the thirteen new reserves suggested was one encompassing the forests of the San Jacinto Mountains.

Based on the findings of the Forest Commission, President Grover Cleveland, just days before he left office, signed a proclamation creating the recommended reserves. Thus, on February 22, 1897, the San Jacinto Forest Reserve was officially established.

It is interesting to note that, unlike the other Southern California reserves, the San Jacinto Reserve did not

Grant I. Taggert (left), first supervisor of the San Jacinto Forest Reserve, and "Con" Silvas, one of the earliest rangers. Silvas was a Soboba Indian. Photo taken in 1899. — HENRY E. HUNTINGTON LIBRARY

come about through strong local pressure. Civic and agricultural leaders in the San Jacinto Valley evidently did not feel their watershed was threatened. Hemet Dam had just been completed and there appeared to be plenty of water to go around. It was national pressure – mainly the recommendation of the National Forest Commission – that brought about the San Jacinto Forest Reserve.

The National Forest Commission, in their report, pointed out that fire and excessive livestock grazing were the major threats to the Southern California forests, and hence to the watersheds. Due largely to the Forest Commission's findings, the Sundry Civil Act of June 4, 1897 was passed, authorizing the appointment of personnel to guard the forest reserves. Control of the reserves was placed under the General Land Office of the Interior Department. Shortly afterwards, Benjamin F. Allen was appointed Special Forest Agent and Supervisor in charge of all the forest reserves in California, Arizona, and New Mexico.

Allen had few instructions other than to prevent fires and control depredations by sheep. He frequently had to write to the Commissioner of the G.L.O. for direction in other matters. In Allen's own words, "our duties are new and undefined; new to the department as well as new to us...."[5]

At first, Allen administered the reserves under his charge single-handedly. Soon he received help from two assistants, one of whom was assigned to the Southern California area. Charles Stedman Newhall, a former preacher and author, was appointed Assistant Special Forest Agent in August 1897, with headquarters in San Bernardino. Not for almost a year was Allen permitted to hire forest rangers for each of the reserves. That authorization finally came on July 18, 1898. The G.L.O. Commissioner told him to select twenty men, instruct them to prevent fires, and place them in the forests where they were most needed.[6]

The earliest forest rangers appointed by the General Land Office of the Department of the Interior usually fell into one of two categories. They were either long-time residents of the local mountain areas, or relatives or friends of high officials in need of favors. In either case, few were qualified for the positions they received. Fortunately for the Southern California reserves, B. F. Allen made an honest effort to appoint individuals who would at least try to do good work. Allen is one of the few G.L.O. men of whom Gifford Pinchot, head of the Department of Agriculture's Forestry Bureau and later to be the first chief of the U.S. Forest Service, spoke highly. He called Allen the best superintendent in the service.[7]

The first forest ranger Allen appointed for the San Jacinto Forest Reserve was Charles H. Thomas, Jr., son of the pioneer cattle rancher, selected in early August 1898. Other early-day rangers appointed in the following months were Frank Brooks, José Antonio Estudillo, José Maria "Con" Silvas, Charles Vandeventer, D. W. Rouse, John Oloan, and "Sulpher Springs" Thompson. The first supervisor for the San Jacinto Reserve was Grant I. Taggart, a political appointee from Northern California. Taggart set up headquarters in San Jacinto. Later, the San Jacinto Reserve headquarters was moved to Valley Vista (1902), and finally to Hemet in 1906.

Charles H. Thomas, Jr. was the first forest ranger appointed to the San Jacinto Forest Reserve in August, 1898. He was the son of the first known white settler in the San Jacinto Mountains. — DAVID SCHERMAN

Keen Camp Ranger Station was one of the first stations built in the San Jacintos. Constructed in 1907-08, it lasted until the opening of the new Keenwild Station in 1958.
— U.S. FOREST SERVICE

The life of the early ranger was not easy. From his meager salary of fifty dollars per month, he was expected to pay for his horse, saddle, and hay. He was also expected to provide his own food and have enough personal gear to be able to camp out wherever his patrol brought him at the end of the day. If he was lucky, he got down to Hemet or San Jacinto once or twice a month.

The San Jacinto Mountains were not plagued by fire or sheep depredation as badly as were the San Bernardino and San Gabriel ranges. Still, large conflagrations did occur, and the newly-appointed rangers were put to test. In September 1899, a very destructive blaze erupted just below Strawberry Valley and roared down hill toward Hemet. It burned for six miles along both sides of Keen Camp Road (now Highway 74).[8] South Fork Canyon, below Lake Hemet, was also swept clean of chaparral.

Gifford Pinchot, head of the Department of Agriculture's Bureau of Forestry, was the big name in American forestry during the last decade of the 19th century and the first decade of the 20th. Pinchot had headed the Bureau since 1898. Every professionally trained forester in government service worked under Pinchot, conducting forestation experiments and programs and making on-site inspections of all existing forest reserves. In fact it was Pinchot's foresters, borrowed from the Bureau, who prepared the first forest ranger information handbook, published by the G.L.O. as the *Forest Reserve Manual* in 1902. The manual contained information about the purpose of the reserves, the duties and responsibilities of a ranger, and rules and regulations governing the forests. This slim volume, the "Bible" of the early forest rangers, was the predecessor of the now lengthy *Forest Service Manual*.[9]

Pinchot's frustration was that he was a forester without forests. He campaigned tirelessly to have the reserves transferred to his Bureau and finally found an ally in Theodore Roosevelt. Shortly after assuming the presidency in 1901, Roosevelt recommended the transfer of the forest reserves from the Department of the Interior to the Department of Agriculture, where they would be under the jurisdiction of Pinchot's Bureau of Forestry. After a succession of scandals in the Interior Department's General Land Office, Roosevelt's support, and Pinchot's constant campaigning among congressmen, the transfer was approved by Congress and signed into law by the President on February 1, 1905. Five months later the Bureau of Forestry became the United States Forest Service.[10]

The Forest Service under the direction of Pinchot began an aggressive management program in the forest reserves. Prospective rangers were now subjected to civil service examinations. They had to be both mentally and physically capable of performing the rigorous duties of their jobs. Forest supervisors had to demonstrate leadership capabilities and knowledge of forestry practices; there were no more political appointments. Rigorously honest himself, Pinchot would tolerate no hint of corruption among his forest officers. In 1906, Pinchot ordered every forest reserve to hold annual meetings, with each forest supervisor and his rangers in attendance, to discuss work accomplished and to be accomplished, the skills of trail building, fire fighting, timber management, etc., and in general to promote the

Vista Grande Ranger Station, on the Banning-Idyllwild Road, as it appeared in 1917. The view is north, with the southeastern end of the San Bernardinos in the background.

This 1903 photograph shows an old cattlemen's cabin in Tahquitz Valley being used as a ranger station. Before the construction of regular ranger stations in 1907, rangers often repaired and occupied abandoned cabins in the mountains. — U.S. FOREST SERVICE

San Jacinto Ranger Station was the headquarters of the San Jacinto Ranger District from 1908 until the construction of the Idyllwild Station in 1934. Since 1938 this has been the Cranston Station, named in honor of former ranger Leon J. Cranston. — U.S. FOREST SERVICE

One of the least known stations was the Banning Ranger Station, located on the old Banning-Idyllwild Road at the base of the mountains. It was in use from 1908 to 1911, with Isaac W. Decker as its only ranger.
— U.S. FOREST SERVICE

Vandeventer Ranger Station as it appeared in 1911. The station, in operation from 1908 to 1927, was on the Santa Rosa Indian Reservation and a cause of friction between the Forest Service and the Indians until its final removal.
— U.S. FOREST SERVICE

Vista Grande fire lookout tower, erected in 1914, was the first built in what is today San Bernardino National Forest. It was located a short distance northwest of the present Vista Grande Ranger Station.

The original Tahquitz Peak lookout tower, built in 1917, with ranger Gilbert J. Spence on the catwalk. This is the longest continuously operating lookout site in San Bernardino National Forest.

"esprit de corps" of the Service.[11] The first such ranger meeting of the San Jacinto Reserve was held in Hemet in 1907.

Beginning in 1906, forest reserve lands were opened to homesteaders, provided the land applied for was suitable for agricultural use. The same year, a grazing permit system was instituted. This was in sharp contrast to the complete ban on this activity just a few years earlier, but in accordance with Pinchot's philosophy that the forests should be wisely managed for public use. Logging operations, a major cause of fire in the San Jacinto forests, were strictly regulated on public lands. However, most of the timber cutting in the San Jacintos, particularly in the Strawberry Valley and Keen Camp areas, was on private lands. Fire control regulations were put into effect and enforced by patrolling rangers.

In the San Jacinto Forest Reserve, after the fire season ended, rangers were put to work building new trails, stringing telephone lines, and constructing ranger cabins. Early historical records of the reserve are scanty, but it appears that the first permanent ranger station in the San Jacinto Mountains was built at Keen Camp in 1907-08. Within the next few years, the San Jacinto (now Cranston), Vista Grande, Banning, and Vandeventer Flat ranger stations were erected. The last two have long since passed out of service.

Early in 1907, a huge block of forested lands stretching from Palomar Mountain to the Mexican border, was added to the San Jacinto Forest Reserve. Encompassing 1,657,000 acres in all, the San Jacinto Reserve became one of the largest in California.

The "forest reserves" were changed to "national

The first meeting of all the San Jacinto Forest Reserve rangers was held in 1907 at the Hemet home of forest supervisor J. R. Bell (seventh from right). Bell's home, still standing today as the McCool House, served as forest headquarters for several years.

The U.S. Army Air Service at March Field, in cooperation with the Forest Service, began daily forest fire detection flights in 1919. The aircraft shown is a DeHavilland DH-4. The flights were discontinued when the squadron was transferred to the East in 1921.

forests" in 1907. Pinchot made this name change to remove from the public mind the idea that the forests were reserved or locked up. Instead, he wanted to emphasize that the "national forests" were being utilized and protected for the use of the American people as a whole. But the newly renamed San Jacinto National Forest lasted just one year.[12]

On July 1, 1908, the San Jacinto National Forest lost its self-identity, never to regain it. Together with the Trabuco Canyon National Forest in the Santa Ana Mountains, President Theodore Roosevelt proclaimed it the Cleveland National Forest, in honor of ex-President Grover Cleveland who had just died. The name change was not well received by local residents when they learned of it several months later. The editor of the *San Jacinto Register* was outraged and urged readers to ignore the proclamation. The newspaper (February 18, 1909) complained that

> Mr. Cleveland himself, if he could rise up in his grave and take in the situation as it exists, would coincide with this opinion when he saw a forest reserve located at the headwaters of the San Jacinto river, in the San Jacinto mountains, whose highest point, San Jacinto peak, pierces the clouds at an altitude of 11,000 feet, standing as a silent sentinel over the beautiful city of San Jacinto, located in the lovely and fertile San Jacinto valley, close by San Jacinto lake, he would decline the doubtful honor of having his name mixed up with such a San Jacinto combination.
>
> If President Roosevelt had understood how thoroughly San Jacintoed this section is, he would never have issued that proclamation changing the name.

California State Senator Miguel Estudillo of Riverside tried but failed to persuade the President to reverse the name change. The San Jacinto would henceforth be a district of a larger forest. The forest headquarters left Hemet and moved to San Diego with new supervisor Harold A. E. Marshall, brought over from Arizona, in charge.

The new Cleveland National Forest instituted a building program that resulted in new ranger stations, residences for rangers, barns, and fire lookout towers. Five lookout towers were erected between 1914 and 1917, two of them in the San Jacinto District. The first was built at Vista Grande, on a little knoll a short distance northwest of the present fire station, in 1914. Vista Grande had long been a lookout point for rangers in the past, and provided and all-encompassing view of the fire-prone western end of the San Jacintos. The second tower in the San Jacintos was erected on Tahquitz Peak, high above Strawberry Valley, in 1917. Visibility in those early days before pollution muddied the skies was excellent, and observers manning the two towers could see over a good portion of Southern California, from the Los Angeles area to the Mexican border and beyond.

Beginning also at this time was a new Forest Service policy offering summer home sites on national forest lands. Starting in 1914, individuals could lease a parcel of land for an annual fee of $15 and build a home on it. The home itself could later be bought or sold, but the land continued to be leased from the government. The San Jacinto District had comparatively few special use

Steven Augustus "Gus" Nash-Boulden was district ranger of the San Jacinto Ranger District of Cleveland National Forest in 1919. In 1925 he became the first supervisor of the newly recreated San Bernardino National Forest.

Rita Morris was the first female employed in San Bernardino National Forest other than office clerks. She served as the Black Mountain lookout in 1929.

tracts, as they were called. A few of the larger tracts were Fuller Creek with 11 lots, Keen Camp with 28, Fern Valley with 18, Lily Creek with 35, and Tahquitz with 59 lots.[13] All but the first two were in the Idyllwild area.

The Forest Service fully realized the importance of early detection as the best method of controlling fires. To augment the fixed-point lookout system, the national forests of Southern California initiated an aerial fire patrol. Beginning in 1919, the Army Air Service, operating out of March Field, began daily fire detection flights over the three Southern California national forests – the Cleveland, the Angeles and the Santa Barbara. The daily flights continued through the end of the 1921 fire season.

Another major administrative change for the San Jacinto Ranger District came in 1925. By proclamation of President Calvin Coolidge, dated September 30, the San Jacinto District was removed from Cleveland National Forest and made part of the newly recreated San Bernardino National Forest. The San Bernardino Forest Reserve had originally been proclaimed by President Benjamin Harrison on February 25, 1893. In 1908, President Theodore Roosevelt had consolidated it with portions of the old San Gabriel National Forest to form the Angeles National Forest. This arrangement later proved too cumbersome to administer effectively, so, in 1925, the San Bernardino National Forest was reestablished. This arrangement has continued to the present time.

Appointed first supervisor of the newly recreated San Bernardino National Forest was Steven Augustus "Gus" Nash-Boulden, who had been head ranger of the San Jacinto District just six years previously. One of Nash-Boulden's first tasks as supervisor was drafting the San Bernardino National Forest Recreation Plan. This document outlined the improvement of old campgrounds and the building of new ones throughout the forest.

During the next few years, the San Jacinto District developed or improved three campgrounds. Hall Campground, located where the Banning-Idyllwild Road crossed Hall Canyon (just above today's Lake Fulmor), Fuller Creek Campground, three miles farther up the Banning-Idyllwild Road, and Pine Flat Campground, just above Strawberry Valley, were the first officially-designated campgrounds in the San Jacinto District. Prior to this time, visitors camped wherever in the forest they pleased. Campgrounds were free and remained so until a fee system was introduced in 1948.

In 1926, Nash-Boulden unveiled the San Bernardino National Forest Fire Control Plan. The plan called for the construction of more roads, firebreaks, and fire lookout towers. That year, the dilapidated Vista Grande lookout was abandoned in favor of a newer, much higher tower on Black Mountain. In an effort to reduce the number of people-caused blazes, a fire permit system was initiated. Campfires were permitted only in designated campgrounds and, during fire season, smoking was prohibited except in public camps, places of habitation, and special posted areas known as "fag stations."

Camp Idyllwild CCC Camp was the first Civilian Conservation Corps facility in the San Jacinto Mountains. Camp Idyllwild opened in 1933 and was located in Alvin Meadow. – WILLIAM NEUHOFF

Despite all these precautions, the forest was plagued by several destructive fires at the end of the decade. The most serious conflagration in the San Jacinto District during this period was the Wilson Creek Fire of 1928, which burned a total of 166,000 acres, 20,000 acres of which were within the boundaries of the San Jacinto District.[15]

The following year the nation was plunged into the Great Depression. For the Forest Service, this difficult time would ultimately prove beneficial. President Franklin D. Roosevelt, like Theodore Roosevelt before him, was a great supporter of the forest conservation movement. One of his projects to provide work for the unemployed, the Civilian Conservation Corps, was targeted specifically at the national forests.

Civilian Conservation Corps (CCC) recruits were from 18 to 25 years of age and came from dependent families. From their salary of $30 per month, $25 was sent to the enrollee's family. Each recruit enrolled for a six month period and was provided food and shelter by the government.

The CCC recruits destined to work in the San Bernardino National Forest were assembled at March Field and given some elemental military training by the Army. During the initial CCC years, 1933 and 1934, they were under the guidance of Army Air Corps Major Henry H. "Hap" Arnold, later of World War II fame. Once organized into companies, the young CCC men were sent out to camps in and around the forest, under the dual control of the Army and either the U.S. Forest Service or the California Division of Forestry.

A typical CCC camp contained 213 individuals: 200 recruits, a commissioned Army commanding officer, 3 non-commissioned Army officers, 5 Army enlisted men, and 5 foremen from either the Forest Service or the state Division of Forestry. Each camp normally contained four bunkhouses for the recruits, an administration building (with officers' quarters and an orderly room), a mess hall, a kitchen, a shower room, a laundry room, and a recreation hall.[16]

Five CCC camps were established in or near the San Jacinto Mountains. The first was known as Camp Idyllwild, located on the old Idyllwild Control Road at Alvin Meadows, opened the last week of May 1933. Within the next few weeks, CCC camps were established at Vista Grande, Kenworthy, and Anza, the latter being co-controlled by state forestry rangers. The last camp, at San Jacinto, opened in October. A camp planned for Bautista Canyon was never built. In addition to the main camps, there were much smaller "spike" camps which were, from time to time, set up for projects in remote areas of the forest. One such spike camp operated in Tahquitz Valley during the summer of 1933 and Round Valley in the summers of 1934 and '35 (see *Game Refuge, State Park, and Primitive Area* chapter).

Probably the most important features of the CCC camps were the fire suppression crews, organized at each camp under the supervision of forest officials. For the first time, the Forest Service had practically unlimited manpower, trained and immediately available, for fighting forest and brush fires. Within less than a month of their formation, the fire crews were tested,

The three large buildings on the right are bunkhouses. The fourth large building is a combination mess hall and bunkhouse. The small structure left of center is the medical facility. On the far left is the recreation hall. Nothing remains at the site today.

extinguishing a wildfire which broke out about a mile from the Camp Anza CCC camp.

During the 1933 season, CCC crews constructed 42 miles of firebreaks, 32 miles of truck trails, 5 miles of hiking trails, 9 miles of telephone lines, and cleared new areas to be made into public campgrounds the following year – Hall Canyon, Fern Basin, and Pinyon Flat.

In 1934, CCC crews from Camp Idyllwild constructed a new Forest Service station in Idyllwild. Upon completion, the San Jacinto Ranger District moved its headquarters from San Jacinto (now Cranston) Station to the new Idyllwild site, where it remains today.

During the next several years, CCCers continued to build improvements throughout the forest. Many miles of trail were constructed in the new San Jacinto State Park and adjacent wilderness areas. Three more campgrounds were completed. New fire lookout towers were erected on Tahquitz Peak, Ranger Peak, Barton (now Barker) Peak, Thomas Mountain, and Red Mountain.

Unfortunately, the greatest period ever in forest improvement did not last long. With America's economic recovery and the growing threat of war, the CCC camps closed down one by one. The last of the camps in the San Jacinto Mountains, Kenworthy, an all Black camp in its final year and a half, was moved to Los Padres National Forest in October 1937. Only Mill Creek and City Creek CCC camps in the San Bernardino Mountains remained open in the San Bernardino National Forest until the outbreak of World War II. The CCC program came to a close nationally on June 30, 1942.[17] The splendid accomplishments of these "sturdy and tan-backed boys" of the CCC are still talked about today.

With the loss of the CCC camps and America's entry into World War II, there was a critical shortage of manpower available to the Forest Service, particularly for fire fighting. "The demand for workers in defense industries has absorbed the labor supply upon which we would normally call," complained wartime supervisor DeWitt Nelson.[18] High school boys were utilized, but they were available during summer vacation only. The Forest Service often had to call on the military from March Field and Camp Haan near Riverside.

The Idyllwild Ranger Station was built by a CCC work crew in 1934 on land donated by C. L. Emerson.
– U.S. FOREST SERVICE

185

San Bernardino National Forest staff meeting, ca. 1955. Sim Jarvi, forest supervisor, is in back row, left end. Next to him is John Gilman, district ranger of the San Jacinto District. Ernie Maxwell is in back row, right end. Front row, third from left, is Don Bauer, fire management officer and San Jacinto District Ranger 1946-52. In middle, bottom row, is Larry Smith, fire management officer of San Jacinto Ranger District. – U.S. FOREST SERVICE

From 1942 through most of 1944, the San Bernardino National Forest was closed to public use except for residents and resort owners and their guests. An advertising campaign promoted forest fire prevention as good for the war effort. Brush was cleared from the shoulders of the major mountain highways.

Still, several large fires occurred. In November 1943, flames erupted at Mountain Center, burning the store, cafe, and gas station, then, whipped by strong winds, swept through Keen Camp, destroying Tahquitz Lodge and a number of cabins. Soldiers from Camp Haan managed to halt the conflagration just short of Idyllwild. Over 8,000 acres were charred.[19] The extensive Bull Canyon Fire of August 1944 started near Anza and burned over the south and west slopes of Santa Rosa Mountain to the Palms to Pines Highway. Camp Haan soldiers again were called in to contain the blaze but not before it had burned 31,000 acres, 7,000 acres within the forest boundary.

World War II brought about new developments in fire control, the most important of which was the use of aircraft, both fixed wing and helicopter, to control forest blazes. Another valuable by-product of the war was the jeep, able to negotiate steep off-road terrain.

The first two decades following the war were marked by a sharp increase in both the resident and the visitor populations in the San Jacintos. The ever increasing visitor use produced a great strain on existing forest camping facilities. Assistant District Ranger James Ruppelt participated in a nationwide recreation survey to determine possible improvement and expansion of the campground system. As a result, Dark Canyon, Marion Mountain, Fern Basin, and Fuller Mill Creek public campgrounds were laid out in accordance with new Forest Service guidelines, allowing for individual and group camping spots complete with stoves, restrooms and waste facilities.

Despite an extensive firebreak system built during the CCC years and carefully maintained afterwards, fires continued to plague the forest – particularly the lower brush-covered slopes. To help prevent and control these blazes, the San Jacinto District created "buzz units," usually two-man patrol units that combined prevention and suppression personnel in one vehicle. By the 1958 fire season, there were six fire stations in the San Jacinto Ranger District: Vista Grande, Idyllwild, Keen Camp, Cranston, Kenworthy, Tripp Flats, and Bautista Canyon. In September of that year, a new station called Keenwild, just above Mountain Center on the road to Idyllwild, replaced the fifty year old Keen Camp station. There was a fire patrolman at each station, as well as one at Pine Cove and one assigned to the high country.

Fire lookout towers, "guardians on the mountaintops," were for many years a mainstay in early fire detection, but no longer is this so. The late 1950s and 1960s witnessed a sharp decline in their numbers, as the Forest Service began to rely more on aircraft to spot blazes. Aircraft had the advantage of mobility and the

The first Black Mountain lookout tower was built in 1926. It was dismantled and rebuilt atop Barton Peak in 1935. The present Black Mountain lookout tower dates from 1962. — U.S. FOREST SERVICE

The 60-foot high Thomas Mountain fire lookout tower was built in 1934. It remained in service into the 1960s. — U.S. FOREST SERVICE

ability to see more of the forest than fixed point stations. Worsening air pollution hampered visibility, particularly of the towers in the lower elevations such as Ranger and Barton peaks. These two lookout towers were abandoned in favor of a new metal tower on Black Mountain, completed in 1962. (The old 1926 wooden tower on Black Mountain had been dismantled and reassembled on Barton Peak by the CCC in 1935.) Thomas Mountain Lookout was closed in the late 1950s except for occasional use during fire emergencies and deer hunting season. By 1970, only Black Mountain, Red Mountain, and Tahquitz Peak remained. Today (1993), only the Tahquitz Peak lookout is manned during fire season in the San Jacinto Ranger District.

As both the resident and visitor population continued to increase, so did the risk of fire. The 1970s proved to be the most devastating fire decade in the history of the San Bernardino National Forest. The largest fire in the Forest's 100-year history was the 1970 Bear Fire in the Big Bear Ranger District of the San Bernardino Mountains, which blackened 53,100 acres.

Ranking as one of the worst conflagrations ever in the history of the San Jacinto Ranger District was the Soboba Fire of August 1974. The arson-caused blaze started in the Valle Vista area at the edge of the Soboba Indian Reservation. It quickly raced uphill through dry brush along two different flanks. The northern flank of the fire moved up Castile Canyon and threatened the community of Poppet Flat. The northeastern flank rushed over Indian Mountain and turned eastward toward the community of Pine Cove. Residents, campers, and some 180 Girl Scouts were evacuated. At the fires's peak, there were 1,300 fire fighters, 92 fire engines, 25 bulldozers, 17 air tankers, and 7 helicopters on duty. Forest Service fire crews were assisted by units of the California Department of Forestry and several local fire departments. Miraculously, only one building at the Girl Scout camp was destroyed, and no lives were lost. The Soboba Fire was finally controlled after scorching more than 18,000 acres of brush and timber at a cost of over $2.5 million.[20]

To combat the increasing fire threat in the forest, new "hot shot" crews, highly trained in the latest fire fighting techniques, were organized. In July 1974, the Vista Grande Hot Shot Crew came into service under the leadership of Kirby More. Over the years, the Vista Grande "Hot Shots" have been called to fight forest conflagrations all over the western United States and are considered one of the very best fire fighting outfits in the U.S. Forest Service.

Providing valuable help to the Forest Service in controlling fires in the San Jacinto Mountains and surrounding foothill areas is the California Department of Forestry. The CDF operates four fire stations in the region: at Pine Cove, Garner Valley, Pinyon Flat, and Anza. The Riverside County Fire Department has operated its volunteer Station #53 in the Garner Valley since 1979. Local fire agencies are also called to help fight mountain and foothill blazes.

Despite these increased fire control efforts, the largest fire in the history of the San Jacinto Ranger District occurred in 1980. The Dry Falls Fire was started by children playing with matches on August 26. Weather conditions, rugged topography, and lack of roads combined to make control of the fire difficult.

Kenworthy Guard Station, 1938. – U.S. FOREST SERVICE

Don Bauer was district ranger of the San Jacinto Ranger District from 1946 to 1952. He served as San Bernardino National Forest supervisor from 1958 to 1974.
– U.S. FOREST SERVICE

From its point of origin east of Palm Springs, the flames raced uphill toward San Jacinto Mountain. In just two days it reached the 8,000-foot level and threatened to engulf Mt. San Jacinto State Park. Instead, the fire moved southward along the east face of the mountain and into the federal wilderness. During the next two weeks the eastern slope of the San Jacintos were burned from Tachevah Canyon south to the "Desert Divide" country as far as Spitler Peak. Because access to most of the burning area was inaccessible to motorized vehicles, suppression was carried out largely by hand crews. At the height of the conflagration there were 56 fire engines (used mainly to prevent the fire from reaching into inhabited areas), 12 bulldozers, 73 hand crews, 15 air tankers, and 12 helicopters. In all, the Dry Falls Fire scorched 28,655 acres.[21]

The Forest Service, the CDF, and local fire fighting agencies have continued to update and improve their fire control methods. Prescribed burns, planned fires set to reduce the amount of flammable vegetation in brushy areas, have been utilized by the San Jacinto Ranger District since 1983. Reforestation of burned slopes has been actively pursued since the '80s, particularly in the Black Mountain, Garner Valley, and May Valley areas. Public information programs aimed at fire prevention have been upgraded.

While fire prevention and control continue to be major concerns of the San Jacinto Ranger District, other issues also require attention. A pine beetle infestation threatens to damage much of the forest. Above all is the problem of managing a forest being overrun by too many people. Forest visitors in the form of sightseers, picnickers, campers, fishermen, hikers, and off road vehicle users often engulf the mountains. San Bernardino National Forest was declared one of the nation's eleven "urban forests" in 1988. Urban forests are all located near major population centers and their major focus is on providing recreational facilities for the millions of forest visitors. Recreational users must be accommodated without damage to the forest – a delicate balancing act. Restrictions on public use, such as the wilderness permit system, are necessary to preserve parts of the forest from being overwhelmed by a swelling tide of humanity.

After much study and input from forest users, the San Bernardino National Forest Land and Resource Management Plan was completed in 1988. The plan addresses such crucial issues as fire control, grazing, mining, recreation, wilderness, and wildlife in the forest and will be reevaluated every fifteen years.

As the San Bernardino National Forest enters its centennial year (1993), it faces challenges undreamed of a century ago. The fragile balance between forest use and forest protection must be maintained. Although Americans have the unalienable right to use their forests, they also have the responsibility to respect and protect them for the enjoyment of generations to come.

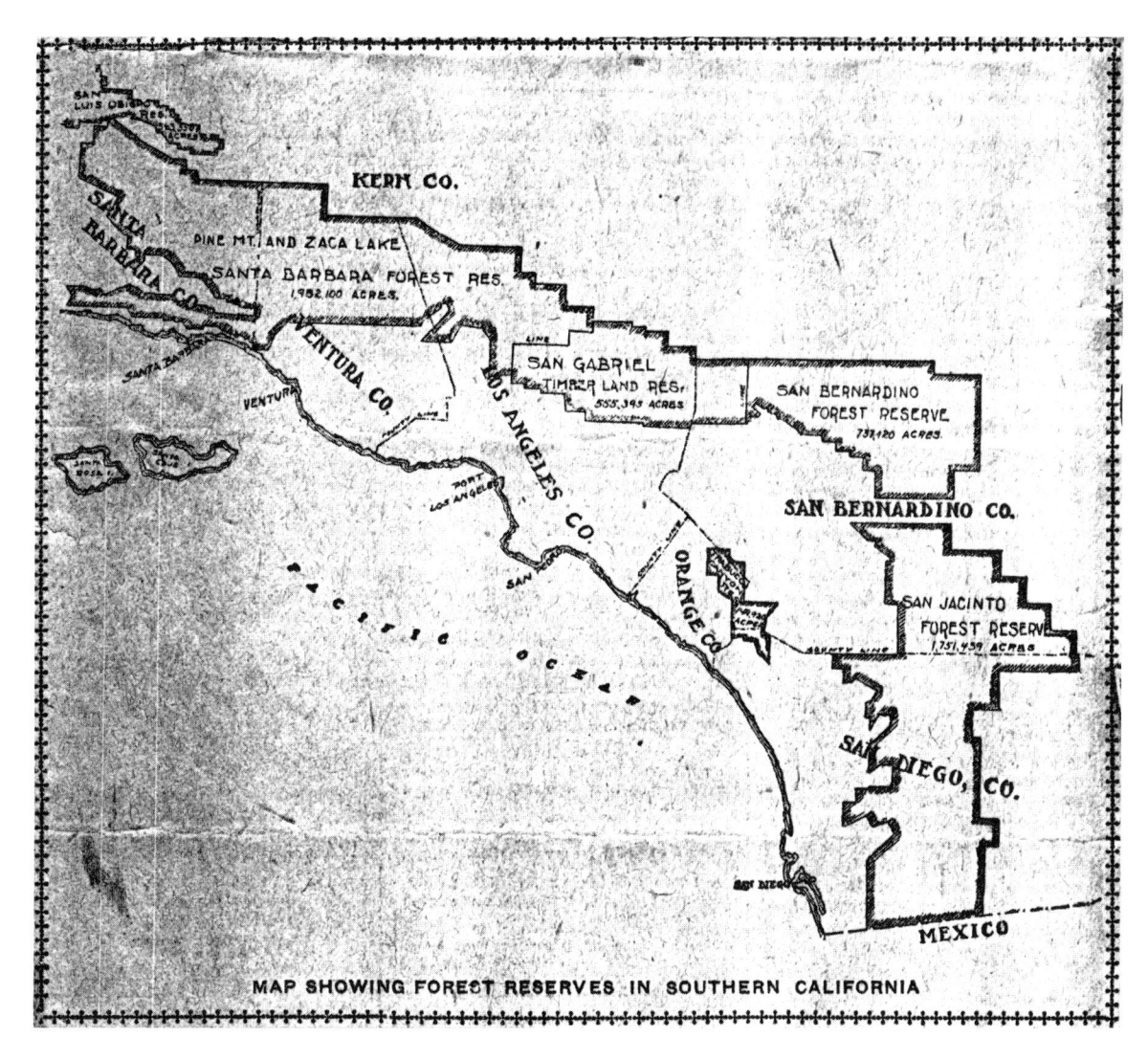

The Forest Reserves of Southern California, 1907. Notice that the San Jacinto Forest Reserve extended to the Mexican border. This arrangement only lasted one year; in 1908 the San Jacinto Reserve lost its self identity and became a ranger district of newly created Cleveland National Forest.

NOTES

1. Ronald F. Lockman, *Guarding the Forests of Southern California: Evolving Attitudes Toward Conversation of Watershed, Woodlands, and Wilderness*, (Glendale: The Arthur H. Clark Co., 1981), p. 71.
2. Gifford Pinchot, *Breaking New Ground* (Seattle: U. of Washington Press, 1947), p. 89.
3. John Muir, *Journals, 1869-1914*, Roll 14 (microfilm), Holt-Atherton Western Research Center, U. Of Pacific, Stockton.
4. Charles S. Sargent, et al, "Report of the National Academy of Sciences," *Senate Document 57*, 55th Congress, 2nd Session, 1898, p. 26.
5. B. F. Allen to S. B. Ormsby, Supervisor of Oregon Forest Reserves, October 25, 1897 (copy on file at Angeles National Forest, Arcadia).
6. B. F. Allen to Binger Hermann, Commissioner of the G.L.O., July 18, 1898 (copy on file at Angeles National Forest).
7. Pinchot, p. 164.
8. E. A. Sterling, *Report on the Fire Conditions in the San Jacinto Forest Reserve in Southern California*, U.S.D.A., Bureau of Forestry, Office of Forest Extension, 1904, p. 3.
9. Pinchot, p. 264-265.
10. John W. Robinson and Bruce D. Risher, "San Bernardino National Forest: A Century of Federal Stewardship," *San Bernardino County Museum Association Quarterly*, 37:4, Winter 1990, p. 17.
11. "Annual Ranger Meetings," Forest Reserve Order No. 39, issued by Gifford Pinchot, April 14, 1906.
12. Robinson and Risher, p. 22.
13. R. H. May & R. H. Cron, "Recreation Survey," correspondence dated October 14, 1937, (copy on file at San Bernardino National Forest, San Bernardino).
14. U.S.D.A. Forest Service California Region, 1931 map of San Bernardino National Forest, issued 1932.
15. Deborah Wettlaufer, *Seventy Years of Fire Management on the San Bernardino National Forest (1910-1980)*, unpublished manuscript, (copy on file at San Bernardino National Forest.)
16. *Hemet News*, June 9 & October 13, 1933.
17. Robinson and Risher, p. 58.
18. *Redlands Daily Facts*, June 2, 1941.
19. *Hemet News*, November 12, 1943.
20. *Hemet News*, August 29, 30, 1974.
21. *Hemet News*, August 28 to September 8, 1980.

On the summit of San Jacinto Peak, ca. 1898. On the right is forester Theodore P. Lukens.
— HENRY E. HUNTINGTON LIBRARY

15

SAN JACINTO PEAK

Naturalist John Muir, upon watching the sunrise from the summit, is said to have exclaimed, "The view from San Jacinto is the most sublime spectacle to be found anywhere on this earth!"[1] Since then, countless others have experienced the same inspiration. The vista is utterly magnificent, extending over hundreds of square miles of mountain, foothill, valley, and desert. On the southwestern horizon, beyond row after row of misty-purple ranges, is the glimmering Pacific. Northwest, the gray hogback of San Gorgonio rises grandly across the trough of San Gorgonio Pass. Eastward sprawls the drab tawniness of the Colorado Desert and its wrinkled hills. Southeast lies the shining platter of the Salton Sea, and beyond, in the distant haze, is Mexico. What gives the panorama a final touch of grandeur is the great north rampart, plunging in jagged cliffs and castillated ridges to Coachella Valley, nearly two miles below.

San Jacinto Peak is no less grand when viewed from below. To the early Indian peoples it was a sacred mountain. Native peoples throughout Southern California looked upon high mountain peaks – particularly Mounts San Antonio (Old Baldy), San Gorgonio and San Jacinto – with a mixture of reverence and mysticism. A creation myth of the Serrano said that their ancestors were led down from the north by a great white eagle belonging to Land God. The eagle landed first on Mt. San Antonio, then flew to San Gorgonio Mountain, each time being followed by the people. With the death of Land God, the eagle flew on to its final resting place atop San Jacinto Peak.[2] The Cahuilla had a similar creation myth, to the effect that their ancestors flew from the north to San Gorgonio Mountain, where they resided for a time before flying on to San Jacinto Peak. The Cahuilla knew the peak as *I a kitch*, or *Aya Kaich*, meaning "smooth cliffs," the home of the meteor *Dakush*, legendary founder of the Cahuilla people. Chief Francisco Patencio of the Desert Cahuilla said, "There is a place near the top, which has no pine trees, a place of about 40 or 50 acres; right in the center of this place is a large smooth rock, about 10 or 15 feet square, not very high from the ground, around three feet. They [ancestral Cahuilla] stayed for a long time."[3] The Luiseño called the peak *Yamiwa;* the Serrano called it *Sovovo*. Even the far away Gabrielino revered it as *Jamiwu*.

Just when the mountain was named *San Jacinto* is unclear. The Franciscan padres of Mission San Luis Rey gave the name to their outlying stock ranch – today's San Jacinto Valley – which was named in honor of the 15th century martyr Saint Hyacinth of Silicia. There is no evidence that the Spanish padres or their Mexican successors knew the peak as San Jacinto.

Early Anglo explorers were quite confused about the name. The peak first appears on Army Lieutenant Edward O. C. Ord's 1849 map as *San Ygnacio Mt.* Lieutenant Robert S. Williamson's Pacific Railroad Survey party of 1853 referred to it as *San Gorgonio* and misjudged its elevation as 7,000 feet. The mistake was corrected in 1855, when Lieutenant John G. Parke's Railroad Survey party passed through San Gorgonio Pass. Dr. Thomas Antisell, expedition geologist, called it *San Jacinto*.[4]

First to name the summit *San Jacinto Peak*, rather than San Jacinto Mountain or Mount San Jacinto, was the U.S. Army's Wheeler Survey, which used the summit as a triangulation point in 1878. They calculated the elevation as 10,987.3 feet above sea level.[5]

Who made the first ascent of San Jacinto Peak will probably never be known. Most likely it was a Cahuilla hunter or spiritual leader centuries before the arrival of the white man. Charles Thomas, owner of the Thomas Ranch in today's Garner Valley, led cattle into the high country as early as 1870 and may have scrambled to the summit. He guided the Wheeler Survey party to the top in 1878, so he must have known the route.

The earliest climb on record was made in September 1874 by a person identified only as "F. of Riverside." The *San Diego Union* (September 16, 1874) gave a long account of the ascent. Briefly, the story is as follows:

John Muir in Palm Springs, photographed by Helen Lukens Gaut in 1905. Did Muir ever climb San Jacinto Peak? The famous quote about the view from the summit being "the most sublime spectacle to be found anywhere on this earth" is attributed to him. He visited Garner and Strawberry valleys with the National Forest Commission in 1896 and Palm Springs in 1905, but that is apparently as close as he got to the mountain. The authors were unable to verify that he ever reached the summit.
— PALM SPRINGS HISTORICAL SOCIETY

The earliest known photograph of a party on the summit of San Jacinto Peak, 1885. — CHARLES VAN FLEET

Five men, including "F," left Riverside on horseback and travelled to Strawberry Valley, then up into the mountains. They reported that "Bears are numerous and rather troublesome." Three of the party left their camp in Tahquitz Valley and followed "a long sloping ridge covered with pine and cedar." About a thousand feet below the top, they were forced to leave their horses and climb on foot. "Climbing very slowly, as the rarified air made the exertion severe, they reached in about an hour the summit first in view, and found, as is usually the case, a higher one beyond. Two of the party were quite exhausted and did not care to go further, but F. determined to push on." After crossing "enormous masses of rock," F. reached the true summit in one and a half hours. After taking in the suberb view and making a compass bearing, F. started to descend. "Running, sliding, rolling and sometimes falling down.... Half an hour brought him to his companions, much alarmed at this prolonged absence and speculating what to do in case he had fallen into some hole and should not soon reappear." The threesome then returned to their horses and descended via a "charming little valley about a mile long and a quarter mile wide, green with tall grass, and with a little stream winding through." This may have been the first description of Tahquitz Valley.

This 1874 ascent and the Wheeler Survey party led by Charles Thomas in 1878 are the only known climbs during the decade of the 1870s. With the growing popularity of Strawberry Valley as a summer resort in the 1880s, ascents became more frequent.

Dr. Walter Lindley, prominent Los Angeles physician who would later build the Idyllwild Sanatorium, ascended the peak in 1888. Lindley and a friend named Warner, along with a young guide recuperating from tuberculosis in Strawberry Valley, rode horseback up the Devil's Slide to Tahquitz Valley, then around the ridge to Tamarack Valley where they spent the night. Early next morning they scrambled to the summit.

> We reached the very top in time to witness the sun rise in its splendor from beyond the Colorado Desert that lay spread out below us in its stupendous barrenness. What is that dark, twisting object, about the size and apparently traveling at about the gait of a snail? It comes nearer, and we see that it is a freight train on the Southern Pacific Railroad near Indio. Our guide starts a boulder over the eastern slope of the mountain, and we hear it bounding through the awful chasms below.... Space will not permit me attempting a description of what we saw from this wonderous height.[6]

The early ascents of San Jacinto Peak were apparently all made from the south, via the Devil's Slide, Tahquitz and Tamarack valleys. In 1891, four Banning young men – Ed Martin, James Gilman, Herbert Gilman, and Marshall French Gilman, the latter, first mayor of Banning – rode horseback up Hall's Grade to the Fuller sawmill and climbed the mountain from the west. They camped just above the sawmill at 7,000 feet.

> Next morning at 6:30 we started on foot for the summit. The climbing was the most difficult I ever encountered. One of the worst places was on a peak below and northwest of the top [probably Folly Peak]. This place was unanimously called 'Hell's Half Section,' and richly deserved the name. No soil, sand or gravel could be seen, and rock was walked on for half a mile.
>
> A short distance farther on, a small cave, or more properly speaking, a series of large cracks in the rock, were seen. The writer entered one of these, travesed it for fifty yards underground, and finally emerged from another opening....

A horseback party from Idyllwild Inn enroute to San Jacinto Peak, ca. 1920. — NELL EMERSON ZIEGLER

On top of San Jacinto Peak, May 17, 1925. The wood structure is a U.S.G.S. triangulation station.
— LOUISE WERNER

> We reached the summit at 2 p.m. The highest point is a large rock, on which is a heap of small stones covering the San Jacinto peak register. A number of names were there, most, if not all of which, had made the summit from the south side.[7]

For those who wanted to stay overnight on or near the summit, warm clothes and a fire were considered necessities. The *San Jacinto Register* (October 1, 1891) reported,

> A big bonfire was plainly visible from San Jacinto peak last week. The fuel for these fires has to be carried up the mountainside 1000 feet and at an incline of nearly 45 degrees. It cannot be an easy matter to thus illumine the big peak. It is a pretty sight, and amply repays the parties for the hard work.... These fires are said to be visible to all the surrounding towns.

The most spectacular route to San Jacinto Peak is via the north-east escarpment, one of the most precipitous mountain ramparts in the United States, rising from the desert to 10,804 feet in five horizontal miles. It has long fascinated mountaineers, who see in its steep gullies, jagged ridges and sheer granite cliffs a resemblance to the eastern face of the Sierra Nevada.

The escarpment was attempted, or at least explored, in 1896. Bertrand Wentworth and a companion departed the train at Whitewater Station and headed on foot toward the face.

> We made our way slowly across the boulders to the line of sycamores shading the pools of Falls Creek; and keeping near its banks we soon entered Falls Creek Cañon. Here on the one side a spur of the mountain rises at a very steep grade to about 4000 feet; on the other, a literal wall towers about fifteen hundred feet. A pebble may easily be cast into the creek from the crest of the precipice. A mile from its foot the cañon terminates suddenly at La Cueva Falls....
>
> In the course of our first day's explorations, we succeeded in reaching the basin at the foot of the principal fall of the La Cueva series. The cliffs form a wall around it about 150 feet in diameter – complete, except the narrow passage where the water escapes to make its next headlong leap. Three hundred feet above this basin, the water, plunging over the cliffs, sparkles brilliantly in the noonday sun....
>
> Four days we explored cañons similar to this one – each rocky and wild beyond description, each abounding in shaded pools of crystal water and noisy cascades, and each effectively blocking the climber.... Whether one advances in Falls Creek or in the cañons of Snow Creek and its several forks, one comes sooner or later to an impassable series of waterfalls.

Bertrand and his friend finally traversed west out of the canyons and onto the timbered slopes northwest of the peak, where they reached an elevation of 8,000 feet before turning back.[8]

Six years later, the prolific writer George Wharton James attempted to climb the escarpment, failed, and ended up climbing San Jacinto Peak via the trailless northwest slope. He described his adventure in his 1906 classic, *The Wonders of The Colorado Desert:*

> Leaving La Cueva, which is at the base of the mountain on its northern side, we enter Falls Creek Canyon, passing beautiful sycamores on the way. The canyon is wild and rugged; a spur of the mountains rising sharply on one side for several thousand feet, and a sheer wall, about fifteen hundred feet high, lining the other side.... To gain the snow ridge one now has to climb and explore. Canyon after canyon, and ridge after ridge are crossed, where icy waters flow down from the snowfields above. The only sure plan is to resolutely edge around to the northwest,... To attempt to go to the summit directly from the north is surely to court defeat, as every canyon seems to terminate in a waterfall, and the ridges are densely covered with manzanita and a chaparral of scrub-oak, greesewood, and buckbrush. This tangled mass varies from five to twelve feet high, and is often impenetrable save with an axe. But the charm and delight of exploring these rugged canyons, enjoying the waterfalls and the clear, pellucid streams of snow-water, and the rare experience of walking into snow tunnels made by the flowing water, where, at a temperature near to freezing, one can look out to ridges upon which he baked at 100 degrees Fahrenheit a few minutes before, make this rugged north slope of San Jacinto the most desirable point of attack to the real lover of mountain climbing.

The hard way up San Jacinto, via Snow Creek on the desert escarpment. The pictures were taken by one of the authors during a 1958 climb.

James, like his predecessor, then traversed west over to the easier northwest slope of the mountain and continued climbing.

> We approach an area where there are few trees, the granite being mainly in evidence. Above this we find ourselves in the real forests where the tall timber grows. And what a change from the scorching desert beneath!... We remember our own discomfort in the heat but a day or two ago, and now! now! we are in the most delicious shade, surrounded by an atmosphere that fairly flows into every hidden place of our body, bringing cool refreshment and sensations of fresh vigor and new life. The pines sing joyously above us, and, as we see the bare ledges of the granite above, capped by the snow-streaked summit, we cry Excelsior! and joyously dash on ahead....
>
> In the final climb of the last one thousand feet or so there are but few trees and when, at last, the summit is reached we feel – what? That we are well repaid? We have been repaid all the way up.... the chief charm to me of being on the summit is that I learn a new respect for the grand mountain itself.... To gain this knowledge is well worth all the labor of the arduous climb.[9]

The first successful ascent of the northeast face, as far as is known, was made by Stewart White of Riverside and Floyd Vernoy of Beaumont in July 1931. White made an unsuccessful attempt via Snow Creek in 1927 and was anxious to try again. White related his experience in a letter to the author:

> On this climb we avoided the brush and stayed on the rock with little difficulty and with only occasional use of a rope. We passed our earlier bivouac site well ahead of our previous schedule.... Climbing on, we spent the night at about 8,000 feet. A few rock walls made a level place big enough to stretch out....
>
> In the morning we completed the climb and enjoyed the wonderful view of the desert. The return was by Dark Canyon where we made note of some fine trout pools.

> As to whether or not our climb in 1931 was a first ascent I do not know. However, as a point of interest, it can be reported that at least one descent was made before that time. The climber was a Boy Scout who became lost at the summit and decided the quick way down to the lights he could see on the desert floor was to go straight down the north face. As I remember, this happened in the late 1920s and the boy walked into the fish hatchery [Snow Creek] carrying a rattlesnake. He had been on the mountain three days.[10]

Stewart White made another ascent via Snow Creek in 1932, and a winter ascent in 1937. A Sierra Club party made up of Howard Sloan, Morgan Leonard and Glenn Rickenbough made the ascent via Snow Creek in April 1932, and R. S. Fink of Santa Ana did it the next month. Two more climbing parties went up in 1933, and several more made it in the late 1930s. Dr. Ernest C. Bower of Altadena, founder of the Ramblers Hiking club, climbed the north face via Snow Creek eleven times between 1940 and 1949, a record no one else approaches.

The climb of San Jacinto Peak via its desert face became quite common after World War II, with six or seven attempts almost every year.

As for ascents of San Jacinto Peak from any direction, Sid Davis, Los Angeles movie producer, holds the record at 626. Davis made most of his ascents the easy way – via the tramway and trail – in the 1960s, '70s and '80s.

Over the years, there have been a number of proposals to develop the summit for scientific or commercial purposes. The first was made in 1899, reported in the *Redlands Citrograph* (September 2): "An observation station to be used in connection with the U.S. Weather Bureau is to be established there, and a rock

Los Angeles movie producer Sid Davis celebrates one of his 626 ascents of San Jacinto Peak. – SID DAVIS

Skiing the ultimate! Chris Kenyon of Pasadena jumps off the summit cornice enroute down Snow Creek to the desert, a dare-devil ski descent that has been accomplished several times since 1988. – CHRIS KENYON

house for the occupants of the station will be erected near the peak." The summit weather station was never built. In 1927 astronomers from the California Institute of Technology in Pasadena visited the summit to determine its feasibility as a location for the 200-inch Hale Telescope, the world's largest at the time. The site finally chosen was Palomar Mountain in San Diego County. In 1929 several Los Angeles businessmen proposed a highway up the mountain with a hotel on top. Fortunately, this grandiose plan never came to pass.

In 1931 and 1932 the San Jacinto Mountain Chamber of Commerce sponsored a Labor Day footrace from Idyllwild Inn to the top of San Jacinto Peak, 18 miles and 5,300 feet of gain. In 1931 it was won by Tom Humphrys, a Hopi Indian, in 3 hours 36½ minutes. Humphrys won again in 1932, breaking his record with a time of 3 hours, 12 minutes.

In 1935 the Civilian Conservation Corps constructed a stone shelter just east of the summit, still there today. The C.C.C. also rebuilt the trail from Saddle Junction to the top.

After World War II, climbs of San Jacinto Peak became almost daily occurrences during the summer months. Boy Scouts, religious groups, Sierra Club parties and all manner of individuals swarmed to the summit in increasing numbers. With the completion of the Palm Springs Aerial Tramway in 1963, even larger crowds reached the top. In recent years, San Jacinto State Park authorities have tried to lessen the impact of too many people by requiring wilderness permits. Still, the summit march goes on. No Southern California hiker worth his salt would miss climbing "San Jack" at least once.

NOTES

1. Weldon F. Heald, "The Lordly San Jactintos," *Westways,* July 1963. We have been unable to verify that John Muir ever climbed San Jacinto Peak. He visited Thomas Ranch with the National Forest Commission in 1896, but stayed only one day and did not approach the mountain. See John Muir Papers, Holt-Atherton Library, University of Pacific, Stockton, Microfilm Roll 14 (1885-1901). The Muir story first appears in K. P. Frederick, *Legends and History of the San Jacinto Mountains* (Long Beach, 1926), p. 4, and has been repeated many times since. Even though Muir may never have visited the peak, the quotation attributed to him accurately portrays the view from the summit.

2. G. Hazen Shinn, *Shoshonean Days: Recollections of A Residence of Five Years Among the Indians of Southern California* (Glendale, 1941), p. 35-36.

3. Chief Francisco Patencio, as told to Margaret Boynton, *Stories and Legends of the Palm Springs Indians* (Palm Springs, 1943), p. 33.

4. See chapter *Government Explorers and Map Makers* for documentation.

5. *Ibid.*

6. Walter Lindley, M.D. "High Altitudes of Southern California," reprint from *Southern California Practitioner* (Los Angeles, 1888), p. 4-5.

7. *San Jacinto Register,* August 20, 1891.

8. Bertrand H. Wentworth, "On Mt. San Jacinto," *Land of Sunshine,* March 1896.

9. George Wharton James, *The Wonders of the Colorado Desert* (Boston, 1906), p. 76-77.

10. Stewart White letter to author, March 7, 1973. Howard Sloan, Morgan Leonard, and Glenn Rickenbough's Snow Creek ascent in April 1932, detailed in Sloan, "Climbing the North Face of Mount San Jacinto," *Sierra Club Bulletin,* February 1933, was long thought to be the first ascent of the northeast escarpment, but the authors accept White's account of his climb a year earlier.

Looking south from the San Jacinto high country. A cloud wave envelops the Desert Divide and the Santa Rosas beyond. In the left distance, the Salton Sea shines like a silver platter in the afternoon sun.
— DICK SHIDELER

Hidden Lake, a mountain gem near the desert escarpment, is the only natural lake in the San Jacintos. In times of drought, it all but dries up.

16

HIGH COUNTRY

Above the desert-facing escarpment and the more gentle seaward slope of the San Jacintos is a sky-island of delectable sub-alpine wilderness, a bit of the High Sierra in Southern California. Here, under white granite summits and bouldery ridges, lie little hanging valleys lush with forest and meadow. Jeffrey pine, incense cedar, white fir and, higher up, lodgepole pine provide a shady canopy, and emerald-green marshes spotted with skunk cabbage delight the eye. The water is icy-cold and the air clean and refreshing, crisp with the chill of elevation.

Those who confine their explorations to the highways that wind around the lower and middle slopes of the San Jacintos will never see this mountain roof-garden. Riders on the spectacular Palm Springs Aerial Tramway can sample a small portion of it, but it is only the hiker or horseback rider who can truly experience this enchanting high mountain wilderness.

In early times, the high San Jacintos were within the realm of the Desert Cahuilla. Hunters ventured high on the mountain in search of deer and other wild game. They climbed the desert face to the forested benches and meadows where deer were grazing, killed and dressed them on the spot, and descended with their kill slung over their shoulders.[1] According to Chief Francisco Patencio, an aged Palm Springs Indian interviewed shortly before his death by historian Margaret Boynton, "The trails of the Indians were everywhere. They led up all the canyons.... A trail led from Chino Canyon up to San Jacinto Peak.... There were two trails from Snow Creek to San Jacinto Peak, one to the right of Snow Creek, and one to the left going up Fall Creek.... There was a hunting trail that led into a trail going to Hidden Lake and San Jacinto Peak from Tahquitz Canyon. Another trail went up Andreas Canyon to San Jacinto Peak."[2] These were all Desert Cahuilla trails; The Mountain Cahuilla, who lived as close as Strawberry and Garner valleys, apparently stayed out of the high regions.

The first non-Indians to enter the summit country were cattle and sheep herders. As early as 1870 and perhaps even earlier, Charles Thomas was driving his hungry herds from Garner Valley to feed on the tall grass of Tahquitz Meadow. There were two cattle trails up the mountain. First used by Thomas and then by others was the notorious Devil's Slide, which climbed from Strawberry Valley over the divide, without benefit of switchback, and down to Tahquitz Meadow. The other cattle trail went from Herkey Creek up over the ridge between Tahquitz and Red Tahquitz peaks via "The Hole-in-The Wall," a rocky notch between the two summits. From Tahquitz Meadow, cattle trails led into Willow Creek and over the ridge into Round and Tamarack valleys – anywhere the tall grass grew. Cowboys who drove their bawling herds up to high pasture in the 1880s and '90s included Frank Wellman (remembered by Wellmans Cienega today), Mryon Onstott, Sam and Dick Meeks, the Tripps, and the Hamiltons. There were at least three cabins built in the high country during the cattle era: two in Tahquitz Meadow and one on Willow Creek. Frank Wellman built the Willow Creek cabin entirely of logs, roof and all. The Meeks are said to have built the larger of the two log cabins in Tahquitz Meadow. The smaller cabin, under the pines at the northwest edge of the meadow, was erected by persons unknown.

Sheep were driven up to high pasture, also. Round Valley was known for a time as Shepherd's Camp; as late as 1907 there were remains of a crude lean-to and a dutch oven there.[3]

After the turn of the century, the Devil's Slide was seldom used as a cattle trail because Idyllwild objected to animals being driven through the growing community. Cowboys continued to use the Hole-in-the-Wall trail into the 1930s.

At the same time cattle and sheep were grazing the high mountain meadows, hunters, campers and moun-

An old cowboy cabin in Tahquitz Meadow, probably built by the brothers Sam and Dick Meeks in the early 1890s.— CHARLES VAN FLEET

tain climbers were scrambling up the Devil's Slide looking for wild game and recreation. Deer were stalked and killed by the hundreds every summer. Grizzly bear inhabited the mountains until the late 1880s. The *San Bernardino Guardian* (September 12, 1874) reported an encounter between John O'Conner, who went hunting above Strawberry Valley, and an angry bruin:

> It seems that, while hunting, he encountered a monster grizzly, which, startled at his near approach, instantly attacked him. O'Conner shot and hit his bearship, but not fatally, for the bear rushed on him, and striking him in the ribs, several of which he broke, knocked him down and seized his arm, which he crushed fearfully. At this juncture, O'Conner's dog, a little white half-breed bull dog..., appeared on the scene, and catching the bear by the hind leg, hung on to it with true bull dog pertinacity. The bear let go of O'Conner to attend to the dog, when O'Conner, though bruised and bleeding, poured another shot into the monster, but failed as before to strike him vitally. The bear now turned from the dog to the man, knocking the latter down and lacerating his scalp fearfully. With one blow of his paw he all but scalped the gallant mountaineer, besides tearing him fearfully about the shoulders and mashing his left arm into a shapeless mass. O'Conner now, knowing his knife the last chance, drew it, and with his fast failing strength, plunged it in the bear's body, who thereupon took flight.

Many early visitors to the high country experienced the strange metallic sounds and vibrations that were attributed to the evil demon Tahquitz of Cahuilla folklore. The *Los Angeles Star* (October 8, 1876) contained an article by A. T. Hawley, who described the unearthly sounds he heard while riding with Charles Thomas above Strawberry Valley. While the two rode up the mountain, a "brazen clang smote our ears."

Thomas said the sound was familiar to residents of the mountain, that the "metallic dissonance... invariably preceeded atmospheric disturbances and changes in the weather." A short time later, Hawley wrote, "the mountain tops were robed in clouds and, lit up with the glare of lightning, echoed great crashes of thunder, leaping from peak to peak." Thomas said that sometimes the clanging was "so unearthly that the whole family got up and dressed themselves."

A horseback rider passing through Tahquitz Valley experienced the mysterious sounds in 1893:

> But hark! What was that? You feel a nameless thrill go through you – there seems some strange oppression in the air; the cattle lift their heads and sniff uneasily, and – ah, a deep boom, then rumbling sound. The ground shakes beneath you as the sound dies away with titanic throbs as of a mighty chain slipping and then stopping while it is hauled up from the bowels of the earth. You find yourself wishing you were safe at home, away from this weird, uncanny region.... the noises and the tremblings continue at intervals all day and all night. ...Perhaps Rip Van Winkle's goblin Dutchmen have moved from the Catskills and are rolling their ninepins in the heart of this higher Western mountain.[4]

William F. Holcomb of San Bernardino rode up from Strawberry Valley to Tahquitz Valley in 1895 and reported the same noises and tremors:

> The next morning, leaving our wagon, we packed our horses and began to ascend. Our course was about northeast for about five miles when we came to the borders of that wonderful, yet to us, beautiful valley, but to the Cahuilla Indians of this part the most terrible and awful place on earth, called by them "Tauquitch," which, in their tongue, means devil. Here it is that you can so frequently hear those rumbling

A second old cabin in Tahquitz Meadow, probably dating from the 1890s. Who built it and when it was built are mysteries. – CHARLES VAN FLEET

Frank Wellman's cabin near the head of Willow Creek dates from the 1890s, possibly earlier. Wellman built it entirely of logs, roof and all. – HENRY E. HUNTINGTON LIBRARY

sounds, not unlike distant thunder, often accompanied with slight shocks or tremors, and supposed in some way connected with the warm springs of San Jacinto.

Sometimes these springs cease to flow. When often, at such times, the rumbling in the mountain is heard and at the same time the waters in San Jacinto springs are troubled, often throwing up pillars of sand from ten to thirty feet high.... Yet the place of the rumbling is distant from the springs about twenty miles. We had the pleasure of hearing one of those rumblings and felt a slight trembling of the earth at the same time.[5]

These sounds and vibrations were noticed by forester Theodore P. Lukens of Pasadena, as reported in the *Hemet News* (May 29, 1903):

Prof. Lukens has been on Mount Tahquitz when the rumblings and noises took place that frighten the superstitious Indians and cause so many to foolishly believe that it is an extinct volcano.

It is understood that President Wheeler and the university [of California] professors will investigate the noises occasionally heard.... It would add greatly to the zest of the investigation if old Tauquitz would give a first class exhibition of noises and rumblings when the distinguished gentlemen visit next July or August.

The scientific investigation never took place. The unearthly disturbances ceased to be noticed shortly after the turn of the century. What were they? A strong possibility is that they were of geologic origin. The San Jacinto Mountains are wedged between two major fault zones – the San Andreas to the north and east, and the San Jacinto to the west and south. Strong earthquakes occurred along the latter fault in 1899 and 1918. Perhaps these quakes relieved some of the presssures under the mountain, which might account for the fact that the rumblings have not been reported in recent years.

Although the source of the weird noises was never investigated by geologists, scientific studies of the flora and fauna did take place around the turn of the century.

Apparently first to study the flora of the high San Jacintos was S. B. Parish, a botanist from San Bernardino. Parish investigated the trees and plants in and around Tahquitz Valley during the summers of 1879 and 1881 but never published a detailed report on his findings.[6]

In 1898, botanist John B. Leiberg made a study of the trees of the newly-created San Jacinto Forest Reserve for the U.S. Bureau of Forestry (precurser of the Forest Service). He was critical of lumbering on the southwestern slopes but found the forests of the high San Jacintos in fine condition.[7]

Harvey Monroe Hall, University of California botanist, catalogued the plant life of the San Jacintos on several expeditions between 1896 and 1901. Hall divided the range into life zone categories that had just been developed by zoologist C. Hart Merriam. He found plant communities in the San Jacintos that ranged from Upper Sonoran at the desert base to a small area of Arctic-Alpine around the summit. "There is probably no place in North America where the alpine and Sonoran floras are in such proximity as they are on San Jacinto Mountain," Hall wrote. He found a few alpine plants on the shaded north face just below the top that represented "The most southern latitude at which the flora of the Alpine Zone is known to occur in North America." Like Leiberg, Hall found the lower forests damaged by extensive lumbering but the high country trees untouched.[8]

Joseph Grinnell and H. S. Swart, University of California zoologists, studied the birds and mammals of the San Jacintos in 1908. They described 169 species of birds and 63 species of mammals in the mountains, ranging from large animals such as big horn sheep, deer and cougar, down to small ones such as the California Little Brown Bat.[9]

In subsequent years, all aspects of the geology, flora

Writer Charles Francis Saunders visits a full Hidden Lake, ca. 1912. — HENRY E. HUNTINGTON LIBRARY

San Jacinto Forest Reserve supervisor Grant Taggart and ranger Con Silvas on the old trail between Round Valley and Tahquitz Creek, ca. 1899.— HENRY E. HUNTINGTON LIBRARY

and fauna of the San Jacintos have been investigated.

As Strawberry Valley became a favorite summer vacation spot, more and more people hiked or rode horseback into the high country. In 1899, the terrible Devil's Slide was tamed with switchbacks, making the ascent much easier. A new pathway, called the "Government Trail" because it was built by forest reserve rangers, climbed the ridge from Saddle Junction to Wellman's Cienega and on to San Jacinto Peak. The old cattle route from Tahquitz Meadow across Willow Creek and around the ridge to Hidden Lake, Round and Tamarack valleys was the most heavily used trail of all. Summer days saw as many as fifty or sixty persons camping in the lush meadows and along the creeks.

Hidden Lake, the little watery gem set in a shallow bowl at the edge of the desert-facing escarpment, was a popular destination. The lakelet was said to have been discovered by George Hannahs, Idyllwild pioneer, in 1889. He first called it Lake Surprise. Grace Hortense Tower visited the lake in 1907 and wrote about it in the *Los Angeles Times Weekly Magazine* (September 29):

> One of the great surprises... is Hidden Lake, which suddenly bursts upon one at a sharp angle in the trail. There it lies in its reed-lined bed, with its fringe of over-hanging trees. The lake is shallow, and every party passing finds its experience incomplete till it has ridden into the middle and has posed for its picture, with horses knee-deep in the clear water. Near the lake is a great bluff, the sheerest and highest precipice outside of the Yosemite Valley.

To cater to the increasing number of high country visitors, Mrs. Joanna Walter set up a tent camp in Tahquitz Meadow in 1908. She offered overnight lodging and meals for a dollar apiece. The *Riverside Daily Press* (July 28, 1908) was quite impressed with Walter's Tahquitz Meadow resort:

> Mrs. Walter has selected for her camp a location second to none in the mountains. In a setting of green, with a spring of ice-cold water nearby, is a mammoth tent subdivided into

Hunting party on the old Devils Slide Trail, 1912. — DIANE MILLER

Deer hunters and their kill at one of the Tahquitz Meadow cabins, 1912.— DIANE MILLER

Pack train leaving Idyllwild Inn for the high country, ca. 1930.

Trout fishing was a major attraction along Tahquitz Creek, ca. 1925.

rooms for guests. The floor is neatly carpeted with burlap and at the farther end of the spacious hallway is a huge fireplace, built from the rocks about the camp. A building of logs and canvas constitutes the dining room and kitchen and is separate from the main tent. Here, it is safe to say, is to be found the most unique stove in existance, made by Mrs. Walter herself.... Mrs. Walter will maintain this camp every summer and is making plans for extensive improvements from season to season.

The newspaper correspondent's optimism was not to bear results. Walter's tent camp was too high in the mountains and too cold at night to attract many guests. The resort folded the next year.

Lee "Dad" Chapman operated his "Idyllwild Hut" in Round Valley during the summers of 1923 and 1924. The *Hemet News* (June 13, 1924) stated that Chapman's Hut "is a favorite camping place for parties enroute to San Jacinto Peak. Comfortable beds and good camp meals tempt one to prolong the stay in that wonderful spot, only two miles from the very summit of the mountain."

George Law, freelance writer and contributor to the *Los Angeles Times* and *Touring Topics,* built a stone and log cabin on a bench near the confluence of Willow and Tahquitz creeks, two miles down from Tahquitz Meadow, in 1915. Law, who owned a ranch near San Juan Capistrano, spent most of his summers at his low-roofed, rustic mountain home, writing his newspaper and magazine articles. He had a winter cabin in Chino Canyon, just above Palm Springs. Law left for Mexico in 1925, and the abandoned cabin above the confluence of Willow and Tahquitz Creek became a shelter for hikers and horsemen. Today the spot, minus the cabin, is known as Laws Camp.[10]

Two miles down Tahquitz Creek from Laws Camp, just above the desert escarpment, is a place known as Caramba. This was Moses S. Gordon's camp while he and a friend named McInnis were building the spectacular Gordon Trail down to Palm Springs in 1916 and 1917. *Caramba!* is a Spanish exclamation indicating shock or surprise; Gordon gave his camp that name because, just beyond the little forested flat, one is shocked to see the terrain abruptly drop to the desert. Moses Gordon had a home in Palm Springs and a cabin in Idyllwild; it was to connect the two that he built his pines to palms trail. A writer from the Riverside Press accompanied Gordon down the trail in 1917 and described it thusly:

Starting from Idyllwild, one takes the short trail known as the Devil's Slide... to a beautiful table land, known as Tauquitz Valley.... Here the trail leads past the log cabin into Hidden Lake Trail, or until you reach Mr. Law's trail... Now there is nothing but an old deer trail until one comes out on a little bit of flat ground on Tahquitz Creek, just as the creek takes its first tumble of some 40 feet down towards the desert, which is nearly 6000 feet below.

This is "Camp Caramba," where M. S. Gordon has a charming camp site, and it is from this point that Mr. Gordon has built his trail winding down to the desert.

Starting first up over a high point, with a most wonderful view of the Coachella Valley, then among the noble pines, you start down the mountain past Sentinel Point, on down to McInnis peak, passing from trees to shrubs, finally to cactus and rocks....

The trail leads on down to the hog-back between Tahquitz canyon and one of the north forks of Andreas canyon, winding down amongst curiously shaped rocks, the Imp and Dog's Head being most prominent, until you finally land at Camp Avispas, meaning wasps, due to the many wasp nests among the cactus.

This is the last water supply before reaching the desert. Also at this point you see your first group of palm trees, which is at an altitude of about 2000 feet.

From Camp Avispas the trail leads on, bringing you closer to the desert at every step, with a most wonderful view of the palisades of Andreas canyon, and her wonderful groups of palms in their long petticoats.

This trail from pines to palms is the first direct connection

A hiking party pauses alongside one of the old cabins in Tahquitz Meadow, 1921.— CHARLES VAN FLEET

George Law built his cabin on a sloping bench above the confluence of Tahquitz and Willow creeks in 1915. Law, a writer, enjoyed his summers here until 1925. This picture was taken in 1921. Today, the spot, minus the cabin, is known as Laws Camp.— EDGAR COOK

George Law and his wife Lela in 1923.— CHARLES VAN FLEET

Looking south from Red Tahquitz Peak. The Desert Divide is in the foreground, the Santa Rosas in the distance.
— DEBOYD SMITH

between the desert of the Coachella valley and the mountain resort of Idyllwild, as the crow flies some twelve miles; but one goes slowly, climbing the distance up over a point 8000 feet, and should allow on horseback, going up, at least 12 or 13 hours, including an hour to rest and water your horse at Camp Caramba.[11]

The Gordon Trail fell into disuse after several years and was abandoned to the elements and the ever-growing brush. It is impassable today. Of all the romantic names Moses Gordon thought up for points along his trail – Sentinel Point, the Imp, Dog's Head, Camp Avispas – only Caramba remains, now a Forest Service trail camp. An effort to reopen the Gordon Trail in the 1960s was thwarted by the Agua Caliente tribal council; Andreas Canyon and lower Palm Canyon, through which the trail passed, are part of the Agua Caliente Reservation. So this "unique short cut from Equator to North Pole, from desert to snow, from palm trees to pines, the trail without a rival in the world," will forever remain a relic of the past.[12]

Another palms to pines pathway was opened in 1933. This was the Chino Trail, built with Riverside County and State funds by a Depression labor gang. The trail climbs from Palm Springs up the ridge east of Chino Canyon to the crest at Long Valley, just east of the present tramway upper terminal.

As hikers, horseback riders, campers, hunters, and even a few cattlemen and their herds continued to use the San Jacinto high country, fears were voiced that this magnificent sub alpine wilderness was being trampled to death. The fears were heightened when the Riverside County Board of Supervisors authorized County Surveyor A. C. Fulmor to survey a highway route from Pine Cove to Tahquitz Valley, Round Valley, and on to the summit of San Jacinto Peak. Fulmor made the survey in 1926 and reported to the supervisors that the road would be feasible and would cost in the neighborhood of $274,000. Supervisor Harvey Johnson of Banning urged that the highway be built and stated that "the road will attract an enormous influx of tourist traffic,... In fact, it would be a remarkable link in the development of mountain roads in Riverside County."[13]

An "enormous influx of tourist traffic" is just what conservationists and supporters of a proposed mountain primitive area did not want. As early as 1908, some of them were proposing national park or national monument status for at least part of the high country.

NOTES

1. Jay W. Ruby, "Aboriginal Uses of Mt. San Jacinto State Park," *U.C.L.A. Archaeological Survey Annual Report, 1961-62*, U.C.L.A. Department of Anthropology and Sociology, 1962.
2. Chief Francisco Patencio, as told to Margaret Boynton, *Stories and Legends of the Palm Springs Indians* (Palm Springs, 1943), p. 70-71.
3. Jim Wellman interview, 1972; Charles Van Fleet interview, 1974; *Redlands Citrograph*, October 26, 1895. For Shepherds' Camp, see *Hemet News*, September 6, 1907.
4. *San Jacinto Register*, July 20, 1893.
5. *Redlands Citrograph*, October 26, 1895.
6. Harvey Monroe Hall, "A Botanical Survey of San Jacinto Mountain," *University of California Publicatons in Botany*, Volume 1 (Berkeley, 1902), p. 5.
7. John B. Leiberg, "San Jacinto Forest Reserve," *20th Annual Report of the United States Geological Survey, 1898-99* (Washington, D.C., 1900), Part 5, p. 455-478.
8. Hall, p. 14, 16.
9. J. Grinnell and H. S. Swarth, "An Account of The Birds and Mammals of The San Jacinto Area of Southern California," *University of California Publications in Zoology*, Volume 10 (Berkeley, 1913). Sarah Rogers Atsatt did a study of the reptiles of the San Jacinto Mountains about the same time. See Atsatt, "The Reptiles of The San Jacinto Area of Southern California," *University of California Publications in Zoology*, Volume II (Berkeley, 1913), p. 31-50.
10. *Hemet News*, July 4, 1919; Idyllwild *Town Crier*, August 12, 1955; Bill Jennings, "Many years ago he erected a stone cabin in the mountains," *Riverside Press-Enterprise* (Valley Edition), July 15, 1972.
11. *Riverside Daily Press*, July 10, 1917; *Hemet News*, August 24, 1917.
12. Ralph Arthur Chase, "San Jacinto, Southern California's Noblest Mountain," *Sierra Club Bulletin*, 1923, p. 352. See also J. Smeaton Chase, *Our Araby: Palm Springs and the Garden of the Sun* (New York, 1923), p. 72-73; and Edmund C. Jaeger, "Forgotten Trails," *Palm Springs Villager*, September 1949, p. 28. For effort to reopen the Gordon Trail, Don Bauer interview, 1984.
13. *Hemet News*, October 1, November 17, December 31, 1926.

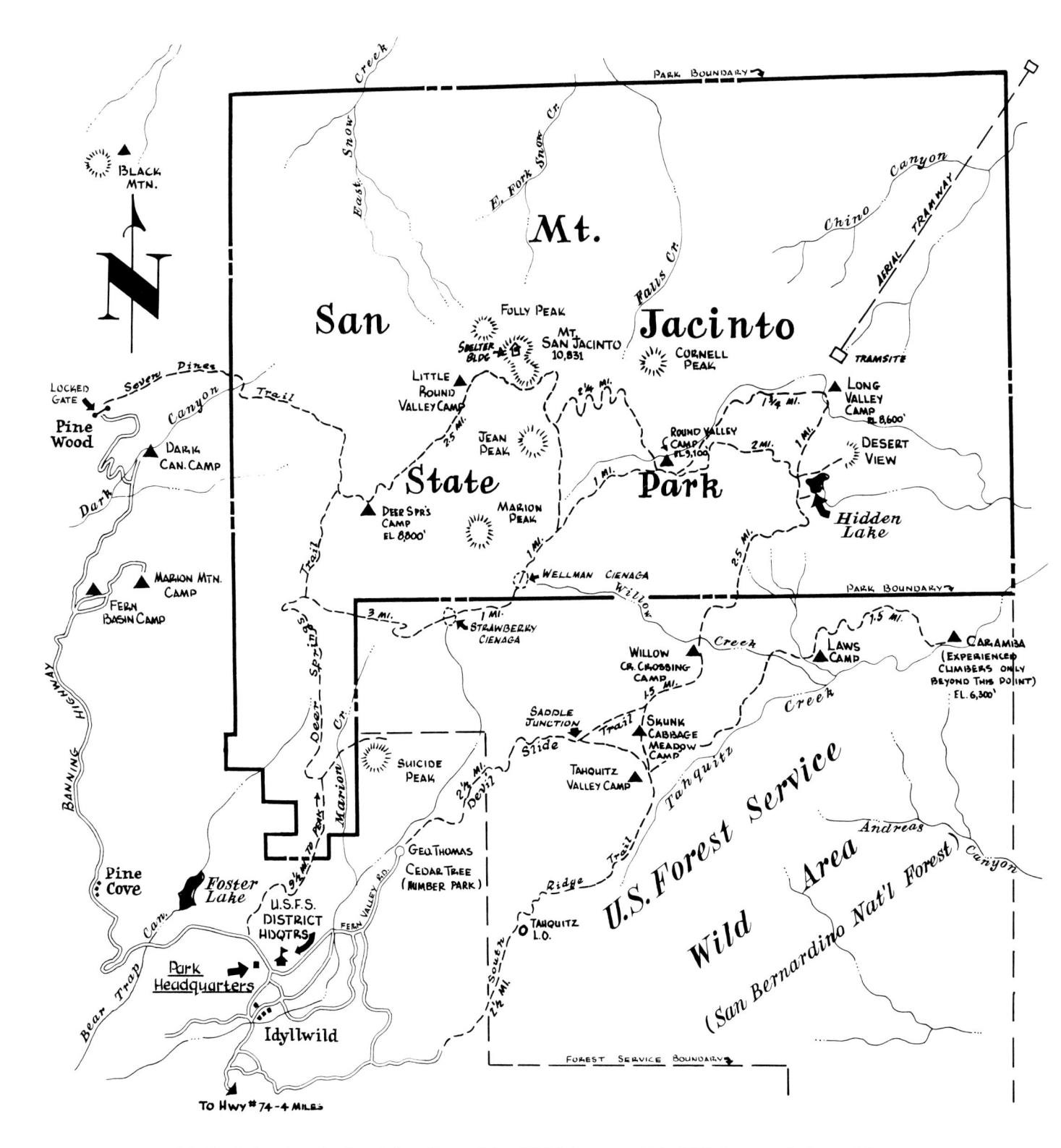

Mt. San Jacinto State Park and the adjacent federal Wild Area, 1962. The Wild Area was designated the San Jacinto Wilderness with the passage of the Wilderness Act of 1964. — U.S. FOREST SERVICE

17

GAME REFUGE, STATE PARK, AND PRIMITIVE AREA

> For me, and for thousands with similar inclination, the most important passion in life is the overpowering desire to escape periodically from the clutches of a mechanistic civilization. To us the enjoyment of solitude, complete independence, and the beauty of undefiled panorama is absolutely essential to happiness.[1]

Robert Marshall – forester, conservationist and wilderness defender – wrote these words almost sixty years ago, but for many people the same passion holds true today. To a growing number, the enjoyment of wilderness is one of the most satisfying forms of recreation and renewal. To spend a day, a weekend, or a week in the forest primeval, away from highways, resorts and noisy public campgrounds, with only the natural sounds of the earth – the wind rustling pine needles, the soft murmur of the stream, the distant howl of a coyote at night, the slight patter of a deer darting through the forest – is pure pleasure for the wilderness buff. More and more urban Americans are discovering that the nourishment afforded by wilderness is a redeeming and enriching experience.

The high San Jacintos represent the prime mountain wilderness area in California south of the Sierra Nevada. The combination of granite, forest, meadow, stream and far-reaching vistas is unexcelled in this part of the state. One might think that this unique piece of the High Sierra set in Southern California would have quickly and without controversy been set aside for protection, but such was not the case. Efforts to preserve this magnificent high country involved hard work, frustration and disappointment before finally reaching success.

As early as 1907, Dr. Walter Lindley, Los Angeles physician and part owner of Idyllwild Inn, told the *Hemet News* (July 26, 1907) that "Riverside [County] has in the San Jacinto Mountains the most beautiful natural park in California outside of the Yosemite Valley," and "With the protection of the Riverside county supervisors and the federal forest rangers it would be possible to have the deer in these mountains so plentiful and fearless that it would be a sight that people would travel far to witness."

In 1908, possibly at the request of Dr. Lindley (the record is missing on this), San Jacinto forest supervisor Harold Marshall forwarded to Washington a proposal for a "Tahquitz Peak and Palm Canyon National Monument," basing the plan on provisions of the Antiquities Act of 1906. The Associate U.S. Forester rejected the plan, writing that the proposed monument was already protected within the forest reserve and that "there does not seem to be anything of any unusual scientific or historical interest connected with the lands in question."[2]

Advocates of protection for the San Jacinto high country were not dissuaded. Francis Fultz, school administrator and self-taught botanist, wrote in the *Sierra Club Bulletin* (January 1920):

> We of the Sierra Club in the south consider the trip to Mount San Jacinto the *ne plus ultra* of our outings....
> Southern California has no national park. There is need for one. True, she has an interest in the parks farther up the state, but she needs one within her own borders.... This one is the San Jacinto Mountains, and I hereby nominate this..., along with a goodly portion of the adjoining desert, for dedication by our Government as a national park.

These early efforts to create a national park out of the high San Jacintos never progressed beyond the talking stage. Instead, interest was focused on setting aside the groves of *Washingtonia filifera* palm trees in Palm and Andreas canyons on the desert side of the mountains. The originator of this idea was Raymond Cree, who owned 65 acres near Palm Springs. Cree loved Palm

An attempt to make Palm Canyon and its tributary canyons, home of the *Washingtonia filifera,* a National Monument was unsuccessful. The Agua Caliente band of Cahuillas, who owned the land, were not consulted.

Canyon and conceived the idea of a national park to encompass not only the canyons, but a vast tract of land extending from San Jacinto Peak south to the Salton Sea. Cree presented his idea to the Riverside County supervisors in 1917. The supervisors expressed interest but felt too much land was included. Cree's grand design was trimmed to include only lower Palm Canyon and its groves of *Washingtonia filifera.* However, America's attention was focused on World War I, and the park idea was shelved for the duration.[3]

With war's end, attention again focused on the park plan. In 1919 the Riverside County supervisors appointed Arthur C. Lovekin to study and work toward a national park or monument to include the *Washingtonia filifera* groves in Palm Canyon. Lovekin was a Canadian by birth who came to Southern California in 1886. He worked as a surveyor and for a few years was a sugar planter in Hawaii before settling in Riverside in 1906. He soon accumulated wealth from real estate investments and opted to devote the latter part of his life to "conserving nature's values."[4]

Lovekin suggested the setting aside of lower Palm Canyon, Andreas Canyon, and San Jacinto Peak as a war memorial park to honor those who died in World War I. The Forest Service objected to the inclusion of any of the lands under its jurisdiction in the proposed memorial park, and the idea of including the high country around San Jacinto Peak was dropped. Instead, a committee made up of Lovekin, Frank Miller of the Mission Inn, and two supervisors came up with a park of 2½ square miles, encompassing the palm groves in lower Palm, Andreas, and Murray canyons. Steven Mather, director of the National Park Service, was invited to Riverside to discuss the proposal. He gave no firm commitment but suggested a national monument, rather than a full-fledged national park, might be fitting for the area.

In January 1920, Representative Kettner of Riverside County introduced a bill in Congress to establish Palm Canyon National Monument. The monument supporters now faced an obstacle they had apparently either overlooked or not cared to consider – the canyon lands they sought were part of the Agua Caliente Indian Reservation. The Agua Caliente Cahuilla could not be divested of their land "without their consent and upon the payment of adequate and just compensation," stated the Commissioner of Indian Affairs.

Undiscouraged, Lovekin found a new ally in Congressman Phillip D. Swing of El Centro, Kettner's successor. Swing introduced a new bill in 1922 calling for a national monument upon attaining "the consent and relinquishment" from the Indians for "a price to be agreed upon."[5] The Agua Caliente, meeting in November 1922, declared themselves "unalterably opposed" to the sale of their canyon lands.

Meanwhile, Palm Springs real estate interests sought to capitalize on the monument proposal. A national monument in Palm Canyon would make their city a

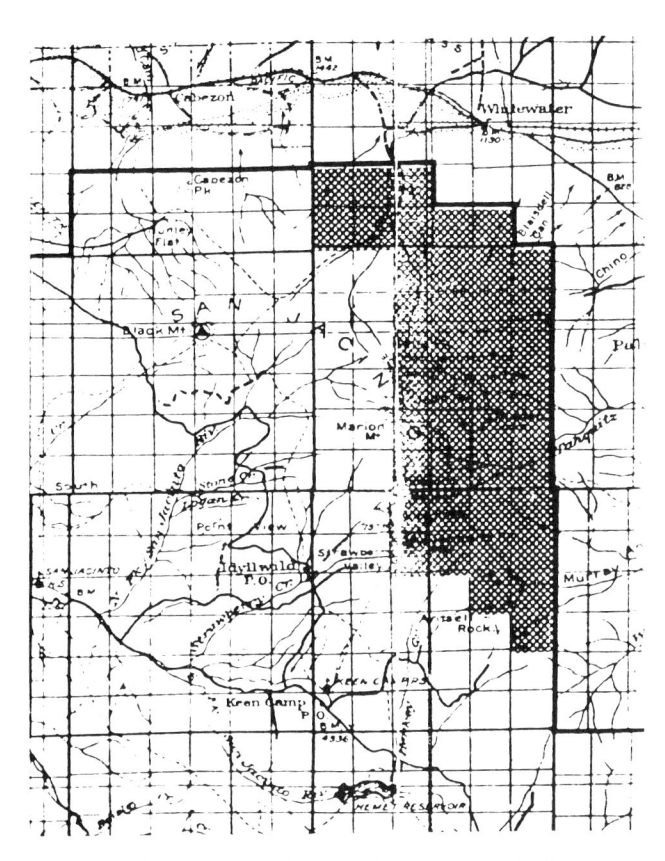

The dark area denotes the Tahquitz State Game Refuge, proclaimed in 1927 after a federal effort failed.
— U.S. FOREST SERVICE

Sierra Club hikers in Tahquitz Valley, May 1925. The Sierra Club was instrumental in getting the Tahquitz State Game Refuge set aside. — EDGAR COOK

tourist mecca, and this fact was highly publicized in selling home and business lots in the growing desert community. Real estate investor William P. Anderson acquired property on the hillside above Andreas Canyon and started subdivision of view lots. There was talk of a hotel at the entrance to Palm Canyon. The private Andreas Club was formed ostensibly to "protect" the canyon; what they really wanted were homesites and a 99-year lease on palm groves within Andreas Canyon itself. Congressman Swing was dismayed by this out and out commercialism, which he looked upon as a scheme to gain public property for private use.

The scheme collapsed in 1923, when the Agua Caliente again refused to part with their ancestral lands.

The whole national monument episode was marked by a thoughtless and disdainful attitude toward Native Americans. Even though the proposed monument was entirely within their lands, no one thought to consult the Agua Caliente until after the national monument bill had reached Congress, and then only because the Bureau of Indian Affairs brought it to their attention. The Agua Caliente's refusal to part with Palm and Andreas canyons was considered by some monument supporters as an attempt on the part of the Indians to get more money, ignoring the fact that the canyons were sacred lands to them. The Andreas Club tried to pose as the Indians' friend and protector, stating that they considered themselves "the big brothers" of the Agua Caliente, a patronizing attitude that must have infuriated these proud native people. Proper regard for minority Americans was still in the future.

The next preservation campaign focused on the protection of deer by the creation of a game refuge in the San Jacintos. The California legislature had, in 1915, designated large areas of the San Gabriel and San Bernardino mountains as game preserves, where hunting was closely regulated. With the San Gabriels and San Bernardinos restricted, Riverside County conservationists feared that hunters would swarm into the San Jacintos and "wipe out all traces of big game in two seasons."[6] In 1917 the state legislature created another game refuge on the eastern slope of the Santa Rosa Mountains to protect big horn sheep.

George Law, a writer who, as we have seen, had a cabin above Willow Creek, then proposed a game refuge that would cover most of the crest and eastern slope of the San Jacintos. Instead of a state refuge, Law sent his proposal for a "Tahquitz National Deer Ranch" to the Secretary of Agriculture for federal action. Law received support from the Sierra Club's Southern California Section. Aurelia Harwood of Claremont, a Sierra Club director and later its first woman president, led the Club campaign.

It must be pointed out that the original proposal was aimed at providing a breeding ground and nursery for deer, and not necessarily to protect the animals from hunters. In Law's words, "The project is not intended to stop hunting, but to insure a perpetual supply of deer and other game. The closed territory lies wholly on the east

Sierra Club party in Tahquitz Valley, 1916. The Club sponsored annual summer trips into the San Jacinto high country from 1916 through most of the 1920s. — MUIR DAWSON

slopes of the main mountain, thus leaving the three most accessible slopes and the lower part of the east, open to hunters during the provided season."[7] Thus, deer would have a safe haven within the refuge in order to produce larger numbers of them to be hunted outside the refuge.

This "breeding ground" concept was not what motivated Aurelia Harwood, who loved animals. She expressed the hope that "this high country will be kept wild and free, and that deer and other native wildlife will have this permanent refuge where every condition is favorable to their safety and welfare." She wanted the mountain "kept untouched forever for the pleasure of the people."[8]

A bill to establish a "Tahquitz National Game Preserve" was introduced in Congress by Representative Phil Swing in 1922. It failed to get out of committee. Swing resubmitted a slightly altered bill and this version was passed by Congress and signed by President Calvin Coolidge on July 3, 1926.

But it turned out to be a hollow victory. The act creating the Tahquitz National Game Preserve had an "Achilles heel" and never took effect. The problem was that alternate checkerboard sections within the preserve belonged to the Southern Pacific, acquired when the railroad was built through the Coachella Valley in 1875. A key provision of the act was that "all land within the exterior boundary... shall first become the property of the United States."[9] The Southern Pacific Land Company, which initially approved the land exchange for land of "equal area," balked when the terms were changed to land of "equal value." Since the sections to be bartered were high on the mountain and considered of little economic worth, the Southern Pacific would not be able to get as much land as it initially expected.

Although federal game protection failed, backers of the game refuge were successful on the state level, after an initial setback. State game refuges, as had been established in the San Gabriel and San Bernardino mountains, did not require public ownership of all lands within their boundaries. Accordingly, Riverside County and Sierra Club supporters of the preserve persuaded state senator Chester Kline of San Jacinto to introduce a bill in the legislature to establish a Tahquitz State Game Refuge. In 1925 the bill passed the legislature only to be pocket vetoed – possibly by oversight – by Governor Friend Richardson. Senator Kline reintroduced the bill in the 1927 legislative session and was successful this time. The Tahquitz State Game Refuge, encompassing 30 square miles of Forest Service and Southern Pacific land on the mountain's eastern slope, was signed by Governor C. C. Young on May 17, 1927.

At last, after a seven year effort, there was a game refuge on San Jacinto, but this was only the first step in preserving the mountain wilderness. It merely prevented hunting within the refuge boundaries, and contained no provision against future development, such as roads and cabins. A highway up the mountain, proposed by some Riverside businessmen, was a very real threat.

The next step was on the federal level: a proposed Forest Service wilderness that would disallow roads or any form of human development other than trails and campsites. The impetus for this came not from local pressure but from several visionary conservationists on the national scene.

On the slopes of Red Tahquitz Peak looking north over Tahquitz Valley to the Marion Mountain Ridge. Most of the area shown here was placed in the San Jacinto Primitive Area in 1931.

Skunk Cabbage Meadow was included in the San Jacinto Primitive Area, proclaimed by the Forest Service in 1931.

The Forest Service in the 1920s had several enlightened spokesmen who preached the value of wilderness preservation. Foremost among these men was Aldo Leopold, graduate of the Yale School of Forestry and at the time a forester stationed in Albuquerque, New Mexico. Leopold proclaimed that undeveloped sections of the national forests were as much an asset as the timber, water, forage, and minerals – a revolutionary concept among foresters at the time. Through Leopold's efforts, the Gila Wilderness Area in Arizona was established by the Southwestern District Forester in 1924 – the first national forest wilderness in the United States.

Aldo Leopold's persistence, along with that of a young and upcoming forester named Robert Marshall, caused the Forest Service leadership to consider wilderness preservation as a worthy goal. William B. Greeley, Chief Forester of the United States, and his deputy L. F. Kneipp came around, at least partly, to Leopold and Marshall's way of thinking. In 1926, Greeley asked all the national forest supervisors in the United States to submit a list of forest lands suitable for wilderness protection.[11]

Even before Chief Forester Greeley's request, a proposal to preserve the San Gorgonio Mountain area in the San Bernardinos had been put forth. The instigator was Harry C. James and his Western Rangers. Canadian-born James came to Los Angeles to work in the motion picture industry in 1913. His real love was the outdoors, and it was not long until he knew well the Southern California mountains. Within a year of his arrival in Los Angeles, James organized a group of local youngsters into the Western Rangers (later renamed The Trailfinders), dedicated to the belief that boys can mature, spiritually as well as physically, through hiking, camping, and mountain climbing. After a climb of San Gorgonio Mountain in 1923, James and his Western Rangers asked that the mountain area be preserved in its primitive state as a national monument. This was, as far as can be ascertained, the first clear-cut public proposal to save a wilderness in Southern California.[12]

San Bernardino National Forest supervisor Steven A. Nash-Boulden, although not receptive to James' proposal, came out with his own plan for forming the San Gorgonio Recreation Area, where no roads would be allowed, in 1925.

After Chief Forester Greeley's request, Nash-Boulden and his staff considered additional areas for a roadless classification. Among these were the Telegraph Peak area in the San Gabriels and the northern Santa Rosa Mountains. San Jacinto was considered, but the Southern Pacific's land holdings there appeared to present a major obstacle. So, San Gorgonio, Telegraph Peak, and the northern Santa Rosas but not San Jacinto were on the list of areas in San Bernardino National Forest suggested for possible wilderness protection.

Forest Service interest in protecting the San Jacinto high country lay dormant for a year, then picked up again in 1928, apparently in response to a well-publicized campaign to include San Jacinto Peak and its surrounding area in a California state park.

The Mount San Jacinto State Park idea had both a state-wide and a local genesis. On the state level, there were already five state-owned parks, all in Northern California, but no unified system of administration. After a campaign by the Save-The-Redwoods League, based in San Francisco, and some Santa Barbara citizens who wanted to preserve Santa Cruz Island, a California State Parks Committee was formed in 1927. A series of legislative acts sponsored by the committee created the State Park Commission, with authority to find suitable park sites, and authorized a $6 million bond issue to purchase potential park land.

Riverside County quickly got on the bandwagon. The County supervisors appointed a committee, chaired by A. C. Lovekin, to cooperate with a Los Angeles group in finding suitable park locations in Southern California. One of the committee appointees, Albert E. Bottel, Riverside County agricultural commissioner and chairman of the forestry board, became the driving force

209

Tahquitz Peak and Lily Rock as seen from the Wellman Cienega Trail. In the far distance is Garner Valley.

behind the movement for a state park on San Jacinto. When the State Park Commission held its first Southern California meeting in Los Angeles in February 1928, Lovekin and Bottel were present to recommend the area adjacent to San Jacinto Peak as a state park.

A San Jacinto Mountain State Park Association was organized in March 1928, with Lovekin as president and Bottel as secretary. The directors, thirty in all, read like a "who's who" of Riverside County, with business leaders from every major community in the county, as well as several from Los Angeles. The spring and summer of 1928 saw a whirlwind campaign to stimulate public support. Bottel led a mass horseback trip to San Jacinto Peak to promote the park, and spoke to many groups. Lovekin traveled to Washington, D.C., visiting Chief Forester Greeley, Senator Hiram Johnson, and Congressman Phil Swing, to suggest that the Forest Service donate its land around San Jacinto Peak for state park purposes. The Southern Pacific Land Company indicated it would be interested in either a fair land exchange or outright purchase of its property on San Jacinto Mountain.

Some Riverside County supervisors and businessmen continued to talk of a road to San Jacinto Peak to give easy access to the proposed state park. But Frederick Law Olmstead Jr., who surveyed the high San Jacintos for the State Park Commission, urged that the park remain in its wilderness state. Olmstead, whose father had been instrumental in saving Yosemite Valley many years earlier, was a nationally famous landscape architect.

Meanwhile, the California State Park bond issue was overwhelmingly approved by the voters in November 1928. A struggle appeared to be brewing over which agency – the Forest Service or the State Park Commission – would administer the San Jacinto high country.

The Forest Service had its own plans for San Jacinto. Just a few days after Lovekin returned from Washington, San Bernardino National Forest supervisor Nash-Boulden proposed the setting aside as a roadless area a 34-square mile tract on the mountain, its boundaries closely approximating those of the Tahquitz State Game Refuge.

In January 1929, the District Forester in San Francisco announced that fourteen wilderness areas would be set aside in the California national forests. Three of them would be in San Bernardino National Forest: San Gorgonio, Telegraph Peak (renamed Cucamonga), and San Jacinto. The latter included San Jacinto Peak and the high areas to the east and south, as Nash-Boulden had suggested.

Neither the State Parks Commission nor the San Jacinto Mountain State Park Association accepted the federal primitive area as a substitute for a state park on San Jacinto. Supported by Congressman Phil Swing, they felt confident that Congress could be persuaded to transfer the federal lands in question to the state.

What looked to be a knock-down, drag-out fight between two governmental agencies – the Forest Service and the State Park Commission – turned out a model in federal-state cooperation. Credit for this went to Newton B. Drury, an instructor of literature at the University of California, Berkeley, and executive secretary of the Save-The-Redwoods League. Drury was appointed as investigating and acquisition officer of the State Park Commission, a capacity he served with distinction from 1929 to 1940, when he became director of the National Park Service. Drury was a master at negotiation, a quality he revealed when he met with Louis A. Barrett, assistant district forester in charge of lands. Friendly talks between Barrett and Drury resulted in agreement on a three-way land exchange to pave the

The stone cabin just below the summit of San Jacinto Peak was erected by the CCC in 1936.

Hidden Lake at its fullest, 1940. – CHARLES MILLER

way for Mount San Jacinto State Park. The Forest Service would give the Southern Pacific a solid four by six mile rectangle on top of the mountain, extending east and west from San Jacinto Peak, in exchange for 12 square miles of land outside the proposed park. The State Park Commission would then purchase this rectangle from the Southern Pacific for a price to be negotiated.[13] (It was necessary to proceed in this manner because federal law prevented the outright sale of forest lands to a private concern, but not a land exchange.)

Drury then came south to consult with members of the San Jacinto Mountain State Park Association. The latter desired a larger park than the 12,000 acres agreed upon by the State Park Commission and the Forest Service, but apparently realized that "half a loaf is better than no loaf at all." Local interests also wanted the park to connect with the Banning-Idyllwild Road for administrative headquarters, camping, and recreational facilities accessible to motorists. Drury agreed to seek this extension of the park boundaries.

Some Riverside County supporters of the state park continued to press for the construction of a road to the top of San Jacinto Peak. But Drury, supported by William Colby, chairman of the State Park Commission and Sierra Club director, strongly favored a wilderness park and were determined to do all in their power to keep roads out of the high country.

In a landmark meeting in Idyllwild in July 1930, Assistant District Forester Barrett, State Park Commissioner Drury, and Assistant Southern Pacific Land Commissioner C. F. Impey reached tentative agreement on the three-way land exchange. The way was finally cleared for Mount San Jacinto State Park to become reality.

Details of the cost, size, and boundaries of the state park were worked out in the fall of 1930. The cost to the state would be $84,218.75. Half of that amount would come from state park bond sales, $40,000 in matching funds would be provided by Riverside County, and the last $2109.37 would be donated by the San Jacinto Mountain Park Association. The park would contain 12,687 acres. To provide access to Idyllwild and the highway, the park boundaries were slightly altered. A mile-wide strip was trimmed off the north side, and 1 7/10 square miles were added as a "corridor" on the southwestern corner. Except for the addition of a small, detached headquarters site in Idyllwild, it would be three decades before Mount San Jacinto State Park was enlarged beyond what was agreed upon by the State, the Forest Service, and the Southern Pacific in 1930.

There remained two steps, both originating in Washington, D.C., before the high country adjacent to the state park would receive federal wilderness protection. In July 1929 Chief Forester Greeley issued Forest Service Regulation L-20 – a landmark in conservation history – providing for the establishment of primitive areas "within which... will be maintained primitive conditions of environment, transportation, habitation, and subsistence, with a view to conserving the value of such areas for purposes of public education, inspiration, and recreation."[14] In accordance with Regulation L-20, the Chief Forester proclaimed the San Jacinto Primitive Area on April 23, 1931.

With the 12,687-acre Mount San Jacinto State Park and the 20,343-acre San Jacinto Primitive Area, adjoining the state park on the north and south and administered by the Forest Service, almost all of the San Jacinto high country was now protected as wilderness.

It took the General Land Office in Washington, D.C. two years to finally give its approval to the exchange of federal and railroad lands. The State did not receive legal title to the park until February 1933.

Entering Mt. San Jacinto Wilderness State Park on the Wellman Cienega Trail, 1968.

Now began a program to build trails and campsites to make the state park and primitive area more accessible to the hiking and horseback riding public. The vast majority of this work, undertaken between the years 1933 and 1936, was accomplished "the sturdy and tan-backed boys" of the Civilian Conservation Corps, a federal work relief program of President Franklin Roosevelt's "New Deal." From CCC camps in Idyllwild (1933), Tahquitz Meadow (1934), and Round Valley (1935 and 1936), work crews of young men under F. L. Niebauer, project superintendent, rebuilt the Devil's Slide trail, constructed the San Jacinto Peak trail via Wellman's Cienega and the Deer Springs trail, repaired other trails, cleared campsites in Tahquitz Meadow and Round Valley, and built the stone shelter hut just below the summit of San Jacinto Peak. About the only planned project they did not accomplish was to build an underground pipeline from Round Valley to Hidden Lake, to supply the latter with year-around water. It was jokingly said that the hordes of CCC boys were sent to landscape the mountain.[15]

Mount San Jacinto State Park was dedicated in an impressive ceremony in Idyllwild on June 19, 1937. Joseph R. Knowland of Oakland, new chairman of the State Park Commission, pledged that the new state park "will never be entered by highways." Albert E. Bottel, representing Riverside County, stated that the park was "set aside as a perpetual wilderness area, whose inmost confines must always be reached either by hiking or pack-train."[16] It seemed that the wilderness status of the park was forever insured.

Two Palm Springs businessmen had other ideas.

NOTES

1. James M. Glover, *A Wilderness Original: The Life of Bob Marshall* (Seattle, 1986), p. 96.
2. Overton Price, Associate U.S. Forester, to H.A.E. Marshall, Supervisor of San Jacinto Forest Reserve, April 20, 1908, in San Bernardino National Forest history file.
3. This chapter and the chapter following constitute in large part a summarization of portions of a doctoral dissertation by Richard Carter Davis, "Wilderness, Politics, and Bureaucracy: Federal and State Policies in the Administration of San Jacinto Mountain, Southern California, 1920-1968," completed at the University of California, Riverside, in 1973. Davis has revised, expanded, and updated his dissertation and his new version, which constitutes a much more elaborate historical analysis, is expected to be published soon under the title *Conservationists at Work: The Defense of California's San Jacinto Mountain Wilderness*.
4. Davis, p. 40-41.
5. Davis, p. 46.
6. Quoted in Davis, p. 59.
7. *Hemet News*, December 2, 1921.
8. Aurelia Harwood, "San Jacinto Game Refuge," *Sierra Club Bulletin*, 1925 annual number, p. 190.
9. Davis, p. 67-68.
10. Michael Frome, *Battle for the Wilderness* (New York, 1974), p. 119-120.
11. Frome, p. 120-121.
12. Davis, p. 75.
13. Davis, p. 126-127. See also Davis, *Newton B. Drury and the Wilderness Preservation Movement, Mount San Jacinto State Park* (Sacramento, 1989), for a summary of Drury's contributions toward the state park.
14. Frome, p. 121.
15. *Hemet News*, July 21 and September 1, 1933, October 25, 1935. See also *Idyllwild Town Crier*, June 19, 1953.
16. Davis, p. 137-138; *Hemet News*, June 25, 1937.

Long Beach Boy Scouts from Camp Tahquitz in the San Jacinto high country, 1939-1940. Top left is a scout group at the CCC camp in Tahquitz Meadow. Top right are some boys preparing dinner at the CCC Round Valley camp. Below left are scouts resting at the Wellman cabin in upper Willow Creek. Below right are three Camp Tahquitz scouts atop Cornell Peak, above Tamarack Valley. — CHARLES MILLER

Tramcars at the halfway point.
— PALM SPRINGS AERIAL TRAMWAY

18

TRAMWAY AND WILDERNESS

The idea of an aerial tramway or "elevator" up the precipitous desert face of San Jacinto Mountain was first expressed by Southern Pacific Railroad officials in 1926. The *Hemet News* (July 2, 1926) reported the railroad's interest:

> The Southern Pacific people figure that it would be a wonderful experience for passengers over their line to stop off at Palm Springs or Cabezon and be transported by deluxe elevator service from the sands of the desert below sea level to the cool shade of pines at an altitude of 10,000 feet.

The newspaper mentioned that Southern Pacific president Paul Shoup and a party of engineers would make a horseback trip from Idyllwild to the summit to study prospects for such an elevator, as they called it. It was suggested that an auto road be constructed to the top "so that tourists could go to the summit by elevator and then take a leisurely trip to Hemet, San Jacinto and Riverside by way of Idyllwild." Nothing ever came of the Southern Pacific proposal, and it was dropped from consideration soon afterwards.

The aerial tramway idea was resurrected in 1934 by Francis F. Crocker, Palm Springs district manager of the California Electric Company. According to a story widely repeated, Crocker was driving from Palm Springs to Banning with publisher Carl Barkow on a hot summer day. He looked up at the glistening white snow on San Jacinto Peak and is said to have exclaimed, "I wish there was some way we could get to the top of that mountain from here in the desert."[1] Crocker talked up the idea of an aerial tramway among his Palm Springs business associates. He found an early convert in Owen Earl Coffman, manager of the Desert Inn and son of Palm Springs pioneer hotel woman Nellie Coffman. Through the efforts of Crocker and Coffman, the Palm Springs Chamber of Commerce set up a committee of businessmen and realtors to look into the tramway prospects.

By 1938 Coffman had raised enough money from Palm Springs hotel owners, businessmen, and realtors to finance a preliminary survey. That summer, Trav Rogers, Palm Springs and Idyllwild stable owner, packed a party of surveyors and tramway supporters into Round Valley to look over the terrain and locate a possible upper terminal. Later, Coffman journeyed to Switzerland and Austria to study aerial trams in the Alps.[2] Palm Springs newspapers were solidly behind the tramway proposal. The *Palm Springs Limelight,* in a flight of fancy, proclaimed Round Valley "perfect ski country" and Hidden Lake "an ice skaters' paradise."[3] (Skiing was never practical on the craggy north and east slopes of the mountain, and Hidden Lake is often dry.)

In the spring of 1940, the New York engineering firm of Modjeska and Masters was employed to survey practical tramway locations. After a month-long study, Modjeska and Masters proposed a two-stage tramway, its base in Chino Canyon at the 2,500-foot level, climbing to a transfer station half way up, with a second stage rising to a point near Long Valley at 8,500 feet elevation. The estimated cost would be $1,360,000 – more than the Palm Springs backers envisioned but considerably less than the eventual final cost.

The proposed route crossed a section of the federal primitive area and the upper terminal was inside Mount San Jacinto State Park, so it was necessary to obtain right-of-way and a land use permit from two governmental agencies, or go over their head through federal and state legislation.

The State Park Commission turned down Palm Springs' initial request when it was presented in 1939. Newton Drury was particularly against the tramway idea, reminding the commissioners of their 1931 understanding with the Forest Service to administer the state park as a primitive area. Drury also influenced the commission to reject an application by Gregory Esgate,

Two Palm Springs businessmen who were most responsible for seeing the tramway project through: Earl Coffman (left) and Francis Crocker. — PALM SPRINGS HISTORICAL SOCIETY

Aerial view of proposed tramway, 1947.

manager of the Idyllwild Inn, to build winter sports facilities in Round Valley. However, Drury left the State Park Commission to become director of the National Park Service in 1940, and the commission lost its leading advocate of wilderness protection.

San Bernardino National Forest supervisor William V. Jones rejected the right-of-way request to cross federal lands, but left the door open. He said he might consider the plan at some future date if it was sanctioned by a governmental agency.[4]

Coffman and Crocker then turned to the state legislature. In January 1941 Riverside state senator John Phillips and assembyman Nelson Dilworth introduced bills to facilitate the building of the tramway. Dilworth's bill would authorize Palm Springs to construct the tramway, and Phillips' legislation would create a Palm Springs Winter Park Authority as a public corporation financed by the sale of bonds. Under Phillips' bill, the Winter Park Authority would be given broad powers not only to build the tramway, but also ski lifts, ski runs, ice skating facilities (Hidden Lake), hotels, lodges, restaurants, and "all other works, properties and structures necessary, convenient, or useful for the development of winter sports, and any other recreational facilities."[5] In effect, a large portion of the state park would be developed into a major winter sports recreation center. Moreover, the Winter Park Authority would be strictly a Palm Springs operation, with all five members of its governing body appointed by the city.

The Phillips-Dilworth bill received little notice outside of Riverside County and easily passed the state senate and assembly with only minor amendments. Not until the bill was on Governor Culbert Olsen's desk did any opposition arise. These objections came mainly from Hemet, San Jacinto, and Idyllwild, and were more concerned with Palm Springs' total control of the operation than with the tramway plan *per se*. Governor Olsen vetoed the bill in May 1941, and pocket vetoed a slightly amended version the following July, stating only that "the bill is not in the best interest of all the people."[6]

Palm Springs considered that it had lost a battle but not the war. Civic leaders from Riverside, Hemet, San Jacinto, and Idyllwild, as well as representatives from the Forest Service, were invited to a conference at Earl Coffman's Desert Inn in April 1943, where differences were smoothed out. The name of the governing body was changed from the Palm Springs Winter Park Authority to the Mount San Jacinto Winter Park Authority, and it would have seven members: two appointed by Palm Springs, two by Riverside County, and three by the governor. Thus, inner-county opposition was quelled.[7] No one at the fateful Desert Inn conference voiced any objection to compromising a designated primitive area.

A bill to create a Mount San Jacinto Winter Park Authority was introduced by assemblyman Nelson Dilworth in the 1943 legislative session. It easily passed both houses but was pocket vetoed by new Governor Earl Warren. Another conference was held at the Desert Inn, this time with representatives from Los Angeles as well as Riverside County. Again, a bill that would mutually satisfy all parties at the conference was agreed upon. San Bernardino forest supervisor William Peterson believed the primitive area would not be compromised by the tramway and later said, "No person voiced any objection to the creation of the Mount San Jacinto Winter Park Authority."[8] A new bill to create the Authority was introduced in the state assembly by Philip Boyd, former Palm Springs mayor and new assemblyman, in January 1945. It speedily passed both houses, with almost no opposition other than a few letters from Riverside Sierra Club members, and was signed into law by Governor Warren on June 25, 1945.[9]

Prepartions to fund and build the tramway began

Harry C. James led the 17-year fight against the tramway. The "lone wolf" conservationist is seen here in Yosemite, 1940. — HARRY C. JAMES

Tramway surveyors near the upper terminal site, 1947. — PALM SPRINGS VILLAGER

right away. Governor Warren appointed tire manufacturer Leonard Firestone and businessmen Harold English and Jack McKenzie to the Authority; Palm Springs chose Earl Coffman and John Chaffey; and Riverside County picked V. W. Grubbs and James Nusbaum. Palm Springs attorney Henry Lockwood acted – without fee, he said – as counsel to clear legal hurdles. Field surveys were undertaken, and the Consolidated Steel Corporation was awarded the contract to build the tramway towers in June 1946. The job was expected to take twenty months and be completed in time for the 1947-1948 winter season.

Rather than twenty months it took seventeen years. The lengthy delay was partly caused by funding problems but mostly by opposition from preservationists who wanted Mount San Jacinto State Park to remain wilderness. During the formative years of the Winter Park Authority, conservationists had been "asleep at the switch," in the words of forest historian Richard C. Davis.[10] But then they awoke with a start.

Wilderness advocates had done little to oppose the tramway, other than writing a few letters and telegrams, until 1944. Then Harry C. James, a conservationist "lone wolf," entered the fray. Most of James' previous conservation battles had involved defending the San Gorgonio Wilderness. He become involved with the San Jacintos when his Trailfinders, a boys outdoor organization, acquired 29 acres just above today's Lake Fulmor in 1941. James was always a believer in wilderness values and resented attempts by developers to infringe on the few high mountain pristine areas left in Southern California. He saw the tramway as a mechanistic intrusion that would destroy, or at least seriously harm, the wilderness nature of this high mountain country.[11]

James wrote letters and contacted others who believed, to some degree, in the wilderness ethic. He found allies in Ernest Maxwell of the Izaac Walton League's Idyllwild Chapter, Richard Elliott of the Desert Sun School in Idyllwild, the latter's daughter Ana Mary Elliott, and Joe Momyer, San Bernardino assistant postmaster and Sierra Club Riverside Chapter leader.

He found a belated ally in the Sierra Club, which seemingly had lost interest in San Jacinto since its crusade for the Tahquitz Game Refuge two decades earlier. The Club, in an effort that can only be termed as half-hearted, attempted without success to influence the state legislature against the Winter Park Authority Act. It was equally unsuccessful in trying to persuade the State Park Commission to oppose the project. In fairness to the Sierra Club, the immediate post-war years found the organization swamped in numerous nationally important conservation battles involving Yosemite, Kings Canyon, Olympic, Glacier, and Grand Teton national parks. They were about to enter the controversy over the Federal Reclamation Bureau's plan to dam the Green River in Dinosaur National Monument, Utah. At the time, the Club felt it simply did not have the resources to battle on every front.[12]

On the national level, James received the support of the Wilderness Society, whose board of directors felt strongly that Mount San Jacinto State Park should remain wild.

In 1950, the preservationists came together in a loosely-organized Mount San Jacinto Protective Association. Harry James, although not wanting to be president, coordinated most of the efforts in opposition to the tramway.

Tramway supporters redoubled their efforts to get the necessary right-of-way, land exchanges, and permits. Led by Palm Springs attorney Henry Lockwood, they beat back a preservationist attempt to influence the State Park Commission. In December 1948, the Com-

Helicopters were used to facilitate the building of the tramway. Above is the heliport at mountain station. To the left, a 'copter (circled) carries supplies to tower #3 site.
— PALM SPRINGS AERIAL TRAMWAY

mission gave unanimous approval for the Winter Park Authority to use a portion of Mount San Jacinto State Park.

Pro-tramway opinion was solidly entrenched among commercial and business organizations. The State Chamber of Commerce and all the local chambers in Riverside County were supporters. The Riverside County supervisors believed that the need for more recreational attractions near growing population centers superceded the need for wilderness. The Winter Park Authority made headway by portraying conservationists as trying to "prevent the pleasure of the many to satisfy the wishes of the few."[13]

The battle continued in the newspapers, in hearings, in letter writing campaigns, in lobbying efforts. Unfortunately we do not have space here to detail all these strategems, but one by one, during the 1950s, the barriers to tramway construction were broken.

Important victories for the tramway proponents were won when the Winter Park Authority and the Forest Service agreed to a land exchange giving the Authority a small corner section for the tramway route, and when the state legislature upheld the Winter Park Authority Act in 1957.

The Winter Park Authority experienced a considerable amount of difficulty in selling bonds to finance the tramway – a fact that the preservationists touted in the hope that the bonds would find no market. The Authority again asked for renewal of the expired contract in 1959. A new plan was formulated that provided for a single stage tram from Chino Canyon to Long Valley, less costly than the original double stage design. The tramway backers were encouraged when the bond market showed improvement at the end of the 1950s.

In 1960 the California Department of Natural Resources reached agreement with the Winter Park

Governor and Mrs. Edmund "Pat" Brown celebrate the opening of the Palm Springs Aerial Tramway on September 12, 1963. Over 400 dignitaries were on hand for the first ride. Here, Governor Brown gets ready to cut the ribbon while Mrs. Brown prepares to christen the first car with champagne.
– PALM SPRINGS HISTORICAL SOCIETY

Authority that allowed bonds to be sold, but the new agreement was more restrictive than the original. The Winter Park Authority now could utilize only four square miles of the state park, rather than the eight square miles as was first authorized. This removed the possibility of ski lifts and runs on the east slope of San Jacinto Peak unless the contract was later altered.

Almost a year passed before the bond issue of $7,700,000 was sold. Private investors put up the money, and no state, county, or city funds were used. The bonds paid 5½ per cent tax-free interest.

In July 1961, the Mount San Jacinto Winter Park Authority met in Los Angeles to receive the funds. The Bank of America was named trustee and handled the financial transactions for tramway construction. At last, the path was cleared for work to begin.

The Winter Park Authority wasted no time. Albert Webb Associates of Riverside was hired to survey the terrain. Geological and foundation studies were conducted by LeRoy Crandall and Associates of Los Angeles and Hood and Schmidt, Inc. of Burbank. The Louis de Roll Company of Berne, Switzerland was engaged to design and build the components and tram cars. Tudor Engineering of San Francisco was hired as consulting engineers.

The biggest job, of course, was the construction of the tramway terminals and towers, the latter perched on precipitous crags on the mountainside. Tough standards had to be met before a contractor could be bonded. Several major firms met these requirements but turned down the job after visiting the site. Two contractors from San Gabriel looked over the mountain face, were confident they could master the job, and applied. The Authority was impressed with their qualifications and positive attitude, and hired L. E. Dixon and Eric M. Emtman as general contractors.

After the contracts were signed, the money safely in the bank, and the paperwork completed, the enormous physical task of erecting the tramway had to be faced. The challenge involved was how to construct the facility over a horizontal distance of two and a half miles with a verticle rise of more than a mile, scaling the east rampart of one of the sheerest mountains in the United States. Henri Bodmer, Swiss tramway expert, looked at the mountain and was said to have exclaimed that "Construction will take four years and at least three lives will be lost."[14] He was wrong on both counts.

What the Swiss expert failed to consider was the use of helicopters to carry men and materials to Long Valley and the five tower construction sites – an innovation that

A car rides the guidewires between towers 2 and 3. The extremely precipitous desert face of the San Jacintos is very evident here.

got the job done in two years without the loss of a single workman's life. Five Bell G-3 helicopters from United Helicopter of Santa Monica made some 22,000 trips up the mountainside, lifting daily work crews and more than 5,500 tons of equipment and material. The first flights hauled a prefabricated 60-man portable work camp to Long Valley, site of the upper terminal. A series of wooden platform heliports were erected at the tower sites, anchored by steel cable to crags with sheer drops of hundreds of feet on three sides. Experience proved that it was most efficient for the 'copters to haul loads not exceeding 850 pounds. Therefore heavy equipment had to be broken down and reassembled on site.

Thirty-five men who lived at the Long Valley construction camp were flown up to the site every Monday morning and back down ever Friday evening. Workers at the tower sites commuted daily from Chino Canyon to the airy heliports and back.

Construction of the five towers and the cables required some 600 tons of steel and over 27 miles of interlocking coil cable, wire rope and strand, produced by United States Steel's American Steel and Wire Division in Trenton, New Jersey. Four lock-coil type track cables, each 13,500 feet long and weighing 58 tons, formed the links from which the two 80-passenger gondola cars were to be suspended. The main lock-coil cables were looped around huge reinforced concrete drums at the upper terminal. At the lower station, the cables were fixed by concrete and steel counterweights weighing 28 tons apiece. The cables were flexible enough to expand or contract eight feet in the event of extremely hot or cold weather conditions. The two tramway cars were linked in a cycle of their own hauling cables, so that as one car went up, the other came down – called a "double jig-back" in engineering terms.

A huge task was stringing the heavy track cables. To pull the cables up the mountainside, a 100-ton capacity hoist was installed at the upper terminal – no small feat in itself. A light line was laid over towers 4 and 5 by helicopter. Then, progressively heavier lines and finally the 58-ton track cables were threaded from tower to tower to the top. This feat had been accomplished many times in suspension bridges such as the Golden Gate, but never before on a precipitous mountain tramway rising 6,300 feet – the longest single lift in the world.

Last to be completed were the terminal buildings in Chino Canyon and Long Valley, designed to adapt to the natural landscape by the Palm Springs architectural firm of Clark, Frey and Williams. The lower station was in a desert drab decor, the mountain station in a boulder and pine setting.

The inauguration of the Palm Springs Aerial Tramway – as it was named – took place on September 12, 1963. Governor Edmund "Pat" Brown and his wife rode the first car up, accompanied by business and

The tram rises from Valley Station (2643') to Mountain Station (8516'), almost 6000 feet gain.

Mountain Station, the tramway's upper terminus, is perched on the rim above Long Valley.

entertainment figures who had paid $1,000 for the privilege. Seven other carloads followed, and the entire entourage was treated to a champagne party with music provided by the United States Marine Corps Band.

The Palm Springs Aerial Tramway, launched with such fanfare, soon found itself on shaky financial ground. The Winter Park Authority's total debt was $8,150,000, with twice yearly interest payments of $224,125 plus $110,000 to amortize the principal. Tramway revenues, from the beginning, were insufficient to pay the indebiture on time. The first semi-annual payment, due October 15, 1963, was late, as were many that followed. Despite publicity all over Southern California, not enough people were riding the tramway.[15]

Just as Harry James and his fellow preservationists had predicted, the Winter Park Authority sought expansion of its facilities on the mountain as a way to increase revenue. Suggested "improvements" included ski lifts and cleared ski runs on San Jacinto Peak, toboggan runs and an ice skating rink in Long Valley, the grooming of Hidden Lake as a picnic area, and even a spectacular 50-room hotel perched on the edge of the escarpment.

If the Winter Park Authority expected the state to acquiesce to these expansion hopes, they were rudely disappointed. The newly formed Department of Parks and Recreation, along with the State Park Commission, indicated in plain terms that they were opposed to any such change in the tramway contract that would allow further intrusions into the park. Part of the reason for this hardening attitude was resentment against what some perceived as arrogance on the part of the Winter Park Authority, particularly its secrecy in handling its affairs. More than that, there was a clearly perceptable change in wilderness attitudes.

With debate on a wilderness bill going on in Congress, attention became more focused on the value of wild areas to urban populations. A growing sentiment toward preserving natural areas permeated the public and government officials alike. In keeping with this new sentiment, the State Park Commission changed the name of the park to Mount San Jacinto Wilderness State Park in December 1963. This was the first unit in the California State Park system to be so designated. No longer would the state look with favor upon attempts to develop its parks for commercial advantage.

The same evolution of wilderness sentiment was going on at the federal level. In 1956 the Forest Service had redesignated the San Jacinto Primitive Area as the San Jacinto Wild Area, in keeping with its U-1 Regulation. This was a change in name only, as the Forest Service reserved the right to add or take away wild areas by simple fiat. The historic Wilderness Act, signed into law by President Lyndon Johnson on September 15, 1964, changed this. The Act designated wilderness on National Forest lands and promised to "secure for the American people of present and future generations the benefits of an enduring resource of wilderness." Wilderness was defined as "an area where the earth and its community of life are untrammeled by man, where man himself is a visitor who does not remain."[16]

In keeping with the Wilderness Act, the San Jacinto Wild Area became the San Jacinto Wilderness. It would take an act of Congress, not Forest Service fiat, to change its boundaries. Now the entire San Jacinto high country – both the State Wilderness Park and the federal wilderness on both sides – was protected from encroachment.

A guided mule ride from Mountain Station into Long Valley. – PALM SPRINGS AERIAL TRAMWAY

Through the middle 1960s, tramway revenues continued to decline. The Winter Park Authority was obliged to default on its loan payment in November 1966. Bondholders threatened to foreclose, but before any such action was taken, tramway revenues began to increase as more visitors used the facility. By 1970, the crisis was over, although the Winter Park Authority did not catch up on its payments until 1983.

As the 1990s begin, the tramway appears to be holding its own. Retirement of the bonded debt is scheduled for 1996. Some conservationists fear that the Winter Park Authority may try to renegotiate its contract with the state to allow the construction of additional facilities. As of now, there appears little likelihood of this happening.[17]

Meantime, things were happening to enhance the wilderness status of the mountain. In 1974, the California legislature passed a bill providing for a state wilderness system and altering the designation of some of the state parks. Most of the higher parts of Mount San Jacinto State Park was given state wilderness status. The state park as a whole was enlarged to 13,521 acres when a new section, reaching down to the Banning-Idyllwild highway, was added in 1963.

The California Wilderness Act, passed by Congress in 1984, added 10,900 acres to the Forest Service administered San Jacinto Wilderness. Most of the new acreage was along the desert divide south of Red Tahquitz Peak, with smaller sections added north and east of Black Mountain. The San Jacinto Wilderness now (1993) totals 43,776 acres. When combined with the Mount San Jacinto State Wilderness of 13,521 acres, protection now extends over a large swath of the most magnificent high mountain region in Southern California.

In recent years, the Forest Service and the California Department of Parks and Recreation, which now administers the state park, have both worked to preserve the wilderness value of the high San Jacintos. This is being done through a wilderness permit system relocating trails and campsites away from fragile meadows, closing overused areas such as Hidden Lake, and encouraging hikers to visit less used parts of the wilderness such as the desert divide country.

On May 30, 1987, Mount San Jacinto State Park celebrated its 50th anniversary with a full day of activity in and around Idyllwild. State Park authorities pledged to rededicate their efforts toward the second fifty years.

Newton Drury Peak, a 10,160-foot summit southeast of the main peak, was dedicated in September 1989, honoring a man who did so much to establish Mount San Jacinto State Park and preserve the high country wilderness.

With the increasing numbers of visitors in the San Jacinto high country, incidents of lost persons and injury accidents became commonplace. During the 1950s mountain searches and rescues were undertaken by the Riverside County Sheriff's Department. In 1961 five men who had participated in Sheriff's Department rescues formed the Riverside Mountain Rescue Unit (RMRU). Over the past 32 years, the RMRU, led by Walt Walker, has provided invaluable service in rescuing lost and injured hikers. The highly-trained unit, an accredited member of the Mountain Rescue Association, presently (1993) has 55 team members, 18 of them Idyllwild residents. The team averages some 40 to 50 responses a year.

Just above Lake Fulmor in Hall Canyon is the James Reserve, its name honoring wilderness defender Harry C. James, who died in 1978. As previously mentioned,

Backpackers camping in Round Valley, in the heart of Mt. San Jacinto State Park. — W.R.C. SHEDENHELM

James and his Trailfinders boys' organization bought 29 acres here in 1941. James moved the Trailfinders' headquarters from Pasadena to this location after completing Lolomi Lodge in 1950. The organization used Lolomi Lodge and surrounding campsites as a base of activity until 1966, when Harry James and his wife Grace sold the property to the University of California for use as a natural reserve. The Jameses continued to live in Lolomi Lodge until Harry's death. Since then, the lodge and adjoining area, named the James Reserve, has become a center for teaching and research under the University of California's Natural Reserve System. In 1980, Trailfinders Lodge was completed, providing living space for students and researchers. In 1987, the James Reserve was enlarged to include 160 acres of Oasis de los Osos, on the north slope of the range twelve miles northwest of Palm Springs. Dr. Mike Hamilton has been director of the reserve since 1982. Hamilton not only guides the efforts of researchers studying the remarkable variety of habitats on the mountain but also has devised a computer program to record in detail the ecology of the San Jacintos. Under Dr. Hamilton, new technologies are being utilized to learn about, to understand, and to preserve the natural environment of the San Jacinto Mountains.[18]

NOTES

1 *Palm Springs Aerial Tramway,* Souvenir Magazine, 1969, p. 11. There are variations on just what Crocker said; The *Riverside Press* (June 30, 1945) quotes him as saying, "There should be some quick and easy way of getting there."

This chapter as well as the chapter preceding constitute in significant part a summarization of portions of the doctoral dissertation by Richard Carter Davis, "Wilderness, Politics, and Bureaucracy: Federal and State Policies in the Administration of San Jacinto Mountain, Southern California, 1920-1968," University of California, Riverside, 1973.

2 Mayor Frank M. Bogert, *Palm Springs: First Hundred Years* (Palm Springs, 1987), p. 222.
3 *Palm Springs Limelight,* January 14, 1939, quoted in Davis, p. 159.
4 Davis, p. 165-166.
5 Quoted in Davis, p. 169.
6 Davis, p. 176-182. See also *Hemet News,* May 16 and July 25, 1941.
7 Davis, p. 182-183.
8 Quoted in Davis, p. 196.
9 Davis, p. 191.
10 Davis, p. 209.
11 Harry C. James, "The San Jacinto Winter Park Summer Resort Scheme," *The Living Wilderness* (Wilderness Society), Winter 1949-50.
12 Harry C. James interview by author, February 1, 1975. James allowed his Sierra Club membership to lapse because of what he said was the Club's "failure to stand up to the principles of John Muir." For a history of Sierra Club conservation battles to 1970, see Michael P. Cohen, *The History of The Sierra Club, 1892-1970* (San Francisco, 1988).
13 Davis, p. 274.
14 Construction of the tramway is largely derived from Bogert, p. 222-226; *Palm Springs Aerial Tramway,* Souvenir Magazine; George B. Ringwald, "Mountain Climbing The Easy Way," *Westways,* December 1963; and various issues of the Palm Springs *Desert Sun,* 1961-63. The *Riverside Press-Enterprise,* September 13, 1963, contains a special supplement on the tramway.
15 Davis, p. 479-486.
16 Michael Frome, *Battle for the Wilderness* (New York, 1974), p. 140-142.
17 Mike Hamilton interview, May 5, 1992.
18 Hamilton.

The second Idyllwild Inn, constructed in 1946, offered the same luxurious accommodations as its predecessor. It changed hands eleven times before its demise in 1976. The Inn was located in Eleanor Park.
— ERNEST MARQUEZ (above), BOB GRAY (below)

19

MOUNTAIN COMMUNITIES

At war's end in 1945, there were fewer than 450 permanent residents living on "The Hill," as Idyllwild, Pine Cove, and Mountain Center became known. Business was slow and real estate sales dormant during the war years. Gas rationing prevented many civilians from making the mountain trip.[1] What saved Idyllwild from total eclipse as a resort center was the influx of servicemen from General Patton's tank corps (training near Twentynine Palms), March Field, Camp Haan, and Hemet Army Air Corps base.

A low point was reached with the burning of Idyllwild Inn, long the community's major hostelry, on May 4, 1945. Dr. Paul Foster, owner and president of the Idyllwild All-Year Resort Company, immediately made plans to rebuild. By the following January, the new, spacious Idyllwild Mountain Inn was completed just east of the old site. The Inn featured a dining room seating 190 people, a coffee shop seating 80, and hotel and cabin accommodations for upwards of 200 guests.

Early in 1946, Dr. Foster sold his Idyllwild All-Year Resort Company to real estate broker Jerry Johnson and two partners. The extensive company holdings included the Idyllwild Mountain Inn, the Idyllwild Water Company, the Idyllwild Market, the Rustic Tavern, the Idyllwild Theatre, 48 cabins, the Idyllwild Stables, 150 subdivided lots, and 320 additional acres for future development. The new syndicate, led by Johnson, then sold Idyllwild Mountain Inn to Bud Funk, long-time Inn manager. Funk leased all the resort cabins and did his best to restore the Idyllwild Mountain Inn to its pre-war glory.

In July 1946, Dr. Foster sold his last mountain holding, Fern Valley Lodge, to James Weir and Allen McMahan. The man who had briefly (1944-1946) owned the heart of Idyllwild is remembered today in the name Foster Lake, dammed in 1946 as a storage reservoir for the Idyllwild Water Company.

According to Ernest Maxwell, Weir and McMahan put in fourteen slot machines at Fern Valley Lodge. Not to be outdone, Bud Funk's Idyllwild Mountain Inn put in several slot machines in a small room off the lobby. It was not long until other Idyllwild restaurants and businesses had a few of the gambling devices, too. Maxwell recalled that "One-third of the take went to the owner of the business, one-third went to the law enforcement personnel of the area, and one-third went to the owners of the slot machines.... Then one day one of the dailies in Los Angeles did an exposé on gambling in Palm Springs and that shut us all down."[2]

Apparently, gambling was not considered morally repugnant, but selling liquor was. Idyllwild religious leaders, joined by their brethren in Hemet and San Jacinto, had long fought the granting of liquor licenses to both Fern Valley Inn and Idyllwild Inn. The ministers renewed their protest when Harold Sanborn applied for a license to sell liquor at the Idyllwild Market.[3]

Idyllwild and Fern Valley were rival communities in the early post-war years. Idyllwild Mountain Inn and Fern Valley Lodge competed for guests. Idyllwild residents shopped at Sanborn's Idyllwild Market, while those living in Fern Valley used Mike and Dorothy Michelsen's Fern Valley Market. Each had its own water company and real estate office. Gradually the distinction between the two sections diminished and by the early 1950s both recognized Idyllwild as their community.

It was real estate sales, long dormant during the war years, that brought real growth to the mountain communities and ushered in Idyllwild's second "Golden Age." Two men dominated Idyllwild real estate during the late 1940s and early '50s: Jerry Johnson and Rollin Humber. "If you wanted to buy in Idyllwild you went to Jerry Johnson; if you desired a lot in Fern Valley you saw Rollin Humber," recalled Ernie Maxwell.[4] Jerry Johnson was president and major owner of the Idyllwild All-Year Resort Company, while Humber, ably assisted by his wife Margaret, managed Strong and Dickinson's Idyllwild Mountain Park Company in Fern Valley. Between them, they sold hundreds of residential lots and sparked a building boom that changed the face of

225

Rollin Humber, along with his wife Margaret, ran the Fern Valley real estate office of the Idyllwild Mountain Park Company for sixteen years. Upon his death in 1955, the Idyllwild Mountain Park Company donated land above Fern Valley that became Humber Park.
— MARGARET HUMBER

Jerry Johnson (center, back) ran the Idyllwild All-Year Resort Company which sold lots in Idyllwild proper. On the right is Bud Funk, manager and for a short time owner of the Idyllwild Inn. Long-time Idyllwild residents Inez and Johnnie Wilson are on the left. Circa 1948.
— INEZ WILSON

"The Hill." One of Johnson's major transactions was the sale of the old Idyllwild Golf Course to a consortium of Beverly Hills and Palm Springs businessmen. The agreement stipulated that the new owners would build homes and Johnson would sell them. This, and other lucrative land deals, made Jerry Johnson "King of The Hill" for several years.

Up in Pine Cove, Bob Appleton and C. A. Hoffman managed sales. Pine Cove developed into a good-sized mountain community after the war, particularly after the completion of the Banning-Idyllwild paved highway in 1950. Paul Kemp's Lookout Cafe was a Pine Cove landmark, as was Art and Mildred Thorn's general store. The Bardwells, A. W. Hoffman, and Earl Dick all had cabins to rent. Later there was Reva Lewis' Pine Cove Tavern.

A new community at the bottom of "The Hill" was Mountain Center, at the junction of State Highway 74 and the road to Idyllwild (State 243). The small community developed after the fiery demise of Keen Camp in 1943. The post office moved to the road junction right after the fire but retained the Keen Camp name. At the request of several residents, the post office was renamed Mountain Center on May 10, 1945, a date which marks the official birth of the new village. Several small resorts and restaurants sprang up in the next few years. Malcom "Mac" Taylor's Mountain Center Lodge, with cafe and cabins, was the best known and lasted 41 years. Taylor, a genial man well liked by his fellow residents, ran the lodge from 1948 to 1977, and Al Wisdom from 1977 until its demise in 1989. Other early businesses were Roy and Iris Bramblett's Chateau Cafe, H. G. Walker's Mountain Center Grocery Store right next to the post office, and Alford Huff's Mom's Place, which received a liquor license apparently unnoticed by Idyllwild religious leaders. A mile east, the old site of Keen Camp and Tahquitz Lodge became Tahquitz Meadows, a Pasadena Y.W.C.A. camp.

Ten miles east on Highway 74 was the tiny community of Thomas Mountain, where Carroll Busch had his Thomas Mountain Tavern and James Lovett ran a store and cabins.

Idyllwild remained by far the largest community in the San Jacinto Mountains. It grew rapidly in the postwar years, surpassing 1200 permanent residents by 1948, and 2,500 by the end of the 1950s.

Two of Idyllwild's most illustrious citizens came to stay in 1946. Ernest and Betty Maxwell first visited the mountain community in the 1930s and liked it so well that, after Ernie's army discharge, they decided to settle there. They bought a home lot in Fern Valley in 1944 and built their home two years later. Ernie was a talented cartoonist whose work had appeared in *Esquire* and *The New Yorker,* and in numerous military publications during the war. He edited a U.S. Army Air Corps base newspaper in Carlsbad, New Mexico, and cartooned all of the World War II aircraft for identification purposes. His wife Betty was a former Broadway actress. Both of the Maxwells were activists and quickly became involved in community activities. They founded the *Idyllwild Town Crier* in October 1946. The newspaper began as a mimeographed sheet produced in the couple's home. "It was lucky I was an artist," Ernie recalled, "If there was an empty space I could just fill it in by drawing."[5] It was only a few years before the *Town Crier* became a full-fledged, respected weekly newspaper that chronicled the growth of the community and the issues that affected Idyllwild residents and visitors. The Maxwells sold the paper in 1972 "because we grew

Betty and Ernie Maxwell at their Fern Valley home, 1948. The Maxwells founded the *Idyllwild Town Crier* in October 1946 and edited it until 1972. They signed their columns BMAX and EMAX. Both of them became deeply involved in community affairs. – IDYLLWILD TOWN CRIER

"Mr. Idyllwild," Ernie Maxwell, 1992. Ernie has been a cherished and very active citizen of Idyllwild for almost half a century. – IDYLLWILD TOWN CRIER

tired of being stuck behind a desk." Besides his newspaper work, Ernie Maxwell founded the Idyllwild Chapter of the Izaak Walton League in 1948 and was the organization's chapter leader for many years. He was president of the Riverside County Fish and Game Commission, pioneered snow surveys for the Forest Service, served on the Fern Valley Mutual Water Company board, was acting president of the Idyllwild Chamber of Commerce, and was secretary of the Idyllwild Arts Foundation. Small wonder that he earned the sobriquet of "Mr. Idyllwild." Today, ostensibly retired, he works in his studio as an artist, cartoonist, and sculptor, signing his artistic creations with his traditional EMAX. What other mountain community anywhere has been enriched as much as Idyllwild has by its beloved Ernie Maxwell?

One early project the Maxwells enthusiastically endorsed was the building of Town Hall as a cooperative community effort. In December 1946, over a hundred residents volunteered their services to lay the foundation for the building. In the following months, community volunteers worked side by side with paid construction workers to complete the structure. Fund-raising activities and entertainments were held from time to time to support the venture. Town Hall was formally dedicated on July 10, 1947, a lasting tribute to the involved citizens of Idyllwild. Since then, it has been used for community meetings and entertainment activities.

Idyllwild, over the years, has seen both stability and great change.

Stability is represented by the likes of Gray's Photo and Gift Shop, in business for 63 years, 54 of them in the present location in the center of Idyllwild. Ernest Benjamin Gray opened his little photo shop, located where the gas company office now stands on Ridgeview Drive, in 1930. His son Bob married Virginia in 1934, and both worked at the little shop. The Grays built their present shop in 1939. The following year Ernest Gray died, and ever since Bob and Virginia have operated the business. Virginia ran it alone during the years 1943 to 1946 while Bob was in the service, a photographer for the Army Signal Corps. Today, Bob and Virginia Gray are cherished figures in the Idyllwild business community.

Another stable fixture is Idyllwild's Village Market, built in the present location in 1941. Under Elmer Horsley, Clarence Bosworth, Harold Sanborn, Lee Dutton, and a succession of more recent owners, the Village Market has served Idyllwild residents and visitors for 52 years.

Other than Gray's Photo and Gift Shop, the Village Market, the Red Kettle coffee shop, Froehlich's Rustic Theatre, and a few other small businesses, downtown Idyllwild has undergone startling change since the early post-war years.

The sprawling Idyllwild Mountain Inn struggled through three decades of hard times. Bud Funk sold out to Bob and Delta O'Donnell in October 1946. The O'Donnells remodelled the Inn, fought for a liquor license which they finally received in 1949, and built more cabins before giving up in 1950, when they sold out to the Idyllwild Arts Foundation. The Arts Foundation tried to attract conventioneers and art groups, but enjoyed little success. In 1951, Martin Sousa bought the ailing Inn, made some improvements but got involved in a controversy over a cocktail bar and lost his liquor license in 1959. A group of Idyllwild investors, led by Leigh Dutton, took over in 1961 but were unable to do any better. In all, the Idyllwild Mountain Inn changed

Ernest and Marguerite Gray started a souvenir and photo shop in 1930. The shop, pictured at right, was located where the gas company office now stands on Ridgeview Drive. — BOB GRAY

Bob and Virginia Gray stand in front of Gray's Photo and Gift Shop, 1992. The beloved Grays are the deans of Idyllwild business people, their little shop serving the public for 54 years.

Bob and Virginia Gray built Gray's Photos and Gifts at the present location in 1939. Here it is pictured shortly after completion. — BOB GRAY

Bob and Virginia Gray in 1934, the year they married. — BOB AND VIRGINIA GRAY

228

Downtown Idyllwild, ca. 1948. Fred Humphrey ran the hardware store and lumber yard.

Idyllwild Town Hall was built as a cooperative community effort in 1946-47. It has long been used for community meetings and entertainment activities.

hands eleven times between its construction in 1945 and its final demise in 1976. The era of big mountain hotels, throughout Southern California, was over. They were too expensive to run, and they no longer appealed to the public. Early in 1976 the San Diego Federal Savings and Loan Association, last owners, tore the structure down.

The main Inn building was removed but the cabins remained. In 1962, well before the Inn's final demise, Glenn and Nina Mae Froehlich bought five acres adjacent to the Inn, including eleven rental units, from Jerry Johnson. They eventually ended up with all the old cabins and added some of their own. After the old hotel building was torn down, the Froehlichs took over the name "Idyllwild Inn" and added "Motel and Cottages" to their sign. The Froehlich's son and daughter-in-law, Keith and Bonnie Froelich, bought the complex in 1980. In 1991 they sold out to Froehlich cousins Don and Joanna White and their son Joel and wife Chris. The Whites' Idyllwild Inn now totals 38 units, three of which date back to 1910 and have the original knotty pine interiors and rock fireplaces. So, the present Idyllwild Inn Motel and Cottages retains a small link with the historic past.

Even more change has taken place in the block just west of Idyllwild Inn, now known as the "Center of Idyllwild." This was the original site of Elmer Horsley's Idyllwild Market, several small businesses and the Idyllwild community swimming pool. In 1946 and 1947 Jerry Johnson and Clifton Russell developed a recreational facility known as Sportland, complete with 5-lane bowling alley, swimming pool, amusement center, and a snack bar. Johnson and Russell sold the recreational complex to Bob Vevers and Percy Van Der Meid in 1948. The new owners scarcely had time to enjoy their acquisition when Sportland burned to the ground in September 1948. A restaurant named the Idyll-hof was

Don Otto's Idyll-hof was located on the present site of the Center of Idyllwild from 1949 through most of the 1950s. — BOB GRAY

Rodney Welch's Carriage Inn occupied the site of the Center of Idyllwild from 1966 to 1975. — BOB GRAY

Schwarzwaldhaus (Black Forest Restaurant), owned by Rudi and Elfie Kloebe, was a predecessor of the Chart House in Fern Valley. — BOB GRAY

Warren Jacoby was the genial host at the Chef in The Forest from 1966 until his untimely death in 1970. Afterwards, it became the Chart House.
— IDYLLWILD PUBLIC LIBRARY

built on the site the following year, run for several years by Don Otto. Avery and Jane Fisher took over the property and completed a new, bigger Sportland in 1962. Besides the swimming pool and bowling alley, the Fishers added a miniature golf course and roller skating rink. Two restaurants were in the complex: The Sportsmen Grill and the Carriage Room, not to mention a burger bar and ice cream emporium. Several small shops and an art gallery were in the complex. Unfortunately, the new Sportland failed to catch on, and the Fishers sold the property to Rodney Welch in 1966. Welch completely remodeled Sportland into a classy restaurant and bar known as the Carriage Inn. The peach-colored Inn featured entertainment and music, and had a unique back-lit fountain that pulsated with the music. Welch ran the Carriage Inn for nine years, then sold it to Glenn Bell, Jr. of Taco Bell in 1975. Bell tore down the Carriage Inn the following year and planned to build a shopping center, but never did.

In 1988 Idyllwild realtor Maureen Jones and Escondido developer Dick Krupp purchased the property and made plans for a large commercial-retail complex to be called the "Center of Idyllwild." The complex, consisting of seven log buildings interconnected by a second-story deck, was completed in November 1992. It houses 18 shops and galleries featuring indigenous art, handmade items, collectables, footwear, children's books, and an historical exhibit. The Center of Idyllwild is constructed entirely of standing dead logs imported from Idaho; no live trees were cut. On one side is a 50-foot by 7.5-foot bas relief mural, reputedly the world's largest, created by chainsaw artist Jonathan La Benne. Because of the Center's log stockade appearance, some have humorously dubbed it "Fort Idyllwild."

Great change has come to Fern Valley, too. Fern Valley Lodge, the original resort, was sold to the

Bill Butler ran Butler Trading Post at Fern Valley Corners in the late 1940s and '50s.

The Idyllwild Community Swimming Pool was in the center of town, where the Center of Idyllwild now stands.
— BOB GRAY

The Kwikset Lock Company turned the old Fern Valley Cafe into an employee retreat in the 1950s.

Paul Kemp's Lookout Cafe was a popular restaurant in Pine Cove during the 1940s. – LAURA SWIFT

Kwikset Lock Company of Anaheim in the 1950s. It has long been used as an employee retreat. The Michelsons' Fern Valley Market went through a number of owners before Robert and Jan Oates extensively remodeled it and added a restaurant known as the Alpine Pantry in 1962. Later, it was the first location of Michelli's Italian Restaurant. The market and restaurant closed down a few years ago and, as of this writing, lies vacant. The present Chart House restaurant has a colorful past. Ernie and Dorothy Jolin opened a hamburger stand there in 1946, which Ralph and Quinnie Sturges turned into the Log Cabin Cafe in 1949. In the early 1960s Rudi and Elfie Kloeble remodeled it into the Schwarzwaldhaus (Black Forest Restaurant). Warren Jacober ran it as the Chef of The Forest from 1966 until his untimely death in 1970. Since then, it has been the Chart House.

One of the most unique resorts on The Hill is The Epicurean and Fern Valley Gardens. Dr. and Mrs. Bell of Pasadena built the Epicurian building and the adjacent Carriage House in 1924, and landscaped the grounds with beautiful shrubs and bushes to give it a park-like atmosphere. The Epicurean and its gardens went through a number of owners over the years before Mitch Susnar remodeled the interior and created the exquisite designs you see today in the two main buildings. Charles and Kirsten Marvin own this remarkable complex today.

Away up at the head of Fern Valley is Humber Park, starting point for hikers and horsemen going to the high country wilderness areas. The park honors Rollin Humber, prominant Fern Valley real estate broker, who died in 1955. The ten acres were donated by the Idyllwild Mountain Park Company, Humber's long-time employer. Riverside County opened the trailhead parking area in 1958. As of this writing (1993) negotiations are underway to turn Humber Park over to the Forest

Mountain Center developed as a small community after Keen Camp burned in 1943. The U.S. Post Office at Mountain Center dates from May 10, 1945.

Malcom "Mac" Taylor ran his Mountain Center Lodge, with cafe and cabins, from 1948 to 1977. – BOB GRAY

231

The bear at the entrance to the Riverside Boy Scouts' Camp Emerson was placed on its pedestal in 1969.

The Epicurean and Fern Valley Gardens, started in 1924, is one of the really unique resorts on The Hill. The beautiful grounds and exquisitely designed buildings are presently owned by Charles and Kirsten Marvin.

Service.

In upper Fern Valley about a mile below Humber Park was Jules Berkeley's Hidden Lodge, built in 1947. Berkeley tried to turn Hidden Lodge and the adjacent slopes into a winter sports center. He hired prominent ski instructor Tommi Tyndall as manager. Tyndall operated a small ski school and developed several short ski runs with rope tows and a toboggan slide. He planned a 2000-foot ski run from the slopes of Tahquitz Peak, but it was never built. Tyndall's effort to turn Idyllwild into a major ski center failed, and the popular ski instructor left for Big Bear in 1950.

Two other unsuccessful attempts to make Idyllwild a winter sports center should be mentioned. Bob O'Donnell and Lem Poates installed a toboggan slide adjacent to the Poates' restaurant and the old Rustic Theatre (now Silver Pines) in 1948. It only lasted a couple of years, as new cabin owners objected to the long slide crossing their property. Halona Hill, developed by Jim Henley, had a rope two and a short ski run, located on the lower west slope of Tahquitz Peak's south ridge. But there was not enough snow most years, so Halona Hill's little ski run fell to the developers in the late 1950s.[6]

The 1960s saw new real estate developments on The Hill. Mary Nelson was exclusive agent for the Big Cedar Glen subdivision, three-quarters of a mile up the Banning-Idyllwild Highway from Idyllwild proper. Nearby was the new Tahquitz Lake Golf Club at Dutch Flat, with a nine-hole golf course, which opened to considerable fanfare in 1960 but closed its doors five years later. Golf, like skiing and tobogganing, simply can not gain a real foothold on The Hill.

Six miles north of Idyllwild on the Banning-Idyllwild Highway, Rodney Welch opened a new subdivision in 1962. Several dozen homesites were sold along a mile and a half stretch of the highway. Welch called his development Alandale for his two sons, Alan and Dale. Nearby Pine Cove boomed with new homes on Marion Ridge, on both sides of the highway.

Down in Garner Valley, James P. Edmundson and the Greatamerican Land Company bought 2,200 acres from the Garner Ranch in 1968. Edmundson announced plans to subdivide the open, pine-dotted ranchland into 3,911 small homesites which would turn Garner Valley into a mountain community larger than Idyllwild. The community would be named Lake Pine Meadows. The development would include a good-sized, man-made lake to be named Lake Idyllwild and an 18-hole golf course.

Greatamerica's mammoth development plan ran into opposition right from the start. Conservationists formed the San Jacinto Mountain Conservation League to oppose the plan. Ecologists at the University of California, Riverside, warned that Garner Valley would become a smog trap if such large-scale development went forth. The Riverside County Park Advisory Commission opposed it and called for a master plan to determine future development in the San Jacinto Mountains.

Despite the strong opposition, the Riverside County Board of Supervisors, in a split vote in July 1970, approved the Greatamerica project. Soon after, charges of undue influence were hurled at the supervisors. A county grand jury investigated and found that Greatamerica had donated $6,250 to the campaign funds of three supervisors who voted in favor of the project. The three supervisors and two others were indicted for bribery and conspiracy, but the charges against four of the men were later dropped and the fifth was acquitted. Nevertheless, a residue of bad taste lingered. Several incumbents lost their reelection bids. In 1971, the new Board of Supervisors voted to rezone Garner Valley which, in effect, nixed the project. Instead of a dense

Jonathan La Benne, the chainsaw artist, carved this 50-foot tree monument in 1989.

Jonathan La Benne carving the design of the new Center of Idyllwild complex, 1992. In the foreground is his exquisitely carved bald eagle, presently perched on the roof.

community of tightly packed homes, the supervisors approved the subdivision and sale of 5-acre lots in the valley and 20-acre parcels on the hillsides. In such manner the sprawling community of Garner Valley has grown over the last two decades. The rural, ranch-like estates retain some of the flavor of the old cattle spread.

It is as a cultural center, not as a real estate development, that The Hill has achieved nation-wide prominence. Foremost among the cultural jewels on the mountain is the Idyllwild School of Music and The Arts (ISOMATA). ISOMATA was the dream turned reality of Max and Bee Krone. Dr. Max T. Krone taught music and conducted the choir at the University of Southern California and for many years was the school's Dean of Fine Arts. His wife Bee was an accomplished musician herself, who conducted music workshops all over the country. Max and Bee Krone visited Idyllwild in 1941 and liked the mountain area so much that they bought a summer home on Marion View Drive. The United States entered World War II a few months later, and the nation's attention was riveted on the world-wide carnage. Amid the horror of war, the Krones dared to think of music, art, and the human spirit. Gradually a dream formed in their minds – a dream of a school unlike most schools, a place where the universal language of music, art, drama, and dance would be taught and practiced amid a beautiful forest setting.

A dream is one thing, turning it into reality is another. The Krones were able to interest Dr. Robert Kingsley, Dean of U.S.C.'s Law School, and twenty-one other faculty members in the project. Pooling their finances, the Krones and their supporters bought 340 acres on Domenigoni Flats, at the lower end of Strawberry Valley, in 1946. Construction of studios and workshops got underway in 1949, and the first summer session took place in 1950.

Students were treated to an intensive course in music and the arts, taught by some of the leading musicians and artists of the day. Among the early notables who appeared at ISOMATA sessions were Alfred Wallenstein, conductor of the Los Angeles Philharmonic Orchestra, violinist Jehudi Menuhin, pianist José Iturbi, composer Meredith Wilson, Benny Goodman, "King of Swing," and Ansel Adams, renowned nature photographer. Long-time instructors at ISOMATA included Robert Evans Homes, choir master who has conducted the "Messiah" as a community project for many years, Marguerite Clapp and Bella Lewitzky (dance), Harry

The Center of Idyllwild under construction, 1992.

233

The Center of Idyllwild, 1993. The commercial complex is made up of seven log buildings interconnected by a second story deck. It holds eighteen shops and galleries, unique in their appeal to visitors. Chainsaw artist Jonathan LaBenne carved the side mural and the host of animals on the roof.

Max and Bea Krone in 1941, when they first visited Idyllwild. The Krones developed the Idyllwild School of Music and the Arts, where the universal language of music, art, drama, and dance would be taught and practiced amid a beautiful forest setting.
— ISOMATA

Sternberg (painting), Susan Peterson (pottery), Burdette Fitzgerald (drama), and Lora Steere (art).

Anywhere from 1,200 to 2,800 students participate in the summer programs. Along with intensive learning activities, students, faculty members, and visiting artists offer dance, theater and musical performances, art exhibits, and lectures, all open to the public. The ISOMATA Arts Academy, founded in 1986, bears the distinction of being the first and only residential high school for the arts in the western United States. It occupies the campus during the traditional September through June school year. ISOMATA's Native Arts Program is nationally recognized. Summer workshops improve the skills of teachers of music, arts, and crafts. The Children's Center provides youths with a full range of cultural activities.

ISOMATA has weathered financial storms. The school became a second campus of the University of Southern California in 1964, with the provision that the campus be self-supporting. By the early 1970s and into the 1980s, ISOMATA had difficulty making ends meet. USC reluctantly severed its connection in 1983. The Idyllwild Arts Foundation, a non-profit private group, resumed ownership of ISOMATA and, with the support of a number of individuals, including many from the Idyllwild community, restored financial stability to the institution. An institution, in every sense of the word, is what ISOMATA has become. 1993 was its 45th consecutive year of conducting classes and workshops in music and the arts, and it holds every promise of continuing to do so in the future. The Associates of ISOMATA, a community support group, donate funds in support of school programs and hold several events each year in Idyllwild.

The Idyllwild School of Music and the Arts (ISOMATA) has developed into one of the major cultural centers of Southern California.

Lora Steere, an artist in sculpture, teaching a young protegé. – ISOMATA

Another cultural institution that brought notoriety to Idyllwild for 44 years was Richard and Edith Elliott's Desert Sun School, later the Elliott-Pope Preparatory School, located in Saunders Meadow. Edith Elliott and her sister Helen Jayne founded the school in Mecca, near the shores of the Salton Sea, in 1930. That first year the school was housed in a tent and had twelve students. Over the years, it acquired a substantial campus and a student body numbering over 100. Looking for another location, Richard and Edith leased, and later bought, the 40-acre Saunders Meadow Lodge and Golf Course in 1944. In 1946 they made a decision to sell the school's desert campus and move their entire operation to Idyllwild. Edith served as headmistress until her death in 1971 and Richard Elliott taught at the school and was a trustee. The Desert Sun School eventually encompassed 100 acres and had facilities that included science laboratories, a computer center, an 18,000-volume library, a gymnasium, swimming pool, stables and riding ring, and seven dormatories to house its 140 students and 27-member faculty. The school's aim was "to create an environment that encourages high levels and standards of achievement within each individual's capability; to develop an awareness within an individual of his own uniqueness and self-concept as to his total nature, intellectual, emotional and spiritual." The name of the fully accredited private high school was changed to the Elliott-Pope Preparatory School in 1983. The change was made to honor the Elliotts and school supporters Edgar and Blanche Pope.

Robert Evans Holmes, with orchestra and choir, leads a performance of Handel's *Messiah*. – ISOMATA

Ansel Adams teaches a class in nature photography, summer 1958. – ISOMATA

Dance taught by the master, Bella Lewitzky. — ISOMATA

Music amid the pines. — ISOMATA

Sadly, the Elliott-Pope School was unable to weather a nationwide recession. Declining enrollment was the chief culprit. Budgeted for 140 boarding students, the school was down to 105 for the 1990-91 school year. With annual tuition per live-in student at $16,800, the reduced enrollment caused a severe shortage of operating funds. When a last-ditch fund raising campaign failed, the Elliott-Pope School was obliged to close its doors on December 31, 1990.

The Desert Sun Science Center, operated by Guided Discoveries Inc. of Upland, now leases the old Elliott-Pope campus at Saunders Meadow. The Center is an outdoor education school, giving fourth through ninth grade students from throughout the Southwest hands-on experiences in nature study, geology, meteorology, and astronomy. Guided Discoveries, whose philosophy is "Education Through Exploration," also operates a science school on Catalina Island.

Another cultural mainstay on The Hill is Ann Lay's Idyllwild Institute-Fiesta, a non-profit organization that conducts summer programs to "install poise, confidence and pride" to hundreds of teen-age girls. Ann Lay, an intensely patriotic woman who has dedicated her life to helping others, started the girls' program in 1953. In 1965, she was able to purchase the 38-acre Four Chimneys estate built by Hollywood movie director Alfred Santell. Since then, this has been the location of Idyllwild Institute-Fiesta. The Institute conducts six week-long sessions for Junior ROTC girls, many of whom are planning to attend the Army, Navy, Marine Corps, Air Force, or Coast Guard academies. Each of the cadets, chosen for scholarship and leadership ability, receives training in leadership, speaking skills, proper manners and etiquette. "I believe that if we can send beautiful girls with these lessons out into America, this country will be a better place," is Ann Lay's conviction.

Idyllwild has long been a magnet for painters and sculptors, too numerous to mention. There is something about the quiet forested basin ringed with granite ridges that brings out creativity.

It is little known now, but Idyllwild was once a center for the construction of craftsman furniture. One of the top furniture craftsmen in the nation, Seldon Belden, founded his Pinecraft Furniture studio in Pine Cove in 1935 and a few years later moved his studio to Idyllwild (located at the corner of Saunders Meadow Road and Highway 243). Belden crafted his distinctive furniture from carefully peeled logs, all of local origin, and applied a clear finish. Pinecraft furniture was in demand all over the United States. Seldon Belden died in 1952, and his son Ted took over, but Seldon's genius at his craft could not be duplicated, and Pinecraft Furniture closed its doors in 1960.[8]

Idyllwild and the surrounding mountain areas have long been a favorite location for youth and religious camps, offering various outdoor educational and recreational activities.

Camp Emerson, now operated by the California Inland Empire Council of the Boy Scouts of America, bears the distinction of being the oldest Scout camp west of the Mississippi, founded in 1921 on land donated by Claudius Lee Emerson. The camp covers 167 acres on both sides of Strawberry Creek and Bear Trap Canyon.

Richard and Edith Elliott in their office at the Desert Sun School in Idyllwild, ca. 1960. The Elliotts opened their Idyllwild campus of the school in 1946 and quickly turned it into one of the best private educational centers in California. Edith was headmistress until her death in 1971; Richard was a teacher and trustee of the school.
– RICHARD ELLIOTT, JR.

Tahquitz Meadows, on the site of old Keen Camp, was a summer camp operated by the Pasadena Y.W.C.A. from 1946 to 1980. – BOB GRAY

The second Boy Scout camp in Idyllwild, Camp Tahquitz of the Long Beach Boy Scout Council, founded in 1925, moved to Barton Flats in the San Bernardino Mountains in 1958. Most of the old camp grounds are now part of Riverside County Park.

Azalea Trails Girl Scout Camp, established by the San Gorgonio Girl Scout Council in 1942, is located in the Dark Canyon area north of Pine Cove.

The largest Girl Scout camp in California is Camp Joe Scherman, located in Morris Canyon just above Garner Valley. The Orange County Council of the Girl Scouts purchased 560 acres from Jim Wellman in 1960 to start the summer camp. Over the years, Camp Joe Scherman, named for the State Forestry ranger who persuaded Wellman to sell part of his cattle ranch, has grown to 700 acres. More than 2,500 Orange County Girl Scouts attend the camp each summer.

The 28-acre Pathfinder Ranch in Garner Valley is used mainly by Southern California members of the Boys Clubs of America.

Idyllwild Pines, a nondenominational religious camp covering 50 acres, is the second oldest camp in Idyllwild, founded in 1923. Its year-around program combines religious training with recreational activities.

Tahquitz Pines, started by Christian Endeavor in 1929, is now operated by the Wycliffe Bible Translators as a missionary training facility. It occupies 22 acres on the east side of Fern Valley.

Camp Maranatha occupies 23 acres in Idyllwild and is owned by the Southern California Conference of the Advent Christian Church.

Buckhorn Camp, 120 acres on Dutch Flat, is run by the Reorganized Church of Jesus Christ of Latter Day Saints. It offers various programs for families and church groups.

470-acre Pine Springs Ranch in Apple Canyon offers programs in sports, photography, and Old West experiences. It is owned by the Southeast Conference of the Seventh Day Adventist Church.

Mesorah Mountain Retreat in Garner Valley offers various programs for adults and children, ranging from religious education to summer soccer and baseball camps.

There are other, smaller camps scattered in forested nooks and flats here and there. In Southern California, only the Barton Flats area of the San Bernardino Mountains has a greater concentration of religious, educational, and youth camps.

As the communities of Idyllwild, Pine Cove, Mountain Center, and Garner Valley grow, they face some of the same issues long experienced by lowland urban areas. Overcrowding, water distribution shortages, rubbish and sewage disposal problems, increased need for adequate fire protection, and preservation of the natural and wildlife habitat scene are things that Hill residents gave little thought to a few decades ago. Now, if the San Jacinto Mountain communities want to preserve their unique setting and life style, these problems must be faced.

The natural lifeblood of any community is its water resources. Living in a community that does not import water has required Hill residents to gain a special appreciation of their present supply and future demand. There are three separate water districts that provide water to Hill communities: The Idyllwild Water District, organized in 1955, the Pine Cove Water District, founded in 1956, and the Fern Valley Water District, formed in 1958. Garner Valley was annexed to the Eastern Municipal Water District in 1969. These districts supply water to their customers through systems of surface water diversions and wells that tap underground sources. Unfortunately these sources are finite, and in

Buckhorn Camp, on the edge of Dutch Flats, is run by the Reorganized Church of Jesus Christ of Latter Day Saints.

Living Free, a sanctuary for abused and abandoned pets, has occupied the old Keen Camp site since 1980.

which usually occur several times each decade, water conservation measures are required. Emergency restrictions limit the watering of lawns, the washing of vehicles, and other types of water waste. The slow but steady growth of the mountain communities poses a serious challenge to the water districts and may result in the eventual need to import expensive water from the MWD or some other outside source. Idyllwild and its sister communities cannot continue to grow without squarely facing this issue.

Recent years of drought, particularly in 1989 and 1990, contributed to the Pine Beetle infestation that periodically ravages the forest trees. The Forest Service and the California Department of Forestry have put out posters and issued bulletins to educate the public on ways to reduce the infestation that threatens the forest. In one case, the destruction of a 180-foot landmark tree that long stood in the middle of South Circle Drive was put to good use. Chainsaw sculptor Jonathan La Benne arranged for the 60-foot base of the forest giant to be moved to Village Center Drive, where he and a team of helpers carved an elaborate monument dedicated to Idyllwild, depicting Cahuilla Indian Chief Algoot, an eagle, a mountain lion, a squirrel, a raccoon, a coyote, and long-time Idyllwild leader Ernie Maxwell. The monument was completed in November 1989.

Fire protection is provided by the Idyllwild Fire Protection District, organized in 1947. The district has a nucleus of professional firefighters who receive help, in time of need, from volunteer firemen. Riverside County maintains fire stations at Pine Cove, Garner Valley, and Anza. In the event of a major forest or brush conflagration, the U.S. Forest Service and California Forestry Department crews are in readiness to protect the mountain communities.

Major growth in Idyllwild and Garner Valley has come in recent years. Because of this, they have been able to learn from the mistakes of mountain communities elsewhere. The Riverside County Planning Commission has taken a hard look at community growth.

Careful zoning and building codes now prevent helter-skelter development, protect residential areas from commercial inroads, and generally try to preserve the unique mountain environment. Kay Ceniceros, Riverside County 3rd District Supervisor, whose territory includes the mountain area, has taken a leading role in helping the mountain communities plan for the future. She was instrumental in setting up the Hill Municipal Advisory Council in 1988. In Garner Valley, the Coordinated Resource Management Planning program (CRMP) is a model of cooperation between public and private land owners.

With a citizenry vitally interested in preserving the mountain way of life, with the close cooperation of governmental agencies, and with a framework of enlightened planning for the future, there is no reason that the Hill communities cannot continue to be desirable places to live, work, and play.

NOTES

1 Margaret Humber interview, Hemet, April 9, 1992.
2 Ernest Maxwell, *Idyllwild Town Crier,* February 18, 1988. See also November 27, 1970.
3 *Hemet News,* February 15, 1946.
4 Ernest Maxwell interview, Idyllwild, March 12, 1992.
5 *Town Crier,* October 26, 1989.
6 Virginia and Bob Gray interview, June 26, 1992.
7 *Riverside Press-Enterprise,* March 8, 1973. The Garner Valley development plan was mentioned by Ralph Nader in his 1971 annual report.
8 John Ripley, "Memorandum of Conversation with Ted Belden, Ventura, California, 1991," typescript in authors' possession.

Line drawing of The Center of Idyllwild, the business complex completed in the fall of 1992. — LUCY BRYANT

The eternal Idyllwild. Ageless Lily Rock looms high over the mountain community. — ERNEST MARQUEZ

The old Idyllwild, ca. 1948. — BOB GRAY (above), HARRY WENDELKEN (below)

239

Lake Fulmor. – ROY MURPHY

20

THE CHALLENGE OF TOMORROW

In recent decades, Americans have seen fit to safeguard our natural heritage and preserve unspoiled scenic treasures as national parks, state parks, and wilderness areas. Nowhere is this more evident than in the San Jacinto-Santa Rosa mountain country. Almost all of the high San Jacintos have been set aside in the form of the San Jacinto Wilderness, administered by the Forest Service and Mt. San Jacinto State Park. More recently, the unique mountain-desert landscape of the Santa Rosas has been given protection with the establishment of the Santa Rosa Wilderness and the B.L.M.'s Santa Rosa National Scenic Area. Also nestled against the southern ramparts of the Santa Rosas is Anza-Borrego State Park.

At the same time, civilization is encroaching on the mountains in ever increasing numbers. Hemet and San Jacinto have boomed in recent years, as have the desert communities from Palm Springs to Indio. In the mountains, the communities of Idyllwild, Pine Cove, Mountain Center, Garner Valley, Pinyon Pines, and the Anza and Terwilliger valleys continue to grow. In the latter two valleys, development is haphazard at best, with homes springing up all over the plains and surrounding hills. Home building continues to take place in Idyllwild, Pine Cove, Garner Valley, fortunately, at a more controlled pace.

This continuing encroachment by new residents and visitors, along with increasing public awareness of natural values, both occurring simultaneously, poses a paradox. How can we save our unique mountain-desert landscape and still allow for more people, larger communities, and more commercial development?

The solution of this dilemma poses a major challenge that we can ignore only at the risk of damaging the quality of mountain living. Hard decisions need to be made. Some form of growth control, along with strict environmental safeguards, is necessary. Wilderness and wildlife must be vigorously protected. The delicate balance that exists between mankind and nature, between development and preservation, must be maintained. If we are willing to make the sacrifices necessary to safeguard our mountain heritage and at the same time better the quality of mountain living, we will have resolved the paradox.

There is no reason why the San Jacintos and Santa Rosas should not continue to be one of Southern California's great natural treasures. The mountain air is crisp and clean, the aroma of pine, cedar, and chaparral is invigorating, the diversity of flora and fauna is a delight to behold, and the vistas are enchanting.

The future of these mountains is in our hands.

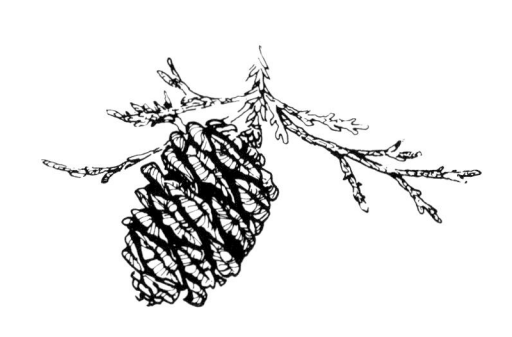

Ascending Snow Creek.

BIBLIOGRAPHY

BOOKS

Bailey, Philip A., *Golden Mirages: The Story of the Lost Pegleg Mine, The Legendary Three Gold Buttes, and the Yarns of and by Those Who Know the Desert*. Ramona: Acoma Books, 1971.

Bauer, John E., *The Health Seekers of Southern California, 1870-1900*. San Marino: The Huntington Library, 1959.

Bean, Lowell John, *Mukat's People: The Cahuilla Indians of Southern California*. Berkeley: University of California Press, 1972.

Bean, Lowell John and Lisa Bourgealt, *The Cahuilla*. New York: Chelsea House, 1989.

Bean, Lowell John and William Mason, *Diaries and Accounts of the Romero Expeditions in Arizona and California, 1823-1826*. Palm Springs Desert Museum, 1962.

Bean, Lowell John, Sylvia Brakke Vane and Jackson Young, *The Cahuilla Landscape: The Santa Rosa and San Jacinto Mountains*. Menlo Park: Ballena Press, 1991.

Beattie, George William and Helen Pruitt Beattie, *Heritage of the Valley: San Bernardino's First Century*. Oakland: Biobooks, 1951.

Becker, Stephen and Jeffrey Birmingham, *The San Jacintos: A History and Natural History*. Riverside: Historical Commission Press, 1981.

Bissell, Charles A. (ed.), *The Metropolitan Water District of Southern California: History and First Annual Report*. Los Angeles: Metropolitan Water District, 1939.

Bolton, Herbert Eugene (ed.), *Anza's California Expeditions*, 5 vol. Berkeley: University of California Press, 1930.

Brown, John Jr. and James Boyd, *History of San Bernardino and Riverside Counties*, 3 vol. Chicago: Lewis Publishing Company, 1922.

Chase, J. Smeaton, *Our Araby: Palm Springs and the Garden of the Sun*. New York: J. J. Little and Ives Company, 1923.

Cleland, Robert Glass, *The Cattle on a Thousand Hills*. San Marino: The Huntington Library, 1951.

Dale, Edward Everett, *The Indians of the Southwest: A Century of Development under the United States*. Norman: University of Oklahoma Press, 1971.

Davis, Carlyle Channing and William A. Alderson, *The True Story of Ramona*. New York: Dodge Publishing Company, 1914.

Elliott, Wallace W., *History of San Bernardino and San Diego Counties*. 1883. Reprint, Riverside: Historical Commission Press, 1965.

Engelhardt, Fr. Zephyrin, *San Luis Rey Mission*. San Francisco: James H. Barry Company, 1921.

Frederick, K. P., *Legends and History of the San Jacinto Mountains*. Long Beach: privately printed, 1926.

Frome, Michael, *Battle for the Wilderness*. New York: Praeger Publishers, 1974.

Gabbert, John Raymond, *History of Riverside City and County*. Riverside, 1935.

Garner, Van H., *The Broken Ring: The Destruction of the California Indians*. Tucson: Westernlore Press, 1982.

Grinnell, J. and H.S. Swarth, *An Account of the Birds and Mammals of the San Jacinto Area of Southern California*. University of California Publications in Zoology, Vol. 10, Berkeley, 1913.

Guinn, J.M., *A History of California and An Extended History of Its Southern Coast Counties*. Los Angeles: Historical Record Company, 1907.

Gunther, Jane Davies, *Riverside County, California, Place Names: Their Origin and Their Stories*. Riverside: Rubidoux Printing Company, 1984.

Hall, Harvey Monroe, *A Botanical Survey of San Jacinto Mountain*. University of California Publications in Botany, Vol. 1. Berkeley, 1902.

Hayes, Benjamin, *Pioneer Notes*. ed. by Margaret Wolcott. Los Angeles: privately printed, 1929.

Hayes, Samuel P., *Conservation and the Gospel of Efciency*. Harvard University Press, 1959.

Heizer, Robert F. (ed.), *Handbook of North American Indians, Vol. 8, California*. Washington: Smithsonian Institution, 1978.

Hemet-San Jacinto Genealogical Society, *San Jacinto Valley, Past and Present*. Hemet, 1989.

Henderson, Randall, *On Desert Trails, Today and Yesterday*. Los Angeles: Westernlore Press, 1961.

Holmes, Elmer Wallace, *History of Riverside County, California*. Los Angeles: Historical Record Company, 1912.

Hooper, Lucile, *The Cahuilla Indians*. Ramona: Ballena Press, 1972. Reprint of 1920 edition.

Huddon, Tom, *Three Paths Along The River: The Heritage of the Valley of the San Luis Rey*. Palm Desert: Desert Southwest Publishers, 1964.

Hughes, Tom, *History of Banning and San Gorgonio Pass*. Banning: Banning Record, n.d. (ca. 1938).

Jackson, Helen Hunt, *Ramona*. Boston: Roberts Brothers, 1884.

James, George Wharton, *Through Ramona's Country*. Boston: Little, Brown and Company, 1909.

James, George Wharton, *Wonders of the Colorado Desert*. Boston: Little, Brown and Company, 1906.

James, Harry C., *The Cahuilla Indians*. Los Angeles: Westernlore Press, 1960.

Leadabrand, Russ, *Guidebook to the San Jacinto Mountains of Southern California*. Los Angeles: Ward Ritchie Press, 1971.

Lewis Publishing Company, *An Illustrated History of San Diego County*. Chicago, 1890.

Lindsay, Diana, *Our Historic Desert: The Story of the Anza-Borrego Desert*. San Diego: A Copley Book, 1973.

Lockmann, Ronald F., *Guarding The Forests of Southern California*. Glendale: The Arthur H. Clark Company, 1981.

Maxwell, Ernie, *Pictorial History of the San Jacinto Mountains*. Idyllwild: privately printed, 1988.

Mathis, Valerie Sherer, *Helen Hunt Jackson and Her Indian Reform Legacy*. Austin: University of Texas Press, 1990.

Parker, Horace, *The Treaty of Temecula*. Balboa Island: The Paisano Press, 1967.

Patencio, Chief Francisco, *Stories and Legends of the Palm Springs Indians,* as told to Margaret Boynton. Palm Springs: Desert Museum, 1943.

Phillips, George H. *Chief and Challengers: Indian Resistance and Cooperation in Southern California*. Berkeley: University of California Press, 1975.

Pinchot, Gifford, *Breaking New Ground*. New York: Harcourt, Brace and Company, 1947.

Pourade, Richard F., *Anza Conquers The Desert*. San Diego: A Copley Book, 1971.

Rabbitt, Mary C., *A Brief History of the United States Geological Survey*. Washington: Government Printing Office, 1980.

Reed, Lester, *Old Time Cattlemen and Other Pioneers of the Anza-Borrego Area*. Redlands: Citrograph Printing Company, 1963.

Reed, Lester, *Old Timers of Southeastern California*. Redlands: Citrograph Printing Company, 1967.

Robinson, John W., *San Bernardino Mountain Trails*. Berkeley: Wilderness Press, 1972.

Robinson, W. W., *The Story of Riverside County*. Los Angeles: Title Trust and Insurance Company, 1957.

Sanchez, Joseph, P., *Spanish Bluecoats: The Catalonian Volunteers of Northwestern New Spain, 1767-1810*. Albuquerque: University of New Mexico Press, 1990.

Saunders, Charles Francis, *The Southern Sierras of California*. Boston: Houghton-Mifflin Company, 1923.

Shinn, G. Hazen, *Shoshonean Days: Recollections of a Residence of Five Years Among the Indians of Southern California*. Glendale: The Arthur H. Clark Company, 1941.

Shumway, Nina Paul, *Your Desert and Mine*. Los Angeles: Westernlore Press, 1960.

Spaulding, Phebe Estelle, *The Tahquitch Maiden: A Tale of the San Jacintos*. San Francisco: Paul Elder and Company, 1911.

Steen, Harold K., *The U.S. Forest Service: A History*. Seattle: University of Washington Press, 1976.

Strong, William Duncan, *Aboriginal Society in Southern California*. Banning: Malki Museum Press, 1972 (reprint of 1929 edition).

Tapper, Violet and Nellie Lolmaugh, *The Friendliest Valley: Memories of the Hemet-San Jacinto Area*. Hemet: Hungry Eye Books, 1971.

United States Department of Agriculture, *The Use Book*. Washington: Government Printing Office, 1906.

United States Department of the Interior, *Forest Reserve Manual*. Washington: Government Printing Office, 1902.

Wheeler, Lt. George M., *Annual Report on the Geographical Surveys West of the 100th Meridian*. Washington: Government Printing Office, 1876.

Whitney, J.D., *Geological Survey of California, Vol. 1, Geology*. Philadelphia: Caxton Press, 1865.

Whitney, Mary E., *Fortune Favors The Brave: A History of the Lake Hemet Water Company*. San Jacinto: Alphabet Printers, 1982.

Williamson, Lt. R.S., *Reports of Explorations and Surveys to Ascertain The Most Practical and Economic Route for a Railroad from the Mississippi River to the Pacific Ocean, Vol. 5*. Washington: Government Printing Office, 1857.

ARTICLES

Bolton, Herbert Eugene, "In the South San Joaquin Ahead of Garces," *California Historical Society Quarterly,* October 1931.

Burgess, Larry E., "Commission to the Mission Indians, 1891." *San Bernardino County Museum Association Quarterly,* Spring 1988.

Brumgardt, John R., "Tea, Crumpets, and San Jacinto Gold: The Short-Lived Town of Kenworthy, California, 1897-1900," *Pacific Historian*, Fall 1976.

Brumgardt, John R. and Greg Robbins, "Gold Camp in the San Jacintos," *High Country*, Winter 1976-76.

Chase, Ralph Arthur, "San Jacinto, Southern California's Noblest Mountain," *Sierra Club Bulletin*, 1923 annual number.

Dyar, Ruth, "Up Snow Creek to the Cairn on San Jacinto," *Desert Magazine*, June 1939.

Fultz, Francis M., "High Places of the South," *Sierra Club Bulletin*, January 1920.

Harwood, Aurelia, "San Jacinto Game Refuge," *Sierra Club Bulletin*, 1925 annual number.

Heald, Weldon F., "The Lordly San Jacintos," *Westways*, July 1963.

Henderson, Randall, "Toro Is Taboo," *Desert Magazine*, July 1938.

Jaeger, Edmund C., "Forgotten Trails," *Palm Springs Villager*, September 1949.

Jaeger, Edmund C., "Saga of Frying Pan Ebbens," *Desert Magazine*, March 1956.

James, Harry C., "Ramona," *Palm Springs Villager*, April 1958.

James, Harry C., "The San Jacinto Winter Park Summer Resort Scheme," *The Living Wilderness* (Wilderness Society), Winter 1949-50.

Jennings, Bill, "All the Mines are not on the Desert," *Desert Magazine*, October 1979.

Jennings, Bill, "Deep Canyon," *High Country*, Winter 1976-77.

Jennings, Bill, "Desert Steve, the Town Founder," *Desert Magazine*, June 1979.

Jennings, Bill, "Kenworthy, once a boom town, isn't even a ghost now," *Riverside Daily Enterprise*, August 6, 1964.

Jennings, Bill, "Many years ago, he erected a stone cabin in the mountains," *Riverside Press-Enterprise, Valley Edition*, July 15, 1972.

Jennings, Bill "Santa Rosa Indian Reservation," *Palms to Pines*, February 1977.

Jennings, Bill, "The Hemet Belle Mine," *Riverside Daily Enterprise*, June 19, 1963.

Johnston, Francis J., "San Gorgonio Pass: Forgotten Route of the Californios," *Journal of The West*, January 1969.

Kinucan, John and Mary Haggland, "El Rancho San Jacinto Viejo: Memories of Miss Ruth M. Pico," *Riverside County Historical Quarterly*, September 1979.

Law, George, "Early Days of Idyllwild," *Hemet News*, August 24, 1923.

Law, George, "Fattening Desert Steers on Mountain Meadows," *Hemet News*, February 9, 1923.

Leadabrand, Russ, "The Pines to Palms Highway," *Westways*, April 1965.

Leiberg, John B., "San Jacinto Forest Reserve," *19th Annual Report of the U.S. Geological Survey, 1897-98;* and *20th Annual Report...*, 1898-99.

Luckoch, V. O., "He Faced-Lifted A Mountain," *Westways*, October 1954.

Maxwell, Ernest, "Justifiable Homicide, California Style," *Desert Magazine*, September 1980.

McShane, Sister Catherine, "The Estudillo Family," *Journal of San Diego History*, Winter 1969.

McKenney, J. Wilson, "Ancestral Home of the Santa Rosa Cahuillas," *Westways*, April 1937.

Pasik, Herb, "Mr. Idyllwild," *Westways*, November 1985.

Patterson, Tom, "Banning-Idyllwild Road is just bits and pieces of earlier route," *Riverside Press-Enterprise*, June 13, 1971.

Patterson, Tom, "Idyllwild was uphill no matter what road," *Riverside Press-Enterprise*, August 22, 1971.

Patterson, Tom, "New land reserve is historical part of the old Banning-Idyllwild Road," *Riverside Press-Enterprise*, September 21, 1980.

Patterson, Tom, "Switchbacks built in 1891 long thought best road to Idyllwild," *Riverside Press-Enterprise*, December 25, 1983.

Quimby, Garfield M., "History of the Potrero Ranch and Its Neighbors," *San Bernardino County Museum Association Quarterly*, Winter 1975.

Quimby, Garfield M., "The Story of Ramona Lubo," *Palms to Pines*, Summer 1977.

Reed, Lester, "The Charles Thomas Family," *High Country*, Spring 1974.

Ringwald, George B., "Mountain-Climbing the Easy Way," *Westways*, December 1963.

Robinson, John W. and Bruce D. Risher, "San Bernardino National Forest: A Century of Federal Stewardship," *San Bernardino County Museum Association Quarterly*, Winter 1990.

Ruby, Jay W., "Aboriginal Uses of Mt. San Jacinto State Park," *U.C.L.A. Archeaological Survey, Annual Report*, 1961-62.

Shanahan, Donald G., "Compensation for the Loss of the Aboriginal Lands of the California Indians," *Southern California Quarterly*, Fall 1975.

Shumway, Nina Paul, "Burro-ing in the Santa Rosas," *Desert Magazine*, May 1939.

Shumway, Nina Paul, "Hard Rock Homesteaders," *Desert Magazine*, September 1939.

Smith, Gerald A., "Juan Antonio: Cahuilla Indian Chief, A Friend of the Whites," *San Bernardino County Museum Association Quarterly*, Fall 1960.

Strong, Dorothy L., "The Original Ramona Tragedy," *High Country*, Summer 1978.

Tollinger, Erika, "Anza Through the Years," *Palms to Pines*, Fall 1976.

Tollinger, Erika, "Our Hill," *Pinyon Gazette*, April 1972.

Tower, Grace Hortense, "To San Jacinto's Peak," *Los Angeles Times Illustrated Magazine*, September 29, 1907.

Wentworth, Bertrand H., "On Mount San Jacinto," *Land of Sunshine*, March 1896.

Whitney, Mary E., "William Franklin Whittier," *California Historical Courier,* September 1986.

Wilson, Henry E. W., "Gold Pockets in the Santa Rosas," *Desert Magazine,* October 1950.

Wilton, Mabel, "Paradise Above the Palms," *Desert Magazine,* July 1944.

Wolcott, Marjorie Tisdale, "The Lugos and Their Indian Ally: How Juan Antonio Aided in the Defense and Development of Rancho San Bernardino," *Touring Topics,* November 1929.

Woolley, Frank M., "Twentieth Century Pioneer," *High Country,* Summer 1978.

PAMPHLETS

Bridge, Norman and Walter Lindley, *The Idyllwild Sanatorium, San Gorgonio [sic] Mountains.* Los Angeles, 1901.

Davis, Richard Carter, *Newton B. Drury and the Wilderness Preservation Movement, Mt. San Jacinto State Park.* Sacramento, 1989.

Herring, Peg, *James San Jacinto Mountains Reserve.* University of California, Natural Reserve System, 1988.

Jackson, Helen Hunt, *Report on the Conditions and Needs of the Mission Indians.* Colorado Springs, 1882. Reproduced by San Jacinto Museum, 1973.

Lindley, Walter, M.D., *High Altitudes of Southern California.* Reprint from Southern California Practitioner, Los Angeles, 1888.

Palm Springs Aerial Tramway Souvenir Magazine. Palm Springs, 1965.

UNPUBLISHED MATERIALS

Carrico, Richard L. et al, *Cultural Resource Overview: San Bernardino National Forest,* prepared under U.S. Forest Service Contract No. 53-9JA9-0-219 by Westec Services, Inc., San Diego, 1982.

Davis, Richard Carter, *Wilderness, Politics, and Bureaucracy: Federal and State Policies in the Administration of San Jacinto Mountain, Southern California, 1920-1968.* University of California Riverside, Ph.D. Thesis, 1973.

McAdams, Henry E., *Early History of the San Gorgonio Pass: Gateway to California.* University of Southern California, MA Thesis, 1955.

Ripley, John, *Memorandum of Conversation with Ted Belden.* Ventura, California, 1991.

Smith, DeBoyd Leon, *A Study of Human Use of the Mount San Jacinto Wild Area.* California State University, Long Beach, MA Thesis, 1957.

Woodward, Lois Ann, *Mount San Jacinto, State Park No. 63.* WPA Project 465-03-3-133, Berkeley, 1937.

NEWSPAPERS

Hemet News
Idyllwild Breezes
Idyllwild Town Crier
Los Angeles Star
Los Angeles Times
Palm Springs Desert Sun
Palm Springs Villager
Redlands Citrograph
Redlands Daily Facts
Redlands Daily Review
Riverside Daily Press
Riverside Press-Enterprise
Riverside Press and Horticulturalist
San Bernardino Guardian
San Bernardino Daily Times
San Diego Union
San Jacinto Register

Also consulted were issues of the *Report of the State Mineralogist* and its successor, *California Journal of Mines and Geology,* that contain material on Riverside County mining activities.

INDEX

A

Agua Caliente 24, 27, 28, 36, 104
Agua Caliente Indian Reservation 107, 116, 119, 206-207
Aguirre, Jose, Manuel, Martin 69-70, 71
Akimo, Proco 56
Alandale 232
Alessandro 113
Alvin Meadow 27, 133, 146, 184
Andreas Canyon 24, 36, 197, 201, 202, 206
Antsell Rock 45
Anza, Juan Bautista 30, 33-35
Anza (town) 74, 184, 186
Anza Valley 31, 50, 57, 107, 116
Army Air Service 183
Arnaiz, Ernest 63
Arnaiz, Manuel 57, 59, 61, 83, 107, 167
Asbestos Mines 84
Asbestos Spring 63, 84
Azalea Trails Camp 237

B

Babtiste (see Anza)
Banning – Idyllwild Highway 149-150, 226
Bautista Canyon 34, 184
Baldwin, E.J. "Lucky" 52
Beale, Edward F. 104
Beatty, Doc 167, 168
Belden, Seldon 236
Black Mountain 187, 222
Bladen Mining District 177
Borrego Valley 31, 33, 34, 167
Buckhorn Camp 237
Bull Canyon 83
Burns, Ruth Curry 138
Byrne, Matthew 109, 110, 114, 115

C

Cabezon, Chief 101, 102, 104, 107
Cahuilla (community) 24, 74, 106
Cahuilla (people) 22-29, 33, 50, 72, 101-120,
163-166, 191, 197
Cahuilla Cowboys 62, 63, 65, 70, 71
Cahuilla Indian Reservation 107, 111-112, 116-118, 119
Cahuilla Valley 27, 33-34, 57, 59, 73-74,
103, 106, 111-112, 147

Calcite 167
California Department of Forestry 187, 188
California Health Resort Company 126, 129
Caramba 201
Carriage Inn 230
Cary, Art and Viola 68
Casa Loma 35, 55, 56
Cattle 49-52, 56-75, 197
Center of Idyllwild 229, 230
Chapman, Lee 201
Chapuli 102
Chilson, Eames 78, 79, 80, 82, 83
Chimney Flat 128, 146, 147
Chino Canyon 24, 36, 120, 197, 203, 215, 218, 220
Chino Trail 203
Civilian Conservation Corps 184-185, 195, 211, 212
Clark, Bud 68, 69
Clark, Frank 67-68, 69, 167, 168
Clark, Fred 67-68, 69, 167, 168
Cleveland National Forest 182-183
Climate 12
Coffman, Owen Earl 215, 216, 217
Collier, John 118
Contreras, Fanny Arnaiz 57, 73-74, 81-82
Contreras, John 57, 73-74
Cornell Peak 45, 213
Corona Hotel 79, 83, 130
Coyote Canyon 24, 31, 33, 34, 68, 102, 163, 168
Crawford, Joseph 145, 146, 147
Crawford Toll Road 91, 123, 145-146, 147, 148, 156
Crocker, Francis 215, 216
Cupeño 23, 101-103

D

Dark Canyon 97-98, 150, 186
Deep Canyon Desert Research Center 174
Desert Sun School 235
Devils Slide 59, 65, 69, 71, 72, 192, 197, 200
Domenigoni, Angelo 123, 128, 130
Domenigoni Flat 123, 128, 130, 133, 139, 233
Dutch Flat 93, 94, 96, 125, 232
Drury, Newton 210, 211, 215-216, 222
Dry Creek 147

E

Ebbens, Theodore "Frying Pan" 167, 168
Elliott-Pope Preparatory School 235-236

Elliott, Richard and Edith 217, 235
Emerson, Camp 133, 136, 138, 236
Emerson, Claudius Lee 98, 99, 133-135, 139
Epicurean & Fern Valley Gardens 231
Esgate, Gregory 139, 215-216
Estudillo, José Antonio 37, 55, 104, 108-109
Estudillo, José Maria 36, 37

F

Fages, Pedro 31-33
Fairview Land & Water Company 155, 156
Fauna 14-19
Fern Valley 25, 26, 134, 138, 183, 229, 230-231
Fern Valley Lodge 138, 140, 229, 230-231
Fig Tree John 166, 167
Fire 20, 184, 186, 187-188, 238
Fleming, Tom 68-69
Flora 13-20
Fobes Ranch 69
Folly Peak 45, 192
Foster, Dr. Paul 140, 225
Foster Lake 225
Fuller Mill Creek 89, 152, 183, 186
Fulmor, Alex C. 150, 151, 203
Funk, Bud 225, 226

G

Gambling 225
Garner, Jack 52, 65, 67
Garner Ranch 52, 60-67, 232
Garner, Robert 52, 60, 62, 64, 65
Garner Valley 24, 26, 45, 49-52, 56, 57, 60-67,
72, 78, 106, 147, 155, 232-233, 237
Garnet Queen Mine 84, 167
Garra Revolt 101-103
Garrett, Richard 89, 123
Geology 5-11, 199
Gold Shot Mine 83-84
Gordon, Moses S. 201
Gordon Trail 201, 203
Grant, Ulysses S. 106
Gray, Bob and Virginia 227, 228
Gray, Ernest and Marguerite 138
Greatamerica 232
Grinnell, Joseph 199
Grizzly Bears 51-52, 72, 198

H

Halfway Spring 133, 146
Hall, Colonel M.S. 87-89, 145
Hall City 88
Halls Camp 88, 89
Halls Grade 87-88, 89, 145, 149, 152
Hall, Harvey Monroe 96, 199
Hamilton, Clara Arnaiz 57, 59
Hamilton, Frank 59, 60
Hamilton, James 57, 59, 147
Hamilton, Joe 59, 61

Hamilton, Lincoln 59, 82
Hamilton School 74, 75
Hamner Ditch 155
Hannahs, George and Sarah 93, 96, 124-135,
129, 134, 200
Hanson, Lewis 78-82
Harwood, Aurelia 207, 208
Hemet 126, 128, 148, 156-158, 160, 178, 182
Hemet Belle Mine 78, 80, 83
Hemet Dam 68, 146, 156-158, 159
Hemet Lake 24, 45, 154-159
Hemet Valley 45, 49, 106
Hemstreet, Gus 128
Herkey Creek 51-52, 64, 65, 68, 72
Hidden Lake 196, 197, 200, 215, 222
Hole in the Wall 65, 68, 197
Horsethief Creek 167, 172
Horsley, Elmer 138, 140, 227
Howell, Wilson 169-170
Humber Park 231-232
Humber, Rollin and Margaret 139-140, 225, 231

I

Idyllwild 126-141, 147, 148, 185, 225-238
Idyllwild Control Road 147, 149, 150
Idyllwild Golf Course 134, 137
Idyllwild Inn (1st) 133, 134, 135, 138-139, 140, 225
Idyllwild Inn (2nd) 224, 225, 227, 229
Idyllwild Institute – Fiesta 236
Idyllwild Lumber Company 98, 99
Idyllwild Pines 133, 136, 138, 237
Idyllwild Sanatorium 126, 138-129, 130, 131, 132
Idyllwild School of Music & the Arts 233-234
Idylwilde Camp 124-125, 126
Indian Rights Association 115

J

Jackson, Helen Hunt 56, 72, 107-110, 111, 112-114
James, George Wharton 51, 96, 111, 113,
163-164, 193-194
James, Harry C. 209, 217, 221, 222
James Reserve 222-223
Jean Peak 45
Joe Scherman, Camp 237
Johnson, James Santiago 37, 38
Johnson, Jerry 140, 225, 226
Johnston, Hancock 64, 68, 71, 72, 130, 155, 156
Juan Antonio 101-104
Juan Bautista 102
Juan Diego 56, 91, 110-111, 113
Juan Diego Flat 111, 112

K

Keen Camp 64, 74, 130, 135, 141, 142, 143,
147, 151, 158, 181, 183, 186, 226
Keen Camp Road 146-147, 149, 150, 156, 179
Keen House 124-125, 126, 127, 130
Keen, John and Mary 124-125, 130

Kenworthy 59, 74, 79-83, 184, 189, 186
Kenworthy, Harold 52, 79-83
Kenworthy School 62, 82, 83
Kinney, Abbot 107, 110, 111

L

La Benne, Jonathan 233, 234
Lake Fulmor 145, 149, 153, 217, 222, 240
Lake Hemet (see Hemet Lake)
Lake Hemet Company 155, 156
Lake Hemet Municipal Water District 160
Lake Hemet Water Company 154, 156-159
Largo, John 117, 118
Largo, Manuel 104, 106
Law, George 64, 201, 202, 207
Lawlor Lodge 153
Laws Camp 201, 202
Lay, Ann 236
Leiberg, John B. 45-46, 199
Lily, Rock 27
Lindley, Dr. Walter 126, 130, 192, 205
Lockwood, Charles 81, 83
Lockwood, Lorinda Fay 81, 82, 83
Long Valley 215, 218, 220, 221
Lookout Cafe 226
Luiseño 23, 103, 106, 108
Lumbering 87-99

M

Magee, Horace 65-66
Marion Mountain 45, 186
Martinez Canyon 170, 172, 174
Mayberry, Edward 68, 146, 154-158
Mayberry Road (see Keen Camp Road)
Maxwell, Ernie and Betty 98, 217, 225, 226-227, 238
McCall's Horse Camp 147
Meeks, Sam and Dick 69, 71, 197, 198
Meier, Martin 93, 96
Michelsen, Dr. Albert 141
Miller, Jack 170
Mission Indians 106, 107, 112, 115, 116
Mt. San Jacinto State Park 204, 209-212, 215, 217, 221
Morongo Reservation 107, 116, 119
Morris Creek 57
Mountain Center 186, 226, 237
Muir, John 73, 177, 191, 192
Mukat 25

N

Nash-Boulden, Steven Augustus 183, 209
Native Lumber Company 96
Nicholas (Old Nicolas) Canyon 106, 163, 164, 165
Nightingale, Arthur 169, 172
Nukil 27

O

Oak Cliff 133, 145, 146, 147, 148
Omstott, Myron 68-69, 97, 197
Ord, Lt. E.O.C. 41

P

Pablo, Will 117
Pacific Railroad Survey 41-42
Palm Canyon 24, 206
Palm Canyon National Monument 205-207
Palms to Pines Highway 151, 153, 159, 169, 186
Peniwell Camp 138
Penrod Canyon 83-84
Palm Springs Aerial Tramway 214-222
Pico, Francisco 55, 56
Pinchot, Gifford 177, 178, 179
Pine Cove 90, 134, 138, 139, 150, 226, 237
Pinyon Flat 27, 57, 63, 70, 73, 164, 166, 169, 173
Pine Springs Ranch 237
Poppet Flats 69
Postle, John and Clara 138, 140
Potrero Ranch 69

Q

Quinn Flat 78, 82

R

Ragsdale, Desert Steve 170-171
Ramona (novel) 51, 56, 91, 111, 112-113
Ramona Lubo 51, 110, 111, 112, 113, 114
Ramona Pageant 114
Ramona Indian Reservation 116
Rayneta 93, 125, 129
Reed, Asa and Naoma 67
Reed, Quitman 67, 72, 73
Report on the Conditions and
   Needs of the Mission Indians 112
Ribbonwood 169-170
Riverside Mountain Rescue Unit 222
Roach, Hiram 97-98
Rockhouse Canyon 24, 106, 163-164, 165, 166, 167, 174
Roundup (cattle) 70
Round Valley 72, 184, 197, 200, 203, 213
Rustic Theater 225, 227, 232
Rutledge, Laura 126

S

Salinas, Jozee 66-67
San Andreas Fault 8-9, 199
San Bernardino National Forest 183-188, 209-211, 216
Sanborn, Harold 225, 227
San Carlos, Pass of 33-34, 68
San Gorgonio Pass 36, 101, 145
San Jacinto (town) 44, 51, 56, 66, 155, 160

San Jacinto Box Factory 93, 95
San Jacinto Fault 10-11
San Jacinto Forest Reserve 59, 73, 96, 177-182
San Jacinto Lumber & Box Company 97-98
San Jacinto Peak 41, 43, 44-45, 190-195,
203, 206, 211, 221
San Jacinto, Rancho 35-37, 55, 104, 108-109, 114, 115
San Jacinto Tunnel 159-160, 161
San Jacinto Valley . . 34, 55-56, 57, 72, 104, 106, 109, 156, 191
San Jacinto Wilderness 204, 209-211, 221, 222
San Luis Rey Mission 35, 108
Santa Rosa Indian Reservation 70, 72, 105, 119, 163, 166, 167, 169, 173
Santa Rosa Mountains 27, 43, 46, 57, 106, 163-175
Santa Rosa Wilderness 173-174
Saunders, Amasa 90, 123, 146
Saunders Meadow 93, 134, 137
Scherman, Anton 90-97, 123, 146
Scherman, Joe 73, 91, 97
Serrano, Celso 117, 118
Sheep 72
Sheriff, Mary 108, 109, 110
Shumway, Nina and Paul 171-172
Sierra Club 205, 207, 208, 217
Silvas, Con 178
Smallpox 104
Smiley Commission 116
Smith, Thomas "Pegleg" 166, 167
Snow Creek 24, 194, 197, 242
Soboba 72, 108-110, 114-115, 117, 118, 161, 187
Southern Pacific Railroad 50, 87-90, 145, 156, 208, 209, 210, 215
Sportland 229, 230
Spitler, George 69
State Park Commission 209, 210, 215, 217, 221
Stamps, Charles, Nester, and Pacific 78
Stanley, Will 116-118
Strawberry Valley 25, 50, 59, 64, 73, 89-96, 98-99, 123-141, 145, 147, 179, 192
Strawberry Valley Hotel 129, 132
Strong & Dickinson 129, 133, 134, 229
Stump Spring 172-173, 174
Sugar Loaf Cafe 170
Swartz, Nicholas 166

T

Taggart, Grant 178, 200
Tahquitz (demon) 27, 28, 72
Tahquitz, Camp 133, 137, 138, 213, 237
Tahquitz Canyon 24, 36
Tahquitz Game Refuge 207-208, 217
Tahquitz Lodge 135, 138, 141, 142, 143
Tahquitz Meadows 141, 226
Tahquitz Mining District 78-79
Tahquitz Peak 27, 64, 182, 185, 187
Tahquitz Pines 134, 136, 138, 237
Tahquitz Valley 59, 64-65, 68, 69, 71, 184, 192, 197, 198, 200, 201, 202, 203, 213
Tamarack Valley 72, 192, 197, 200
Tarabel, Sebastian 33
Taylor, Malcom "Mac" 226

Temecula, Treaty of 103-104
Temple, Sam 56, 59, 91, 95, 110-111, 112, 113, 123, 146
Terwilliger, Jacob and Almira 67
Terwilliger Valley 31, 67-68
Thomas, Charles 49-52, 56, 64, 69, 106, 107, 145, 155, 191, 192, 197, 198
Thomas, Charles Jr. 178, 179
Thomas, Genoveva 49
Thomas Mountain 59, 185, 187
Thomas Ranch 49-52, 81
Thomas Valley (see Garner Valley)
Toro Peak 27, 163, 169, 172
Tourmaline 84-85
Town Hall 227
Tripp Flat 34, 57, 58, 186
Tripp, Ozro 56, 57, 107
Tripp, Ray 58
Tripp, Samuel V. 56-57, 58, 111, 113, 123, 155
Tripp, Shasta 56, 58, 107
Tripp, William 56, 57, 58, 68, 97

U

Ubach, Fr. Anthony 108
United States Forest Service 179-189, 208-211
United States Geological Survey 44-45, 47

V

Vandeventer, Charles 168, 169, 178
Vandeventer Flat 24, 31, 168-169
Vandeventer, Frank 167-168
Victoriano, Chief 108
Vista Grande 182, 184, 186
Vista Grande "Hot Shots" 187

W

Weather 11-12
Weaver, Paulino 37-38
Webster, William and Mary 68
Wellman, Frank 57, 59, 71, 91, 95, 146, 197, 199
Wellman, Jim 59, 60, 62, 167
Wellmans Cienega 72, 200
Wheeler Survey 43-44, 191, 192
Whitewater Ranch 65
Whitney, Josiah Dwight 41, 43
Whittier, William 68, 126-127, 154-158
Williams, Isaac 37
Williamson, Lt. R.S. 41
Willow Creek 59, 71, 197, 199, 207, 213
Winter Park Authority 216, 218, 219, 221, 222
Wood, Walter 134

Horses, Garner Ranch. – JOZEE SALINAS

A departed friend, sorely missed. Jim Jenkins (1952-1979) in Round Valley, with Cornell Peak on the skyline, 1974.

THE SAN JACINTOS completes the trilogy on Southern California mountain ranges, complimenting THE SAN GABRIELS and THE SAN BERNARDINOS, published by Glen Owens and The Big Santa Anita Historical Society. It's been a long journey and a richly rewarding one.

R. 3 W.
R. 2 W.
R. 1 W
R. 1 E.
T.L.P.
SGP
Beaumont
SGP
T.L.P.
Banning
S A N
Moreno
Mt. Davis
Mt. Russell
2685
Eden Hot Springs
Mt. Eden
Laborda
Canyon
Lamb Canyon
POTRERO
SAN JACINTO
NUEVO
SAN JACINTO NUEVO
Colony
Heights
VALLEY
Mystic Lake
LIMEKILN
Potrero Cr.
Y POTRERO
PGS M
Lakeview
Poppet
Flat
T.L.P.
Lookout
T.L.P.
Relief Hot
Springs
Casa Loma
Mt. Rudolph
2629
SAN
JACINTO
DeMamont
Claremont
Poppet Cr.
LAKEVIEW MOUNTAINS
Springs
PGS
sM
PGM
T.L.P.
San Jacinto
SGP
SAN
JACINTO
Bowers
INDIAN RES.
Standard
VIEJO
6262
Juniper
Flat
CAL. R.R.
(SAN JACINTO DIVISION)
Park
Hill
TLP
VALLEY
Hemet
SGP
PGM
TLP
R.S.
North Fork
Tollgate Road
M
TLP
Merifee
Double
Butte
Egan
JACINTO
Reservoir Butte
SGP M
Winchester
Hemet Butte
PLEASANT VALLEY CO'S. CANAL
SAN JACINTO
Diamond
Valley
SAN
Polly
Butte
VALLEY
Bautiste
Cactus Valley
Mica Butte
DOMENIGONI
VALLEY
Bell Mt.
LEON MINE
PALOMA VALLEY
Spring
Bautista
Bosley Cr.
Horse Cr.
Leon
Creek
California Gem Mines
Red
Mountain
French Valley
Rawson Canyon
Black Mt.
Bachelor Mt.
Willow Canyon
R.S.
Reed Valley
Warm Springs Cr.
Los Alamos Valley
Auld
Tucalota Cr.
Sage
Murrieta
Hot Sulphur Springs
Glenoak Valley
Spring
Valley
Wilson Cr.
TEMECULA
Lewis
Long Valley
Roundtop
Oak Mt.
PAUBA
SGP
Temecula
M
Nigger Canyon
TEMECULA RV.
Wilson
Valley
Lancaster
Valley
COAHUILA